Neal Bedford

Vienna

The Top Five

1 MuseumsQuartier
An art space to rival anything Europe has to offer

2 Hofburg
Seat of one the longest-reigning monarchies the world has ever seen

3 Naschmarkt
Breakfast on the run or while away the hours in the city's colourful market

4 Stephansdom
Vienna's glorious Gothic cathedral, and its beloved icon

5 Schönbrunn
Wander the halls and gardens of imperial grandeur at its bombastic best

Contents

Introducing Vienna   5

City Life   7

Arts   21

Architecture   31

History   37

Districts   47

Walking & Cycling Tours   105

Eating   115

Entertainment   137

Shopping   159

Sleeping   171

Excursions   183

Directory   197

Language   211

Index   231

Map Section   237

Published by Lonely Planet Publications Pty Ltd
ABN 36 005 607 983

Australia Head Office, Locked Bag 1, Footscray,
Victoria 3011, ☎ 03 8379 8000, fax 03 8379 8111,
talk2us@lonelyplanet.com.au

USA 150 Linden St, Oakland, CA 94607,
☎ 510 893 8555, toll free 800 275 8555,
fax 510 893 8572, info@lonelyplanet.com

UK 72–82 Rosebery Ave, Clerkenwell, London,
EC1R 4RW, ☎ 020 7841 9000, fax 020 7841 9001,
go@lonelyplanet.co.uk

France 1 rue du Dahomey, 75011 Paris,
☎ 01 55 25 33 00, fax 01 55 25 33 01,
bip@lonelyplanet.fr, www.lonelyplanet.fr

The Authors

NEAL BEDFORD

Neal's love affair with Vienna started in 1994, when he arrived in the city all bright-eyed and bushy tailed to fill a vacant au pair job. Not speaking a word of German (except for *Eins, Zwei, Polizei, Drei, Vier, Brigadier*), he was anxious and afraid of being lost in a strange city, surrounded by people mumbling something he couldn't understand. His fears were totally unfounded: his employers soon became his second family, his English-course buddies introduced him to more locals than he could keep track of, and before he knew it, he felt perfectly at home. He even learnt some German.

Over the years Neal has enjoyed numerous year-long stints in this fair city, only to leave for what he thought were greener pastures. But the magic of Vienna (whose pull is stronger than he'd like to admit) is a magnet too hard to resist. For the past two years he's called Ottakring/Hernals home, and wouldn't exchange his rooftop apartment, with views of the Wienerwald, Votivkirche and busy Ottakringer Strasse, for anything.

CONTRIBUTING AUTHOR
JANE RAWSON

It's not every city that understands the profound beauty of reinforced concrete or the potential of the public toilet for gorgeousness. Vienna does, and that's why Jane loves it. Wandering aimlessly through Eastern and Central Europe, she was lured to the city by the promise of coffee shops that serve hot chocolate with a chaser of rum, and in no time at all fell head-over-heels in love with Egon Schiele and Wiener Werkstätte cutlery sets. Jane wrote the Arts and Architecture chapters.

PHOTOGRAPHER
RICHARD NEBESKY

Richard was born one snowy night in the grungy Prague suburb of Zizkov, but surprisingly he didn't have a camera in his hand. It was, however, not long after he got out of his cot that his father, an avid photo enthusiast, gave him his first point-and-shoot unit. Ever since, he's kept a camera by his side on treks, ski adventures, cycling trips and while researching Lonely Planet books around the globe. He has also worked for various magazines, travel guide book publishers and on many social photography projects.

Introducing Vienna

'The streets of Vienna are paved with culture; in other cities they are paved with asphalt.' So remarked the Austrian writer Karl Kraus (1874–1936). Around half a century later, the band Ultravox summarised the city with the magical line 'Oh, Vienna'. Both are perfect summaries of a city without cultural equal, a city where monumental imperial heritage, glorious operas and moving classical music walk the streets like living entities, spreading their energy and spirit to every last nook and cranny of this stunning metropolis. But it's not just a city living off its past, it's also a capital shaking off the decay of decades of complacency and comfort, and embracing a new global world in all its colourful richness and diversity.

Think of Vienna and a gamut of images surge forward to flood the memory banks: angelic choirboys thrilling a crowd of onlookers, proud white stallions strutting in measured sequence, grand imperial palaces and bombastic baroque architecture too beautiful to ignore, Art-Nouveau masterpieces of depth and quality, art galleries with unfathomable collections, and of course strong coffee, delicate pastries and divine cakes. Then there's the music. Just let it roll off your tongue: Mozart, Beethoven, Haydn, Schubert, Strauss, Brahms, Mahler, Schönberg. For lovers of classical music, it doesn't get *any* better than this.

But Vienna is so much more than its past. Thankfully, the wise denizens of this golden city haven't settled on their laurels and let themselves sink sleepily into their impressive history. Like the rest of the Western world, they want a taste of what's out there, and they want it on their own turf. Asian diners, kebab houses and conveyor-belt sushi joints compete with, but don't overpower, the traditional *Beisl* (beer house) and *Heuriger* (wine tavern). The upwardly mobile while away the wee small hours in hip, unpretentious bars before moving on to pumping clubs where DJs work their magic with the latest sounds. Modern art houses constantly host contemporary artists who aren't afraid to push the boundaries of art to its thought-provoking limits.

Yes, there's still a Vienna that's stuck in time, a Vienna ruled by old ladies and their chattering, unstoppable gossip. But this only adds to the city's charm. Where would the city be without its genteel ladies, unashamedly churning over the latest trip to the doctor in the local Aida café? Up the canal without a paddle.

My Essential Vienna

- Kunsthistorisches Museum (p77)
- Naschmarkt (p166)
- MuseumsQuartier (p79)
- Schönbrunn (p100)
- Stephansdom (p53)

Yet Vienna isn't all about urban life and high culture. With almost half the city given over to green spaces (more than any other European capital); the mighty blue Danube (Donau) slicing the city in two; and Beethoven's inspiration, the Wienerwald (Vienna Woods), on its western fringes; it's also a city for the pursuit of the great outdoors. And then there's the vast expanse of vineyards, which makes Vienna the largest wine-growing city in the world.

It doesn't matter when you arrive, the city looks just as glorious – some would say even more so – under a layer of snow as it does under the gaze of a midsummer sun. And the constant turnstile of festivals and events rivals anything most other European cities can offer. Come Christmas the good burghers of Vienna roll out the welcoming mat to *Christkindlmärkte*, Christmas markets full of tradition and charm, and the all-important mulled wine; when summer shines through so does a plethora of musical events. In between, cultural and musical festivities line up beside each other, all vying for attention. The only drawback to the summer is the holiday season: many of the city's world-famous institutions, such as the Vienna Boys' Choir, the Lippanzer Stallions and the Staatsoper, all take breaks, so if you're dead keen to catch any of the above, plan your trip to avoid this period.

Lowdown

Population 1.55 million

Time zone Central European Time (GMT + 1 hour)

3-star double room Around €90-100

Melange coffee Around €3

Slice of Sacher Torte €3

Opera ticket €2-254

U-Bahn ticket €1.50

Common sight Dogs, dogs, and more dogs

Don't Joke about Hitler; his deeds are still within living memory

Vienna is simply a magical city, a place where culture, history, art and the nightlife buzz are mixed into one beautiful melting pot. If you've only a few days, don't bother sleeping too much, just get out there and experience Vienna in all its wonderful splendour.

NEAL'S TOP VIENNA DAY

I start my day at around 9am with an omelette at Kent, before picking up some fruit at the Brunnenmarkt for the day's outing. I then jump on the J and head straight to the Leopold Museum and spend far too long gazing in awe at Schiele's work, before stepping outside onto the MuseumsQuartier's courtyard for a bit of sun and a quiet coffee. My feet lead me across the Ringstrasse and into the Innere Stadt via the Hofburg and the National Bibliothek's glorious Prunksaal. A few quick phone calls will determine who's up for lunch at Expedit and a beer at the Kleines Café afterwards. As the afternoon heat scorches the city, I make a beeline for the Alte Donau (Old Danube) for a long, lazy swim before making my way north to Stammersdorf and its traditional *Heurigen* for refreshments. After a hasty shower at my apartment, the night's entertainment begins at the rhiz bar where the bartenders know me far too well. A quick flick through *Falter* and a club is chosen; Flex invariably wins the popularity vote. If my energy lasts I party the night away, and head to Café Dreschler or Goodmanns for an early-morning snack before falling into bed thoroughly exhausted.

City Life

Vienna Today	8
City Calendar	9
January & February	9
March & April	9
May & June	9
July & August	10
September & October	11
November & December	11
Culture	11
Identity	11
Lifestyle	12
Food & Drink	13
Fashion	15
Sport	16
Media	16
Language	17
Economy & Costs	17
Government & Politics	18
Environment	18
The Land	18
Green Vienna	19
Urban Planning & Development	19

City Life

VIENNA TODAY

They say everything has a life cycle, and so it is with Vienna. Once the brightest diamond in Europe's cultural crown for centuries, it fell on hard times with the decline of its keepers, the Habsburgs. With the exception of Red Vienna in the 1920s, when the city prospered under the most successful socialist government Europe has ever seen, the city wallowed in the cultural backwaters for much of the 20th century.

Over the last 10 years, however, Vienna has picked itself up by the bootlaces, dusted itself off and charged headlong into the 21st century with gusto reminiscent of its former glory days. The bar and club scene has literally exploded across the city, leaving traditional pockets such as the Bermuda Dreieck floundering in its wake, unable to keep up with the pace. Now locals are almost spoiled for choice (they'd be the last ones to admit it though), with areas like the Gürtel and around Schleifmühlgasse filled with progressive bars and live-music venues. Electronic music has carved major inroads into the music scene, and Vienna is fast becoming a hub for the music genre; clubs such as Flex regularly attract Europe's best DJs and loudest bands. The Viennese, back from world trips, soon tired of *Schnitzel* on the menu every night and began exploring the token Chinese restaurants and Turkish kebab houses in town. Before long, new flavours and spices were popping up all over the city (and continue to do so), whetting the Viennese appetite.

Art, a major link in Vienna's cultural armour, continues to go from strength to strength, and fortunately the councillors of Vienna have never been shy about forking out for art and public space. Their greatest achievements in the 21st century – the reopening of the Albertina, home to the world's greatest graphic art collection, and the completion of the Museums-Quartier, the eighth largest cultural complex in the world – have not only complemented the city's incredible art treasure chest, but helped to create an art scene of epic proportions.

Through all this improvement and new-found openness to the world, Vienna has remained an incredibly safe city. Crime has been on the increase in the past 10 years, but it has had little impact on the freedom and safety of the Viennese. People can go almost anywhere night or day and feel unthreatened; women still walk home alone at night without fear of harassment, and the elderly ride the trams and buses safe in the knowledge no-one is out to rob them.

As open and friendly as Vienna has become, not everything comes up roses. There is still a xenophobic fear of certain ethnic groups among some citizens, who consider every black African a drug dealer, and every Turkish or Yugoslav citizen a drain on the city's coffers. Unfortunately, this hatred has extended into sections of the police force; in 1999 an African died while being deported, and another in 2003 during an arrest process. In recent years the FPÖ (Freedom Party), formerly headed by Jörg Haider, has played on this fear, targeting foreigners and asylum-seekers during election time. In 2000 it rode the tide of xenophobia right to the doorsteps of parliament, forming a coalition government with the ÖVP (People's Party). This, however, seemed a catalyst for Vienna's sleeping liberals, who demonstrated en masse on Heldenplatz (some 200,000 turned up) against the FPÖ's racist streak. In the 2001 council and 2002 national elections, FPÖ lost major ground in the popularity stakes and is currently fighting for political stability.

Hot Conversation Topics

- **Specials** – what's on sale at Ikea and Hofer?
- **Prices** – how much everything has gone up since the introduction of the euro.
- **Nappies** – will the city council be able to force *Fiaker* (horse and carriage) drivers to fit their horses with them this summer?
- **The Viennese** – the Viennese complaining about the Viennese.
- **Bicycles** – what's the latest equipment and who has it.

Cyclists and Würstelstand (sausage stand) at Donauinsel (p87)

CITY CALENDAR

Festival-wise, it seems as though Vienna never sleeps. The entire year is jam-packed with events and happenings, all vying for the attention, and attendance, of locals and visitors alike. The cultural heritage of the city has given birth to many classical music events and a much-loved ball season, but the range doesn't stop there – jazz and rock festivals, gay parades and communist and art gatherings pepper the city's calendar. For a full list of public holidays, see the Directory (p198). The following is by no means a complete listing of annual events; check the Tourist Info Wien website, www.wien.info, for a more comprehensive list.

Top Five Quirky Events

- **Fasching** – a time to dress up as a tree, oil slick or your favourite comic character and bar hop across the city.
- **Lange Nacht der Museen** – one night in the year when museums across the country throw open their doors to all and sundry.
- **Life Ball** – outrageous outfits, celebrities galore, and all in the noble cause of raising funds for AIDS.
- **Soho in Ottakring** – a multicultural residential neighbourhood transforms itself into a centre for contemporary art and nightlife.
- **Volksstimmefest** – a surreal hippy/communist festival with a very laid-back feel and plenty of live acts.

JANUARY & FEBRUARY

FASCHING

The Fasching season, a carnival time of costumes and parties, actually runs from November to Ash Wednesday, but February is traditionally the time when most of the action takes place. Look for street parties and drunken Viennese in silly get-ups.

OPERNBALL

☎ 514 44 78-80; 01, Staatsoper

Of the 300 or so balls held in January and February, the Opernball (Opera Ball) is number one. Held in the Staatsoper, it's a supremely lavish affair, with the men in tails and women in shining white gowns.

MARCH & APRIL

FRÜHLINGSFESTIVAL

Alternating each year between the Musikverein and the Konzerthaus, this Spring Festival of classical concerts generally runs from the end of March to the beginning of April.

OSTERKLANG FESTIVAL

☎ 427 17; www.osterklang.at; 01, Stadiongasse 9

Orchestral and chamber music recitals fill some of Vienna's best music halls during this, the 'Sound of Easter', festival. The highlight is the opening concert, which features the Vienna Philharmonic.

MAY & JUNE

DONAUINSELFEST

For the younger generation, the Donauinselfest on the Donauinsel (Danube Island) occupies

9

the top spot on the year's events' calendar. Held over three days on a weekend in late June, it features an absolute feast of rock, pop, folk and country performers, which attracts almost three million onlookers. Best of all, it's free!

LANGER NACHT DER MUSIK
☎ 870 70 30; langenachtdermusik@orf.at
On 10 May, between 7pm and 2am, bars and concert venues host a heap of bands playing every kind of music genre conceivable. Tickets (adult/child €14/12; available at venues) grant entry into all performances. An information booth is set up on Heldenplatz two days before the event.

LIFE BALL
www.lifeball.org; 09, Porzellangasse
This AIDS-charity event is one of the highlights of the gay and lesbian calendar and is often graced by international celebrities. It's normally held in the Rathaus around the middle of May and attracts some colourful and flamboyant outfits.

QUEER IDENTITIES
☎ 524 62 74; www.identities.at
Identities is easily Vienna's second largest film festival, showcasing queer movies from around the world. It normally takes place at the beginning of June.

REGENBOGEN PARADE
At the end of June Vienna is taken over by the Regenbogen Parade (Rainbow Parade), a predominantly gay and lesbian festival attracting some 150,000 people. Expect loads of fun, frolicking and bare skin.

SOHO IN OTTAKRING
☎ 0699 19 53 35 94; www.sohoinottakring.at, German only; 16, Haberlgasse 76
The multicultural streets bordering the Gürtel in the Ottakring district come to life in May and June with Soho in Ottakring. Hairdressing salons, disused offices and fishmongers are transformed into art galleries, bars, band venues and art shops, all of which attracts an arty crowd.

VIENNA MARATHON
☎ 421 95 00; www.vienna-marathon.com
The city's top road race is held in May.

WIEN IST ANDERSRUM
☎ 966 01 10; www.andersrum.at, German only; 04, Grosse Neugasse 29

Wien ist Andersrum is a month-long extravaganza of gay and lesbian art, which takes up all of June. Most performances stick to the genre of stage and song.

WIENER FESTWOCHEN
☎ 589 22-22; www.festwochen.or.at; 06, Lehárgasse 11
From May to mid-June the Vienna Festival hosts a wide-ranging program of the arts, based in various venues around town. Expect to see quality performance groups from around the world. It's considered to be one of the highlights of the year.

JULY & AUGUST
IMPULSTANZ
☎ 523 55 58; www.impulstanz.com; 07, Museumstrasse 5/21
Vienna's premiere avant-garde dance festival attracts an array of internationally renowned troupes and newcomers between mid-July and mid-August. Performances are held in the MuseumsQuartier, Volkstheater and a number of small venues.

JAZZ FEST
☎ 712 42 24; www.viennajazz.org; 08, Lammgasse 12/8
From the end of June to mid-July, Vienna relaxes to the smooth sound of jazz, blues and soul flowing from the Staatsoper and a number of clubs across town.

KLANGBOGEN FESTIVAL
☎ 427 17; www.klangbogen.at; 01, Stadiongasse 9
The KlangBogen Festival ensures things don't flag during the summer holidays. Running from July to August, it features operas, operettas and orchestral music in the Theater an der Wien and Musikverein, plus a few other locations around town.

MUSIKFILM FESTIVAL
01, Rathausplatz
Once the sun sets in July and August, the Rathausplatz is home to screenings of operas, operettas and concerts. They're all free, so turn up early for a good seat. Food stands and bars are close at hand, which are swamped by hoards of people creating a carnival-like atmosphere.

VOLKSTIMMEFEST
☎ 0676 696 90 02; www.kpoe.at, German only
For a weekend around the end of August/beginning of September, the Communist Party lets its hair down in the Prater and parties like

there's no tomorrow. The festival, which has been running since 1945, features some 30 live acts and attracts a bizarre mix of hippies and staunch party supporters.

SEPTEMBER & OCTOBER
LANGE NACHT DER MUSEEN
http://langernacht.orf.at, German only
On the evening of 20 September, some 370 museums nationwide open their doors to visitors between 6pm and 1am. One ticket (adult/child €12/10; available at museums) allows entry to all of them, and includes public transport around town. You'll be hard pushed to visit all 58 museums in Vienna though.

VIENNALE FILM FESTIVAL
☎ 0800 664 003; www.viennale.at
The country's biggest and best film festival, Viennale features fringe and independent films from around the world in October. See p153 for more details.

NOVEMBER & DECEMBER
CHRISTKINDLMÄRKTE
Vienna's much-loved Christmas market season runs from mid-November to Christmas Day. See p169 for more details.

SILVESTER
The city council transforms the Innere Stadt into one big party venue for Silvester (New Year's Eve). It's an uproarious affair, with more than enough alcohol consumed, and far too many fireworks let off in crowded streets.

WIEN MODERN FESTIVAL
☎ 242 002; www.konzerthaus.at; 03, Lothringerstrasse 20
The Wien Modern Festival takes an opposing view to many of the city's music festivals by featuring modern classical and avant-garde music. The festival is held throughout November, with many performances in the Konzerthaus.

CULTURE
IDENTITY
Vienna is a melting pot of Central and Eastern European societies, the result of 600 years of Habsburg rule.

Today, out of a population of just over 1.5 million, almost a quarter (366,000) is born outside Austria. The largest ethnic communities by far are Yugoslavian (around 70,000) and Turkish (close to 40,000), followed by Bosnian and Croatian. This, however, says nothing of second- or third-generation 'foreigners' who are now fully integrated into the Viennese way of life, and no longer associate themselves with their ancestor's homeland.

A Penchant for...
The Viennese can be a strange bunch, and often their interests and tastes are even stranger. Here are just three:

Death It's a well-known fact the Viennese have a morbid fascination with death. Where else in the world would you find a museum dealing specifically with funerals and the undertaker's profession (see Bestattungsmuseum p92)? Funerals are big business in the city and for many the bigger the better, and *eine schöne Leich*, which literally means 'a beautiful corpse', is a must. Tombstones are often grandiose affairs and Sunday trips to the cemetery commonplace.

Politeness For all their grumpiness, the Viennese love *Höflichkeit* (politeness). Shop assistants, waiters and the like always greet people with *Grüss Gott* or *Guten Tag* (good day) and expect the same in return. Occasionally you'll hear *Servus*, but that's normally reserved for greetings between friends. *Auf Wiedersehen* will follow you out the door. When a new introduction is made, people shake hands; this even applies in younger, informal company. *Prost* is the common toast, and always make eye contact when clinking glasses – some may consider you insincere otherwise.

Toilet doors You'd expect all toilet doors to be marked with H for *Herren* (Gentlemen) or D for *Damen* (Ladies) to make things simple and clear but, no, more and more bar and café owners are taking great pleasure in confusing their patrons. Some do have H and D, or man and woman silhouettes, but they're hidden behind posters, on the floor, or blend in perfectly with stickers and graffiti. Others have nothing at all, or cryptic codes, which is the last thing you need when your bladder is bursting.

Traditionally, Vienna, along with the rest of Austria, has been a stronghold of the Catholic religion, and it still plays an important part in the lives of many. In the latest census, 73.6% of the population classed themselves as Roman Catholic, 4.7% Protestant and 4.2% Muslim. Religion starts early in a person's life, and even the religious rights of children are protected: from age 12 to 14 a change of religion cannot be imposed upon any child and upon reaching 14, children have full independence to choose their own faith.

The Viennese personality is like a mixed bag of sweets: you just never know what you're going to get and often it comes as a surprise. A shop assistant might be overly friendly towards you, but downright rude to your friend, or a waiter may grumble at a small tip one week but smile generously at the same amount the following week. Through it all, it's best to take the Viennese with a pinch of salt because that's how the Viennese handle the Viennese. Humour is another feature of the Viennese identity, known as *Wiener Schmäh* – cutting, dark, often aimed at themselves and thoroughly charming.

If a stereotype for the Viennese had to be thrown up though, it would probably land on 'grumpy'. For some reason they have a tendency to dwell on the negative side of life and they like everyone around them to know it. Of course, this characteristic won't apply to every Viennese you come across, but it does seem to prevail throughout most levels of society.

LIFESTYLE

Quality is the key to life in Vienna. Fast food and videos certainly have their place, but many Viennese prefer dinner out and a trip to the cinema. Theatre, opera, art exhibitions and classical music concerts are enjoyed by all sectors of society. Weekends are a much-guarded work-free zone, often spent away with friends and family or pursuing lazy outdoor activities – swimming and sun-bathing, walking and cycling, but nothing overly strenuous. If a public holiday falls on a Thursday, many companies will give the Friday off to its employees, known as a *Fenster Tag* (Window Day). Come summertime the city practically moves to the Mediterranean for a well-earned holiday. All this is possible because of healthy pay packets: employees receive 14 monthly salary payments per year, an extra pay in June known as *Urlaub Geld* (holiday money) and the other, *Weihnacht Geld* (Christmas money), in November.

On the whole, Vienna is an accepting and safe society (unless you're from the East or Africa, see p8 for details). Gays and lesbians hardly receive any harassment and maternity leave is an astounding two years, which can be taken by either the father or the mother. Fights in bars are almost unheard of, even though the Viennese love their beer and wine, and it's common to see elderly folk using public transport for evening excursions.

Living conditions are generally of a high standard and rents comparatively low. Home ownership is not a big issue as in some cases it's cheaper to rent a property than buy it outright. Even students can afford their own flat.

Sigmund Freud

Sigmund Freud was born in Freiberg, Moravia, on 6 May 1856 and at the age of three moved with his family to Vienna. He graduated as a Doctor of Medicine in 1881 and five years later set up his first office as a neurologist at 01, Rathausstrasse 7. Later that year he married Martha Bernays, who went on to bear him six children. In 1891 he moved his practice to 09, Berggasse 19, where he created one of his greatest gifts to mankind, psychoanalysis.

Although many academics and physicians were hostile towards his published works, Freud was able to gather around him a core of pupils and followers. Among their number was the Swiss psychologist Carl Jung, who later severed his links with the group because of personal differences with Freud. In 1923 Freud was diagnosed as having cancer of the palate, an affliction that caused him great pain and forced him to undergo surgery over 30 times. The illness prompted him to mostly withdraw from public life; his daughter Anna (a child psychiatrist) often appeared in his stead at meetings and conventions.

The arrival of the Nazis in 1938 instigated a mass evacuation by many of Vienna's Jews. Freud was allowed to immigrate to London on 4 June, accompanied by Anna. The rest of his children also managed to escape, but other family members weren't so fortunate – four of his elderly sisters were detained in the city, and finally killed in a concentration camp in 1941. Freud breathed his last breath in London on 23 September 1939.

The Viennese and their Dogs

It has been said that the Viennese love their dogs more than their children, and even though this is an exaggeration, they certainly adore their canine friends. This can clearly be seen on the streets and in restaurants, where owners are invariably ignored while their dogs are smothered with affection by total strangers.

As much as the Viennese love their dogs, they abhor cleaning up their mess. John Sparrow must have been in Vienna when he penned 'that indefatigable and unsavoury engine of pollution, the dog'. Approximately 8.3% of households own a dog, which, at a conservative calculation, equates to 65,000 dogs. Multiply this by the amount of times they need to do number twos every day, and you have *a lot* of doggy poo on footpaths, between parked cars, on grass verges, in parks and even in doorways. This is quite incredible considering 870,000 sq metres of parkland in Vienna is designated dog zone – places where dogs are free to sniff butts, go to the loo and do doggy things. So it's good to remember to drag your eyes away from Vienna's architectural delights now and then to make sure you're not stepping in something unsavoury on your sightseeing wanderings.

FOOD & DRINK

If truth be told, Vienna doesn't really have a cuisine of its own, but rather a conglomeration of the best the old empire could beg, steal and borrow from its foreign lands. There are original Viennese dishes, but, for example, the world famous *Wiener Schnitzel* is from Milan, *Knödel* (dumplings) originated in Bohemia, *Gulasch* (goulash) and *Paprika Huhn* (paprika chicken) are from Hungary and the delightful *Palatschinken* (pancakes) come all the way from Romania. This isn't intended to run down the Viennese kitchen – far from it – but to show that its cuisine has developed like every other aspect of this great city; it has rolled with the times, taken the best of the bunch and made it its own.

On the whole, traditional Viennese cuisine is quite heavy, hearty and strongly meat-based. *Wiener Schnitzel*, the ubiquitous Viennese dish of a cutlet of veal *(Kalb)*, pork *(Schwein)*, or turkey *(Puten)* covered in a coating of egg and breadcrumbs and fried, is a national dish. Goulash, a beef stew with a spicy sauce flavoured with paprika, is also on most Viennese menus. It would be rude not to try the dumplings here, but you may have no choice in the matter anyway as they are an essential element of many meals, and can appear in soups and desserts as well as main courses. *Nockerl* are a home-made pasta with a similar taste to *Knödel*.

Potato is a staple side dish and appears fried, boiled, roasted, as *Geröstete* (sliced small and sautéed) or in salads, such as *Petersilkartoffel* (potatoes with parsley). A typical side salad to the *Wiener Schnitzel* is *Kartoffelsalat* or *Erdapfelsalat*, both names for potato salad. The latter is specific to Austria, and literally means 'earth apple salad'; if you want to get in with the locals, ask for *Erdapfelsalat* rather than *Kartoffelsalat*. The obligatory *Sauerkraut*, a sour-tasting cabbage, is commonplace.

The most famous Austrian dessert is the *Strudel*, baked dough filled with a variety of fruits – usually apple *(Apfel)* with a few raisins and cinnamon. *Palatschinken* are a thinner version of the common pancake and are another popular dessert, but are often eaten as a main dish as well. And Vienna wouldn't be Vienna without the *Sacher Torte* (see the boxed text this page).

Viennese cuisine is also seasonal. Come early autumn and mushrooms not only appear in the Wienerwald, but also on menus.

Sacher Torte – More Than Just a Cake

The *Sacher Torte* is a cake with a torrid history. Two vicious 'wars' were fought between Hotel Sacher and the Demel café, in 1938 and 1953, over the origin of the cake. The 1953 war turned on a vital question: should the apricot jam be directly under the icing or in the middle of the cake?

In 1887, 200 to 400 *Sacher Torten* were baked daily in the kitchen of Hotel Sacher for distribution as far afield as Berlin, Paris and London. These days, 12 pastry chefs produce 500 to 600 a day, and as many as 3000 during Christmas.

So what's the big deal? *Sacher Torte* is basically just a rich chocolate cake with apricot jam in it. But Hotel Sacher claims that Japanese spies have infiltrated the kitchen in attempts to uncover the mysteries of the cake – what are the four chocolates used in the cake's mixture? And what is the secret of the jam? (The hotel says the jam used in its cake is 68% fruit.)

A Culinary Institution

The *Würstelstand* (sausage stand), Vienna's equivalent of a fast-food joint, is a familiar sight throughout the city. They're the perfect place for a quick bite to eat on the run; a pastime imbedded in the Viennese way of life.

These shrines to fatty bangers may sell up to a dozen types of sausage. Each comes with a chunk of bread and a big dollop of mustard *(Senf)* – which can be sweet *(süss* or *Kremser Senf)* or hot *(scharf)* – and are washed down with a beer. Tomato ketchup and mayonnaise can be requested. The thinner sausages are served two at a time, except in the less expensive 'hot dog' version, when the sausage is placed in a bread stick.

Take your pick from the *Frankfurter*, a standard thin, boiled sausage; the *Bratwurst*, a fat, fried sausage; and *Burenwurst*, the boiled equivalent of *Bratwurst*. *Debreziner* is a thin, spicy sausage from Hungary. *Currywurst* is *Burenwurst* with a curry flavour, and *Käsekrainer*, a favourite of 3am snackers, is a sausage infused with cheese. *Tiroler Wurst* is a smoked sausage. Not a sausage, but sold at *Würstelstände* is *Leberkäs* (literally 'liver cheese'), a kind of meatloaf often made from horse meat. There's even a stand for vegetarians, called *Vürstelstand*.

If you want to surprise and perhaps impress the server, use the following Viennese slang to ask for a *Burenwurst* with sweet mustard and a crust of bread: *'A Hasse mit an Sóassn und an Scherzl, bitte'*. But you probably won't get it – crusts are generally reserved for regular customers.

Late autumn heralds the beginning of the wild game season and the prevalence of *Martinigansl*, succulent roast goose. Spring starts off the season for asparagus, while summer sees a grand array of fruits.

So, where to try all these delectable dishes? Look no further than the humble *Beisln*, simple beer houses of uncountable cultural value. The word originates from the Yiddish for 'little house', and Viennese from all classes of society frequent the places. The décor and furniture is generally simple and wooden, and servings cater to gourmands. If you'd prefer to combine wine and Viennese cuisine, then the *Heuriger* (wine tavern) is for you. See the Entertainment chapter (p137) for more information.

When the Viennese are not up for a large meal of *Schnitzel* and *Erdapfelsalat*, they opt instead to visit one of their greatest loves, the *Kaffeehaus* (coffee house). These are as much

Sacher Torte from Café Sacher (p120)

a part of Viennese life as football is for the Brits and BBQs are for Aussies; see the box text on p118 for more information.

Fortunately for visitors and locals, Viennese cuisine is not the only dish on the menu. The last few years have seen a long-overdue explosion in world food, and the Viennese are simply lapping it up. Explore the city's backstreets and it won't take long till you stumble across Asian diners, Turkish kebab houses and Italian trattoria. This new-found love of foreign tastes is slowly making its presence felt in domestic kitchens across town; a stroll through the Naschmarkt, Vienna's greatest market and purveyor of exotic fruit and spices, is ample proof of this.

FASHION

All in all, the Viennese are a tidy, conservatively dressed bunch. Vienna's certainly not as chic as Paris and Milan, or as outrageous as London and New York, but it's not as provincial as many of the larger Eastern European cities either.

It's not uncommon to spot Viennese (of all ages it seems) getting around in *Tracht*, the traditional Austrian dress. This consists of *Dirndl* (colourful folk-dress) for women, and *Lederhosen* (three-quarter-length leather trousers), walking socks and heavy woollen jackets for men. This is fine in the countryside, but a little suss in a major European capital. Come wintertime, old ladies dust off their fur coats and parade them like prized kills, and in parts of working-class neighbourhoods, there's no cure for the '80s hangover – mullets, moustaches, coloured perms and shell suits just won't go away.

This of course is no representation of the entire population. Much of the new generation has taken fashion to heart, and wants to look as good as the models in those glossy mags. Chains such as H&M, Zara and Mango are bursting at the seams on Saturday mornings with Viennese looking for the latest and greatest T-shirt or jacket. Colour is also making an appearance; moody and brooding 20- and 30-somethings are swapping their blacks and greys for lighter, happier shades. Like the entire world, everyone has a mobile, but they're not so much a fashion statement or an accessory as a practical tool.

Fashion boutiques and designers are quite thin on the ground. Names to look out for include Helmut Lang (p163), Eva Blut (p169) and Turkish-born Alit Kutoglu, and while Blut is big in Japan, Lang is the only designer to enjoy any great success in the international arena. The MuseumsQuartier hosts the occasional fashion show and the Austrian Fashion Week is held around the end of September and the beginning of October.

Helmut Lang

For a guy born in Vienna, educated the Catholic way and schooled in finance, Helmut Lang has done exceptionally well for himself in the fashion arena. Stores in New York, Paris, Milan, Munich and Vienna are proof of his resounding, and resilient, success.

Helmut Lang's desire to be an artist was strong from the beginning, but, as he put it, he 'was so in awe' of artists that his initial career moves were towards the world of finance. The creative juices couldn't be denied however, and unable to find the perfect jacket and T-shirt, he decided to make his own. His designs were such a hit with friends that Lang felt a change of career was in order, and it wasn't long before he opened his first shop. In 1986 he staged his first catwalk show in Paris, and while it went down a treat with fashion gurus, he stayed resident in Vienna for some time. The pull of the New York fashion scene was too much though, eventually dragging him across the Atlantic in the late '90s. In 1998 Lang produced his first New York show and the following year he made fashion headlines (and fashion history) by staging his show in mid-September, two months before any other New York show and well before any in Europe. In April 2000 Lang entered the elite Council of Fashion Designers of America, the first non-American to receive such an honour.

His current collection is characterised by severe lines and minimal use of colour, which couldn't be further from the traditional Austrian *Dirndl* and *Lederhosen*. Many outfits are monochromatic, or a combination of black and white, but are by no means simplistic; avant-garde and cutting edge best describe many of his creations. His latest designs can be seen at www.helmutlang.com.

SPORT

The Viennese aren't what you'd call sports-mad, but the city does have its fair share of fanatical supporters, particularly when it comes to football and skiing. And while the parks certainly aren't full of people pursuing leisurely physical activity, the locals do enjoy walking, swimming, cycling, in-line skating and racket sports.

Summer is pretty much a dead time for spectator sports. However, with the arrival of autumn and winter, things heat up, so to speak. The national football league, the Austrian Bundesliga, kicks off at the end of autumn and runs until the beginning of spring with a break during the severe winter months; two of the country's better teams, Austria Memphis and Rapid, are based in Vienna. A local derby is quite an affair, and while the actual football isn't the most scintillating, the match certainly brings out the best and worst in fans.

With much of the country given over to mountainous splendour, it's no surprise to learn that snow sports are hugely popular in Austria. Almost every Austrian you meet has skied since they could walk, and the average child will literally ski circles around you on the slopes. The best skiing is in the western reaches of the country, where most competitions are held. Vienna has a couple of tiny slopes and a handful of mountains within a couple of hours' drive.

See the Sports (p155) and Health & Fitness (p155) sections of the Entertainment chapter for information on sporting venues and various outdoor activities.

MEDIA

Vienna has a long history in media. The *Wiener Zeitung* (www.wienerzeitung.at), first published in 1703, is the oldest newspaper in the world still regularly produced. With such a long and solid journalistic background, it's no surprise that Vienna receives a wide and varied view on political and social matters by its media.

Founded in 1957, ÖRF (Österreichischer Rundfunk; Austrian Broadcasting Corporation; www.orf.at, German only) is the country's independent public broadcaster. For decades it held a monopoly on radio and TV until the government passed a law in January 2002 cancelling such rights. To date, however, ÖRF has received only minimal competition. It owns a grand total of 13 radio stations (Österreich1, Ö3, FM4, RÖI and nine regional radio stations) and the county's only two non-cable and satellite TV channels, ÖRF1 and ÖRF2.

The press media is quite another matter. Alongside a plethora of regional papers, eight national papers vie for Austria's paper-reading audience. Of these eight, two follow tabloid-style reporting and the rest stick to quality over quantity, which results in fierce competition and generally good investigative journalism. Papers receive state grants, but this is under review.

The Neue Kronen Zeitung

The *Neue Kronen Zeitung* (*Krone*; www.krone.at), a celebrated daily tabloid, is a power unto itself. Its influence on the nation is said to be so great that no national decision or project can go ahead without its consent, and ultimately the consent of its founder and owner, Hans Dichand.

The figures speak for themselves: of a nation of around eight million, three million buy newspapers daily and of that three million, one million purchase a copy of the *Krone*. In percentage terms, that makes the *Krone* the widest-read newspaper per capita in the world. The paper's owners, Hans Dichand and WAZ (each own 50%), also publish the *Kurier*, the country's second-largest paper. Together, the *Krone* and *Kurier* reach around half the paper-reading population of Austria daily.

So what's all the fuss about? It seems the Viennese, like the rest of the world, love a bit of scandal and gossip. It could be said that the *Krone* is a less-aggressive (but just as powerful) version of the UK's *Sun*: light on solid newsworthy items, heavy on attention-grabbing headlines, celebrity gossip, cars and sports. There's even a section devoted to dogs.

The real fuss, however, is the paper's power to influence. Some sectors of society have voiced concern that too much influence lies in the hands of Dichand, and his views are at times far too nationalistic. This may be a moot point, as he recently retired and passed the reins over to his son Michael Dichand. It hasn't been a smooth changeover for Michael Dichand though, as, in his short term as editor-in-chief, he has managed to ruffle the feathers of WAZ, accusing them of dealings with the Balkan mafia.

With all this competition and high standards, it's hard to believe that the *Neue Kronen Zeitung* (see p16), a thoroughly tabloid spread, is easily Austria's most-read newspaper. Of the weekly news magazines, *News*, owned by Germany's Gruner und Jahr publishers, is the largest of its kind per household readership in Europe. The Newspapers & Magazines section in the Directory chapter (p197) provides a short but succinct list of papers available in Vienna.

LANGUAGE

German is the official language of Austria, but each region has a distinct dialect of its own. The Viennese dialect has many similarities to High German, but also many differences. It is certainly slower and more relaxed than its High German counterpart (it has all the qualities of a lazy drawl), but it is also more charming. The Viennese love to sprinkle their dialect with lively, evocative words and expressions which are often gobbledegook to other native German speakers. It's also peppered with French words, such as *Melange* and *Tottoir*, which is a hangover from the days when Maria Theresia encouraged her court to throw a bit of French into the conversation.

Within Vienna itself there exists a further dialect, Tiefwienerisch: a thick, sometimes unintelligible dialect that slowly oozes out between the lips, weighed down with expressive sayings that would make your mother blush. This is the language of the working class, but the nonworking class folk of the city just love it, and use it at every opportunity.

Vienna has traditionally been a melting pot of many nationalities, which has created a population where speaking two languages is almost the norm; three, sometimes four is not that rare. For around 22% of the population German is not their native tongue. This level of proficiency extends through much of society – you may find yourself being accosted by a beggar asking for money, who, upon your ignorance to his requests in German, will switch to English or French.

If you don't speak much German, or none at all, don't worry. Nowadays English is taught from kindergarten level and a high percentage of the younger population speaks English quite well. The older generation unfortunately did not have the same advantages, but they'll probably be able to understand your requests if you keep them simple. See the Language chapter (p211) at the back of this book for vocabulary and pronunciation tips.

How Much?

Box of Mozart Kügeln – €7.30

Bag of Mozart Kügeln seconds at the Manner Fabriksverkauf shop – €2

One litre of unleaded petrol – Around €0.80

A *Käsekrainer* (cheese sausage) at a *Würstelstand* (sausage stand) – €3 to €3.50

A *Krügerl* (half-litre of beer) at a *Beisl* (beer house) – Around €3

An *Achterl* (small glass of wine) at a *Heuriger* (wine tavern) – €1 to €1.50

Copy of the *Falter* – €2.05

Ticket to the Opernball – €215

20-minute *Fiaker* (horse and carriage) ride – €40

72-hour transport ticket – €12

ECONOMY & COSTS

Austria has one of the strongest economies in the EU and Vienna is Austria's financial centre. Citizens enjoy good welfare services and health care, and a benign pensions and housing policy.

Vienna is a base for precision engineering, metal products and the manufacture of electrical and electronic goods. Banking and insurance are also important, as is the service industry. The port of Vienna is the largest facility for container transloading in inland Europe, and has increased in importance with the opening of the Main canal connecting the Rhine and the Danube (Donau). Tourism is well down the list as a money spinner for the city, although it is definitely on the increase.

By European standards, Vienna isn't a particularly expensive city. It's cheaper than Paris, London or Rome, and more expensive than Prague or Budapest. Shopping aside, accommodation will be the most expensive item on your budget. Food isn't that pricey, and if you take advantage of *Mittag Menü* (midday menus) you'll save quite a bit of cash and still eat exceptionally well. Museum entry fees can soon add up, so it may pay to be a little choosy. Many theatres and classical music halls sell tickets at discounted prices a few hours before performances, and have a standing-room-only section where tickets go for a song. These options help to stretch your euro that little bit further; see also the boxed text on p53 for ideas. Note that children pay lower prices and students and senior citizens often receive discounts. Public transport is an absolute bargain in Vienna.

On average, staying at a 2/4-star hotel (double room), eating out twice a day, taking in a show and a couple of museums, and downing a few cups of coffee will set you back around €150/230 per day.

GOVERNMENT & POLITICS

As well as being the capital city of Austria, Vienna is (and has been since 1922) one of nine federal provinces *(Bundesländer)*. Every Austrian federal province has its own head of government *(Landeshauptmann)* and provincial assembly *(Landtag)*, therefore the mayor of the city is also the governor of a federal province and Vienna's City Council is a provincial assembly.

Vienna's current mayor is Michael Häupl of the SPÖ (Social Democratic Party). Elections take place every five years; the last, in 2001, resulted in the SPÖ winning 52 seats, the FPÖ 21 seats, the ÖVP 16 seats, and the Greens 11. In a city with such a solid socialist history, a collective sigh was audible throughout Vienna following SPÖ's outright victory. The previous elections, in 1996, had ushered in the first post-war coalition between SPÖ and ÖVP, a right-wing political machine. SPÖ failed to win an absolute majority and had to deal with not only a coalition with its traditional arch-rival, but also a strong opposition in FPÖ (it had won 29 seats). FPÖ has gained international notoriety under its former leader Jörg Haider, who has expressed admiration for Adolf Hitler's labour policies and made several trips to see Iraq's former dictator Saddam Hussein while he was still in power. Haider, the governor of Carinthia province, resigned as head of the FPÖ in early 2000, following the international outcry generated by the FPÖ becoming part of the federal coalition government. He remains, however, the party's most influential figure.

The Viennese are the country's staunchest supporters of socialism and are generally a rather cynical, expressive and questioning bunch when it comes to politics. It's not uncommon to hear a heated conversation over the affairs of the state or city at restaurants and bars. People are rarely shocked, or even bothered, with the private lives of their politicians and couldn't care less who is having an affair with whom – their concern is how policy making will affect their day-to-day lives, and the future of their city.

ENVIRONMENT
THE LAND

Vienna (elevation 156m) occupies an area of 415 sq km in the Danube Valley, the most fertile land in Austria. More than 700 hectares are under vineyard cultivation in the Vienna region, and nearly 90% of the wine produced is white. The largest wine-growing area is Stammersdorf in the northeast of the city.

To the west and north of the city are the rolling hills of the Wienerwald, the much-adored Vienna Woods. These are the only hills to speak of; the rest of the city is relatively flat. The Danube divides the city into two unequal halves, with the old city and nearly all the tourist sights to the west of the river. The Danube Canal (Donaukanal) branches off from the main river and winds a sinewy course south, forming one of the borders of the historic centre, the 1st district (known as the Innere Stadt). The long, thin Donauinsel, which splits the Danube in two as it courses through Vienna, is a recreation area populated with beaches, playgrounds and pathways. Just to the east of the island is a loop of water called the Alte Donau (Old Danube), known for its beaches and water sports in summer and its ice skating in winter.

Almost half the city is given over to green spaces, more than any other European capital. Major parks include the Prater, a massive belt of green just to the southeast of the Innere Stadt, and Lainzer Tiergarten, a forested area home to wild animals and enthusiastic walkers in the far western reaches of the city.

GREEN VIENNA

The Viennese, along with the rest of the country, are well informed about environmental issues, recycling and alternative energy sources.

Recycling is well established in Vienna – 295,000 tonnes of waste are recycled annually. Residents diligently divide tin cans, paper, glass and plastic from the rest of their refuse for recycling purposes. This isn't only dictated by conscience – they are compelled to do so by law. In addition, hazardous materials such as aerosols must be put aside to be collected twice a year by the municipal authorities and second-hand clothing bins are scattered throughout the city. Most beer and water glass containers (and some of the bigger plastic bottles) have a return value.

Vienna's widespread use of environmentally friendly trams and buses powered by gas has helped keep the city's air reasonably clean, and the Wienerwald does its part as an efficient 'air filter'. The city's water supply, which flows directly from the Alps, is one of the cleanest in the world, although many of the older houses still have lead pipes. This has resulted in one in every 10 houses recording lead in the water supply, but levels are generally too low to cause harm.

Vienna's pride and joy, the Fernwärme incinerator (p95), has one of the lowest emission levels of any incinerator worldwide. This plant reprocesses waste matter, burning 260,000 tonnes of waste annually to supply heating for more than 40,000 homes in Vienna.

URBAN PLANNING & DEVELOPMENT

For such an old city, Vienna is extremely well laid out and highly practical. An exception is the Innere Stadt, with its twisting, one-way system of narrow streets and pedestrianised areas, but these traits only add to the district's charm.

Hundertwasser-designed Fernwärme incinerator (p95)

Vienna is a rather compact city lined with apartment blocks and housing estates. Only a small percentage of the population enjoy a house with a white picket fence and back garden, but this doesn't seem to bother those who don't. Any real urban development to speak of in the last decades has taken place east of the Danube. Unfortunately, planning didn't match the rest of the city and instead the eastern districts consist of wide boulevards, unattractive estates and plenty of gaps.

'Constant Improvement' seems to be the motto of the city council these days. It has financed seminal architectural projects, such as the Gasometer (p98), Bücherei Wien (p95) and MuseumsQuartier (p79), creating superb public spaces while managing to retain the buildings' original ambience. 'URBION', an EU incentive to modernise the West Gürtel area, is another such project. Since 1995 the Gürtel's *Bogen* (disused arched spaces below the tracks of the U6 U-Bahn) have been miraculously transformed into bars, restaurants and art spaces. Developments in the pipelines include major overhauls to Vienna's main train stations, something everyone agrees is long overdue.

Arts

Music & Theatre   22
Visual Arts   24
Literature   27
Cinema & TV   28

Arts

Guilt, self-loathing, a pathological distaste for being Austrian and a fondness for dogs: these are the themes you'll see again and again in Viennese art, whether it's cinema, literature or painting. WWII and Austria's voluntary embrace of Nazism have created a generation of artists trying to come to grips with their heritage, and it shows in the violent self-hatred of the Actionism art movement, the sadomasochistic obsessions of film director Michael Haneke and the general hatred of humanity in author Elfriede Jelinek's novels.

While the Viennese love their contemporary visual arts and cinema – regularly taking a look at both – visitors are more likely to encounter Viennese music. Contemporary pickings are slim (legendary DJs Kruder & Dorfmeister are definitely the cream of the crop), but Vienna's musical history is rich, glorious and immensely accessible. Beethoven, Mozart, Haydn and the Strauss family all did their stints in this city, and Vienna isn't about to let you forget it. Visit the Vienna Philharmonic and you certainly won't want to.

Golden statue of Johann Strauss (p83)

MUSIC & THEATRE

Above all else, Vienna is known for music, and an unmissable Viennese musical experience is a visit to the Vienna Philharmonic. This is one of the best-known orchestras in the world, and plays to packed houses wherever it tours. Started as an experiment in 1842, it grew in popularity in Vienna but did not venture on its first foreign tour until 1898, under the baton of Gustav Mahler. The Philharmonic has the privilege of choosing its conductors, whose ranks have included the likes of Mahler, Richard Strauss and Felix von Weingartner. The instruments used by the Philharmonic generally follow pre-19th-century design and more accurately reflect the music Mozart and Beethoven wrote. Most of its members have been born and bred in Vienna, making it a truly Viennese affair.

It is a sign of the perhaps disproportionate importance of music to this city that after both world wars, when resources were so low that people were starving, money was still put aside to keep up performances at the Staatsoper. Today, you can't avoid music in Vienna, as you pass by buskers playing the classics or singing opera in the streets and Mozart lookalikes peddling tickets to concerts.

The Habsburgs started patronising court musicians way back in the 13th century, and by the 18th and 19th centuries this investment was drawing composers to Vienna from all over Europe and making music a very fashionable hobby. Among those who came in search of Habsburg ready money were Mozart, Haydn, Schubert and Beethoven;

Top Five CDs

- *Die Zauberflöte* (The Magic Flute; EMI Classics version conducted by Otto Klemperer), Mozart
- *'The Trout' Quintet*, Schubert
- *Falco 3*, Falco (try to get the original LP with the full version of *Rock me, Amadeus*, rather than the CD)
- *The K&D Sessions*, Kruder & Dorfmeister
- *Pierrot Lunaire*, Arnold Schoenberg (1992 Nonesuch recording with Jan DeGaetani)

between 1781 and 1828 they produced some of the world's greatest classical music. The Johann Strausses, father and son, kept the ball rolling when they introduced the waltz to Vienna.

The *Heurigen* (wine taverns) in Vienna have a musical tradition all their own – *Schrammelmusik* – with musicians wielding a combination of violin, accordion, guitar and clarinet playing maudlin tunes that are the perfect accompaniment to drunkenness.

Vienna hasn't had a huge impact on international jazz, rock or pop music (unless you count the striking but tragically short career of Falco, the brains behind *Rock me, Amadeus*), but the small local rock scene is alive and kicking. Particularly popular is Ostbahn Kurti (or Kurt Ostbahn, depending on how he feels at the time), who sings in a thick Viennese dialect. The mainstream Austrian pop of Wolfgang Ambros, Georg Danzer and Reinhard Fendrich also draws large crowds.

Cheat Sheet of Viennese Composers

If you want to strike up a conversation with a local while waiting in line at the *Bankomat* (ATM) or pausing over a *Melange* (cappuccino) in a coffee house, memorise some of these facts and you'll be good to go.

Christoph Willibald von Gluck Knowing about Gluck will really get you in good with the intelligentsia, because although next to no-one has heard of him, this composer paved the way for all the big names by reconstructing opera: he replaced recitatives (which broke up the story and placed the emphasis on the singer) with orchestral accompaniments that kept the story moving along. His major works include *Orfeo* (1762) and *Alceste* (1767).

Wolfgang Amadeus Mozart Not just the star of a blockbuster movie, Mozart (1756–91) wrote some 626 pieces; among the greatest are *The Marriage of Figaro* (1786), *Don Giovanni* (1787), *Così fan Tutte* (1790) and *The Magic Flute* (1791). The *Requiem Mass*, apocryphally written for his own death, remains one of the most powerful works of classical music. Have a listen to Piano Concerto Nos 20 and 21, which comprise some of the best elements of Mozart: drama, comedy, intimacy and a whole heap of ingenuity in one easy-to-appreciate package.

Josef Haydn People in the know think Haydn (1732–1809) is one of the three greatest classical composers; he wrote 108 symphonies, 68 string quartets, 47 piano sonatas and about 20 operas. His greatest works include Symphony No 102 in B-flat Major, the oratorios *The Creation* (1798) and *The Seasons* (1801), and six Masses written for Miklós II.

Ludwig van Beethoven Beethoven (1770–1827) studied briefly with Mozart in Vienna in 1787; he returned in late 1792. Beethoven produced a lot of chamber music up to the age of 32, when he became almost totally deaf and – ironically – began writing some of his best works, including the Symphony No 9 in D Minor, Symphony No 5 and his late string quartets.

Franz Schubert Schubert (1797–1828) was born and bred in the city and really knew how to churn out a tune: he composed nine symphonies, 11 overtures, seven Masses, over 80 smaller choral works, over 30 chamber music works, 450 piano works and over 600 songs – that's over 960 works in total – before dying of exhaustion at 31. His best-known works are his last symphony (the Great C Major Symphony), his Mass in E-flat and the 'Unfinished Symphony'.

The Strausses and the waltz The waltz first went down a storm at the Congress of Vienna (1814–15). The early masters of the genre were Johann Strauss the Elder (1804–49) and Josef Lanner (1801–43). Johann Strauss the Younger (1825–99) composed over 400 waltzes, including Vienna's unofficial anthem, *The Blue Danube* (1867), and *Tales from the Vienna Woods*. Strauss also excelled at operettas, especially the eternally popular *Die Fledermaus* (The Bat; 1874) and *The Gypsy Baron* (1885).

Anton Bruckner Bruckner (1824–96) was a very religious man, known for lengthy, dramatically intense symphonies (nine in all) and church music. Works include Symphony No 9, Symphony No 8 in C Minor and Mass in D Minor.

Johannes Brahms At the age of 29, Brahms (1833–97) moved to Vienna, where many of his works were performed by the Vienna Philharmonic. Best works include *Ein Deutsches Requiem*, his Violin Concerto and Symphony Nos 1 to 4.

Gustav Mahler Mahler (1860–1911) is known mainly for his nine symphonies, and – though German-born – was director of the Vienna State Opera from 1897 to 1907. His best works include *Das Lied von der Erde* (The Song of the Earth) and Symphony Nos 1, 5 and 9.

The Second Vienna School Arnold Schönberg (1874–1951) founded the Second Vienna School of Music and developed theories on the 12-tone technique. His Pieces for the Piano Op 11 (1909) goes completely beyond the bounds of tonality. Viennese-born Alban Berg (1885–1935) and Anton Webern (1883–1945) also explored the 12-tone technique. At the first public performance of Berg's composition *Altenberg-Lieder*, the concert had to be cut short due to the audience's outraged reaction.

Vienna is making small waves on the DJ and clubbing scene worldwide, and attracts well-known international acts. Local DJs Kruder & Dorfmeister and the Sofa Surfers have both enjoyed international success and are slowly putting Vienna on the map of modern music.

Vienna's tradition in the theatre was – and still is – bolstered by the quality of operas and operettas produced in the golden age of music; without music, Viennese theatre would have very little to say for itself. However, Vienna has a huge range of federal, municipal and private theatres supporting the work of playwrights and librettists; in fact, the Burgtheater (see p152) is the premier performance venue in the German-speaking world. The Akademietheater (see p152), under the same management, is a more intimate venue that generally stages contemporary plays. The Theater in der Josefstadt (see p153) is known for the modern style of acting evolved by Max Reinhardt. The Theater an der Wien (see p151) favours musicals.

The first great figure in the modern era was the playwright Franz Grillparzer (1791–1872), who anticipated Freudian themes in his plays, which are still performed at the Burgtheater. Other influential playwrights who still regularly get an airing are Johann Nestroy, known for his satirical farces, and Ferdinand Raimund (*King of the Alps and the Misanthrope*).

Many Viennese authors are also playwrights – perhaps the Viennese fondness for the avant-garde encourages the crossing of artistic boundaries. Arthur Schnitzler, Thomas Bernhard, Elfriede Jelinek and Peter Handke (see Literature, p27) have all had their plays performed at the Burgtheater.

VISUAL ARTS

Vienna has a thriving contemporary arts scene with a strong emphasis on confrontation, pushing boundaries and exploring new media – incorporating the artist into the art has a rich history in this city. Standing in stark contrast to the more self-consciously daring movements such as Actionism, Vienna's extensive Neue Wilde group emphasises traditional technique and media. To get a great overview of what's happening now in Viennese art, visit the Sammlung Essl (see p104).

Up-and-coming artist Eva Schlegel is a real name to watch. She is working in a number of media, exploring how associations are triggered by images. Some of her most powerful work has been photos of natural phenomena or candid street shots printed onto a chalky canvas then overlaid with layers and layers of oil paint and lacquer; they manage to be enjoyable at both a sensual and intellectual level.

One of Vienna's best-known contemporary artists, Arnulf Rainer, worked during the 1950s with automatic painting (letting his hand draw without trying to control it). Later delving into Actionism, foot-painting, painting with chimpanzees and the creation of death masks, Rainer has more recently been photographing and reworking classic pieces by Schiele, van Gogh and Rembrandt.

Top Five Museums & Galleries

- Leopold Museum (p80)
- Albertina (p58)
- Museum für angewandte Kunst (p82)
- Secession (p34)
- Sammlung Essl (p104)

Rainer's work expands on the important Viennese existentialist ('what's the point of it all?') tradition. One of the most notable early existentialists and expressionists was Egon Schiele (1890–1918), whose gritty, confrontational paintings and works on paper created a huge stir in the early 20th century. Schiele worked largely with the human figure, and many of his works are brilliantly executed minimalist line drawings splashed with patches of bright colour and usually featuring women in pornographic poses. He also produced many self-portraits and a few large, breathtaking painted canvases, most of which can be seen in the Leopold Museum (see p80). For more on Schiele's life and work, see Oberes Belvedere (p91) and the Leopold Museum (p80). The other major exponent of Viennese expressionism was playwright, poet and painter Oskar Kokoschka (1886–1980), whose sometimes turbulent works show his interest in psychoanalytic imagery and baroque-era religious symbolism. Kokoschka's work is also collected by the Leopold.

Actionism has been an important movement in Viennese art since the late 1950s (see the boxed text p26). Once an important member of the group, Gunter Brus now uses the more traditional media of painting and drawing for his still abrasive, shocking message. Much of Brus's work these days is *Bilddichtungen* (image poems), combining lurid images with strong, graphic text that is an integral part of the picture. Some viewers may see Brus's work as violent, self-hating pornography; others comment on the brilliant tension he creates between desire and repulsion.

While the Viennese have an unmistakable penchant for the avant-garde, there is still space in the city's contemporary art world for more-traditional works. In the 1980s, when painting was supposedly dead as an art form (replaced, apparently, by conceptual art, multimedia and installation art), the Neue Wilde group performed CPR on its still-warm corpse, creating a style of painting which was more about the paint on the canvas than the concept behind it. The Neue Wilde – which includes painters such as Siegfried Anzinger, Herbert Brandl, Maria Lassnig and Otto Zitko – is committed to maintaining the Austrian painting tradition, whether figurative or abstract, and their work crosses a variety of subject matter and styles. Brandl, for example, paints large-scale landscapes where literal representations of mountains and forests dissolve into abstract metaphors and symbols.

The Neue Wilde takes as inspiration thousands of years of traditional Viennese painting, stretching back to the Middle Ages. If you're interested in seeing the work of Medieval Viennese artists, the Orangerie in Unteres Belvedere (see p92) has a collection of Gothic religious art from the period. In the Renaissance period, the Viennese shifted their focus from biblical to natural; the Danube School combined landscapes and religious motifs. While Austria didn't produce the same calibre of baroque artists as other central European countries, some striking church frescoes were painted by Johann Michael Rottmayr and Daniel Gran. Franz Anton Maulbertsch, working on canvas, was well known for his mastery of colour and light and his intensity of expression. In the mid-19th century, the Biedermeier (or *belle époque*, as it was known elsewhere) era was dominated by Georg Ferdinand Waldmüller (1793–1865), whose evocative, idealised peasant scenes are in the Historisches Museum der Stadt Wien (see p93) and Oberes Belvedere (see p91).

While these days it's seen as slightly kitsch or commercial, Vienna's take on Art Nouveau remains one of the city's most famous – and popular – art movements. After decades of devotion to classical styles, Vienna's art scene was ripped apart by a group of young artists who, in 1897, seceded from the Art Academy and began working in the Art-Nouveau style. The style, called Jugendstil and later Secessionism in Vienna, featured organic motifs such

Sculpture outside Sammlung Essl art gallery (p104)

Viennese Actionism

Viennese Actionism spanned from 1957 to 1968 and was one of the most extreme of all modern art movements. It was linked to the Vienna Group, formed in the 1950s by HC Artmann, whose members experimented with surrealism and Dadaism in their sound compositions and textual montages. Actionism sought access to the unconscious through the frenzy of an extreme and very direct art; the actionists quickly moved from pouring paint over the canvas and slashing it with knives, to using bodies (live people, dead animals) as 'brushes', and using blood, excrement, eggs, mud and whatever came to hand as 'paint'. The traditional canvas was soon dispensed with altogether and the artist's body instead became the canvas. This turned the site of art into a deliberated event (a scripted 'action', staged both privately and publicly) and even merged art with reality.

It was a short step from self-painting to inflicting wounds upon the body, and engaging in physical and psychological endurance tests. For 10 years the actionists scandalised the press and public, inciting violence and panic – but they got plenty of publicity. Often poetic, humorous and aggressive, the actions became increasingly politicised, addressing the sexual and social repression that pervaded the Austrian state. The press release for *Art in Revolution* (1968) gives the lowdown on what could be expected at a typical action: '[Gunter] Brus undressed, cut himself with a razor, urinated in a glass and drank his urine, smeared his body with faeces and sang the Austrian national anthem while masturbating (for which he was arrested for degrading state symbols and sentenced to six months detention)'. This was, not entirely surprisingly, the last action staged in Vienna.

as flowing hair, tendrils of plants, flames and waves, and no-one embraced the sensualism more than Gustav Klimt (1862–1918). Perhaps Vienna's most famous artist, Klimt was traditionally trained, and his early drawings, some of which can be seen at the Albertina and the Leopold, show what a fine portraitist he was. But he soon developed his own colourful and distinctive style, full of naked female figures, flowing patterns and symbolism.

The influence Secessionism had on design can still be felt in Vienna. Though sculpture in the city had its strongest period in the baroque – the Donner Fountain by George Raphael Donner (see p92) and Balthasar Permoser's statue of Prince Eugene in the Unteres Belvedere (see p92) are striking examples – and neoclassical eras (see the equestrian statue of Emperor Josef II in Josefsplatz by the Hofburg p58), design didn't really hit its stride until the Biedermeier period of the mid-19th century. Viennese artists produced some extraordinary furniture during this period; deep, well-padded armchairs were particularly popular (examples can be seen in the Museum für angewandte Kunst, see p82).

The most lasting impression, however, has been left by a group of Secessionist artists who, in 1903, founded the Wiener Werkstätte (Vienna Workshop). Originator Josef Hoffman (see p34), along with core members Gustav Klimt and Kolo Moser, set out to change the face of domestic design. They wanted Jugendstil to appear not only in galleries and public buildings but in homes (albeit only well-off homes) all over the city. Determined that art wasn't just for walls, they made curtains, furniture, wallpaper, tiles, vases, trays, cutlery and bowls into objects of beauty, declaring, 'We recognise no difference between high art and low art. All art is good.'

Highly ideological, the WW (as they came to be known) joined a Europe-wide anticapitalist, anti-industrial movement espoused by designers such as English Arts and Crafts guru William Morris. They promised equality of designers and craftsmen and paid their workers reasonably for their output. The WW thought they could improve the taste of the middle and lower classes – rapidly becoming accustomed to mass-produced, slightly shoddy homewares – by promoting individual design and quality craftsmanship for everyday objects. Hang the cost, they held that style was paramount.

The result was works of sublimely simple beauty – pure, abstract, geometric pieces, many of which you can now see in the Museum für angewandte Kunst (see p82). At the same time, artists such as Oskar Kokoschka were working for the WW producing postcards and graphic books influenced by Japanese woodcuts and Austrian folk art.

Bickering over how to price these gorgeous items (the WW was constantly running at a loss) tore the workshop apart, and in 1907 Moser left. After 1915 the workshop popularised and became, in essence, simply an interior design company. In 1932 the WW closed, unable to compete with the cheap, mass-produced items being churned out by other companies.

LITERATURE

Lacking the variety of German literature or the vein of 'isn't tragedy hysterical?' running through Czech literature, Viennese writing seems to be bowed down by the weight of its authors' history. Living under an autocratic empire, dealing with the end of an autocratic empire, the guilt of Anschluss, the horror of Nazism, the emotional damage (and its legacy) dealt by WWII, neo-Nazism and the general nastiness of human beings and bleakness of life are all very, very popular themes in Viennese literature. Not content to deal with difficult subject matter, Viennese authors have regularly embraced obscure and experimental styles of writing. Overall, the Viennese oeuvre is earnest, difficult and disturbing, but quite frequently intensely rewarding.

The *Nibelungenlied* (The Song of the Nibelungs) was one of Vienna's earliest works, written around 1200 by an unknown hand and telling a tale of passion, faithfulness and revenge in the Burgundian court at Worms. But Austria's literary tradition really took off around the end of the 19th century, the same time as the Secessionists (see Visual Arts, p24) and Sigmund Freud were creating their own waves. Karl Kraus was one of the period's major figures; his apocalyptic drama *Die letzten Tage der Menschheit* (The Last Days of Mankind) employed a combination of reports, interviews and press extracts to tell its tale – a very innovative style for its time. Peter Altenberg was a drug addict, an alcoholic, a fan of young girls and a poet who depicted the bohemian lifestyle of Vienna. Hermann Broch (1886–1951) was very much a part of Viennese café society. A scientist at heart, Broch believed literature had the metaphysical answers to complement new scientific discoveries. His masterwork was *The Death of Virgil*, begun in a Nazi concentration camp in 1938 and finished in 1945, after his emigration to the USA.

Top 10 Books

- *Dicta and Contradicta*, Karl Kraus (1909) – fans of Dorothy Parker and Oscar Wilde will want to get their hands on this book of aphorisms by the 1920s satirist and social critic. Selections suitable for toilet-wall scribbling include 'Art serves to rinse out our eyes'.
- *The Play of the Eyes*, Elias Canetti (1985) – the third in this Nobel-Prize winner's autobiographical trilogy, 'Eyes' is set in Vienna just before the Anschluss. Covering the span of human experience, many believe it is a work of genius.
- *The Death of Virgil*, Hermann Broch (1945) – not just a novel, but a complete overhaul of what a novel can be, *The Death of Virgil* is one of German-language literature's stylistic ground-breakers (though it has some similarities to James Joyce's English-language *Ulysses*). Covering the last day of the poet's life, this book is hard, hard work.
- *Bambi*, Felix Salten (1923) – banned by the Nazis but beloved by alleged Nazi-sympathiser Walt Disney, this is the book that launched the movie that launched a million crying sprees. Nonpurists should look out for the scratch-and-sniff version, *Bambi's Fragrant Forest*.
- *The Radetzky March*, Phillip Roth (1932) – a 1932 study of one family affected by the end of an empire, the themes of *The Radetzky March* are applicable to any society emerging from a long-hated, but at least understood, regime. In some ways, it is about life after God.
- *The Third Man*, Graham Greene (1950) – put some time aside to read the book Greene designed as a screenplay: there is a lot of intriguing and easily-missed detail in this complex story of death, morality and the black market in the rubble of post-war Vienna.
- *Beware of Pity*, Stefan Zweig (1938) – almost Russian in its melancholic psychological complication, *Beware of Pity* weighs logic against emotion in this tale of a hedonistic soldier who lacks direction until he becomes accidentally entangled with a lame girl.
- *Across*, Peter Handke (1986) – another cheery Viennese novel, *Across* follows an observer of life drawn into 'real being' after he whimsically murders someone. Pretty darn postmodern.
- *The Devil in Vienna*, Doris Orgel (1978) – A book for older kids, *The Devil in Vienna* is the story of two blood-sisters in 1938 Vienna, one Jewish, the other from a Nazi family, and their attempts to maintain their friendship. May get kids all riled up, in a 'why is the world so unjust?' way.
- *Lust*, Elfriede Jelinek (1993) – she's a witty and clever writer, but Elfriede Jelinek hates all her characters. *Lust* is the story of a rural woman preyed on by her husband and lover, told without a gram of sympathy for the filthy habits of humans. Jelinek also wrote the book upon which Cannes-awarded film *The Piano Teacher* was based.

Robert Musil (1880–1942) was one of the most important 20th-century writers, but he only achieved international recognition after his death, when his major literary achievement, *Der Mann ohne Eigenschaften* (The Man without Qualities), was – at seven volumes – still unfinished. Heimito von Doderer (1896–1966) grew up in Vienna; his magnum opus was *Die Dämonen* (The Demons), an epic fictional depiction of the end of the monarchy and the first years of the Austrian Republic. A friend of Freud, a librettist for Strauss and a victim of Nazi book burnings, Stefan Zweig (1881–1942) had a rich social pedigree. A poet, playwright, translator, paranoiac and pacifist, Zweig believed Nazism had been conceived specifically with him in mind and when he became convinced in 1942 that Hitler would take over the world, he killed himself. Joseph Roth (1894–1939), primarily a journalist, wrote about the concerns of Jews in exile and of Austrians uncertain of their identity at the end of the empire. His recently re-released *What I Saw: Reports from Berlin* is part of an upsurge of interest in this fascinating writer.

Perhaps it's something in the water, but the majority of contemporary Viennese authors (at least, those translated into English) are grim, guilt-ridden, angry and sometimes incomprehensibly avant-garde. Thomas Bernhard (1931–89) was born in Holland but grew up and lived in Austria. He was obsessed with disintegration and death, and in later works like *Cutting Timber* turned to controversial attacks against social conventions and institutions. His novels are seamless (no chapters or paragraphs, few full stops) and seemingly repetitive, but surprisingly readable once you get into them.

The best-known contemporary writer is Peter Handke (born 1942). His postmodern, abstract output encompasses innovative and introspective prose works and stylistic plays. The provocative novelist Elfriede Jelinek dispenses with direct speech, indulges in strange flights of fancy and takes a very dim view of humanity, but she is worth persevering with. Elisabeth Reichart is considered an important – if obscure and ferocious – new writer, producing novels and essays concerned with criticism of the patriarchy and investigations of Nazi-related Austrian guilt, both during WWII and more recently.

CINEMA & TV

Modern Viennese cinema is a bleak landscape of corrupt and venal characters beating their children and dogs while struggling with a legacy of hatred and guilt. That's a slight exaggeration, but contemporary film does seem to favour naturalism over escapism, violent sex over flowery romance, ambivalence and dislocation over happy endings where all the ends are tied.

The Third Man

'I had paid my last farewell to Harry a week ago, when his coffin was lowered into the frozen February ground, so that it was with incredulity that I saw him pass by, without a sign of recognition, among the host of strangers in the Strand.' Thus wrote Graham Greene on the back of an envelope. There it stayed, for many years, an idea without a context. Then Sir Alexander Korda asked him to write a film about the four-power occupation of post-war Vienna.

Greene had an opening scene and a framework, but no plot. He flew to Vienna in 1948 and searched with increasing desperation for inspiration. Nothing came to mind until, with his departure imminent, Greene had lunch with a British intelligence officer who told him about the underground police who patrolled the huge network of sewers beneath the city and the black-market trade in penicillin. Greene put the two ideas together and created his story.

After filming one night, director Carol Reed went drinking in the *Heuriger* (wine tavern) area, where he discovered Anton Karas playing a zither. Although Karas could neither read nor write music, Reed flew him to London to record the soundtrack. The bouncing, staggering refrain that became Harry Lime's theme dominated the film, became a chart hit and earned Karas a fortune.

As a final twist of serendipity, the most memorable lines of dialogue came not from the measured pen of Greene, but from the improvising mind of Orson Welles as Harry Lime: 'In Italy for 30 years under the Borgias they had warfare, terror, murder, bloodshed – they produced Michelangelo, Leonardo da Vinci and the Renaissance. In Switzerland they had brotherly love, 500 years of democracy and peace, and what did that produce? The cuckoo clock. So long Holly.' And in Vienna they had the ideal setting for a classic film.

That said, the film industry is lively and productive, turning out Cannes-sweepers like Michael Haneke, of *The Piano Teacher* fame, and festival darlings like Jessica Hausner, director of the confronting *Lovely Rita*. A healthy serving of government arts funding certainly helps, as does the Viennese passion for a trip to the *Kino* (cinema), where local, independent films are as well attended as blockbusters by Graz-boy-made-good, Arnie Schwarzenegger. A yearly festival, Viennale, draws experimental and fringe films from all over Europe, keeping the creative juices flowing, while art-house cinemas like the gorgeous Jugendstil Breitenseer Lichtspiele (see p153) keep the Viennese proud of their rich cinematic history.

That history has turned out several big names ('big' in that they've moved to America and been accepted by Hollywood). Director Fritz Lang made the legendary *Metropolis* (1926), the story of a society enslaved by technology, and *The Last Will of Dr Mabuse* (1932), during which an incarcerated madman spouts Nazi doctrine. Billy Wilder, writer and director of massive hits like *Some Like it Hot*, *The Apartment* and *Sunset Blvd*, was Viennese, though he moved to the States early in his career. Hedy Lamarr (not to be confused with Hedley Lamarr of *Blazing Saddles* fame) – Hollywood glamour girl and inventor of submarine guidance systems – was also born in Vienna. Klaus Maria Brandauer, star of *Out of Africa* and *Mephisto*, is another native. And Vienna itself has been the star of movies such as *The Third Man*, *The Night Porter* and *Before Sunrise*.

These days, the big name is Michael Haneke, whose films tend to feature large doses of sadism and masochism. His film *The Piano Teacher*, based on the novel by Viennese writer

Top 10 Movies

- *The Third Man* (1949) – wander through the ruins of post-war Vienna, split in four by the Allied powers and kept alive by a thriving black market. Pulp fiction writer Holly Martins searches for his possibly mysteriously killed friend Harry Lime, played by an incomparable Orson Welles. Directed by Carol Reed.
- *Before Sunrise* (1995) – alternative American director Richard Linklater tells the story of two travellers – one American, one French – who meet by accident on a one-night stop in Vienna and can't help falling in love. Surprisingly sweet, with some great shots of the city.
- *Indien* (1993) – two of Vienna's greatest comedy artists, Häder and Dorfer, are government workers on the road around Vienna and the surrounding countryside checking kitchen hygiene standards. Very funny but quietly tragic. Directed by Paul Harather.
- *Lovely Rita* (2001) the next big thing, director Jessica Hausner shot her first feature film on digital with non-actors and an improvised script. *Lovely Rita* tells the story of a young Viennese woman struggling to escape her bourgeois life through love, but who ends up murdering her parents.
- *Foreigners out!* (2002) – documentary about a protest event staged in Vienna in 2000 on the election of Jorg Haider. A concentration camp for asylum seekers was installed near the Opera; immigrants – in a parody of *Big Brother* – could be voted out of the country. Worth seeking out. Directed by Paul Poet.
- *Twinni* (2003) – a period piece set in 1980, *Twinni* is the story of a Viennese teenager who moves to the country in the midst of her parents' divorce. Achingly awkward Jana suffers the attentions of a boy and the scorn of the Catholic church in this sweet film. Directed by Ulrike Schweiger.
- *The Piano Teacher* (2001) – winning scads of awards at Cannes, director Michael Haneke's most recent film continues his preference for groundbreaking, eye-opening, discomfiting projects. From the novel by Elfride Jelinek (see Literature, p27), this is the story of a masochistic young woman who suppresses, warps and destroys all her feelings in the search for artistic perfection.
- *Dog Days* (2001) – on Vienna's hottest day in years, the suburbs combust. Six intertwined stories of bondage, sexual abuse, private investigators, car theft and marital breakdown make up a surprisingly humorous film. Directed by Ulrich Seidl.
- *The Man with Two Brains* (1983) – if Steve Martin – as Dr Michael Hfuhruhurr, groundbreaking cranial surgeon – was going to fall in love with a brain in a bottle, then get mixed up with the insane Elevator Killer, where else would he do it but Vienna? You know you want to see it again. Directed by Carl Reiner.
- *Siegfried* (1924) – Austrian director Fritz Lang turns his hand to the legendary *Nibelungenlied* (see Literature, p27). It may be silent and black and white and not have any special effects, but this remains one of the best action films ever made.

Elfriede Jelinek (see Literature, p27) won three awards at Cannes. Documentary-maker Ulrich Seidl has made *Jesus, You Know*, following six Viennese Catholics as they visit their church for prayer, and *Animal Lovers*, an investigation of Viennese suburbanites who have abandoned human company for that of pets. Lately he has branched into features with *Dog Days*. Jessica Hausner has made several short films and recently released her first feature, *Lovely Rita*, the story of a suburban girl who kills her parents in cold blood. Her films critique Vienna: she says the city lacks imagination and courage.

If Viennese cinema is original and edgy, Viennese TV is anything but. With only two stations, both state-run (plus a recently introduced cable alternative), demand for locally produced content is low. Programming is dominated by foreign shows dubbed into German, though you can also catch interminable broadcasts of parliament, Austrian talk shows, local variants on reality TV or specials on folk music (that said, Viennese news coverage is excellent). If Vienna has a local hit show, it's *Komissar Rex*, the bizarrely genre-fluid, violent crime/kids' comedy series featuring a ham-roll-stealing Alsatian dog and plenty of local scenery. (Australian readers can catch Rex on SBS TV.) But the classic of Viennese serial TV is *Ein echter Wiener geht nicht unter* (A Real Viennese Never Goes Under), a '70s soap opera about Mundl, a Viennese from the darkest depths of Vienna's working class, and family. Scripted almost entirely in local dialect, even other Austrians can't understand a word of what's going on.

Architecture

Medieval & Before	32
Baroque & Rococo	32
Neoclassical and the Ringstrasse	32
Jugendstil: the Viennese Art Nouveau	34
The Secession	34
Modern Architecture	35

Architecture

MEDIEVAL & BEFORE

If you're keen on really, really early architecture, the earliest you're likely to find in Vienna is Roman. Ruins are being excavated in a couple of places in the Innere Stadt: at Michaelerplatz (p62), Am Hof 9 (p63) and Hoher Markt. There's very little Romanesque architecture visible to the naked eye these days, but if you visit some churches – such as Stephansdom (p53) and Michaelerkirche (p62) – and use your imagination, you might be able to picture the Romanesque buildings that formed these churches' foundations.

Top 10 Notable Buildings

- Belvedere (p91)
- Rathaus (p75)
- Kunsthistorisches Museum (p77)
- Stephansdom (p53)
- Majolikahaus (p94)
- Postsparkasse (p74)
- Kirche am Steinhof (p103)
- Spittelau incinerator (p36)
- Karl-Marx-Hof (p104)
- Haas Haus (p36)

While the medieval Gothic style swept through Europe during the Middle Ages, it didn't really take hold in Austria until the accession of the Habsburgs. The most impressive – and accessible – Gothic structure in Austria is Vienna's Stephansdom, with its pointed steeple and multicoloured roof tiling. Typically Austrian Gothic, it has three naves of equal height; step inside and it's not hard to picture the type of services that would have taken place in this dim, atmospheric church in medieval times.

BAROQUE & ROCOCO

After a long siege in the 17th century, German and Polish soldiers kicked the Turks out of Vienna in the year 1683, ending centuries of threat to the city's security. Money and energy previously spent on defence was poured into urban redevelopment, resulting in a building frenzy. Learning from the Italian model, Johann Bernhard Fischer von Erlach (1656–1723) developed a national style called Austrian baroque. This mirrored the exuberant ornamentation of Italian baroque with a few local quirks, including coupling dynamic combinations of colour with groovy undulating silhouettes. Examples of Fischer von Erlach's work in Vienna include the Nationalbibliothek (national library; p60) and Karlskirche (p93). Another prominent baroque architect was Johann Lukas von Hildebrandt (1668–1745), responsible for the palaces of Belvedere (p91) and Schwarzenberg (p82), and the Peterskirche (p57).

Rococo, the extreme version of baroque, was a great favourite with Maria Theresia. She chose this fussy style of gilt and curlicues for most of the rooms of Schloss Schönbrunn (p101) when she commissioned Nicolas Pacassi to renovate it in 1744. Austrian rococo is sometimes referred to as late-baroque Theresien style.

NEOCLASSICAL AND THE RINGSTRASSE

All this baroque and rococo extravagance was bound to cause a backlash. From the 18th century (but culminating in the 19th), Viennese architects – like those all over Europe – turned to a host of neoclassical architectural styles. In the mid-18th century, archaeological finds – such as the city of Troy in Turkey – inspired a revival of classical (Greek and Roman) aesthetics in many forms of art. In architecture, this meant cleaner lines, squarer, bulkier buildings and a preponderance of columns (particularly popular in the late 18th century, when romantic classicism relied heavily on Doric and Ionic Greek-style columns). The Technical University and Luigi Pichl's Diet of Lower Austria at 13 Herrengasse are examples of the neoclassical style.

Paul Sprenger's Landeshauptmannshaft next door at 11 Herrengasse is neo-Renaissance, another popular 'neo' style of the time, known in German as Rundbogenstil.

Meanwhile, the Industrial Revolution was marshalling the forces of technological development across Europe to house its factories and workers. As mechanisation upped the pace of the manufacturing industry, the new capitalists demanded more and more factories to produce their goods. In Austria, people flooded into Vienna from the countryside, drawn by the promise of jobs. Demand for housing skyrocketed, and cheap, mass-produced homes swelled the city's newly formed suburbs (see p88). Innovations in the manufacture of iron and glass allowed for taller, stronger buildings, and architects took full advantage.

When Emperor Franz Josef I took the Austro-Hungarian throne in 1848, the building boom reached a whole new level. As Habsburg Emperor, Franz Josef's power was almost unequalled: when he took it into his head to overhaul a city, that city was overhauled. Franz Josef's ambition to one-up Napoleon's makeover of Paris led

Dome of Karlskirche (p93)

to him planning, in 1849, what would become one of Europe's most homogeneous inner-city designs. The set piece of the new Vienna was (and still is) the Ringstrasse (p65). In the mid-19th century, Vienna was still essentially a medieval city in layout, with an inner area surrounded by fortifications. Franz Josef's plan called for the fortifications to be demolished and replaced with a ring road lined with magnificent imperial buildings. A competition was held to design the new Ringstrasse; once the winner, Ludwig Förster, was chosen, demolition of the old city walls began in 1857.

Although Förster was the overall designer, the buildings were created by a smorgasbord of successful architects. Taking a tram ride around the Ring will give you a quick lesson in the architectural styles popular at the time. Some of the earlier buildings are neo-Renaissance (Rundbogenstil) style – stop by Heinrich von Herstel's Herrengasse Bank, for example. But the typical style for the Ringstrasse is High Renaissance. This style features rusticated lower stories; look further up and you'll see lots of columns and pilasters. Theophil von Hansen's Palais Epstein, Gottfried Semper's Naturhistorisches Museum (Museum of Natural History; p76) and Karl von Hasenauer's Kunsthistorisches Museum (Museum of Art History; p77) are perfect examples of High Renaissance design.

While High Renaissance is the overarching theme, some of the more interesting buildings on the Ring stray from this style. Von Hansen also designed the Ring's Parlament (p75), one of the last major Greek Revival works built in Europe (take a close look at the statuary out front – perhaps horse punching was part of the traditional Greek Olympiad). While neogothic was immensely popular elsewhere in Europe, especially Britain, Vienna has very few examples of the style. Von Herstel's Votivkirche (p66) is one of the best, but the showiest is Friedrich von Schmidt's unmissable Rathaus (City Hall; p75), with its dripping spires and spun-sugar façades. The Ring also features a few neobaroque buildings: the most notable example is Eduard van der Nüll's Staatsoper (State Opera House; p151), though it's also worth having a look at Gottfried Semper's Burgtheater (p152). While Franz Josef was Emperor he had a new wing added to the Hofburg (see p58). The architect, Karl von Hasenauer, stuck very closely to a traditional baroque look, though there are some 19th-century touches – a certain heavy bulkiness to the wing – that reveal it is actually neobaroque. Neorococo runs riot in the Hotel Imperial (p176), at Kärntner Ring 16, built in 1863 as a princely palace and these days one of the city's most luxurious hotels.

Work on the Ringstrasse and associated buildings comprised one of the biggest building booms in the history of Europe. Thanks to the sheer volume of architecture created during this period, Vienna – despite massive destruction wrought in two world wars, including heavy bombing raids by the Allies towards the end of WWII which damaged almost every public building in the city and destroyed 86,000 houses – is still a showcase of European neoclassicism.

JUGENDSTIL: THE VIENNESE ART NOUVEAU

While the neoclassical style continued into the late 19th century, by the 1880s Art Nouveau was beginning to bubble up. The clean lines and elegant sturdiness of neoclassicism still held appeal for architects who appreciated history and tradition, but some designers were tired of the style's restrictions. At the same time, the Industrial Revolution had spawned a trend towards cheaply made, mass-produced architecture and design, and towards a philosophy of utilitarianism above aestheticism. While it rejected the tradition of neoclassicism, Art Nouveau was in some ways a very nostalgic, elitist movement, longing for the old days of individual craftsmanship and for style above utility.

Vienna's branch of the Europe-wide Art-Nouveau movement, known as Jugendstil ('Young Style'), had its genesis from within the Viennese Academy of Fine Arts. The Academy was a strong supporter of neoclassicism and wasn't interested in supporting any artists who wanted to branch out, so in 1897 a group of rebels, including Gustav Klimt, seceded. Architects, such as Wagner, Olbrich and Hoffman, followed. Originally Jugendstil focused more on interior and exterior ornamentation than on the actual structure of buildings. Its motifs were organic – flowing hair, tendrils of plants, flames, waves – and signature materials included iron, stucco and plain and stained glass. One of the premier exponents of Jugendstil was Otto Wagner (see p35).

THE SECESSION

By the second decade of the 20th century, Wagner and others were moving towards a uniquely Viennese style, called Secession. Many artists felt Jugendstil had become too elitist; others thought it had been debased by commercialism, as more and more 'Jugendstil-look' artefacts were produced. Secessionism stripped away some of the more decorative aspects of Jugendstil and concentrated more on functionalism, clarity and geometry.

Joseph Maria Olbrich and Josef Hoffman had both been pupils of Otto Wagner, but as the 20th century developed so did their confidence and initiative, and they eventually ended up educating Wagner in the Secession style. Olbrich designed the showpiece of the Secession, the Secession Hall (see p76), used to display other graphic and design works produced by the movement. The building is basically functional and modern – at least, far more so than earlier Jugendstil works – though it retains some striking decorative touches, such as the giant 'golden cabbage' on the roof. Interestingly, many scholars believe Gustav Klimt drew the conceptual sketches for the building, and that Olbrich took Klimt's ideas and turned them into architectural reality. Ever the functionalist, Olbrich (like his mentor Wagner) also worked on Vienna's public transit system, designing Westbahnhof, one of the city's major train and underground stations.

Josef Hoffman was inspired by the British Arts and Crafts movement, led by William Morris, and also by the stunning Art-Nouveau work of Glaswegian designer Charles Rennie Mackintosh. But by 1901 Hoffman had abandoned the flowing forms and bright colours of Art Nouveau to concentrate on black and white and the square, becoming one of the earliest exponents of the Secession style. He is best known for setting up the Wiener Werkstätte (Vienna Workshop) design studio, but he was also an architect of note. His major work is in Brussels, but some of his lesser structures can be seen on the outskirts of Vienna. The Hohe Warte urban planning project, wherein Hoffman designed a whole suburb with a 'back-to-nature' outlook, occupied him from 1901–05, and in 1903 he designed the Purkersdorf Anatorium (now restored), a health spa built from largely undecorated reinforced concrete, with the emphasis on planes and lines and only sparse ornamentation of black-and-white tile and delicate geometric fenestration. Hoffman's folkloric, anti-urban-sophisticate outlook on design was later parlayed

Otto Wagner

Otto Wagner (1841–1918) was one of the most influential Viennese architects at the end of the 19th century (also known as the *fin de siècle*). He was trained in the classical tradition, and became a professor at the Akademie der bildenden Künste (Academy of Fine Arts; p75). His early work was in keeping with his education, and he was responsible for some neo-Renaissance buildings along the Ringstrasse. But as the 20th century dawned he developed an Art-Nouveau style, with flowing lines and decorative motifs. Wagner left the Academy to join the looser, more creative Secession movement in 1899 and attracted public criticism in the process, one of the reasons why his creative designs for Vienna's Historical Museum were never adopted. In the 20th century, Wagner began to strip away the more decorative aspects of his designs, concentrating instead on presenting the functional features of buildings in a creative way.

The most accessible of Wagner's works are his metro stations, scattered along the network. The metro project, which lasted from 1894 to 1901, included 35 stations as well as bridges and viaducts. Wagner's stations were to blend in with the surrounding architecture, wherever they were built. All of them, however, feature green-painted iron, some neoclassical touches (such as columns), and curvy, all-capitals *fin-de-siècle* fonts. The earlier stations, such as Hüttledorf-Hacking, show the cleaner lines of neoclassicism, while Karlsplatz, built in 1898, is a curvy, exuberant work of Secessionist gilding and luminous glass.

Wagner's Majolikahaus (1898–99; p94) was one of his first Secessionist works. The façade of this apartment block, at Linke Wienzeile 40, is covered in a pink floral motif painted on majolica tiles. Inside, stair railings and elevator grilles are extraordinarily decorative, flowing like vines. Next door, the Linke Wienzeile Building at 38 was created by Wagner and Kolo Moser and is covered in gilded leaves and flowers – inside and out. Ten years later, Wagner designed another residence, this time at Neustiftgasse 40 – while the Linke Wienzeile blocks were designed for the elite, Neustiftgasse was built for workers. The contrast between the two – due both to the clientele and Wagner's shift in architectural focus – is striking. By 1910 Wagner was committed to a futuristic style, and Neustiftgasse is all flat planes and straight lines, with very little ornamentation. The well-lit interior is decorated with marble and metal in greys, blues and white, studded with metal rivets and floored with parquetry.

Perhaps Wagner's most impressive work is the Postsparkasse (p82) at Georg-Coch-Platz 2. Built between 1903 and 1912, this bank looms over the plaza, its exterior of thin panels of marble studded with aluminium rivets topped by statues of protective goddesses. Inside, a reinforced concrete and aluminium courtyard is roofed in glass; all the building's doors, balustrades and radiators are also aluminium.

into a periodical, *Hohe Warte*, and picked up by the Austrian National Socialist Party – apparently Hoffman had no objection to his work being used to endorse Nazi principles.

The fourth notable Secessionist – and the one most violently opposed to ornamentation – was Czech-born, Vienna-based designer Adolf Loos. In 1908 Loos wrote a polemic against the rest of the Secessionists, *Ornament and Crime*, slamming the movement's dedication to decorative detail. He was of the opinion that ornament was a waste of labour and material, and that high-quality materials were far more beautiful than any kind of decoration. Loos's work features minimal, linear decoration and geometric shapes. He preferred to work in high-quality materials including marble, glass, metal and wood. Up until 1909, Loos mainly designed interiors – one of the most accessible is the dim but glowing American Bar (see p140), a place of heavy ceilings and boxy booths just off Kärntner Strasse. Also worth a look are the public toilets he designed on the Graben: just look for the sign near the Plague Column (see p56). In the 1910s Loos developed a passion for reinforced concrete, and began designing houses with no external ornamentation. The result was a collection of incredibly flat, planar buildings with square windows – the Loos Haus (see p62), built between 1909 and 1911, is a notable example. Loos's *Raumplan*, or 'plan of volumes', was a system he developed for internally organising houses. Using this plan he later built the split-level Rufer and Moller houses.

MODERN ARCHITECTURE

The dominance of the Social Democrats in the city government of the new Republic gave rise to a number of municipal building projects, not least the massive Karl-Marx-Hof (p104) apartment complex. In the early 1970s Viennese architecture got a new burst of life, with architects taking on the challenge of building mass housing that was both functional and beautiful. Robert Krier's low-line housing estates at Hirschstettenerstrasse, built in 1982 with inward-looking courtyards, are a striking example.

Dome of Kirche am Steinhof (p103)

Since the late 1980s a handful of multicoloured, haphazard-looking structures have appeared in Vienna; these buildings have been given a unique design treatment by maverick artist Friedensreich Hundertwasser. Hundertwasser felt that 'the straight line is Godless' and faithfully adhered to this principle in all his building projects, proclaiming that his uneven floors 'become a symphony, a melody for the feet, and bring back natural vibrations to man'. Although he complained that his more radical building projects were quashed by the authorities, he was commissioned to re-create the façade of the Spittelau incinerator. This was opened in 1992; it's the most nonindustrial-looking heating plant you'll ever see

Austria's premier postmodern architect is Hans Hollein. The geometric shapes and bright glasswork of the Austrian Tourist Bureau Central Office (1976–79) and the Retti Candleshop, with its façade of sheet aluminium and doorway of two R's back-to-back, are among his earliest centrally located works. The two jewellery stores Hollein designed for Schullin have been described as 'architectural Fabergés': their smooth, granite façades appear riven and melting. Opposite Stephansdom, Hollein's best-known work is the Haas Haus, whose façade seems to be peeling back to reveal the curtain wall of glass below.

Hollein's opinion of modern Viennese architecture was quoted in a 1963 edition of *Arts + Architecture* magazine as follows: 'Today for the first time in the history of mankind, at this moment when immensely developed science and perfected technology offer the means, we are building what we want, making an architecture that is not determined by technique, but that uses technique – pure, absolute architecture. Today, man is master over infinite space.'

History

The Recent Past   38

From the Beginning   39
The Early Years   39
The Babenbergs   40
The Early Habsburgs   41
Turks, Counter-Reformation & Baroque   41
The Years of Reform   42
The Crumbling Empire   42
The Republic   44
The Rise of Fascism   45
Post-WWII   45

History

THE RECENT PAST

With its entry into the EU in 1995, Austria entered a new age of politics. This move was endorsed by the populace, who voted a resounding 66.4% in favour of EU membership in the June 1994 referendum. Since then, however, people have been rather more ambivalent about the advantages of EU membership – the introduction of the euro placed doubt in the minds of many.

After the 1999 national elections, Austria suffered international criticism when the far-right Freedom Party (FPÖ) formed a new federal coalition government with the Austrian People's Party (ÖVP) under the leadership of Chancellor Schlüssel. The new administration, though democratically elected, was condemned before it even had the opportunity to put a foot wrong. The EU immediately imposed sanctions against Austria by freezing all high-level diplomatic contacts.

The problem arose from the then leader of the FPÖ, Jörg Haider, and his flippant and insensitive remarks towards foreign members of state, his comparison of Winston Churchill's war record with that of Adolf Hitler, and his xenophobia. However, many Austrians, irrespective of their views towards the FPÖ, were upset at the EU's pre-emptive move, believing that Austria would not have been targeted had it been a more important player in European affairs. In any event, sanctions proved not only futile but counterproductive, and they were withdrawn by the EU in September 2000.

In the 2002 elections the FPÖ's popularity took a nose dive, dropping to a mere 10.1% (from 26.9% in 1999). The ÖVP was the winner all round, snatching 42% of the vote and ensuring another term in government. Haider instantly offered his resignation as head of the FPÖ, and soon after a second term of the ÖVP-FPÖ coalition began in earnest. Infighting and scandal has dogged the FPÖ since then, causing national support to plummet to even greater depths. Yet Haider pulled another rabbit out of the hat, winning the Carinthian governor's election in early 2004. While this has had no direct effect on staunchly socialist Vienna, it has certainly sent another minor shock wave through the populace.

Top Books on Vienna's History

- *A Nervous Splendour: Vienna 1888–1889* (1979), *Thunder at Twilight: Vienna 1913–14* (1989), Frederic Morton – Highly enthralling accounts of seminal dates at the end of the Habsburg rule. The first deals with the Mayerling affair, and the second with the assassination of Franz Ferdinand in Sarajevo.
- *Guilty Victim: Austria from the Holocaust to Haider*, Hella Pick (2000) – An excellent analysis of Austria during this period.
- *Last Waltz in Vienna*, George Clare (1981) – A moving account of a Jewish upbringing in the interwar years leading up to the Anschluss.
- *The Austrians: A Thousand Year Odyssey*, Gordon Brook-Shepard (1998) – One of the few books to tackle the history of Austria from the Babenburgs through to the country's entry into the EU. Great for a general overview.
- *Vienna and the Jews, 1867–1938: A Cultural History*, Steven Beller (1989) – An insightful look into the cultural contributions Vienna's Jewish community made to the city.

TIMELINE	AD 8	803	996
	Vindobona becomes part of the Roman province of Pannonia	Charlemagne establishes the 'Ostmark' territory in the Danube Valley	'Ostarrichi' first mentioned in documents

FROM THE BEGINNING

THE EARLY YEARS

The 25,000-year-old statuette, the *Venus of Willendorf,* is evidence of inhabitation of the Danube Valley since the Palaeolithic age. Vienna, situated at a natural crossing of the Danube (Donau), was probably an important trading post for the Celts when the Romans arrived around 15 BC. The Romans established Carnuntum as a provincial capital of Pannonia in AD 8, and around the same time created a second military camp 40km to the west. Called Vindobona (derived from the Vinid tribe of Celts), it was centred on the heart of what is now Vienna's Innere Stadt: the Hoher Markt was its middle, and it was bordered by Tiefer Graben to the northwest, Salzgries to the northeast, Rotenturmstrasse to the southeast and Naglergasse to the southwest. Part of its southwestern border had no natural defence, so a long ditch, the Graben (p56), was dug. A civil town sprang up outside the camp, which flourished in the 3rd and 4th centuries. Around this time a visiting Roman Emperor, Probus, introduced vineyards to the hills of the Wienerwald (Vienna Woods).

In the 5th century the Roman Empire collapsed and the Romans were beaten back by invading tribes. During the Dark Ages, the importance of the Danube Valley as an east–west crossing meant that there were successive waves of tribes and armies trying to wrest control of the region.

The rise of Charlemagne, the king of the Franks, marked the end of the Dark Ages. He soon brushed aside all those in his path and in 803 established a territory in the Danube Valley west of Vienna, known as the Ostmark (Eastern March). The Ostmark was constantly overrun by Magyars until King Otto the Great won a decisive battle in 955 and ended Magyar raids. However, the region received no mention in imperial documents until 996, when it was referred to as 'Ostarrichi'. The forerunner of the city's modern name – 'Wenia' – first appeared in the annals of the archbishopric of Salzburg in 881.

Roman ruins on Michaelerplatz (p62)

1137	1155–56	1276	1365
Vienna is first documented as a city	Vienna becomes a residence of the Babenburgs	Rudolf I of Habsburg occupies Vienna. The Habsburgs reign until 1919	Foundation of University of Vienna

THE BABENBERGS

Some 21 years after Otto's victory, the Ostmark was handed over to Leopold von Babenberg, a descendant of a noble Bavarian family. The Babenberg dynasty was to rule for the next 270 years.

The Babenbergs were a skilful bunch, and it wasn't long before their sphere of influence expanded: in the 11th century most of modern-day Lower Austria (including Vienna) was in their hands; a century later (1192) Styria and much of Upper Austria was safely garnered. Heinrich II 'Jasomirgott' (so called for his favourite exclamation, 'Yes, so help me God') was the most successful of them all, convincing the Holy Roman Emperor to elevate the territory to a dukedom and moving his court to Vienna in 1156.

Vienna was already an important and prosperous city by this stage, welcoming artisans, merchants and minstrels. In 1147 Stephansdom (St Stephen's Cathedral), then a Romanesque church, was consecrated and a city wall was built. A king's ransom flowed into the city in 1192: Richard the Lion-Heart, on his return home from the Crusades, was captured by the then ruler, Leopold V. He had purportedly insulted the Babenberg ruler at the Siege of Arce, and an astronomical figure was required for his release. Leopold used the money to found Wiener Neustadt. Under Leopold VI, Vienna was granted a city charter in 1221, ensuring more prosperity.

In 1246 Duke Friedrich II died in battle, leaving no heirs. This allowed the ambitious Bohemian king, Ottokar II, to move in and take control. He bolstered his claim to Austria by marrying Friedrich II's widow. Ottokar, however, refused to swear allegiance to the new Holy Roman Emperor, Rudolf of Habsburg, and his pride proved costly – Ottokar died in a battle against his powerful adversary at Marchfeld in 1278. Rudolf's success on the battlefield began the rule of one of the most powerful dynasties in history, a dynasty that would retain power right up to the 20th century.

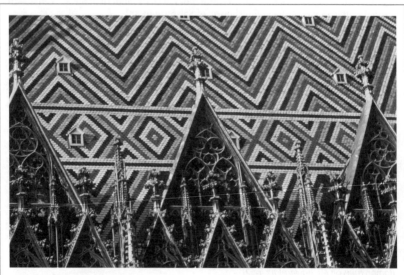

Detail of Stephansdom roof (p53)

1420–21	1529	1551	1670
The first large-scale persecution of Jews in Vienna (Wiener Geserah)	First Turkish siege of Vienna	Jesuits invited into Vienna. The Counter-Reformation begins	Second expulsion of Jews ordered by Leopold I

THE EARLY HABSBURGS

Rudolf left the government of Vienna to his son Albrecht, who proved an unpopular ruler. His successor, Albrecht II, was far more competent, and while he gained the nickname 'the Lame' due to his polyarthritis, he was also known as 'the Wise'. He procured Carinthia and Carniola in 1335 and laid solid foundations for his successor, Rudolf IV.

Rudolf IV, despite living only 26 years, founded the University of Vienna in 1365 and the new Stephansdom in 1359. However, he is more famous for his forgery of the *Privilegium maius*, a document supposedly tracing the Habsburg lineage back to early Roman Emperors.

In 1453 Friedrich III was elected Holy Roman Emperor, the status Rudolf IV had attempted to fake. Furthermore, he persuaded the pope to raise Vienna to a bishopric in 1469. Friedrich's ambition knew few bounds – his motto, *Austria Est Imperator Orbi Universo* (AEIOU), expressed the view that the whole world was Austria's empire. To prove this he waged war against King Matthias Corvinus of Hungary, who managed to occupy Vienna from 1485 to 1490.

What Friedrich could not achieve on the battlefield, his son, Maximillian I, acquired through marriage. His marriage gained him Burgundy, while his son Peter's gained Spain (and its overseas lands), and the marriage of his grandchildren attained the crowns of Bohemia and Hungary. This prompted the proverb, adapted from the *Ovid*: 'Let others make war; you, fortunate Austria, marry!'

With the acquisition of so much land in such a short time, control of the Habsburg Empire soon became too unwieldy for one person to handle. In 1521 the Austrian territories were passed from Karl V to his younger brother, Ferdinand, who soon faced problems of insurrection and religious diversity in Vienna. He promptly lopped off the head of the mayor and his councillors and placed the city under direct sovereign rule.

TURKS, COUNTER-REFORMATION & BAROQUE

Rebellion and religion were not the only problems facing Ferdinand. The Turks, having overrun the Balkans and Hungary, were on the doorstep of Vienna by 1529. Although the city managed to defend itself, the 18-day siege highlighted glaring holes in Vienna's defences. With the Turks remaining a powerful force, Ferdinand moved his court to Vienna in 1533 and beefed up the city's walls.

Soon after the siege, Ferdinand went about purging Vienna of Protestantism, a hard task considering four out of every five burghers were practising Protestants. He invited the Jesuits to the city, one step in the Europe-wide Counter-Reformation that ultimately led to the Thirty Years' War (1618–48). Maximillian II eased the imperial stranglehold on religious practice, but this was reversed in 1576 by the new emperor, Rudolf II, who embraced the Counter-Reformation. Rudolf ruled from Prague so the dirty work in Vienna was left to Archduke Ernst, who was highly successful.

In 1645 a Protestant Swedish army marched within sight of Vienna but did not attack – by this time though Vienna was once more in the hands of the Catholics. Leopold I, whose reign began in 1657, seemed to forget about the previous religious troubles and the threat of the Turks, and went about beautifying his surroundings. He instigated the beginning of the baroque era, building a whole new wing of the Hofburg (Imperial Palace), and spent lavishly on histrionic operas. He did, however, take time out from his toys to expel Vienna's Jews in 1670.

The end of the 17th century saw Vienna suffer terribly. In 1679 a severe epidemic of the bubonic plague killed between 75,000 and 150,000, and four years later the city was once again under siege from the Turks. However, Vienna rebuffed the attack, and the removal of the Turkish threat helped bring the city to the edge of a new golden age.

1679	1683	1740–90	1791
The black plague ravages Vienna	Second Turkish siege of Vienna	Age of reform under the guidance of Empress Maria Theresia and her son Joseph II	The Magic Flute is performed for the first time at the Theater auf der Wien

The Turks & Vienna

The Ottoman Empire viewed Vienna as 'the city of the golden apple', though it wasn't the *Apfelstrudel* they were after in their two great sieges. The first, in 1529, was undertaken by Suleiman the Magnificent, but the 18-day endeavour was not sufficient to break the resolve of the city. The Turkish sultan subsequently died at the siege of Szigetvár, but his death was kept secret for several days in an attempt to preserve the morale of the army. This subterfuge worked for a while. Messengers were led into the presence of the embalmed body, which was placed in a seated position on the throne, and unknowingly relayed their news to the corpse. The lack of the slightest acknowledgment of the sultan towards his minions was interpreted as regal impassiveness.

At the head of the Turkish siege of 1683 was the general Kara Mustapha. Amid the 25,000 tents of the Ottoman army that surrounded Vienna he installed his 1500 concubines. These were guarded by 700 black eunuchs. Their luxurious quarters contained gushing fountains and regal baths, all set up in haste but with great opulence.

Again, it was all to no avail – perhaps the concubines proved too much of a distraction. Whatever the reason, Mustapha failed to put garrisons on the Kahlenberg and was surprised by a quick attack from a German army led by Charles of Lorraine and supported by a Polish army led by King Sobieski. Mustapha was pursued from the battlefield and defeated once again, at Gran. At Belgrade he was met by the emissary of the sultan. The price of failure was death, and Mustapha meekly accepted his fate. When the Austrian imperial army conquered Belgrade in 1718 the grand vizier's head was dug up and brought back to Vienna in triumph, where it is preserved in the Historisches Museum der Stadt Wien (but is no longer exhibited).

THE YEARS OF REFORM

The beginning of the 18th century heralded further baroque projects, including the Belvedere Palace, Karlskirche and Peterskirche. At the helm of the empire was Karl V, a ruler more concerned with hunting than the plight of Vienna's citizens. Having produced no male heirs, his biggest headache was ensuring his daughter, Maria Theresia, would succeed him. To this end he drew up the *Pragmatic Sanction*, cosigned by the main European powers. Of course, most who signed had no intention of honouring such an agreement, and after Maria Theresia ascended to the Habsburg throne in 1740, she had to fight off would-be rulers in the War of the Austrian Succession (1740–48). She had hardly caught her breath when the Seven Years' War (1756–63) was fought to retain Habsburg lands (though Prussia won Silesia in this conflict).

Maria Theresia is widely regarded as the greatest of the Habsburg rulers, ringing in a golden era in which Austria developed as a modern state. In her 40 years as empress, she (and her wise advisers) centralised control, reformed the army and economy, introduced public schools, improved civil rights and numbered houses (initially for conscription purposes). Her son, Joseph II, who ruled from 1780 to 1790 (he was jointly in charge from 1765), was even more of a zealous reformer. He issued the Edict of Tolerance (1781) for all faiths, secularised religious properties and abolished serfdom. Yet Joseph moved too fast for the staid Viennese and was ultimately forced to rescind some of his measures.

The latter half of the 18th century (and beginning of the 19th) witnessed a blossoming musical scene never before, and never again, seen in Vienna or Europe. During this time, Gluck, Haydn, Mozart, Beethoven and Schubert all lived and worked in Vienna, producing some of the most memorable music ever composed.

THE CRUMBLING EMPIRE

Napoleon's rise in the early 19th century spelled hard times for Vienna. He inflicted embarrassing defeats on the Austrians and occupied Vienna twice, in 1805 and 1809. Due to the Frenchman's success, Franz II, the Habsburg ruler of the time, was forced into a bit of

1805 & 1809	1814–15	1848	1857
Napoleon occupies Vienna	Congress of Vienna	Revolution across the Empire. Franz Josef I succeeds to the throne and overthrows revolution	City walls demolished to make way for Ringstrasse development

crown swapping; he took the title of Franz I of Austria in 1804 but had to relinquish the Holy Roman Emperor badge in 1806. The cost of the war caused the economy to spiral into bankruptcy, from which Vienna took years to recover.

The European powers celebrated Napoleon's defeat in 1814 with the Congress of Vienna, and the capital regained some measure of pride. The proceedings were dominated by the skilful Austrian foreign minister, Klemens von Metternich.

Although culture and the arts, pursued by the comfortable middle classes, flourished (the so-called Biedermeier period), the lower classes were suffering. Metternich had established a police state and removed civil rights, and wages and housing were poor. Revolution broke out in March 1848: the war minister was hanged from a lamppost, Metternich was ousted and Emperor Ferdinand I abdicated. The subsequent liberal interlude was brief, until the army reimposed an absolute monarchy. The new emperor, Franz Josef I, was just 18 years old.

Franz Josef promptly quashed the last specks of opposition, executing many former revolutionaries. He soon eased off his harsh reproaches and in 1857 ordered the commencement of the massive Ringstrasse developments around the Innere Stadt. He also re-established the city council (Gemeinderat) in 1861, but only 1% of Viennese – all privileged landowners – were eligible to vote.

The years 1866–67 were telling on the empire's powers: not only did it suffer defeat at the hands of Prussia, but it was forced to create the dual Austro-Hungarian monarchy, known as the Ausgleich (compromise). Vienna, however, flourished through the later half of the 19th century and into the 20th. Massive improvements were made to infrastructure – trams were electrified, gasworks built and fledgling health and social policies instigated. Universal male suffrage was introduced in Austro-Hungarian lands in 1906. The city hosted the World Fair in 1873, which coincided with the major glitch of the era – a huge stock-market crash. Culture boomed; the *fin de siècle* years produced Freud, Klimt, Mahler, Brahms, Strauss and Wagner.

The assassination of Franz Ferdinand, nephew of Franz Josef, in Sarajevo on 28 June 1914, put an end to the city's progress. A month later Austria-Hungary declared war on Serbia and WWI began.

Red Vienna

With Austria's Fascist, Nazi and, more recently, far-right political history, It's surprising to learn that Vienna was a model of social democratic municipal government in the 1920s, the most successful Europe has ever witnessed. The period is known as Rotes Wien, or Red Vienna.

The fall of the Habsburg Empire left a huge gap in the governing of Vienna. The Social Democratic Workers' Party (SDAP) soon filled it by popular demand, winning a resounding victory in the municipal elections in 1919. Over the next 14 years they embarked on an impressive series of social policies and municipal programs, particularly covering communal housing and health, aimed at improving the plight of the working class. Their greatest achievement tackled the severe housing problem Vienna faced after the war by creating massive housing complexes across the city. The plan was simple: provide apartments with running water, toilets and natural daylight, and housing estates with parkland and recreational areas. This policy not only gained admiration from within Austria, but also throughout Europe. Many of these colossal estates can still be seen in the city; the most celebrated, the Karl-Marx-Hof (p104), was designed by Karl Ehn and originally contained 1600 apartments. Karl-Marx-Hof is by no means the biggest – Sandleiten-Hof in Ottakring and Friedrich-Engels-Hof in Brigittenau are both larger.

If you're interested, the Architekturzentrum Wien (p80) organises guided tours of the main Red Vienna housing complexes.

1910–14	1914–18	1918	1919
Vienna's population breaks the two million barrier, the greatest it has ever been	WWI	Karl I, the last Habsburg emperor, resigns	Treaty of St Germain signed; the Social Democrats take control of the Vienna City Council

THE REPUBLIC

Halfway through WWI Franz Josef died, and his successor, Karl I, abdicated at the conclusion of the war in 1918. The Republic of Austria was created on 12 November 1918, and although the majority of citizens pushed for union with Germany, the victorious allies prohibited such an act. The loss of key lands such as Czechoslovakia, Poland, Hungary and Yugoslavia caused severe economic difficulties – the new states declined to supply vital raw materials to their old ruler and Vienna's population was soon on the verge of famine.

By 1919 the franchise was extended to women; now all Viennese adults could vote for the city government by secret ballot. The socialists (Social Democrats) gained an absolute majority and retained it in all free elections up until 1996. Their reign from 1919 to 1933 was by far the most industrious (see the boxed text on p43).

The rest of the country, however, was firmly under the sway of the conservatives (Christian Socialists), causing great tensions between city and state. On 15 July 1927, in a very dubious judgment, right-wing extremists were acquitted of an assassination charge. Demonstrators gathered outside the Palace of Justice in Vienna (the seat of the Supreme Court) and set fire to the building. The police responded by opening fire on the crowd, killing 86 people (including five of their own number). The rift between Vienna's Social Democrats and the federal Christian Socialists grew.

The Jews of Vienna

Vienna's love-hate relationship with its Jewish population is a tale of extreme measures, a tale which began almost 1000 years ago.

Shlom, a mint master appointed by Duke Leopold V way back in 1194, is the first documented Jew to have lived in Vienna. For the next few hundred years the Jewish community lived in relative peace inside the city, even being allowed to build a synagogue, until 1420 when Albrecht V, the Habsburg ruler of the time, expelled them. The 300 or so that remained were burned to death the following year. Over the ensuing centuries Jews slowly drifted back to the city and prospered under Habsburg rule. Both parties were happy with the arrangement – the Jews had a safe haven, and the Habsburgs could rely on Jewish financial backing. However it all turned sour with the arrival of Leopold I and his bigoted wife, Margarita Teresa, who blamed her miscarriages on Jews. In 1670 Jews were once again expelled from the city, but the act weakened the financial strength of Vienna, and the Jewish community had to be invited back.

The following centuries saw Jews thrive under quite benign conditions (compared to those of other Jewish communities in Europe at the time); in the 19th century Jews were given equal civil rights and prospered in the fields of art and music. It was in Vienna that Theodor Herzl published his seminal Der Judenstaat (The Jewish State) in 1896, which laid the political foundations for Zionism and ultimately the creation of Israel. But the darkest chapter in Vienna's Jewish history was still to come. On 12 March 1938 the Nazis occupied Austria, and with them came persecution and curtailment of Jewish civil rights. Businesses were confiscated (including some of Vienna's better-known coffee houses) and Jews were banned from public places, obliged to sport a Star of David and go by the names of 'Sara' and 'Israel'. Violence exploded on the night of 9 November 1938 with the November Pogrom, known as the Reichskristallnacht. Synagogues and prayer houses were burned and 6500 Jews arrested. Of the 180,000 Jews living in Vienna before the Anschluss, more than 100,000 managed to emigrate before the borders closed in May 1939. Another 65,000 died in ghettos or concentration camps and only 6000 survived to see liberation by Allied troops.

In 1998 the Austrian government finally set up the Historikerkommission (Historian's Commission; www.historikerkommission.gv.at/english_home.html) to investigate crimes committed against Jews during the Nazi occupation, but nothing substantial has come of it yet. Today, Vienna's Jewish community numbers only 7000, but it's slowly expanding due to an influx of Jews to Leopoldstadt. With any luck, this immigration will continue to bolster numbers and once again establish a healthy community in this golden city.

1934	1938	1945	1955
Civil War breaks out. Catholic conservatives win	Hitler invades Austria. Anschluss with Germany	End of WWII. Austria is re-established and Vienna is divided into quarters	Austrian State Treaty (Staatsvertrag) signed

THE RISE OF FASCISM

Political and social tensions, coupled with a worldwide economic crisis, weakened the Social Democrats, giving federal chancellor Engelbert Dollfuss the opportunity he was looking for, and in 1933 he dissolved parliament on a technicality. In February 1934 civil war erupted, with the Schutzbund, the Social Democrat's militias, up against the conservatives' Heimwehr. The Schutzbund were soundly beaten, and the party outlawed. However, Dollfuss' reign was short-lived – in July of the same year the Nazis assassinated him in an attempted coup. His successor, Schuschnigg, buckled under increasing threats from Germany, including National Socialists in his government, in 1938.

On 12 March 1938 German troops marched into Austria, encountering little resistance. Hitler, who had departed Vienna many years before as a failed and disgruntled artist, returned to the city in triumph, and held a huge rally at Heldenplatz on 15 March in front of 200,000 ecstatic Viennese. Austria was soon incorporated into the German Reich under the Anschluss.

The arrival of the Nazis was to have a devastating affect on Vienna's Jews in particular, though many non-Jewish liberals and intellectuals were also targeted. After May 1938, Germany's Nuremberg racial laws were also applicable in Austria (see the boxed text on p44). Austria joined Germany's WWII machine from 1939 to 1945, and towards the end of the war Vienna suffered a heavy toll from Allied bombing raids; most major public buildings, plus around 86,000 homes, were damaged or destroyed. On 11 April 1945 advancing Russian troops liberated the city.

POST-WWII

It wasn't long after liberation that Austria declared its independence from Germany. A provisional federal government was established under Socialist Karl Renner, and the country was restored to its 1937 frontiers and occupied by the victorious Allies – the Americans, Russians, British and French. Austria was divided into four zones, one for each occupying power. Vienna, within the Soviet zone, was itself divided into four zones. This was a time of 'four men in a jeep', so aptly depicted in Graham Greene's *The Third Man*.

Holocaust memorial in Judenplatz (p64)

1979	1995	2001	2004
Vienna International Centre, home to the UN, opened	Austria enters the EU	Vienna's Innere Stadt becomes a Unesco World Heritage listed site	Heinz Fischer elected Austrian President – first Social Democrat to hold the position since 1986

Delays caused by frosting relations between the superpowers ensured that the Allied occupation dragged on for 10 years. It was a tough time for the Viennese – the Russians sporadically raped and looted, the rebuilding of national monuments was slow and expensive, and the black market dominated the flow of goods. On 15 May 1955 the Austrian State Treaty was ratified, with Austria proclaiming its permanent neutrality. The Allied forces withdrew, and in December 1955 Austria joined the UN. As the capital of a neutral country on the edge of the Cold War front line, Vienna attracted spies and diplomats: Kennedy and Khrushchev met here in 1961, Carter and Brezhnev in 1979; the International Atomic Energy Agency set up shop in 1957, as did the UN in 1983.

Austria's international image suffered following the election in 1986 of President Kurt Waldheim who, it was revealed, had served in a German Wehrmacht unit implicated in WWII war crimes. But a belated recognition of Austria's less-than-spotless WWII record was a long time in coming. In 1993 Chancellor Franz Vranitzky finally admitted that Austrians were 'willing servants of Nazism'. Since then, however, Austria has at least tried to make amends for its part in atrocities against the Jews. The years 1993 and 2003 saw Jewish museums opened in the heart of Vienna, and in 1998 the Austrian Historical Commission, set up to investigate and report on expropriations during the Nazi era, came into being.

Itineraries	48
Organised Tours	50

Innere Stadt — 52
Stephansplatz	53
East of Stephansplatz	54
Kärntner Strasse, Graben & Kohlmarkt	55
Hofburg	58
Michaelerplatz to Mölker Bastei	61
Rotenturmstrasse to Schottenring	63

Ringstrasse — 65
Danube Canal to Schottentor	66
Schottentor to Parlament	75
Parlament to Schwarzenbergplatz	75
Kunsthistorisches Museum	77
MuseumsQuartier	79
Schwarzenbergplatz to the Danube Canal	82

Between the Danube Canal & the Danube — 83

Across the Danube — 86
Floridsdorf	87
Donaustadt	87

Inside the Gürtel — 88
Landstrasse	89
Schloss Belvedere	91
Wieden	92
Mariahilf	94
Neubau	95
Josefstadt	95
Alsergrund	95

Outside the Gürtel — 97
Favoriten	98
Simmering	98
Hietzing	99
Schönbrunn	100
Penzing	103
Ottakring	103
Döbling	103
Liesing	104

Districts

Districts

Vienna, standing imperiously in the Danube Valley, has its head resting on the gentle, wooded hills of the Wienerwald (Vienna Woods) to the west and its feet dipping in the deep, fast-flowing Danube (Donau) River to the east.

This is a pleasantly whimsical look at Vienna's geography, but it's not entirely true. The Danube actually divides the city into two unequal halves, with around a third of Vienna to its east and the rest to its west. The Wienerwald protects the city's western and northern borders, while to the south Vienna slowly merges with flat, cultivated land. The old city centre, the Innere Stadt, is also the city's geographical centre and is flanked by the Ringstrasse (Ring Road) to the north, west and south. To the east is the Danube Canal (Donaukanal), a diversion of the great river. Combined, the Innere Stadt and the Ringstrasse possess the lion's share of Vienna's sights and attractions. Beyond the Ringstrasse are residential districts and a larger traffic artery, the Gürtel (literally meaning 'belt'), which is fed by the flow of vehicles from the outlying motorways. East of the Danube Canal are residential districts and the Danube itself.

Vienna has 23 *Bezirke* (districts), but to make things easier for ourselves and for the traveller, we've grouped them under geographical headings. First comes the **Innere Stadt**, a compact central district which is more like an open-air museum than a city centre, followed by the **Ringstrasse**, a wide boulevard lined with grandiose architectural achievements. We then move onto the area **Between the Danube Canal & the Danube**, encompassing a residential district rich in Jewish history and fabulous public parks, before heading **Across the Danube** to Vienna's modern expanse largely ignored by tourists. Next comes the area we've classed as **Inside the Gürtel**, a swath of outlying districts where well-to-do Viennese live side by side with broke students, and we finish with the areas beyond them, grouped under the heading **Outside the Gürtel**.

> ## Top Five for Children
>
> - **Donauinsel** (p87) Playgrounds, swimming areas, bicycle and in-line skate hire, and miles of pathways – what more could you ask for?
> - **Haus der Musik** (p55) Vienna's top interactive museum with loads of fun and challenging activities.
> - **Schönbrunn Kindermuseum** (p102) Where the little tykes can learn how to behave like right royal princes and princesses.
> - **Wurstelprater** (p85) A fun park with amusement rides and silly games the kids will go crazy over.
> - **Zoom** (p82) Vienna's premiere children's museum, and one big arts and crafts lesson.
>
> If you speak German, *Falter's Kinder in Wien* book is the only resource you'll ever need for any aspect of your child's life in Vienna. It's available from book stores.

ITINERARIES

One Day

If you've only one day to explore Vienna, we have three pieces of advice for you: start early, finish late and remember that discovering the back alleys and cul-de-sacs of the Innere Stadt can be more rewarding than most museums. If you'd like to see the big attractions, then stick to the following itinerary. Begin the day with a *Melange* (Viennese cappuccino) and a *Buttersemmel* (buttered roll) at a traditional *Kaffeehaus* (coffee house) — **Café Central** (p121) or **Café Sperl** (p129) would be a good choice. Jump on tram 1 or 2 and circle the **Ringstrasse** (p65) for a brief, but rewarding, informal tour of the boulevard's buildings. Then duck down **Kärntner Strasse** (p57), Vienna's much-heralded shopping street, to **Stephansdom** (p53) and climb its steeple for views across the rooftops. Meander along **Graben** (p56) and **Kohlmarkt** (p57), with a few side-street detours along the way, to the **Hofburg** (p58) and pick a museum that takes your fancy. Next, head across the Ringstrasse and Maria-Theresien-Platz to the **MuseumsQuartier** (p79) for a well-deserved lunch break. Depending on your tastes, either take in the **Leopold Museum** (p80) or jump on the U-Bahn and head for **Schloss Schönbrunn** (p101). Recharge the batteries at one of the many **Innere Stadt restaurants** (p119) before attending a performance at the **Staatsoper** (p151).

Three Days

After filling your first day with the must-sees (see the one-day itinerary p48), start your second day with either the Leopold Museum or Schloss Schönbrunn, whichever one you opted out of on day one. Return to the Hofburg and discover the Nationalbibliothek's **Prunksaal** (p60), before lunching at the **Naschmarkt** (p128). After lunch take in some much-needed fresh air in the **Prater** (p85) and treat yourself to a ride on the **Riesenrad** (p85). In the evening head to the outskirts of the city and dine in one of Vienna's many **Heurigen** (wine taverns; p144); don't forget to sample the local wine.

Flohmarkt at Naschmarkt (p166)

On the morning of the third day spend as long as you deem fit at the **Kunsthistorisches Museum** (p77) in order to truly appreciate its goldmine of art. Lunch at **Zu den Zwei Leisln** (p134) and walk off that monstrous *Wiener Schnitzel* in the **Volksgarten** (p75), before viewing Klimt's sumptuous *Beethoven Frieze* in the **Secession** (p76). If there's time, make for **Kahlenberg** (p104) to beat the setting sun. Your final evening can be spent in one of the **Gürtel's progressive bars** (p139) or the plethora of nightspots in and around the Naschmarkt.

A Divided City

Vienna is comprised of districts *(Bezirke)*, 23 of them in fact. Number one is the Innere Stadt, or 1st district as it's more commonly known, and the rest basically fan out from there in an almost spiral shape. Generally speaking, the higher the district number the further it is from the centre. Addresses come in three parts: district, street name and street number/apartment number in that order – eg 01, Kärntner Strasse 43/12 means flat 12, number 43 on Kärntner Strasse in the 1st district. We have stuck to this arrangement throughout the book. If you only have the postcode of an address it's possible to work out the district. Postcodes consist of four digits, with the middle two indicating the district; eg a postcode of 1010 means the place is in district one, and 1230 refers to district 23. Also note that the same street number may cover several adjoining premises, so don't give up if you come across an apartment block if you're looking for a restaurant as it may just be next door.

Districts not only divide the city geographically, but also socially. They often, but not always, signify social and financial status, and the numbers are no indication of any order. The 13th (Hietzing) and 19th (Döbling) districts are generally regarded as the *crème de la crème*, with the 18th (Währing) and 3rd (Landstrasse) coming a close second. Also-rans include the 8th (Josefstadt) and 9th (Alsergrund). The 15th (Rudolfsheim-Fünfhaus) and 16th (Ottakring) districts attract not only immigrants but also young Viennese looking for some ethnic diversity, while the 10th (Favoriten), 11th (Simmering) and 12th (Meidling) are regarded as the underbelly of the city and home to *Prolos* (a not particularly complimentary Viennese word for the working class). A resident of Hietzing probably wouldn't be seen dead in Simmering, and vice versa.

The rest of the districts fall somewhere in between, except the Innere Stadt, which is a law unto itself. Viennese tend to associate it with tourists, shopping and an evening out rather than day-to-day living – except for the ones living there, of course.

One Week

When your fourth day rolls around it's time to get out of town. Take a bike, boat, bus or car along the Danube Valley to the picturesque towns of **Krems** (p189), **Dürnstein** (p188) and **Melk** (p186). On the fifth day escape Vienna's urban confluences again, but this time in the opposite direction to Burgenland, where the **Neusiedler See** (p190) and its quaint villages surrounded by vineyards await. If your sixth day coincides with a Saturday, combine breakfast and a flea market at the **Naschmarkt** (p166), then cross town to the gardens and galleries of the **Belvedere** (p91) or head to the Innere Stadt to explore the newly renovated **Albertina** (p58). This is a city where 'macabre' and 'imperial' comfortably exist in the same sentence, so an afternoon trip to the **Kaisergruft** (p56) should follow. And, not to forget, this *is* a city of music; spend the evening at the **Konzerthaus** (p150) or **Musikverein** (p150).

The seventh day is mop-up day: enjoy anything that takes your fancy. If you need some guidance, spend the day shopping, sunning yourself on the **Donauinsel** (Danube Island; p87) or **Alte Donau** (Old Danube; p87), or simply wandering through the atmospheric back alleys of the Innere Stadt.

ORGANISED TOURS

Whether your preference be bus, boat, foot or horse-drawn carriage (known locally as *Fiaker*), Vienna has an organised tour to suit. Each serves a specific purpose: bus tours cover a lot of ground and take in the further-flung sights; boat tours use the Danube Canal and Danube to great effect; walking tours take full advantage of the Innere Stadt's flat topography and plethora of pedestrianised zones; bike tours are a leisurely way to see much of the city at your own pace; and *Fiaker* are just a pleasant, old-fashioned way to get around.

It's also possible to organise your own tram tour; trams 1 and 2, which circle the Innere Stadt along the Ringstrasse, are perfect self-guided tours of the Ringstrasse's architectural delights, and the Walking & Cycling Tours chapter (p105) offers five tours throughout the city.

Bus Tours

CITYRAMA Map pp240-3
☎ 534 13; www.cityrama.at; 01, Börsegasse 1; tours adult €33-109, child €15-45

Cityrama offers a range of half- and full-day tours of Vienna and attractions within a day's striking distance of the city, including Salzburg, Budapest and Prague. Some tours require an extra fee for admission into sights, such as training at the Spanish Riding School. See the website for times and details.

HOP ON HOP OFF VIENNA LINE
Map pp240-3
☎ 712 46 83; www.viennasightseeingtours.com; 01, Opernring; 1hr/2hr/all-day tickets adult €12/15/20, child €7/7/7; ⌚ 10am-5pm; U1, U2, U4 Karlsplatz, Karlsplatz trams

The Vienna Line buses pass by 13 sights in Vienna. Tickets range from one hour to all day, and you can hop on and off the buses as many times as you wish in that time.

Buses circle the Innere Stadt, with a detour to Stephansplatz, departing on the hour, every hour, Monday to Thursday, and every half-hour Friday to Sunday, from outside the Staatsoper. Buses at 11am, 1pm, 3pm and 5pm continue onto sights east of the Innere Stadt, such as the UNO city and Prater, while the noon, 2pm and 4pm buses take in Schönbrunn and Belvedere.

REISEBUCHLADEN Map pp240-3
☎ 317 33 84; reisebuchladen@aon.at; 09, Kolingasse 6; tours €27; ⌚ 10am-6pm Mon-Fri, 9.30am-12.30pm Sat; U2 Schottentor, Schottentor trams

This travel agency conducts alternative sightseeing tours, such as 'Traum und Wirklichkeit' (Dream and Reality), which concentrates on Red Vienna and Jugendstil (Art Nouveau) architecture, and a Hundertwasser tour. The guide is not afraid to reveal uncomplimentary details about Vienna. Schedules depend upon demand and tours are in German unless there are enough English speakers.

VIENNA SIGHTSEEING TOURS
Map pp240-3
☎ 712 46 83; www.viennasightseeingtours.com; tours €32

Run by the same company that organises the Hop On Hop Off tours, Vienna Sightseeing Tours offers a wide variety of half- and full-day tours in English with free hotel pick-up. Its website lists all the tours and times.

Boat Tours

DDSG BLUE DANUBE Map pp240–3
☎ 588 80; www.ddsg-blue-danube.at; 01, Schweden-brücke; full tour adult/child €14/7, half tour €10/5, children under 10 free; tours 11am & 3pm May-Sep; U1, U4 Schwedenplatz, Schwedenplatz trams

DDSG *Blue Danube* circumnavigates Leopold-stadt and Brigittenau districts using the Danube Canal and the Danube as its thoroughfare. It's more of a relaxing break than a huge sightseeing tour. The half tour (two hours) ends at Reichsbrücke, the full tour (3¼ hours) back at Schwedenbrücke.

Its 'Hundertwasser Tour' is similar to the one above, the biggest difference being the boat has been given the Hundertwasser design treatment. It departs at 10am and 2pm daily from Schwedenplatz from mid-April to September, and only on Friday, Saturday and Sunday in October. The tour takes around 1½ hours and costs €14.50/7.25 per adult/child. Half tours are also available, costing €10.80/5.40. You can either board at the Schwedenplatz or at Reichsbrücke.

DONAU SCHIFFAHRT PYRINGER-ZOPPER Map pp240–3
☎ 715 15 25-20; www.donauschiffahrtwien.at; 01, Schwedenplatz; grand tour adult/child €14/7, small tour €10/5; tours 10.45am Apr-Oct, 10.45am & 2.45pm mid-Jun–early-Sept

Pyringer-Zopper does almost identical Danube circuits to DDSG *Blue Danube* and departs from either Schwedenplatz or Reichsbrücke.

Guided Walking Tours

MUSIC MILE VIENNA
three hr €5, extra hr €1.50

Reminiscent of Hollywood's 'walk of fame', this trail of marble stars runs from Stephansdom to Theater an der Wien and commemorates some 70 musical geniuses related to Vienna in one way or another. The stars are embedded in the footpath, often adjacent to where the composer, singer or musician lived or worked, and audio guides and booklets provide background information on the person. The audio guides and booklets are available from the following locations between 10am and 7pm: Musikmeile Wien Servicestelle (Map pp240–3; 01, Stephansplatz); Wien-Ticket Pavillon (Map pp240–3; 01, Herbert-von-Karajan-Platz) and Theatershop, Theater an der Wien (Map pp240–3; 01, Linke Wienzeile 6).

VERLIEBT IN WIEN
☎ 889 28 06; www.verliebtinwien.at; adult/child €10.50/5

Margarete Kirschner offers various themed walks covering such topics as Medieval Vienna, Art Nouveau and Erotic Vienna. Tours take around 1½ to two hours, leaving at 10am and 2.30pm daily from the corner of Hotel Sacher (p174) and Kärntner Strasse. Book direct or try through your hotel.

VIENNA TOUR GUIDES
☎ 876 71 11; www.wienguide.at; adult/child €11/6

Vienna Tour Guides are a collection of highly knowledgeable guides who conduct 40 different guided walking tours, 11 of which are in English. Everything from Art-Nouveau architecture to Jewish traditions in Vienna is covered. The monthly *Wiener Spaziergänge* (Vienna's Walking Tours) leaflet from the tourist office details all of these, gives the various departure points, and also indicates those tours conducted in English. Tours last about 1½ hours and some require a valid public transport pass and extra euros for entrance fees into sights.

The 'Third Man Tour', based on the film of the same name, is conducted in English by Dr Brigitte Timmermann (☎ 774 89 01; brigitte@viennawalks.tix.at) and is about the most popular tour offered. It departs at 4pm Monday and Friday from the U4 Stadtpark station (Johannesgasse exit); a torch and good footwear are prerequisites. At €16 it costs a little extra, but takes in all the main location spots used in the film, including the underground sewers, home to 2½ million rats. You'll discover that the sewers are not linked together, so it is impossible to cross the city underground as Harry Lime did in the film.

Other Tours

FIAKER
20-min/40-min/1-hr tour €40/65/75

More of a tourist novelty than anything else, a *Fiaker* is a traditional-style open carriage drawn by a pair of horses. Drivers generally speak English and point out places of interest en route. Lines of horses, carriages and bowler-hatted drivers can be found at Stephansplatz, Albertinaplatz and Heldenplatz at the Hofburg.

OLD-TIMER TRAMS
☎ 790 91 05; www.wiener-tramwaymuseum.org; adult/child €15/5; U1, U2, U3 Karlsplatz, Karlsplatz trams

On weekends and holidays from May to October trams from 1929 trundle through Vienna

More for Your Money

Want to go everywhere, do everything, shop at every store? Consider purchasing a Vienna Card (€16.90), which is valid for three days and includes public transport and a plethora of discounts on museums, shops and cafés. For more information, see the Discount Cards section in the Directory chapter p197.

If you plan to see more than one or two sights associated with the Kunsthistorisches Museum, consider purchasing a Gold, Silver or Bronze ticket. The Gold ticket (€23) allows entry to the Kunsthistorisches Museum, Schatzkammer and Neue Burg museums, as well as the Museum für Völkerkunde, Wagenburg in Schönbrunn and the Theatermuseum. The Silver ticket (€21) covers everything the Gold ticket does, minus the Wagenburg. Third place Bronze (€19) will get you into the Kunsthistorisches Museum, Schatzkammer, Neue Burg museums and the Museum für Völkerkunde.

In general, children up to the ages of 14 to 18 are charged the children's entrance fee, and concession prices cover senior citizens (over 65), students up to the age of 27 and disabled people. Family tickets usually mean two adults and two children; children under four normally enter free of charge.

taking people on one-hour tours of the city. They depart from the Stadtbahn Pavillons on Karlsplatz at 11.30am and 1.30pm on Saturday and 9.30am, 11.30am and 1.30pm on Sunday.

PEDAL POWER Map pp244-5
☎ 729 72 34; www.pedalpower.at; 02, Ausstellungs-strasse 3; tours with own bike adult/student/child €23/19/12, incl hired bike €16/14/12; U1 Praterstern, tram 0, 5, 21

Pedal Power conducts half-day bicycle tours in and around Vienna from May until September. Tours start at 10am daily and there are five tours on offer: Innere Stadt and the Prater; Donau Park and Lobau; Donauinsel and Klosterneuburg; Donauinsel and the *Heurigen* (wine taverns) of Stammersdorf; and Classical Music Memorials and the Zentral-friedhof. Child seats and helmets cost €4 extra apiece.

INNERE STADT

Eating p119; Shopping p161; Sleeping p173

The Innere Stadt – and Vienna for that matter – started life as a Roman camp centred on what is now Hoher Markt, and since those barbaric days it has never looked back. It has endured power struggles, riots, wars, bombings and plagues and come through them all with its head held high and dignity intact. And whichever way you look at it – geographical, historical, financial, religious, imperial – the Innere Stadt still remains the very heart of Vienna.

There is something timeless and magical about the place, which nothing else in Vienna even comes close to. Take a stroll down its back alleys and cobblestoned cul-de-sacs on a cold winter evening as the fog set-

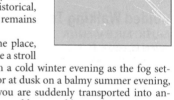

tles, or at dusk on a balmy summer evening, and you are suddenly transported into another world: one of horse-drawn carriages and Mozart and Beethoven recitals, when an imperial family ruled over this regal city. You can easily see why the entire district has been designated a World Heritage Site since 2001.

Many locals avoid the Innere Stadt, claiming it to be only for tourists with its overpowering open-air museum status. But the truth is quite the contrary. Sure, every second building seems to be more ornate, elaborate and just plain gorgeous than the

Innere Stadt Top Sights

- Being amazed at the sheer volume of books in the **Prunksaal** (p60)
- Climbing **Stephansdom's** (p53) tall spire
- Discovering your hearing range at the **Haus der Musik** (p55)
- Losing yourself in the **back alleys** and cobble-stoned **cul-de-sacs** of the Innere Stadt
- Wandering the art-covered hallways of the newly renovated **Albertina** (p58)

next, but it's also a district full of life. It has a good helping of fine museums, inviting restaurants, top-notch bars and quality shops. Combine all these and you have a district which is there to be enjoyed, as well as appreciated.

Of the highlights within the Innere Stadt, the imperial Hofburg, Gothic Stephansdom and the pedestrianised streets in between should definitely not be missed. But don't forget to take time out to stop, sip a coffee and soak up the rich ambience.

Orientation

The Innere Stadt is a compact district – it's only 1800m across at its widest point – and easily manageable on foot. In fact, you're better off leaving your car at home: pedestrian zones and a confusing one-way system make driving in the Innere Stadt hell. The Ringstrasse, with the help of the Danube Canal, conveniently form the borders of this district.

The heart of the Innere Stadt is Stephansdom, which dominates the main square, Stephansplatz. Kärntner Strasse, the Innere Stadt's main pedestrianised street, runs south from Stephansplatz, and connects the square with the Ringstrasse. Rotenturmstrasse heads north from Stephansplatz to the Danube Canal. Graben and Kohlmarkt, the Innere Stadt's other main pedestrianised thoroughfares, are to the west of Stephansplatz and end at Michaelerplatz and Michaelertor, entrance to the Hofburg. The mighty Hofburg occupies much of the district's southwest corner. At the western end of Graben is Bognergasse, which quickly transforms itself into Freyung, which in turn leads directly into Schottengasse. These four streets link Stephansplatz with Schottentor, a public transport hub on the northwest section of the Ringstrasse. To the southwest of Schottentor is Mölker Bastei, one of the few remnants of the old city walls.

STEPHANSPLATZ

DOM- & DIÖZESANMUSEUM

Map pp240-3

☎ 515 52-36 89; 01, Stephansplatz 6; adult/concession/child €5/4/2.15; ⏲ 10am-5pm Tue-Sun; U1, U3 Stephansplatz

The Cathedral and Diocesan Museum of Vienna is a treasure-trove of religious art pieces spanning a period of over 1000 years. While the collection is blessed with extraordinary articles, such as the earliest European portrait, that of Duke Rudolph IV (1360), and two Syrian glass vessels (1280–1310), thought to be among the oldest glass bottles in the world, after a while it all seems to blend into one. If you're into religious art, however, this must be on your itinerary.

STEPHANSDOM Map pp240-3

☎ 515 52-35 20; www.stephanskirche.at, German only; 01, Stephansplatz; admission free; ⏲ 6am-10pm Mon-Sat, 7am-10pm Sun; U1, U3 Stephansplatz

The most beloved and recognisable structure in all of Vienna is the Gothic masterpiece Stephansdom, or Steffl (little Stephen), as the locals call it. It is the geographical and emotional heart of the city itself.

Stephansdom (St Stephen's Cathedral) was built on the site of a 12th-century church and this church's remains – the Riesentor (Giant's Gate) and the Heidentürme (Towers of the Heathens) – are incorporated into the present structure. Both features are Romanesque in style; the **Riesentor** (literally 'Giant's Gate' – rumour has it the gate was named because a mammoth's tibia, which was mistaken for a giant's shin, once hung here) is the main western entrance, and is topped by a tympanum of lattice patterns and statues. The church was re-created in Gothic style at the behest of Habsburg Duke Rudolf IV in 1359; the duke laid the foundation stone and earned himself the epithet of 'The Founder' in the process.

The dominating feature of the church is the skeletal **Südturm** (south tower). It stands

136.7m high and was completed in 1433 after 75 years of building work. Ascending the 343 steps will bring you to the cramped viewing platform for an impressive panorama (🕙9am to 5.30pm; adult/concession €3/1). It was to be matched by a companion tower on the north side, but the imperial purse withered and the Gothic style went out of fashion, so the half-completed tower was topped off with a Renaissance cupola in 1579. Austria's largest bell, weighing in at a hefty 21 tonnes, is the **Pummerin** (boomer bell) and was installed here in 1952. The north tower, accessible by lift, is open from 9am to 6pm April to October, until 6.30pm July and August, and from 8.30am to 7pm November to March (adult/child €4/1.50).

From the outside of the cathedral, the first thing that will strike you is the glorious **tiled roof**, with its dazzling row of chevrons on one end and the Austrian eagle on the other; a good perspective is gained from the northeast of Stephansplatz. The cathedral suffered severe damage during a fire in 1945, but donations flowed in from all over Austria and the cathedral was completely rebuilt and reopened in just three years.

The interior matches the exterior to a T, although on a cloudy, grey day, you may be hard pushed to fully appreciate the elaborate detail due to a distinct lack of light. Taking centre stage is the magnificent Gothic **stone pulpit**, fashioned in 1515 by Anton Pilgram. The expressive faces of the four fathers of the church (Saints Augustine, Ambrose, Gregory and Jerome) are at the centre of the design, but the highlight is Pilgram himself peering out from a window directly below the platform. He also appears at the base of the organ loft on the northern wall, seemingly holding up the entire organ on his own narrow shoulders. Take a closer look at the pulpit's handrailing: salamanders and toads fight an eternal battle of good versus evil up and down its length. The baroque **high altar**, at the very far end of the nave, shows the stoning of St Stephen. The chancel to its left has the winged Wiener Neustadt altarpiece, dating from 1447; the right chancel has the Renaissance red marble tomb of Friedrich III. Under his guidance the city became a bishopric (and the church a cathedral) in 1469. Don't forget to study the decorations and statue groups on the outside of the cathedral: at the rear the agony of the Crucifixion is well captured, although some irreverent souls attribute Christ's pained expression to toothache. Guided tours of the

cathedral in English are at 3.45pm daily from April to October; otherwise, tours in German leave at 10.30am and 3pm Monday to Saturday and 3pm Sunday (adult/child €4/1.50). Evening tours at 7pm every Saturday from June to September are also offered, and include a climb to the top of the south tower (€10/4). Organ concerts are a special treat, and are held at 8pm every Wednesday from May to October. Note that much of the nave is closed to the public during mass, which is held up to seven times a day.

Last, but by no means least, is the cathedral's **Katakomben** (catacombs), which are open daily but can only be visited with a tour guide. The entrance is near the lift to the north tower; tours leave every 15 to 30 minutes between 10am and 11.30am and 1.30pm and 4.30pm Monday to Saturday, and afternoons only on Sunday (€4/1.50). The catacombs house the remains of countless plague victims, kept in a mass grave and a bone house. Also on display are rows of urns containing the internal organs of the Habsburgs. One of the many privileges of being a Habsburg was to be dismembered and dispersed after death: their hearts are in the Augustinerkirche in the Hofburg and the rest of their bits are in the Kaisergruft.

EAST OF STEPHANSPLATZ

DOMINIKANERKIRCHE Map pp240-3
☎ 512 91 74; 01, Postgasse 4; admission free; 🕙 daily; U3 Stubentor, tram 1, 2, bus 2A
Dominikanerkirche (Dominican Church) was built on the site of an earlier church and completed in 1634. The expansive interior is incredibly baroque, with white stucco, frescoes, and even the imperial double-headed eagle on the ceiling. The Dominicans first came to Vienna in 1226 under the invitation of Leopold VI of Babenberg.

FIGARO HAUS Map pp240-3
☎ 535 62 94; 01, Domgasse 5; adult/concession €4/2; 🕙 9am-6pm Tue-Sun; U1, U3 Stephansplatz, bus 1A
Figaro Haus is famous for its former occupant Mozart, who spent 2½ happy and productive years here. The house gained its name from one of the pieces he penned while living here, *The Marriage of Figaro*. There's not a lot to see inside except a few of the composer's manuscripts, but you're paying a pittance to enter. Figaro Haus is a municipal museum. Please try to repress the urge to sing *Figaro, Figaro, Figaro* outside the premises.

FLEISCHMARKT Map pp240-3
U1, U4 Schwedenplatz, Schwedenplatz trams

Fleischmarkt (it gained its name from an old meat market based here), which runs parallel the Danube Canal and crosses Rotenturmstrasse, is blessed with a cluster of **Art-Nouveau buildings**. No 14, built by F Dehm and F Olbricht between 1889 and 1899, exhibits gold and stucco embellishments, while No 7 (Max Kropf; 1899) was the childhood home of Hollywood film director Billy Wilder from 1914 to 1924. Arthur Baron was responsible for Nos 1 and 3 (1910), now home to a bank and a Spar supermarket. Other notables on the street include the Greek Orthodox Church (see p55), Griechenbeisl (see p120) and the Main Post Office.

FRANZISKANERKIRCHE Map pp240-3
☎ 512 45 78-11; 01, Franziskanerplatz; admission free; ⏰ 7.30-11.30am & 2.30-5.30pm; U1, U3 Stephansplatz

This small Franciscan church tucked away on Franziskanerplatz behind Stephansdom dates from the early 1600s. Its Renaissance façade hides a surprisingly rich baroque interior that has left almost every nook and cranny untouched. The archaeological findings of a recent dig at the church can be viewed by appointment only, and choir recitals are a regular feature.

GREEK ORTHODOX CHURCH Map pp240-3
01, Fleischmarkt 13; U1, U4 Schwedenplatz, Schwedenplatz trams

A rather hidden door at No 13 on Fleischmarkt is the entrance to this unusual find. Built in 1861 by Vienna's Greek community, the interior of the church is a glittering display of Byzantine design and the façade a colourful brickwork. The inside can only be seen in its full glory during Sunday services; during the week only the ornate entrance way can be viewed. Next door is a quaint and famous old tavern, the Griechenbeisl (see p120).

HAUS DER MUSIK Map pp240-3
☎ 516 48-0; www.hdm.at; 01, Seilerstätte 30; adult/ concession €10/8.50; ⏰ 10am-10pm; tram 1, 2, bus 3A

It took a while in coming – considering the significant contribution Vienna made to the world of music – but finally the city organised itself a museum devoted to music, the Haus der Musik.

The museum is spread out over four floors and all descriptions are in English and German. The 1st floor plays host to the Vienna Philharmonic, though it's rather brief and more interesting things are on the floors above.

Floor 2 is where the fun begins. The first room you enter is the 'foetus' room; no, you won't get born again, but you'll experience sounds and noises heard by babies in the womb. It's the perfect place to lie down and relax for a while. The following rooms delve into the physics of sound and use touch screens and loads of hands-on displays to explain the mechanics of sound. Here you can test the limits of your hearing, and play around with sampled sounds in order to record your own CD (€7.30).

Floor 3 moves onto the classics – Vienna's classical composers that is. The greats all receive their own room; the lives, loves and geniuses of Haydn, Mozart, Beethoven, Schubert, Strauss and Mahler are detailed in a thoughtful and informative manner. Best of all though is the 'virtual conductor': a video of the Vienna Philharmonic responds to a conducting baton and keeps time with your movements. You soon realise conducting is not as easy as it looks.

Floor 4 has experimental and electronic music, which you can also modify yourself. Singing trees, sound sticks and beeping buttons are just some of the hands-on 'instruments' at your disposal.

You could easily spend three hours here. Every Tuesday from 5pm to 9pm the museum is half price, and it also hosts the occasional children's program – see the website for details.

KÄRNTNER STRASSE, GRABEN & KOHLMARKT
ALBERTINAPLATZ
Bus 3A

Albertinaplatz is the sight of the troubling work **Monument against War and Fascism** (Map pp240–3) by Alfred Hrdlicka, created in 1988. This series of pale block-like sculptures commemorates Jews and other victims of war and fascism. The dark, squat shape with the barbed wire is a Jew washing the floor; the greyish block originally came from the Mauthausen concentration camp.

BAWAG FOUNDATION Map pp240-3
☎ 532 26 55; www.bawag-foundation.at; 01, Tuchlauben 7A; admission free; ⏰ 10am-6pm; bus 1A, 2A, 3A

Well located in the very heart of the Innere Stadt is this gallery, financed by the Bawag Bank. It features contemporary artists from both the international and local scene and has a regular influx of temporary exhibitions on display. Works range from sculpture pieces to photo exhibitions and film.

GRABEN
U1, U3 Stephansplatz, bus 1A, 2A, 3A

Graben, which runs northwest from the junction of Stock-im-Eisen-Platz and Kärntner Strasse, started life as a protective ditch (*Graben* means 'ditch' in German) for the Roman encampment. Today it is a bustling pedestrianised street lined with expensive shops and historical and Jugendstil buildings. Particularly impressive is the neo-Renaissance **Equitable Palais** (Map pp240–3) at No 3; duck inside and take a peek at the ornately tiled inner courtyard. Note the blackened and aged stump encased in glass on the eastern corner of the building; apprentice journeymen during the Middle Ages would hammer nails into the stump in order to ensure a safe homeward journey. Other buildings of note include the neoclassical **Erste Österreichisches Sparkasse** (Map pp240–3; 1836) on the corner of Tuchlauben, complete with a gilded bee symbolising thrift and industriousness, and the Jugendstil **Grabenhof** (Map pp240–3; 1876) at No 14, built by Otto Wagner using the plans of Otto Thienemann.

Two unmissable features at street level are the **Pestsäule** (Map pp240–3) and **Adolf Loos' public toilets** (Map pp240–3). The Pestsäule (Plague Column), near the junction of Graben and Habsburgergasse, commemorates the ending of the plague and was erected in 1692. Designed by Fischer von Erlach, it is one of the finest of its kind in Europe. The toilets are not far northwest of the statue, and are an impressive, and practical, use of Jugendstil design.

JÜDISCHES MUSEUM Map pp240-3
☎ 535 04 31; www.jmw.at; 01, Dorotheergasse 11; adult/concession €5/2.90; ◷ 10am-6pm Sun-Fri, to 8pm Thu; U1, U3 Stephansplatz

The Jüdisches Museum (Jewish Museum), taking up three floors of Palais Eskeles, uses holograms and an assortment of objects to document the history of the Jews in Vienna, from the first settlements at Judenplatz in the 13th century up to the present. The ground floor is filled with the Max Berger collection: a rich compilation of Judaica mainly dating from the Habsburg era. Temporary exhibitions are presented on the 1st floor, with the 2nd floor dividing its space between more temporary exhibitions and 21 holograms depicting the history of the Jewish people in Vienna.

A combined ticket of €7/4 per adult/child allows entry to the museum, the synagogue and a second Jewish museum on Judenplatz.

KAISERGRUFT Map pp240-3
☎ 512 68 53; www.kapuziner.at/wien, German only; 01, Neuer Markt; adult/concession/child €3.60/2.90/1; ◷ 9.30am-4pm; U1, U3 Stephansplatz, bus 2A

The Kaisergruft (Imperial Burial Vault) beneath the Kapuzinerkirche (Church of the Capuchin Friars) is where the residents of the Hofburg (Imperial Palace) eventually ended up. Opened in 1633, it was instigated by Empress Anna (1585–1618), and her body and that of her husband, Emperor Matthias (1557–1619), were the first to be entombed. Since then, all but three of the Habsburg dynasty found their way here; the last Emperor, Karl I, was buried in exile in Madeira and Marie Antoinette (daughter to Maria Theresia) still lies in Paris. The remains of Duc de

Shoppers and tourists on Graben mall (above)

Reichstadt, son of Napoleon's second wife Marie Louise, were transferred to Paris as a publicity stunt by the Nazis in 1940. The last Habsburg to be buried in the crypt was Empress Zita, wife of Karl I, in 1989. Needless to say, she received a right royal sendoff by the city and its citizens.

It's interesting to observe how fashions change through the ages even in death – tombs range from the unadorned to the ostentatious. By far the most elaborate caskets are those portraying 18th-century baroque pomp, such as the huge double sarcophagus containing Maria Theresia and Franz Stephan, with fine scenes engraved in the metal and plenty of angels and other ornamentation. The tomb of Charles VI is also striking and has been expertly restored. Both of these were the work of Balthasar Moll. Most visitors come to see the tombs of Franz Josef I and his much-adored wife Empress Elisabeth; both are constantly strewn with fresh flowers.

The only non-Habsburg of the 138 people here is the Countess Fuchs, a formative influence on the youthful Maria Theresia.

KÄRNTNER STRASSE

U1, U3 Stephansplatz, U1, U2, U4 Karlsplatz, Karlsplatz trams

No other street in Vienna receives such attention as Kärntner Strasse (Graben is the leading contender). Unfortunately this is due more to hype – and being the main thoroughfare between the Staatsoper and Stephansplatz – than to the attraction of the street itself. At one time Kärntner Strasse was the place to shop, lined with the finest establishments within the city's confines, but these days High St names have taken over. One exception is J & L Lobmeyr at No 26 (see p163), seller of exquisite Werkstätte pieces. It's still a pleasant street to stroll down (with so many people, it's actually more of a weave) and enjoy the diverse array of busker performances; harp players and puppeteers are the norm.

KOHLMARKT

U3 Herrengasse, bus 1A, 2A, 3A

Pedestrianised Kohlmarkt received its name from the charcoal market that once existed here. The charcoal is long gone, replaced by luxury shops which rival the Graben establishments. Best of all though is the view along Kohlmarkt towards Michaelertor and the Hofburg, which is arguably one of the most arresting sights in Vienna.

Of particular note is the café **Demel** (see p121), maker of fine cakes and server of great coffee at No 14. It ranks among the best *Kaffeehäuser* (coffee houses) in Vienna, but also attracts swarms of tourists. At No 9 is the **Artaria House**, home to the city's leading map maker and seller, Freytag & Berndt (see p163). Its Jugendstil façade was created by Max Fabiani.

PETERSKIRCHE Map pp240-3

☎ 533 64 33; 01, Petersplatz; admission free;
🕑 10am-1pm & 4-7pm; U1, U3 Stephansplatz, bus 1A, 2A, 3A

Peterskirche (St Peter's Church; 1733), on Petersplatz, is one of the finest baroque churches in Vienna, outshone only by Karlskirche (see p93). It is said that Charlemagne founded the first church that stood on this site, an event depicted in the exterior relief on the southeast side. A large majority of the church was completed by the celebrated baroque architect Johann Lukas von Hildebrandt, and the dome's fresco was painted by JM Rottmayr. The fresco's colours have dulled over the years, but it still manages to impress.

THEATERMUSEUM Map pp240-3

☎ 512 88 00; www.theatermuseum.at, German only; 01, Spiegelgasse 1; adult/concession/family €4.50/3.50/9; 🕑 10am-5pm Tue-Sun, until 8pm Wed; U1, U2, U4 Karlsplatz, bus 3A

The baroque Lobkowitz palace, which houses the Theatermuseum (Theatre Museum), is as much a delight to visit as the museum itself. Built between 1691 and 1694, it was the first of its kind in Vienna, and gained its name from the noble family who occupied its esteemed halls from 1753 onwards. The Eroicasaal, with its frescoed ceiling, is a sight to behold, and Beethoven conducted the first performance of his Third Symphony in the banquet hall.

The palace has served time as the French embassy and the Czech embassy, and as a fashion museum during WWII, but since 1991 has housed a museum devoted to the history of Austria's theatre. On display are costumes, props and set designs mixed in with theatre memorabilia, such Gustav Mahler's farewell message to the Vienna Opera company. A small room hidden towards the back of the 1st floor contains an ensemble of puppets from puppeteer Richard Teschner. These are works of intricate detail – John Malkovich would wet himself – and range from magicians to orangutans. They are often used in performances; inquire at the ticket desk for times. The museum is included in the Gold and Silver tickets (see the boxed text on p52).

HOFBURG Map pp240-3

Like Schloss Schönbrunn and the Belvedere, the Hofburg (Imperial Palace) is something that has to be seen to be believed. This impressive repository of culture and heritage was the home to one the most powerful empires Europe has ever seen: the Habsburgs based themselves here for over six centuries, from the first emperor (Rudolph I in 1279) to the last in 1918 (Charles I). In that time new sections were periodically added, resulting in the hotchpotch of styles and the massive dimensions. The palace now houses the offices of the Austrian president and a mix of fine museums.

The Hofburg owes its size and architectural diversity to plain old one-upmanship. Habsburg rulers took a dislike to inhabiting their predecessor's quarters and would build themselves new, grandiose digs to show the rest of the Europe their power and prowess. The oldest part is the **Schweizerhof** (Swiss Courtyard), named after the Swiss guards who used to protect its precincts. Dating from the 13th century and recently renovated, this small courtyard gives access to the **Burgkapelle** (Royal Chapel) and the **Schatzkammer** (Imperial Treasury). Its Renaissance entrance, known as the Swiss Gate, dates from 1553. The buildings encircling the Schweizerhof are collectively known as the **Alte Burg** (Old Palace).

Adjoining the Schweizerhof is a much larger courtyard, **In der Burg**. It sees most of the human traffic entering the Hofburg because of its easy access to Michaelerplatz and Kohlmarkt to the northeast, and Heldenplatz to the southwest. The courtyard is centred on a large **monument to Emperor Franz**, the last in a long line of Holy Roman emperors, and is the main entrance to the **Kaiserappartements**.

To the southeast of the Schweizerhof is **Josefsplatz**, a small square named after Joseph II, which gained cellular immortality through the film *The Third Man*. It was here, outside Palais Pallavicini, that Harry Lime faked his own death. In close proximity to Josefsplatz are the **Albertina**, **Augustinerkirche**, **Nationalbibliothek**, **Spanish Riding School** and **Lippizzaner Museum**.

The most active phase of building was carried out from the second half of the 19th century to WWI, culminating in the **Neue Burg**. Plans called for the building of a further wing, the mirror image of this curving façade on Heldenplatz, but the Habsburg era ended before it could be instigated. Facing each other with eternal stares on Heldenplatz are the **monuments of Prince Eugene of Savoy** (closest to the Neue Burg) and **Archduke Karl**. The Neue

Burg houses the **Museum für Völkerkunde** and the three **Neue Burg museums**, and its balcony holds an infamous distinction: it was from here that Hitler addressed a rally during his triumphant 1938 visit to Vienna after the Anschluss.

ALBERTINA Map pp240-3

☎ 534 83-544; www.albertina.at; 01, Albertinaplatz 3; adult/concession/child €7.50/6.50/5.50; ☺ 10am-6pm, until 9pm Wed; U1, U2, U4 Karlsplatz, bus 3A

Opened in 2003 after extensive and lengthy renovations, the Albertina is an extension of the Hofburg to the south, once used to house imperial guests. It is now home to the greatest collection of graphic art in the world. The collection, founded in 1768 by Maria Theresia's son-in-law Duke Albert of Sachsen-Teschen, consists of an astonishing 1½ million prints and 50,000 drawings, including 145 Dürer drawings (the largest collection in the world), 43 by Raphael, 70 by Rembrandt and 150 by Schiele. There are loads more by Leonardo da Vinci, Michelangelo, Rubens, Bruegel, Cézanne, Picasso, Matisse, Klimt and Kokoschka.

Because of the sheer number of prints and drawings in the Albertina's archive, only a small percentage can be displayed at any one time. Exhibitions, which normally follow a theme or artist, are therefore changed every three months and also feature works from other collections. Whatever's on show, it's sure to be worth the entrance fee. The DO & CO Albertina (see p119) and Filmmuseum (see p154) are within the confines of the Albertina.

AUGUSTINERKIRCHE Map pp240-3

☎ 533 70 99; www.kirchenmusik-augustin.at, German only; 01, Augustinerstrasse 3; admission free; U1, U3 Herrengasse, bus 2A, 3A

The Augustinerkirche (Augustinian Church) is one of the older parts of the Hofburg, dating from the early 14th century. Although Gothic in style, the interior was converted to baroque in the 17th century, and its original appearance was restored in 1784. It is here that the hearts of the Habsburgs rulers are kept in the Herzgrüftel (Little Heart Crypt); viewings are by appointment only. Important tombs include that of Maria Theresia's daughter Archduchess Marie Christina, designed by Canova. Tours of the church, in German, are available by prior arrangement, and cost €1.50/0.50 per adult/concession.

The church hosts regular evening classical music concerts, and the 11am Mass on Sunday is celebrated with a full choir and orchestra;

the choir practices on a regular basis and times are posted on the church door.

BURGKAPELLE Map pp240-3

☎ 533 99 27; 01, Schweizerhof; Guided tours €2; ⏰ 11am-3pm Mon-Thu, 11am-1pm Fri Sep-Jun; U3 Herrengasse, bus 2A, 3A

The Burgkapelle (Royal Chapel) originally dates from the 13th century and received a Gothic make-over from 1447 to 1449, but much of this disappeared during the baroque fad. The vaulted wooden statutory survived and is testament to those Gothic days. This is where the Vienna Boys' Choir sings at Mass (see p150) every Sunday at 9.15am between September and June. Unfortunately, you can only visit the chapel with a tour guide or during choir performances.

GLOBENMUSEUM Map pp240-3

☎ 534 10-397; 01, Josefsplatz 1, 3rd fl; adult/concession/family €2.50/1.50/4; ⏰ 11am-noon Mon-Wed & Fri, 2-3pm Thu; U3 Herrengasse, bus 2A, 3A

Part of the Nationalbibliothek (National Library) complex is this museum dedicated to cartography, the Globe Museum. Among the plethora of 19th-century globes and maps in the collection are a couple of gems a few centuries older. Look for the globe made for Emperor Karl V by Mercator in 1541 and a map of the world produced in 1551, also for Karl V.

KAISERAPPARTEMENTS Map pp240-3

☎ 533 75 70; 01, Innerer Burghof, Kaisertor; adult/concession/child €7.50/5.90/3.90; ⏰ 9am-7pm; U3 Herrengasse, bus 2A, 3A

The rooms in the Kaiserappartements (Imperial Apartments), once occupied by Franz Josef I and Empress Elisabeth, are as opulent as you might expect, with fine furniture, hanging tapestries and bulbous crystal chandeliers, but they all seem to blend into one after a while. The dining room has a table for 20 laid out in suitably elegant fashion, and the Audienzzimmer contains the high desk Franz Josef used to receive petitions, a ritual he only relinquished on his death bed. Unless you have an appetite for such things, you may be better off skipping the apartments and spending your valuable time taking in the interior finery of Schloss Schönbrunn instead.

The adjoining **Hoftafel- und Tafelkammer** (Court Tableware and Silver Depot) collection is included in the entry price. Laying a table with some of this silver and porcelain would certainly impress the in-laws: the largest silver service here can take care of 140 dinner guests.

Hourly guided tours are only in German; English-speakers can hire an audio guide (both cost €2.50).

LIPIZZANER MUSEUM Map pp240-3

☎ 533 78 11; www.lipizzaner.at; 01, Reitschulestrasse 2; adult/concession/family €5/3.60/10; ⏰ 9am-6pm; U3 Herrengasse, bus 2A, 3A

If you're into horses, don't pass this museum over. Everything you wanted to know about Lipizzaner stallions, the tricks they perform in the Spanish Riding School and the stud farm where they're reared, is here to be uncovered. There's English text, but the content is a little thin. Windows allow a view directly into the stallion stables, albeit obscured by thick glass and fine mesh. Tours in German leave at 11am from the ticket office and are available in other languages on request. Audio guides are available for €2 and a combined ticket for the museum and to watch a training session at the Spanish Riding School across the road costs €14.50/11.60/8 per adult/concession/child.

MUSEUM FÜR VÖLKERKUNDE
Map pp240-3

☎ 534 30-0; www.ethno-museum.ac.at; 01, Heldenplatz; adult/concession/family €8/6/16; ⏰ 10am-6pm Wed-Mon; tram D, J, 1, 2, bus 2A

The Museum für Völkerkunde (Museum of Ethnology), with its wide-ranging collection of exhibits on non-European cultures, makes good use of the furthest reaches of the Neue Burg. Exhibits are broken down into nationalities, and cover such countries as China, Japan and Korea, and also the Polynesian, Native American and Inuit cultures. The highlight of the museum is the centrepiece of the Central America section, an Aztec feather headdress once worn by Emperor Montezuma. Tours in German are normally available at 11am (extra €2) and temporary exhibitions are commonplace. An audio guide is included in the price, but does not cover temporary exhibitions.

MYTHOS SISI Map pp240-3

☎ 533 75 70; 01, Innerer Burghof, Kaisertor; adult/concession €7.50/3.90; ⏰ 9am-5pm, until 5.30pm Jul & Aug; U3 Herrengasse, bus 2A, 3A

Many of the older generation of Austrians (particularly its film makers) have an obsession with the wife of Emperor Franz Josef I, Empress Elisabeth (1837–1898), or Sisi, as she was affectionately named. Now they, and you, can bathe in the glory of her personal effects.

The first six rooms of the **Kaiserappartements** (see this page) have been turned over to a museum devoted to the beloved empress. A reconstruction of her luxurious coach, which carried her on many a journey, is impressive, but it's the small details that steal the show: a reconstruction of the dress she wore on the eve of her wedding, her sunshade, fans and gloves. There's even a replica of her personal fitness room complete with rings and bars, testament to her obsession with keeping slim.

Of course, the museum would not rate in Vienna without her death mask, taken after her assassination in Geneva in 1898.

NATIONALBIBLIOTHEK Map pp240-3

☎ 534 10 397; www.onb.ac.at; 01, Josefsplatz 1; adult/concession/family €5/3/9; ☽ 10am-4pm, until 7pm Thu May-Oct, 10am-2pm, until 7pm Thu Nov-Apr; U3 Herrengasse, bus 2A, 3A

The Nationalbibliothek (National Library) once served as the imperial library and is now the largest library in Vienna. The real reason to visit these esteemed halls of knowledge is to gaze on the majesty of the **Prunksaal** (Grand Hall). Commissioned by Charles VI, this baroque hall was the brainchild of Johann Bernhard Fischer von Erlach, who died the year the first brick was laid, and finished by his son Joseph in 1735. It holds some 200,000 volumes and the sheer size of the hall is breathtaking. Leather-bound scholarly tomes line the walls, and the upper storey of shelves is flanked by an elegantly curving wood balcony. Rare ancient volumes (mostly 15th-century) are stored within glass cabinets, with pages turned to beautifully drawn sections of text. A statue of Charles VI, looking like the hall's guardian, stands under the central church-like dome, which itself has a fresco depicting the emperor's apotheosis (by Daniel Gran).

The often-missed **Esperanto Museum** (enter from Michaelertor; admission free; ☽ 10am-4pm Mon & Fri, 10am-6pm Wed), devoted to the artificial language created by Dr Ludvik Zamenhof back in 1887, is also part of the library. The first book in Esperanto, written by Dr Zamenhof himself, is displayed in the museum.

NEUE BURG MUSEUMS

☎ 525 24-484; 01, Heldenplatz; adult/concession/family €8/6/16; ☽ 10am-6pm Wed-Mon; tram D, J, 1, 2, bus 2A

Instruments of all shapes and sizes are to be found at the **Sammlung Alter Musikinstrumente** (Collection of Ancient Musical Instruments; Map pp240-3), the first of three-museums-in-one in the Neue Burg. The forward-thinking Archduke Ferdinand of Tyrol started the whole thing off by collecting rare instruments, and now it ranks among the finest Renaissance collections in the world. The instruments were designed more for show than for actually producing music; horns shaped like serpents and violins with carved faces are some of the elaborate pieces on display. Note the baroque cabinet incorporating a keyboard from the early 17th century (in Saal XI) – it's beautiful, but a strange combination.

The admission price includes entry to two adjoining collections. The **Ephesus Museum** (Map pp240–3) contains artefacts from Ephesus and Samothrace supposedly donated (some say 'lifted') by the Sultan in 1900 after a team of Austrian archaeologists excavated the famous site in Turkey. The highlight of the museum is a massive frieze honouring the defeat of the Parthians by Lucius Verus and his Roman army. Noted as one of the finest museums of its kind in the world, the **Hofjagd und Rüstkammer** (Arms and Armour; Map pp240–3) collection dates mostly from the 15th and 16th centuries and has some superb examples of ancient armour; note the bizarre pumpkin-shaped helmet from the 15th century.

Audio guides are available for €2 and the three museums are included in the price of a Gold, Silver or Bronze ticket (see p52).

SCHATZKAMMER Map pp240-3

☎ 533 79 31; 01, Schweizerhof; adult/concession/family €8/6/16; ☽ 10am-6pm Wed-Mon; U3 Herrengasse, bus 2A, 3A

The Schatzkammer (Imperial Treasury) is among the best of its kind in Europe. Containing secular and ecclesiastical treasures of priceless value and splendour, the sheer wealth exhibited in the collection of crown jewels is staggering: Room 7 alone has a 2860-carat Colombian emerald, a 416-carat balas ruby and a 492-carat aquamarine, probably enough to wipe the debt of a third-world country.

Room 11 holds the highlight of the Treasury, the imperial crown. Dating from the 10th century, it has eight gold plates and precious gems alternating with enamel plaques to show religious scenes. The private crown of Rudolf II (1602) is a more delicate piece, with gems interspersed by four beautifully engraved gold bas-reliefs, showing Rudolf in battle and at three of his coronations.

Room 5 contains mementos of Marie Louise, the second wife of Napoleon; the best piece here is the cradle donated by the city of Paris to their son. The golden bees around the sides are a standard motif of Napoleonic state artefacts. Room 8 has two unusual objects formerly owned by Ferdinand I: a 75cm-wide bowl carved from a single piece of agate, once thought to be the Holy Grail, and a narwal tusk (243cm long), once claimed to have been a unicorn's horn.

The Sacred Treasury almost outshines the rest of the museum, with its collection of rare, and hard to believe, religious relics. Fragments of the True Cross, one of the nails from the Crucifixion, a thorn from Christ's crown and a piece of tablecloth from the Last Supper all vie for your attention. There are also some rather more worldly artefacts on display, like the extremely elaborate Column of the Virgin Mary made from gilded silver, which stands over 1m tall and is encased with 3700 precious stones – a modest conversation piece fit for any mantelpiece.

An audio guide is included in the price and the Schatzkammer is part of the Gold, Silver and Bronze discount tickets (see p52). Allow anything from 30 minutes to two hours to get around.

SCHMETTERLINGHAUS Map pp240-3
☎ 533 85 70; www.schmetterlinghaus.at; 01, Burggarten; adult/senior/student/child 3-6 €4.70/4/3.30/2.20; ☽ 10am-4.45pm Mon-Fri, 10am-6.15pm Sat & Sun Apr-Oct, 10am-3.45pm Nov-Mar; U1, U2, U4 Karlsplatz, Karlsplatz trams

Unfortunately the Jugendstil Palm House where this butterfly house resides is more interesting than the actual display. There are hundreds of butterflies and the shop stocks a great range of butterfly paraphernalia, but the temperature is quite unbearable, the species range fairly limited and it's quite a small display area. It's located in the Burggarten, behind the Neue Burg. Only for the butterfly-mad.

SPANISH RIDING SCHOOL Map pp240-3
☎ 533 90 31; www.srs.at; 01, Michaelerplatz 1; adult/concession from €24/12; performances 6pm Fri, 11am Sat & Sun May, 11am Sat & Sun Apr, 11am & 6pm Fri & Sun Sep, 11am Sun Mar, Jun, Oct & Dec; U3 Herrengasse, bus 2A, 3A

The world famous Spanish Riding School (Spanische Hofreitschule) is a Viennese institution truly reminiscent of the old Habsburg era. This unequalled equestrian show is performed by Lipizzaner stallions, a crossbreeding of Spanish, Arab and Berber horses. The horses were first imported from Spain (hence 'Spanish') by Maximilian II in 1562, and in 1580 a stud was established at Lipizza (hence 'Lipizzaner'), now in Slovenia.

A Lipizzaner performance is an absolute must for any hippophile (others may think it's a show with horses doing dog-tricks). These graceful stallions perform an equine ballet to a program of classical music while the audience cranes to see from pillared balconies, and chandeliers shimmer above. The mature stallions are all snow-white (though they are born dark and turn white at age four) and the riders wear traditional garb, from their leather boots up to their bicorn hats.

Reservations to see them perform need to be booked up months in advance; tickets can be ordered on the website. Otherwise, ask in the office about cancellations: unclaimed tickets are sold around two hours before performances.

Tickets to watch a training session can be bought the same day (adult/concession/child €11.50/8.50/5) at gate No 2, Josefsplatz in the Hofburg. Training is from 10am to noon Tuesday to Saturday. Queues are very long early in the day, but if you try at around 11am most people have gone and you can get in fairly quickly – indicative of the fact that training is relatively dull except for a few isolated high points. If you only want to grab a few photos, you can try waiting to see them cross between the school and the *Stallburg* (stables), which usually happens on the half-hour.

MICHAELERPLATZ TO MÖLKER BASTEI
BUNDESKANZLERAMT Map pp240-3
01, Ballhausplatz 2; U3 Herrengasse

Across the square from Minoritenkirche (see p62) is the Bundeskanzleramt (Federal Chancellor's Office). It's notable mainly for its historical significance as a seat of power since the time of Maria Theresia. Prince Metternich had his offices here, and it is where Chancellor Dollfuss was murdered by the Nazis on 25 July 1934. In 2000 the square outside became the meeting point for demonstrations (every Thursday) against the inclusion of the FPÖ (Freedom Party) in the federal government.

KUNSTFORUM Map pp240-3
☎ 537 330; www.kunstforum-wien.at; 01, Freyung 8; adult/concession/family €8.70/7.30/16; ☽ 10am-9pm; U3 Herrengasse, bus 2A, 3A

Often forgotten among the palaces and churches which line Freyung, the KunstForum is a stalwart of the Vienna art scene and hosts a number of temporary exhibitions throughout the year. The overall exhibit theme is not confined to one genre, but leaps and bounds between them with ease.

LOOS HAUS Map pp240-3
01, Michaelerplatz; U3 Herrengasse, bus 2A, 3A
The one and only Adolf Loos created this modernist gem between 1909 and 1911. Though it is widely accepted as a work of genius today, it was labelled as a downright abomination at the time of its conception. Its intentionally simple façade offended Franz Josef I deeply, and critics described it as a 'house without eyebrows', referring to its lack of window detail. Work was even stopped until Loos agreed to add 10 window boxes. Today the house is occupied by a bank on the ground floor and temporary exhibition halls on the upper floors, and can be visited during normal opening hours.

MICHAELERKIRCHE Map pp240-3
01, Michaelerplatz; admission free; ☺ 10.30am-4.30pm Mon-Sat, 1-5pm Sun May-Oct, dawn-dusk Nov-Apr; U3 Herrengasse, bus 2A, 3A
Michaelerkirche is the oldest building on Michaelerplatz (as long as you discount the Roman ruins as buildings), and dates from the 13th century. Its rather dark interior won't hold your interest for long, but, depending on your tastes, tours of its morbid and slightly disturbing crypt will. The tour (in German) takes you past numerous coffins, some of which have rusted away to reveal their long-deceased occupants in all their deathly splendour, and piles of bones of those who could not afford proper burials.

Tour guides like to spice things up by turning out the lights at the worst possible moment. Tours depart at 1pm and 3pm Monday to Friday, November to April, and at 11am, 1pm, 2pm, 3pm and 4pm Monday to Friday, May to October; it costs €4/2.50 per adult/child.

MICHAELERPLATZ
U3 Herrengasse, bus 2A, 3A
Michaelerplatz is ringed with a grand collection of sights and its uneven cobblestones are often crowded with snap-happy tourists. To the west is the neobaroque Michaelertrakt and Michaelertor, one of the Hofburg's main entrances. The building is lined by statues of Hercules in various acts of maiming some poor creature or another, and at its edges are evocative fountains to the Power of the Land and Power of the Sea. Turning in a clockwise direction from Michaelertor is Café Griensteidl (see p121), followed by Loos Haus and Michaelerkirche (see p62). The centre is occupied by Roman ruins unearthed during the digging of the U3 line.

MINORITENKIRCHE Map pp240-3
☎ 533 41 62; 01, Minoritenplatz; admission free; ☺ 3-6pm Sat, services Sun; U3 Herrengasse
The Minoritenkirche (Minorite Church) is a 14th-century church that later received a baroque face-lift. If you think the tower looks a little short, you're right on the button: the top was 'shortened' by the Turks in 1529. The most noteworthy piece inside is a mosaic copy of Leonardo da Vinci's *Last Supper*, commissioned by the one-and-only Napoleon.

Michaelerplatz with Hofburg in the background (p62)

The church often hosts classical concerts and choir recitals throughout the year; schedules are posted outside and tickets cost around €20.

PALAIS FERSTAL Map pp240-3
01, Herrengasse/Freyung; U3 Herrengasse, bus 1A, 2A, 3A

Palais Ferstal dates from 1860 and is better known for its occupants: it's the home to Café Central (see p121) and the Freyung Passage. The passage is ornately decorated and lined with elegant shops of style and sophistication, including Xocolat (see p165).

PALAIS HARRACH Map pp240-3
☎ 525 24-0; 01, Freyung; temporary exhibitions adult/concession/family €7/5/14.50; ✆ 10am-6pm; U3 Herrengasse, bus 1A, 2A, 3A

Palais Harrach is connected by the Freyung Passage to Palais Ferstal but outdates its neighbour by some 170 years. The upper floors of the palace have been taken over by the Kunsthistorisches Museum and are now used for temporary exhibitions (audio guides are an extra €2); the courtyard is filled with galleries, antique dealers and designer fashion.

PALAIS KINSKY Map pp240-3
01, Herrengasse; U3 Herrengasse, bus 1A

On the left as Herrengasse opens out into Freyung you'll see the classic baroque façade of Palais Kinsky, built by Johann Lukas von Hildebrandt in 1716. Recently restored to its former glory, the highlight of this quite superb palace is the stairway off to the left of the first inner courtyard; rising three storeys, its elegant banisters are graced with statues at every turn. The palace is now filled with highbrow art shops and classy restaurants.

PASQUALATI HAUS Map pp240-3
☎ 535 89 05; 01, Mölker Bastei 8; adult/child €2/1; ✆ 9am-12.15pm & 1-4.30pm Tue-Sun; U2 Schottentor, Schottentor trams

Beethoven made the 4th floor of this house his residence from 1804 to 1814 (he apparently occupied some 30 places in his 35 years in Vienna) and during that time composed Symphonies 4, 5 and 7 and the opera Fidelio, among other works. His two rooms have now been converted into a museum, which is lightly filled with memorabilia. The house is named after its longtime owner (with a long-winded name) Josef Benedikt Freiherr von Pasqualati, and it is a municipal museum.

SCHOTTENKIRCHE Map pp240-3
☎ 534 98-600; 01, Freyung; adult/child €4/2; ✆ 10am-5pm Thu-Sat, 10.30am-1pm Sun; U2 Schottentor, bus 1A

Freyung isn't particularly Scottish these days (the closest it comes is the Irish pub Molly Darcy's around the corner), but back in the 12th century Scotland was well in with the 'In' crowd in these parts. At the time Schottenkirche (Church of the Scots) was founded by Benedictine monks (the monks were probably actually from Ireland, then known as Scotia Maior), though the present façade dates from the 19th century. The interior is typically elaborate (exactly what you'd expect from the Benedictines) and free to enter; a small art and artefacts museum in the adjoining monastery, with religious pieces from the church and monastery, charges admission.

ROTENTURMSTRASSE TO SCHOTTENRING

AM HOF
U3 Herrengasse, bus 1A, 2A, 3A

Am Hof was once a powerful stronghold of the Babenberg rulers of Vienna who built a fortress on the square before moving to the Hofburg, but its history dates back to the Roman era and a few excavations can be seen at the **Feuerwehr Centrale** (Fire Brigade Centre; Map pp240-3; 01, Am Hof 9; adult/child €2/1; ✆ 11am-1pm Sat & Sun). These days it's the largest square in the Innere Stadt with little life and plenty of parked cars. There are, however, a few buildings of note, such as the 16th-century **former civic armoury** (Map pp240-3) on the north side at No 10, with an impressively elaborate façade. The **Kirche Am Hof** (Map pp240-3; ✆ services 7am Mon-Thu, 7am & 6pm Fri, 6pm Sat, 9am, 11am & 6pm Sun), on the southeast side, is even more impressive – the baroque façade was adapted from its fire-damaged Gothic predecessor.

The **Mariensäule** (Mary Column) in the centre of the square is dedicated to the Virgin Mary and was erected in 1667.

ANKERUHR Map pp240-3
01, Hoher Markt 10-11; bus 1A, 2A, 3A

The picturesque Art-Nouveau Ankeruhr (Anker Clock) was created by Franz von Matsch in 1911. It's named after the Anker Insurance Co, which commissioned it. Over a 12-hour period, figures slowly pass across the clock face, indicating the time against a static measure showing the minutes. Figures represented range from Marcus Aurelius (the Roman emperor who died in Vienna in AD 180) to Josef Haydn, with Eugene of Savoy, Maria Theresia and others in between. Details of who's who are outlined on a plaque on the wall below. Tourists flock here at noon, when all the figures trundle past in succession and organ music from the appropriate period is piped out.

ARCHIV DES ÖSTERREICHISCHEN WIDERSTANDS Map pp240-3

☎ 534 36-903 19; www.doew.at, German only; 01 Wipplingerstrasse 8; admission free; ☷ 9am-5pm Mon-Thu; bus 2A, 3A

Housed in the Altes Rathaus (Old City Hall), the Austrian Resistance Archive documents the little-known anti-fascist resistance force during the Nazi regime. There are plenty of photos and memorabilia detailing the movement, and a small section on the rise of fascism in the period before WWII, but the museum could do with some modernising. Some 2700 resistance fighters were executed by the Nazis and thousands more sent to concentration camps.

JUDENPLATZ

Bus 2A, 3A

The old Jewish quarter, Judenplatz, is just off the northeast corner of Am Hof. Here you'll find an attractive square, underneath which are excavations of a medieval synagogue which have been turned into the Museum Judenplatz (see p64). In the centre of the square is the **Holocaust-Denkmal** (Map pp240–3), a pale, bulky memorial to Austrian Jews who perished in the Holocaust, which received mixed reviews when it was unveiled in October 2000 (see the boxed text this page). On the north side of Judenplatz is the former **Böhmische Hofkanzlei** (Bohemian Court Chancery). Walk round to Wipplingerstrasse to see its striking façade by JB Fischer von Erlach.

MUSEUM JUDENPLATZ Map pp240-3

☎ 535 04 31; 01, Judenplatz 8; adult/concession €3/1.50; ☷ 10am-6pm Sun-Thu, 10am-2pm Fri; bus 2A, 3A

The main focus of this Jewish museum is the excavated remains of a medieval synagogue that once took pride of place on Judenplatz. Built around 1420, it didn't last long: Duke Albrecht V's 'hatred and misconception', as the museum puts it, led him to order its destruction in 1421. The basic outline of the synagogue can still be seen, lit with subdued lighting, and a small model of the building helps to complete the picture. Documents and artefacts dating from 1200 to 1400 are on display, and there is a short computer-graphics film on life in Jewish Vienna in the Middle Ages. Don't pass over the spacey interactive screens explaining Jewish culture at the bottom of the stairs as you walk in. A combined ticket for €7/4 per adult/child allows entry to the museum plus the Stadttempel and Jüdisches Museum.

NEIDHART-FRESKEN Map pp240-3

☎ 535 90 65; 01, Tuchlauben 19; adult/child €2/1; ☷ 9am-noon Tue-Sun; bus 2A, 3A

This unassuming house on Tuchlauben hides quite a remarkable decoration: the oldest ex-

---

Holocaust Stories in 'Nameless Library'

When you reach Vienna's Judenplatz, you'll be confronted by the squat, boxlike structure that is Austria's first Holocaust memorial. Finally unveiled in October 2000 after several years of dispute, it pays homage to the 65,000 Austrian Jews who were killed during the Anschluss.

The stark, pale concrete sculpture doesn't offer the relief of a curved line or pleasing ornamentation. 'This monument shouldn't be beautiful', said Nazi-hunter Simon Wiesenthal at the unveiling. 'It must hurt.' British sculptor Rachel Whiteread created the 'nameless library' – a structure in the shape of a library where the spines of books face inwards – to represent the untold stories of Holocaust victims. It has the names of Austrian concentration camps written across its base.

The monument sits on the site of a recently discovered medieval synagogue where dozens of Jews committed suicide in 1421 to escape forcible baptism by the Christians. This has brought objections to the monument from several members of the Jewish community, who claim it stands on a sacred site. And they're not the only ones – Viennese residents have also expressed considerable criticism of the sculpture, complaining that it would ruin business in the area.

Vienna's mayor Michael Haupl said at the unveiling that the memorial is 'necessary for Austria', an unfortunate reminder that anti-Semitism has played such a role in the country's history. He said that no-one can deny any longer that the atrocities that took place in Austria 60 years ago, and that the new memorial will 'send a message to the world'.

tant secular murals in Vienna. The frescoes, dating from 1398, tell the story of the minstrel Neidhart von Reuental (1180–1240) and life in the Middle Ages, in lively and jolly scenes. The fresco has lost some colour and is patchy in parts, but it's in fine condition for its age. Neidhart is a municipal museum.

PUPPEN & SPIELZEUG MUSEUM
Map pp240-3

☎ 535 68 60; www.puppenmuseumwien.com; 01, Schulhof 4; adult/child €4.70/2.35; ☉ 10am-6pm Tue-Sun; U3 Herrengasse, bus 1A, 2A, 3A

The Doll and Toy Museum, next door to the Uhren Museum (see p65), may sound like it's something for the kids, but in reality it's not. The collection is quite intriguing, with dolls from around the world, but there's no hands-on fun with the toys. Look for the *Kasperl* booth – the equivalent of Punch and Judy – which is a favourite with Viennese of all ages.

ROMAN RUINS Map pp240-3

☎ 535 56 06; 01, Hoher Markt 5; adult/concession €2/1; ☉ 9am-12.15pm & 1-4.30pm Tue-Sun; bus 1A, 2A, 3A

Under the central courtyard of Hoher Markt, a small expanse of Roman ruins dating from the 1st to the 5th century is open to the public. The ruins are thought to be part of the officers' quarters of the Roman legion camp at Vindobona and consist of crumbled walls and tiled floors. There's a small but selective exhibit on artefacts found during the excavations. The ruins are part of the municipal museum group of Vienna.

RUPRECHTSKIRCHE Map pp240-3
01, Ruprechtsplatz; U1, U4 Schwedenplatz, Schwedenplatz trams

A few steps to the north of Fleischmarkt is Ruprechtskirche (St Rupert's Church), the oldest church in Vienna. Records dating from 1137 first mention the church's existence, but some historians believe some of the founda-tions date back to as early as 740. What is for certain is that the lower levels of the tower date from the 11th century and the roof from the 15th. With its simple layout, ivy-clad walls and cobblestoned surrounds, it's more impressive from the outside, which is fortunate as it's rarely open to the public.

STADTTEMPEL Map pp240-3

☎ 535 04 31; 01, Seitenstettengasse 4; adult/concession €2/1; ☉ 11.30am-3pm Mon-Thu; U1, U4 Schwedenplatz, Schwedenplatz trams, bus 2A

By the end of WWII Stadttempel was the only synagogue spared from destruction by the Nazis. It's no surprise therefore that it is the main place of worship for the ever-expanding Jewish community in Vienna. Built in 1824 by Josef Kornhäusel, the bland façade provides no hint of the fine Biedermeier interior within. The Stadttempel is included in the combined ticket for the Jüdisches Museum and Museum Judenplatz; entrance is by guided tour only.

Even if you don't venture into the synagogue, the quiet cobblestone pedestrian streets in these parts are made for exploring. They're also a welcome break from the tourist chaos which often descends on much of the Innere Stadt. Just ignore the armed police wandering these parts: it's a safety measure for the synagogue.

UHREN MUSEUM Map pp240-3

☎ 533 22 65; 01, Schulhof 2; adult/child €4/2; ☉ 9am-4.30pm Tue-Sun; U3 Herrengasse, bus 1A, 2A, 3A

Behind the Kirche Am Hof is the small cobblestoned Schulhof where the Uhren Museum (Clock Museum) is located. Opened in 1921, the museum fills three floors of the Harfenhaus, one of the oldest buildings in Vienna, with an astounding 21,200 clocks and watches, ranging from the 15th century to a 1992 computer clock. If you enjoy your peace and quiet, try not to be there at the striking of the hour. The Uhren Museum is a municipal museum.

RINGSTRASSE

Eating p123; Shopping p167; Sleeping p176

The Ringstrasse, or Ring as it's known locally, is a wide, tree-lined boulevard encircling much of the Innere Stadt and follows the line of the old city walls. It's also the address of one momentous piece of architecture after the next; spend an hour or two strolling along its shaded pathways and you'll soon discover the architectural styles that dominated Europe's past.

The majestic architecture you see today is largely due to the efforts of Emperor Franz Josef I. The Ringstrasse

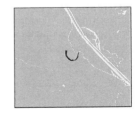

originally began life as defensive walls way back in the 16th century, but by 1857 Franz Josef decided these military fortifications had become redundant and needed to be torn down. The exercise grounds, or *Glacis* as they were known, which separated the Innere Stadt from the suburbs, also needed to go; his idea was to replace them with grandiose public buildings that would better reflect the power and the wealth of the Habsburg Empire. The Ringstrasse was laid out between 1858 and 1865, and in the decade that followed most of the impressive edifices that now line this thoroughfare were under construction. Franz Josef had extremely deep pockets to match his elaborate plans – consider this for an archi-

Ringstrasse Top Sights
 - Delighting in the sheer extent of the **Kunsthistorisches Museum** (p77) collection - Enjoying the **Ringstrasse** from the comfort of tram 1 or 2 - Exploring the **MuseumsQuartier** (p79), one of the world's top exhibitor spaces - Spending hours discovering the likes of Schiele, Klimt and Kokoschka at the **Leopold Museum** (p80) - Wondering how Klimt's *Beethoven Frieze* was ever thought a temporary exhibition at the **Secession** (p76)

tectural shopping list: Staatsoper (built 1861–69), Musikverein (1867–69), Museum für angewandte Kunst (1868–71), Akademie der bildenden Künste (1872–76), Naturhistorisches Museum (1872–81), Rathaus (1872–83), Kunsthistorisches Museum (1872–91), Parlament (1873–83), Universität (1873–84), Burgtheater (1874–88), Justizpalast (1875–81) and the Heldenplatz section of the Neue Burg (1881–1908).

Ironically, WWI intervened and the empire was lost before Franz Josef's grand scheme was fully realised: a further wing of the Hofburg had been planned (which would have sat directly on the Ringstrasse, taking up what is now the Volksgarten), and the palace and the giant museums opposite were to be linked by a majestic walkway, rising in arches over the Ring. Nevertheless, what was achieved is quite beyond belief.

To fully appreciate the sheer scale of this endeavour, you should take a tour of at least some of the Ringstrasse by foot. The whole ring is about 5km long, but the grandest section, between the university and the opera, is less than 2km. Instead of walking, you can pedal along the bike path on either side of the Ringstrasse, or take tram No 1 (clockwise) or No 2 (anticlockwise). Our tour of the Ringstrasse, set out below, travels in an anticlockwise direction from the Schottenring U-Bahn stop on the Danube Canal to the Urania cinema and bar complex, once again on the banks of the Danube Canal.

Orientation

A collection of nine roads linked together to form a horseshoe around the Innere Stadt make up the Ringstrasse. Closing the open end of this horseshoe is the Danube Canal. Schottentor and Karlsplatz, in the northwestern and southern stretches of the Ringstrasse respectively, are major public transport hubs where bus, tram and U-Bahn lines converge.

While the MuseumsQuartier, Akademie der bildenden Künste and Secession do not directly lie on the Ringstrasse, we have included them in this section because of their easy accessibility from the Ringstrasse.

DANUBE CANAL TO SCHOTTENTOR

VOTIVKIRCHE Map pp240-3

09, Rooseveltplatz; 🕲 9am-1pm & 4-6.30pm Tue-Sat, 9am-1pm Sun; U2 Schottentor, Schottentor trams

In 1853 Franz Josef I survived an assassination attempt when a knife-wielding Hungarian failed to find the emperor's neck through his collar – reports suggested that a metal button deflected the blade. The Votivkirche (Votive Church) was commissioned in thanks for

his lucky escape; Heinrich von Ferstel designed this twin-towered Gothic construction, which was completed in 1879. The interior, which is too bleak and spacious to be welcoming, is bedecked in frescoes and bulbous chandeliers. The tomb of Count Niklas Salm, one of the architects of the successful defence against the Turks in 1529, is in the Baptismal Chapel. Take note of the interesting stained-glass windows: one to the left of the altar tells of Nazism and the ravages of war.

(Continued on page 75)

Districts – Ringstrasse

1 Maria Theresia statue and Naturhistorisches Museum dome (p76) 2 Rathaus (p75) 3 Opernring on the Ringstrasse (p65) 4 People enjoying Vienna's Volksgarten (p75)

1 *Horse-drawn carriage outside Schloss Schönbrunn (p101)*
2 *Detail of the golden-leaf dome of the Secession building (p76)*
3 *City bike racks, Innere Stadt (p52)* 4 *Sculpture on the roof of the Postsparkasse building (p82)*

1 *Golden statue of Johann Strauss in the Stadtpark (p83)* *2* *Gothic window of Ruprechtskirche (p65)* *3* *Modern Haas Haus (p36)* *4* *Exhibition poster for Kunsthistorisches Museum (p77)*

IORGIONE
NSTHISTORISCHES MUSEUM

1 A funfair ride in the Wurstel-prater (p85) 2 Flakturm (flak tower) in Augarten (p84)
3 Porcelain from the Wiener Porzellanmanufaktur Augarten (p86) 4 View of the Danube from the Donauinsel (p87)

1 *Belvedere gardens (p91)*
2 *Hundertwasser-designed Fernwärme incinerator (p95)*
3 *Hundertwasser Haus (p90)*
4 *Karlskirche on Karlsplatz (p93)*

1 Kleines Café (p142) 2 Waiter carrying beers at the Schweizerhaus (p126) 3 Crowded outdoor tables at Café Gloriette (p135) 4 Wine selection at Sirbu (p145)

1 Shops lining the Kärntner Strässe (p57) **2** The bright façade of Hotel Adlon (p177) **3** The lobby of the famous Hotel Sacher (p174) **4** Up-market shopping on Kohlmarkt (p162)

1 Renaissance arches of the Schloss Schallaburg (p187) 2 The Haus des Meeres in Esterhazypark (p94) 3 The picturesque village of Dürnstein (p188) 4 The Danube Valley in the Wachau region (p188)

(Continued from page 66)

SCHOTTENTOR TO PARLAMENT

PARLAMENT Map pp240-3

☎ 401 10-25 70; www.parlinkom.gv.at, German only; 01, Dr-Karl-Renner-Ring 3; tours €2; tours 9am, 10am, 11am, 1pm, 2pm, 3pm Mon-Fri mid-Jun–mid-Sep; U2, U3 Volkstheater, tram D, J, 1, 2, 46, 49

The parliament building is the least impressive of the bombastic buildings on the Ringstrasse – it seems almost too squat to be here. Nevertheless, its neoclassical façade and Greek pillars, designed by Theophil Hansen in 1883, are quite striking, as is the beautiful **Athena Fountain** (Map pp240–3) directly in front of the building, which was sculptured by Karl Kundmann. Grecian architecture was chosen, as Greece was the home of democracy; Athena is the Greek goddess of wisdom. It was hoped that both qualities would be permanent features of Austrian politics. The four statues flanking Athena are of horse breaking (though some would say horse punching). Guided tours (leaving from Gate 1) are cancelled when the parliament is in session.

Parlament is the seat of the two federal assemblies, the Federal Council (Bundesrat) and the National Council (Nationalrat). On its southern side is the German Renaissance **Justizpalast** (Palace of Justice; Map pp240–3), home of Austria's Supreme Court.

RATHAUS Map pp240-3

☎ 525 50; www.wien.gv.at; 01, Rathausplatz; tours 1pm Mon, Wed, Fri; U2 Rathaus, tram D, 1, 2

For sheer grandness, the Rathaus (City Hall) steals the Ringstrasse show. This neogothic structure, completed in 1883 by Friedrich von Schmidt, was modelled on Flemish city halls. Its main spire soars to 102m, that's if you include the pennant held by the knight at the top. You're free to wander through the seven inner courtyards, but you must join a guided tour to catch a glimpse of the interior, with its red carpets, gigantic mirrors, and frescoes (tours leave from the Rathaus information office on Friedrich-Schmidt-Platz). The largest of the courtyards sometimes hosts concerts.

Between the Rathaus and the Ringstrasse is the **Rathaus Park**, with fountains, benches and several statues. It is split in two by Rathausplatz, which is lined by statues of notable people from Vienna's past. Rathausplatz is the sight of some of the city's most frequented events, including the Christkindlmarkt (Christmas Market; see p169), Musikfilm Festival (see p10) and the Wiener Eistraum (Vienna Ice Dream; see p157).

UNIVERSITÄT WIEN Map pp240-3

☎ 427 78 150; www.univie.ac.at; 01, Dr-Karl-Lueger-Ring 1; U2 Schottentor, Schottentor trams

Even though the Universität Wien (University of Vienna) building was completed in 1884, it's classed as 'new'. The university actually dates back to 1365; the original building still exists at 01, Bäckerstrasse 20. The new university is Italian Renaissance in style and was constructed during the Ringstrasse developments. It contains some beautiful rooms and a peaceful inner courtyard, but the highlight is the Grosser Festaal, blessed with ceiling frescoes by Klimt. Unfortunately it's usually out of bounds to the public and only used for graduation ceremonies, but try your luck and sneak in anyway.

VOLKSGARTEN Map pp240-3

01, Dr-Karl-Renner-Ring; ☼ 6am-10pm Apr-Oct, 6am-8pm Nov-Mar; U2, U3 Volkstheater, tram D, J, 1, 2, 46, 49

The Volksgarten (People's Garden) occupies a venerable position between the Burgtheater and Heldenplatz. It's attractively laid out, with a riot of rose bushes and several statues, including one of Empress Elisabeth in the northwest corner. In winter the roses are lovingly protected with hessian sacks, transforming them into rows of covered heads on poles. It's also home to the **Temple of Theseus** (Map pp240–3), an imitation of the one in Athens (commissioned by Napoleon), and to one of Vienna's largest clubs and its accompanying pavilion bar (see p144).

PARLAMENT TO SCHWARZENBERGPLATZ

AKADEMIE DER BILDENDEN KÜNSTE Map pp240-3

☎ 588 16-0; www.akademiegalerie.at, German only; 01, Schillerplatz 3; adult/concession/child under 10 €5/3/free; ☼ 10am-4pm Tue-Sun; U1, U2, U4 Karlsplatz, Karlsplatz trams

The Akademie der bildenden Künste (Academy of Fine Arts) has a smallish picture gallery largely passed over by most in favour of the bigger galleries. Hieronymus Bosch's impressive *The Last Judgement* altarpiece is here, as well as works by Guardi (scenes of 18th-century Venice), Cranach the Elder, Titian

Hitler's Vienna

Born in Braunau am Inn, Upper Austria, in 1889, with the name Adolf Schicklgruber (his father changed the family name when they moved to Germany in 1893), Adolf Hitler moved to Vienna when he was just 17. Six unsettled, unsuccessful, poverty-stricken years later he abandoned the city and moved to Munich to make a name for himself. He later wrote in *Mein Kampf* that his Vienna years were 'a time of the greatest transformation that I have ever been through. From a weak citizen of the world I became a fanatical anti-Semite'. Hitler briefly returned in 1938 at the head of the German army, to be greeted by enthusiastic crowds.

Although Vienna would be happy for the world to forget about its association with Hitler, an increasing number of tourists are retracing the Vienna footsteps of the infamous fascist. He spent several years living in a small, dimly lit **apartment** (Map pp246–7) at Stumpergasse 31, in the 6th district. It's a private block, but frequent visits by curious tourists have prompted plans (unrealised as yet) to turn the apartment into a museum.

Hitler was a regular visitor to the opera, and despite his penury, preferred to pay extra to stand in sections that were barred to women. **Café Sperl** (see p129) is another address on the Hitler itinerary: here he would loudly express his views on race and other matters. Among his gripes was probably the nearby Akademie der bildenden Künste (Academy of Fine Arts), which twice rejected an application by the would-be artist, dismissing his work as 'inadequate'. Although convinced that proper training would have made him into a very successful artist, these rejections caused Hitler to write to a friend that perhaps fate may have reserved for him 'some other purpose'.

and Rembrandt. Flemish painters are well represented, particularly Rubens. Van Dyck and Jordaens also get a look-in. The building itself has an attractive façade and was designed by Theophil Hansen (of Parlament fame). It was this academy that turned down would-be artist Adolf Hitler twice, forcing him to find a new career (see the boxed text this page). Directly in front of the academy, **Schiller's statue** takes pride of place on Schillerplatz.

Audio guides are available for an extra €2, and tours, in German only, take place at 10.30am every Sunday.

BURGGARTEN Map pp240-3

01, Opernring; 6am-10pm Apr-Oct, 6am-8pm Nov-Mar; tram D, J, 1, 2, bus 57A

This small garden tucked behind the Hofburg is a leafy oasis from the hustle and bustle of the Ringstrasse and Innere Stadt. The marble **statue of Mozart** is the park's most famous tenant, but there's also a **statue of Franz Josef** in military garb. Lining the Innere Stadt border of the Burggarten is the Schmetterlinghaus (p61) and the ever-popular Palmenhaus (see p102).

NATURHISTORISCHES MUSEUM

Map pp240-3

☎ 521 77-0; www.nhm-wien.ac.at; 01, Burgring 7; adult/senior/concession €8/6/3.50; 9am-6.30pm Thu-Mon, 9am-9pm Wed; U2, U3 Volkstheater, tram D, J, 1, 2

The Naturhistorisches Museum (Museum of Natural History) is the scientific counterpart of the Kunsthistorisches Museum (Museum of Art History) opposite. The building is a mirror image

of the art history museum, and while some of the exhibits inside are quite extraor-dinary their actual presentation could do with a touch of modernisation. As you would expect in a natural history museum, there are exhibits on minerals, meteorites and assorted animal remains in jars. In the gems collection, the Colombian emerald, believed to be a present from the Aztec ruler Montezuma to the Spanish conquistador Hernán Cortés, is overshadowed by the bouquet of precious stones presented to Franz Stephan by Maria Theresia. It consists of a staggering 2102 diamonds and 761 other gems. Zoology and anthropology are covered in detail, including specimens of the extinct Moa and Dodo and the rare Komodo dragon, and there's a children's corner, some good dinosaur exhibits and a room with 3D projections of microorganisms. The 25,000-year-old statuette 'Venus of Willendorf' is here (see Dürnstein in the Excursions chapter p188) – though she's a mere youngster compared to the 32,000 BC statuette 'Fanny' from Stratzing (the oldest figurative sculpture in the world). Only photos of the statuette are on display; the real McCoy is in storage. Though seemingly inappropriately named, the nickname Fanny actually comes from her unusual pose, supposedly reminiscent of the Austrian ballerina Fanny Elssler.

SECESSION Map pp240-3

☎ 587 53 07; www.secession.at; 01, Friedrichstrasse 12; admission exhibition & frieze €5.50, exhibition only €4; 10am-6pm Tue-Sun, until 8pm Thu; U1, U2, U4 Karlsplatz

In 1897, 19 progressive artists broke away from the Künstlerhaus and the conservative artistic establishment it represented and formed the Vienna Secession. Their aim was to present current trends in contemporary art and leave behind the historicism that was then in vogue in Vienna. Among their number were Gustav Klimt, Josef Hoffman, Kolo Moser and Joseph M Olbrich (a former student of Otto Wagner). Olbrich was given the honour of designing the new exhibition centre of the Secessionists. It was erected just a year later and combined sparse functionality with stylistic motifs.

The building is certainly a move away from the Ringstrasse architectural throwbacks. Its most striking feature is a delicate golden dome rising from a turret on the roof that deserves better than the description 'golden cabbage' accorded it by some Viennese. Other features are the Medusa-like faces above the door with dangling serpents instead of earlobes, the minimalist stone owls gazing down from the walls, and the vast ceramic pots supported by tortoises at the front. The motto above the entrance asserts: *Der Zeit ihre Kunst, der Kunst ihre Freiheit* (To each time its art, to art its freedom).

The 14th exhibition (1902) held in the building featured the famous *Beethoven Frieze* by Klimt. This 34m-long work was only supposed to be a temporary display, little more than an elaborate poster for the main exhibit, Max Klinger's Beethoven monument. Fortunately it was bought at the end of the exhibition by a private collector and transported – plaster, reeds, laths and all – in eight sections to the buyer's home. In 1973 the government purchased the frieze and spent 10 years restoring it to its original glory, and since 1983 it has been on display in the basement. The frieze has dense areas of activity punctuated by mostly open spaces, reminiscent of something plastic partially melted and stretched out over a fire. It features willowy women with bounteous hair who jostle for attention with a large gorilla, while slender figures float and a choir sings. Beethoven would no doubt be surprised to learn that it is based on his Ninth Symphony.

The small room you enter before viewing the frieze tells the story of the building. It served as a hospital during WWI and was torched by the retreating Germans during WWII (the gold dome survived the fire). The ground floor is still used as it was originally intended: presenting temporary exhibitions of contemporary art. It's an incredible achievement of modern functionality and a perfect compliment to the art: spacious, airy, bright and uninhibiting. It's amazing to think it was created over a century ago.

KUNSTHISTORISCHES MUSEUM Map pp240-3

☎ 525 24-403; www.khm.at; 01, Burgring 5; adult/concession/family €10/7.50/20; ☺ 10am-8pm Tue-Sun, until 9pm Thu; U2 Museumsquartier, tram D, J, 1, 2

The Kunsthistorisches Museum (Museum of Art History) ranks among the finest museums in Europe, if not the world, and should not be missed. The Habsburgs were great collectors, and the huge extent of lands under their control led to many important works of art being funnelled back to Vienna.

The building itself is delightful and was designed to reflect the works it displays, with older architectural styles faithfully reproduced. No expense was spared in construction and all the marble here is genuine. Ceilings are superbly decorated with murals and stucco embellishments. Halfway up the stairway to the 1st floor you'll see Canova's sculpture *Theseus & the Minotaur*. On the walls above the arches are the portraits of some of the more important artists exhibited in the museum, such as Dürer, Rembrandt and Raphael. The murals between the arches were created by three artists, including a young Gustav Klimt (north wall), painted before he broke with classical tradition.

It's impossible to see the whole museum in one visit: after a while the paintings will all meld into one and lose their appeal. The best idea is to concentrate on specific areas. Temporary exhibitions (which may cost extra) sometimes cause reorganisation of rooms, and famous works are occasionally lent to other museums. Various guides and plans are for sale in the shops – you'll probably be able to make do with the *Kunsthistorisches Museum Vienna* booklet in English for €1.50, which includes a floor plan of the museum, and information on sister collections (eg the Schatzkammer and Sammlung Alter Musikinstrumente in the Hofburg, and the Wagenburg in Schönbrunn). Guided tours in English are currently available, but this may change in the future; they leave from the information desk at 11am Tuesday and at 3pm Friday and Saturday (€2). If none are available, just pick up an audio guide, which is included in the admission price. The museum is part of the Gold, Silver and Bronze discount ticket (see p52), and a ticket covering it and the Leopold Museum is available for €16.50/10.50 per adult/child.

Children's events are often organised by the museum, and free children's tours of various sections are held every Thursday at 3pm (five- to eight-year-olds) and Saturday (nine- to 12-year-olds); they are only in German.

Ground Floor

The west wing (to your right as you enter) houses the Egyptian collection, including the burial chamber of Prince Kaninisut. Amid the many sarcophagi and statues in this section are the peculiar mummified remains of various animals (falcon, baboon, cat etc) and examples of the Book of the Dead on papyrus.

Next come the Greek and Roman collections, including sculptures, urns, vases and Etruscan art. One of the most impressive pieces is the *Gemma Augustea cameo* (Room XV), made from onyx in AD 10, with delicately carved white figures on a bluish-brown background.

The east wing contains a collection of sculpture and decorative arts covering Austrian high baroque, Renaissance, mannerism and medieval art. There is some exquisite 17th-century glassware and ornaments, and unbelievably lavish clocks from the 16th and 17th centuries (Rooms XXXV and XXXVII). But the prime item here is the salt cellar (Room XXVII; 1543) by Benvenuto Cellini, made in gold for Francis I of France. It depicts two naked deities: the goddess of the earth, reclining on elephants, with a small temple by her side where the pepper was kept, and Poseidon, god of the

sea, making himself comfortable on a team of sea horses with the salt in a bowl by his trident. Hidden beneath the base are small wheels, so the cellar could be pushed easily around the table. This beautiful work of art begs an envious question: if the humble cruet set looked as good as this, what did the rest of the dining room look like?

First Floor

The Gemäldegalerie (picture gallery) on this floor is the most important part of the museum – you could lose yourself for hours wandering round whole rooms devoted to works by Bruegel, Dürer, Rubens, Rembrandt, Van Dyck, Cranach, Caravaggio, Canaletto, Titian and many others. Some rooms have information cards in English giving a critique of particular artists and their work.

EAST WING

The east wing is devoted to German, Dutch and Flemish paintings. Room X contains the collection of Pieter Bruegel the Elder's works, amassed by Rudolf II, which is unrivalled in the world. A familiar theme in the artist's work is nature, as in his cycle of seasonal scenes, three of which are shown here. *The Hunters in the Snow* (1565) portrays winter; the hunters return towards a Dutch-like frozen lake with frolicking skaters, beyond which rise some

Kunsthistorisches Museum (p77)

very un-Dutch-looking mountains. The viewer's eye is drawn into the scene by the flow of movement – a device commonly exploited by Bruegel. This is also seen in the atmospheric *The Return of the Herd* (1565), illustrating a glowering autumnal day. Bruegel's peasant scenes are also excellent, such as *The Battle Between Carnival & Lent* (1559), where the centre and foreground are dominated by carnival tomfoolery, with the dour, cowled and caped figures in religious processions pushed to the edges of the scene.

The next gallery (Room XI) shows Flemish baroque, in vogue some 80 years later, with warm, larger-than-life scenes such as *The King Drinks* by Jacob Jordaens (with the revellers raising their glasses to a motto in Latin that translates as 'None resembles a fool more than the drunkard') and *The Fishmarket* by Frans Snyders.

Albrecht Dürer (1471–1528) is represented in Room 16. His brilliant use of colour is particularly shown in *The Holy Trinity Surrounded by All Saints*, originally an altarpiece. The *Martyrdom of 10,000 Christians* and *The Adoration of the Holy Trinity* are other fine works.

The paintings by the mannerist Giuseppe Arcimboldo in Room 19 use a device well explored by Salvador Dali: familiar objects are arranged to appear as something else. But Arcimboldo did it nearly 400 years earlier! His series of four composite pictures *Summer*, *Winter*, *Water* and *Fire* (1563–66) cleverly show faces composed of objects related to those particular themes.

Peter Paul Rubens (1577–1640) was appointed to the service of a Habsburg governor in Brussels, so it is not surprising that the museum has one of the best collections of his works in the world. He was a very influential figure because of his synthesis of northern and Italian traditions. His works can be seen in Rooms XIII and XIV and in Room 20. Try to spot the difference between those he painted completely himself (eg note the open brushwork and diaphanous quality of the fur in *Ildefonso Altar*) and those that he planned and finished off, but were mostly executed by his students (like the vivid but more rigid *Miracle of Ignatius Loyola*, a dramatic baroque picture displayed along with Rubens' initial study for the scene).

Rembrandt has several self-portraits in Room XV. Vermeer's *The Allegory of Painting* (1665–66) is in Room 24. It's a strangely static scene of an artist in his studio, but one that transcends the mundane by its composition and use of light.

WEST WING

Room I has some evocative works by Titian, of the Venetian school. He uses colour and broad brush strokes to create character and mood, rather than distinct outlines. In Room 2 is *The Three Philosophers* (1508), one of the few authenticated works by Giorgione.

In Room 4 is Raphael's harmonious and idealised portrait *Madonna in the Meadow* (1505). The triangular composition and the complementary colours are typical features of the Florentine High Renaissance. Compare this to Caravaggio's *Madonna of the Rosary* (1606) in Room V, an example of new realism in early baroque; note the dirty soles on the feet of the supplicants. Caravaggio emphasises movement in this picture by a subtle deployment of light and shadow.

Susanna at her Bath (1555) by Tintoretto can be found in Room III. It re-creates the Old Testament tale of Susanna being surprised at her ablutions by two old men. The picture successfully portrays both serenity and implicit menace. Tintoretto employs mannerist devices (contrasting light, extremes of facial features) to achieve his effect.

Room VII has paintings by Bernardo Bellotto (1721–80), Canaletto's nephew. He was commissioned by Maria Theresia to paint scenes of Vienna, and several are shown here. Note the way landmarks are sometimes compressed to create a more satisfying composition; the view from the Belvedere is not a faithful reproduction. The pastoral view of Schönbrunn is in stark contrast to its urban situation today.

Room 10 has portraits of the Habsburgs. Juan Carreño's portrait of Charles II of Spain really shows the characteristic Habsburg features: a distended lower lip and jaw and a nose that would be more at home in an aviary. Most of the young women in Diego Velázquez's royal portraits are wearing dresses broad enough to fit around a horse, but the artist still manages to make the subjects come to life.

MUSEUMSQUARTIER

☎ 523 58 81-17 30, within Austria 0820-600 600; www.mqw.at; 07, Museumsplatz 1; ☺ information & ticket centre 10am-7pm; U2 Museumsquartier, U2, U3 Volkstheater, tram 49, bus 2A, 48A

It may have only been operating since 2001, but already the MuseumsQuartier (Museums Quarter) has gained the third spot on Vienna's most-visited list (after Schönbrunn and the Kunsthistorisches Museum). But being blessed with excellent museums, great cafés and warm public spaces, that comes as no real surprise.

The MuseumsQuartier lies within the confines of the former imperial stables, just behind the Kunsthistorisches and Naturhistorisches Museums. The stables, designed by Fischer von Erlach, housed a reputed 600 horses, and contained two rooms just for the emperor's personal stock – one for his white stallions and the other for his black. The construction of the new complex began in earnest in 1998 – after much controversy and to-ing and fro-ing between its supporters and opposition – and was completed in 2001, to the tune of €145 million. It's now the eighth largest cultural complex in the world, with over 60,000 sq metres of exhibition space, and houses the Leopold Museum, MUMOK (Museum of Modern Art), Kunsthalle, Zoom, Architekturzentrum Wien, Tanzquartier Wien (see p152) and a number of cafés. Towards the front on the complex is Quartier 21, a mall-like space given over to shops and temporary exhibitions. Currently under construction is the Theaterhaus für junges Publikum (Theatre for the Young) and towards the back of the complex, on Breite Gasse, the much anticipated Glacis Beisl.

MuseumQuartier's rectangle piazza is constantly used for happenings and hosts both a winter and summer program of events (see the website for details). It's particularly popular during the summer months when tourists and locals alike get to work on their tans.

If you plan to see a number of attractions in the MuseumsQuartier, consider purchasing one of the following: **MQ Kombi Ticket** (€25), includes entry into every museum except for Zoom (which only has a reduced ticket price) and a 30% discount on performances in the Tanzquartier Wien; **MQ Art Ticket** (€18), allows admission into the Leopold Museum, MUMOK, Kunsthalle and reduced entry into Zoom, plus 30% discount at the Tanzquartier Wien; **MQ Duo Ticket** (€12), covers everything the Art ticket does, minus the Kunsthalle. Tours of the MuseumsQuartier in English leave at noon on Saturday and Sunday and cost €3.

ARCHITEKTURZENTRUM WIEN
Map pp240-3
☎ 522 31 15; www.azw.at; 07, Museumsplatz 1; exhibitions adult/student €5/3.50; ⏰ 10am-7pm, until 9pm Wed; U2 Museumsquartier, U2, U3 Volkstheater, tram 49, bus 2A, 48A

The Architekturzentrum Wien (Vienna Architecture Centre) takes up much of the MuseumsQuartier north of MUMOK, collectively encompassing three halls used for temporary

exhibitions, a library and Café Una (see p124). Exhibitions focus on international architectural developments and change on a regular basis. The extensive library is open to the public 10am to 5.30pm Monday, Wednesday and Friday and until 7pm on Saturday and Sunday. The centre also organises walking tours through Vienna on Sunday, covering various architectural themes, but they are in German only.

KUNSTHALLE Map pp240-3
☎ 521 89 33; www.kunsthallewien.at; 07, Museumsplatz 1; Hall 1 adult/ concession €6.50/5, Hall 2 €5/3.50, combined ticket €8/6.50; ⏰ 10am-7pm Fri-Wed, until 10pm Thu; U2 Museumsquartier, U2, U3 Volkstheater, tram 49, bus 2A, 48A

Caught between the Leopold and MUMOK is the Kunsthalle (Art Hall), a collection of exhibition halls used to showcase local and international contemporary art. While it doesn't have the sheer impact of the Tate Modern in London or the Centre Pompidou in Paris, its high ceilings, open space and pure functionality have been rated among the top institutions for exhibitions in Europe. Programs, which run for three to six months, tend to focus on photography, video, film, installations and new media. Guided tours, in German, leave at 3pm on Saturday and Sunday and cost €1.80.

LEOPOLD MUSEUM Map pp240-3
☎ 525 70-0; www.leopoldmuseum.org; 07, Museumsplatz 1; adult/concession €9/5.50; ⏰ 10am-7pm Wed-Sun, until 9pm Fri; U2 Museums-quartier, U2, U3 Volkstheater, bus 2A

The Leopold Museum easily steals the show in the MuseumsQuartier: The museum is named after Rudolf Leopold, a Viennese ophthalmologist who, on buying his first Egon Schiele for a song as a young student in 1950, started to amass a huge private collection of mainly 19th-century and modernist Austrian artworks. In 1994 he sold the lot – 5266 paintings – to the Austrian government for €160 million (sold individually, the paintings would have made him €574 million), and the Leopold Museum was born.

The building is in complete contrast to the MUMOK, with a white, limestone exterior, open space (especially the 21m-high glass-covered atrium) and natural light flooding most rooms. Considering Rudolf Leopold's love of Schiele, it's no surprise the museum contains the largest collection of the painter's work in the world. Most are to be found on the top floor; look for

Leopold Museum (p80)

Selbstportrait mit Judenkirschen (Self-Portrait with Winter Cherries) and *Kardinale und Nüne* (Cardinal and Nun), two masterpieces of the expressive artist. Klimt is also represented; his *Tod und Leben* (Death and Life) on the ground floor is by far the most impressive. Simple, yet highly emotional sketches from both artists are displayed in the basement.

Other artists well represented include Albin Egger-Lienz (1868–1922), Richard Gerstl (1883–1908) and, arguably Austria's third greatest painter (after Klimt and Schiele), Oskar Kokoschka (1886–1980). Egger-Lienz had a knack for capturing the essence of rural life; this is seen in his stark *Pietà*, considered by Leopold as his greatest work. Kokoschka had a long life in the painting arena, but his earlier works steal the show; his *Selbstportrait mit ein Hand* (Self-Portrait with One Hand) from 1918 is his most substantial piece. Works by Loos, Hoffmann, (Otto) Wagner, Waldmüller and Romako are also on display.

Audio guides are available for €2, and the museum has a highly rated café. A joint ticket covering this museum and the Kunsthistorisches Museum costs €16.50/10.50 per adult/child. At 10.30am every second and third Sunday of the month guided tours for children are offered (€5). The kids are given the lowdown on many of the artists' works and then given the chance to create their own masterpieces.

MUMOK Map pp240-3

☎ 525 00-0; www.mumok.at; 07, Museumsplatz 1; adult/concession €8/6.50; ⏱ 10am-6pm Tue-Sun, until 9pm Thu; U2 Museumsquartier, U2, U3 Volkstheater, tram 49, bus 2A, 48A

The dark basalt rock edifice that houses the Museum moderner Kunst (MUMOK; Museum of Modern Art) is something the Borg from Star Trek would be proud of: sheer grey walls, sharp corners and a powerful presence. The exterior will certainly impress, but as a whole MUMOK fails to please. Inside, many of the exhibition rooms on its five floors, which house Vienna's premiere collection of 20th century art, are cramped and devoid of natural light – great for cave dwellers but not for the average Joe. The exhibition is centred around fluxus, nouveau realism, pop art and photo-realism, but expressionism, cubism, minimal art and Viennese Actionism are also represented. The best of the bunch is an extensive collection of pop art featuring the likes of Warhol, Jasper Johns and Rauschenberg. If you've never seen Viennese Actionism, this is your chance as MUMOK holds the largest collection of such art in the basement. Be prepared though: Actionism is a melting pot of animal sacrifice, bloody canvases, self-mutilation and defecation, and certainly not everyone's cup of tea. Other well-known artists represented throughout the museum include Picasso, Klee, Magritte, Ernst and Giacometti.

ZOOM Map pp240-3

☎ 524 79 08; www.kindermuseum.at; 07, Museums-platz 1; adult/child €3.50/5; programs from 8am-4pm; U2 Museumsquartier, U2, U3 Volkstheater, bus 2A

Zoom holds the prestigious title as Vienna's first museum devoted to kids. Actually, it's not so much a museum as an arts and crafts session, with a lot of playing thrown in. Children are guided through themed programs, and get the chance to make, break, draw, explore and basically be creative. Topics range from animation to zoology and change throughout the year. Programs begin every 1½ to two hours from 8.30am to 4pm; there are normally four programs a day Monday to Friday and five on both Saturday and Sunday. Advance bookings for the more popular ones are highly recommended, but you can also just turn up and try your luck. Zoom is aimed at kids between the age of zero and 14 and most staff speak English.

SCHWARZENBERGPLATZ TO THE DANUBE CANAL

MUSEUM FÜR ANGEWANDTE KUNST
Map pp240-3

☎ 711 36-0; www.mak.at; 01, Stubenring 5; adult/concession €7.90/4; 🕙 10am-6pm Wed-Sun, 10am-midnight Tue; U3 Stubentor, tram 1, 2

Think your wine glasses are ornate? Or your dinner set something quite extraordinary? Your sofa and chairs too precious to even consider the guests using? Well, think again. The Museum für angewandte Kunst (MAK; Museum of Applied Arts) has an extensive collection of practical, everyday items turned art forms that will set you straight, and perhaps even give you some ideas for your own private castle. The building which MAK shares with its excellent café (see p125) – a High Renaissance construction dating from 1871 – offers some fine features in its own right, especially the ceilings.

Each exhibition room is devoted to a different style, eg Renaissance, baroque, oriental, historicism, empire, Art Deco and the distinctive metalwork of the Wiener Werkstätte. Contemporary artists were invited to present the rooms in ways they felt were appropriate, which has resulted in the creation of eye-catching and unique displays. For example, in the Biedermeier room, Jenny Holzer placed electronic signs near the ceiling so 'they can be ignored' while Barbara Bloom's display of Art-Nouveau chairs is back-lit and presented

behind translucent white screens. This takes nothing away from the actual objects on display, but rather complements their beauty. The 20th-century design and architecture room is impressive; Frank Gehry's cardboard chair is a gem. The museum's collections encompass tapestries, lace, furniture, glassware and ornaments, and Klimt's *Stoclet Frieze* is upstairs.

In the basement is the Study Collection, which groups exhibits according to the type of materials used: glass and ceramics, metal, wood and textiles. Actual objects range from ancient oriental statues to sofas (note the red-lips sofa). There are some particularly good porcelain and glassware pieces, with casts showing how they're made.

MAK is one of the few big museums with free entry one day a week – on Saturday.

POSTSPARKASSE Map pp240-3

01, Georg Coch Platz; admission free; 🕙 8am-3pm Mon-Fri, until 5.30pm Thu; U1, U4 Schwedenplatz, tram N, 1, 2, 21

The celebrated Post Office Savings Bank building is the work of none other than Otto Wagner, who oversaw its construction between 1904 and 1906, and 1910 and 1912. The design and choice of materials were both innovative for the time; compare the modern appearance of the Postsparkasse with the austere and powerful former **Kriegsministerium** (Imperial War Ministry) on the Ring opposite, which was built around the same period. The grey marble façade is held together by some 17,000 metal nails while the inside is filled with sci-fi aluminium heating ducts and naked stanchions – this is pared down functionality *par excellence*. The main savings hall can be perused during office hours and there is an information counter.

SCHWARZENBERGPLATZ
tram D, 1, 2, 71

The view from Schwarzenbergplatz is more interesting than the square itself; facing south from the Ringstrasse, you'll notice a huge fountain, known as the **Hochstrahlbrunnen** (Map pp240–3), and behind it, a rather gaudy monument, the **Russen Heldendenkmal** (Russian Heroes' Monument; Map pp240–3). The fountain was commissioned in 1873 to commemorate Vienna's first water mains and the monument is a reminder that the Russians liberated the city at the end of WWII. The latter is certainly not in the hearts of many Viennese. Directly in front of the fountain on Schwarzenbergplatz is a **statue of Karl von Schwarzenberg** (Map pp240–3), leader in the Battle of Leipzig (1813), from which the square gained its name. In the distance is **Palais Schwarzenberg**, co-created by JB Fischer von Erlach and Johann Lukas von Hildebrandt and now a luxurious hotel (see p178). After all that strenuous eye-work, stop in at **Café Schwarzenberg** (see p125) for coffee and cake, or a beer.

STADTPARK
01, Parkring; U3 Stubentor, U4 Stadtpark, tram 1, 2
The largest of the Ringstrasse parks is the Stadtpark (City Park), stretching from Johannesgasse to Weiskirchnerstrasse. Opened in 1862, it is an enjoyable recreation spot, with winding paths and a pond – great for strolling or relaxing in the sun and a favourite lunch-time escape for Innere Stadt workers. Of the several statues within the park (eg Schindler, Bruckner, Schubert), the most recognisable is the **Johann Strauss Denkmal** (Map pp240–3), a golden statue of Johann Strauss under a white arch. It's easily the most photographed statue in the park, and probably in the whole of Vienna. The **Kursalon** (see p150), in the southwest corner, hosts regular waltz concerts and there's a small children's playground on the eastern side of the Wien Fluss (Vienna River), which cuts through the park on its way to the Danube Canal.

BETWEEN THE DANUBE CANAL & THE DANUBE
Eating p125; Shopping p167; Sleeping p177

Crossing the Danube Canal from the Innere Stadt to the districts of Brigittenau and Leopoldstadt is almost like entering another city. Normally, such close proximity to the heart of a once grand empire would result in a little of the magic of the city rubbing off, but this is not the case with these districts. These are residential neighbourhoods, largely bereft of individual sights of interest to the average visitor, where anything that could have attracted was flattened during the war by the Nazis or the allied bombing raids of WWII.

But scratch the surface a little or spend even a small amount of time wandering its busy residential streets and a whole new neighbourhood springs to light. Leopoldstadt, easily the greater of the two districts, is steeped in history. It gained its name from Leopold I, an anti-Semite who dispelled the Jews from a ghetto in the area in 1670. Long the scapegoats of Vienna's elite and general populace alike, God's chosen people had slowly been drifting back to the city after their expulsion in the 15th century, and the beginning of the 21st century has seen a new influx of Jews. This has added a new lease of life to a floundering district, which in the past decades has accommodated wave after wave of immigrants from Turkey and the Balkans. Karmelitermarkt, a busy food market in the heart of the district, is where kosher and halal signs harmoniously hang side by side and Vienna's ethnic diversity is on show.

Leopoldstadt's monumental attractions are its parks. Prater, Vienna's seminal outdoor playground, is a combination of dense woodlands intermittently dispersed with swaths of green fields and the Wurstelprater, a funfair bordering on the tacky side of things. Praterstern, at the northern edge of the Prater, is a rough and ready transport connection hub and a notorious drug dealer and junky haunt. Its back alleys are still home to a scene slowly disappearing from Vienna's streets: a red light district, which is a touch on the shady side. Augarten, a park bordering Brigittenau, is far more genteel. Its wide pathways and manicured fields are regularly populated with a cross section of Vienna's society.

> ## Between the Danube Canal & the Danube Top Sights
>
> - Kicking back, enjoying a film and relaxing under the stars at **Kino Unter Sternen** (p154)
> - Pumping up the adrenaline levels on the rides at the **Wurstelprater** (p85)
> - Strolling along the tree-shaded pathways of the **Augarten** (p84)
> - Taking a ride on one of Vienna's icons, the **Riesenrad** (p85)

Orientation
Together, the districts of Leopoldstadt and Brigittenau form an island surrounded by the Danube Canal and the Danube.

Brigittenau makes up the northern third of the island while Leopoldstadt stretches from opposite the Innere Stadt to within sight of the city's southern border. Much of Leopoldstadt is given over to the Prater. Almost at the heart of the island is the Praterstern, the area's main public transport junction, and Wien Nord, one of Vienna's many train stations. Both are currently enjoying much-needed renovations.

ATELIER AUGARTEN/GUSTINUS AMBROSI-MUSEUM Map pp244-5

☎ 216 40 22; www.atelier-augarten.at, German only; 02, Scherzergasse 1a; adult/concession €4.50/2.50; ⏲ 10am-6pm Tue-Sun; tram N, 5

Sculptures by Austrian-born Gustinus Ambrosi (1893–1975) are the highlight of the works displayed at Augarten's Atelier, in the western corner of Augarten park. His bronze and stone sculptures are complemented by the museum's sculpture garden, which features European sculptures from the 20th and 21st centuries. The Atelier also regularly features temporary exhibits from international artists – check the program on the website.

Entry to the Atelier is included in the combined Belvedere ticket (see p91).

AUGARTEN Map pp244-5

www.augarten.at; Main entrance 02, Obere Augartenstrasse; ⏲ 6am-dusk Apr-Oct, 6.30am-dusk Nov-Mar; tram 31, bus 5A

Augarten is Leopoldstadt's second park, and has a somewhat less boisterous atmosphere than its bigger brother, the Prater. It gained its present shape in 1712, making it the oldest baroque garden in Vienna, and opened its doors to the public in 1775. The park is dotted with open meadows and crisscrossed with tree-shaded paths but your eyes will be drawn to the austere *Flaktürme* (flak towers; Map pp244–5) in its northern and western corners. Other buildings to note are the Augarten baroque palace, home to the Vienna

Boys' Choir, the nearby Saalgebäude, where the Augarten Porzellanmanufaktur (see p86) has set up shop, and the Atelier, housing the Gustinus Ambrosi-Museum.

Vienna's most popular open-air cinema, **Kino unter Sternen** (see p154), hosts classic movies over the summer months near the flak towers, and fills the park with people and food stalls.

JOHANN STRAUSS RESIDENCE

Map pp240-3

☎ 214 01 21; 02, Praterstrasse 54; adult/concession €2/1; ⏲ 9am-12.15pm & 1-4.30pm Tue-Sun; U1 Nestroyplatz, bus 5A

Strauss called Praterstrasse 54 his residence from 1863 to 1878 and composed *the* waltz, the *Blue Danube Waltz*, under its high ceilings. Inside you'll find an above-average collection of Strauss and ballroom memorabilia, including his grand piano and oil paintings from his last apartment which was destroyed during WWII. The rooms are decked out in period furniture, which matched the era Strauss resided here. This is a municipal museum.

PLANETARIUM Map pp244-5

☎ 729 54 94; www.planetarium-wien.at, German only; 02, Oswald-Thomas-Platz 1; adult/child/family €8/6/21; U1 Praterstern, tram O, 5, 21

The Planetarium, Vienna's extraterrestrial and interstellar viewfinder, is located on the edge of the Wurstelprater behind the Riesenrad. Shows, normally at 9.30am, 11am, 3pm and 7pm or 8pm, change on a regular basis, but

Flaktürme

It can be quite a shock, and a little unnerving, to walk around the corner and be confronted with a gigantic relic from WWII, a *Flakturm* (flak tower). Built from 1943 to 1944 as a defence against air attacks, these bare monolithic blocks stand like sleeping giants among the residential districts of Vienna. Apart from their air-defence capabilities, they were built to house up to 30,000 troops, had an underground hospital and munitions factory and could control their own water and power supply. And they were built to last: the 5m-thick walls of reinforced concrete mean that they are almost impossible to pull down. So they remain standing as an uncomfortable reminder of the Nazi era, featureless but for four circular gun bases at the top corners (these protrusions are strangely reminiscent of Mickey Mouse's ears).

Six flak towers still exist; two in Augarten (p84) and one just off Mariahilfer Strasse in Esterhazypark (housing the Haus des Meeres, p94) and another behind the MuseumsQuartier in Stiftskaserne (Map pp240–3). Of the last two in Arenbergpark (Map pp248–9), one is used by MAK for temporary exhibitions (⏲ 3-7pm Thu May-Nov); even if you're not interested in what's on show, it's worth paying the entrance fee just to see the inside of one of these WWII dinosaurs.

normally focus on our closest neighbours or star constellations and where Earth fits in amongst all that black stuff. Be aware that all shows are in German only.

Joint tickets for the Planetarium and Riesen-rad are available for €13/11/7.50 per adult/child over 12/child under 12; tickets for the Planetarium and Lilliputbahn cost €9.50/7.50/6.50.

PRATERMUSEUM Map pp244-5

☎ 726 76 83; 02, Oswald-Thomas-Platz 1; adult/concession/child under 6 €2/1/free; ☼ 9am-12.15pm & 1-4.30pm Tue-Fri, 2-6.30pm Sat & Sun; U1 Praterstern, tram 0, 5, 21

Sharing the same building as the Planetarium is this municipal museum that traces the history of the Wurstelprater and its woodland neighbour, the Grüner Prater. For all the life and splendour the Prater has seen, unfortunately its museum has only a rather dull mix of photos and stories mainly from the 19th century. The antique slot machines, some of which are still functioning, are the museum's saving grace.

PRATER

www.wiener-prater.at; U1 Praterstern, tram 0, 5, 21

Prater is a term commonly used to encompass two distinct areas of one of the city's favourite outdoor playgrounds: the Wurstelprater and the green, woodland park on its outskirts.

The **Wurstelprater** (Map pp244–5), or Volksprater as it's also known, is a large amusement park with all sorts of funfair rides, ranging from modern big dippers to merry-go-rounds and test-your-strength machines, which could easily date from the early 20th century. Bumper cars, go-karts, haunted houses, games rooms and mini-golf attractions abound, as do hotdog and candyfloss stands. There's also a 4km Lilliputbahn (mini railway; joint tickets with the Planetarium are available), which connects the park with Ernst Happel Stadium. Kids go bananas over the place. Rides cost around €1 to €5. One of the most popular attractions, however, is free: colourful, bizarre, deformed statues of people and creatures in the centre of the park, on and around Rondeau and Calafattiplatz.

Depending on your tastes, the 60 sq km of woodland park may be more appealing. Formally the royal hunting grounds of Joseph II, the Prater was first opened to the public in 1766 and has never looked back. Viennese flock here to walk, run, cycle, in-line skate or simple soak up the sun in the park's open green fields or tree-shaded alleys. Even though the park attracts a multitude of people, it's still possible to find a private patch of green, particularly in its southwestern reaches.

The Prater is home to the Riesenrad, the Planetarium, the Pratermuseum, Ernst Happel Stadium, the Lusthaus and the Schweizerhaus (see p126).

RIESENRAD Map pp244-5

☎ 729 54 30; www.wienerriesenrad.com; 02, Prater 90; adult/child/family €7.50/3/19; ☼ 9am-midnight May-Sep, 10am-10pm Mar, Apr & Oct, 10am-8pm Nov-Feb; U1 Praterstern, tram 0, 5, 21

Dominating the Prater is the Riesenrad (Ferris Wheel), one of Vienna's symbols and an absolute must for any visitor to the city. Built in 1897 by Englishman Walter B. Basset, the wheel rises to 65m and takes about 20 minutes to rotate its 430-tonne weight one complete circle. This gives you ample time to snap some fantastic shots of the city laid out in front of you. It survived bombing in 1945 and recently received a make-over which included dramatic lighting and a café at its base. If you think you're experiencing *déjà vu* upon spotting the great wheel, you're not: it achieved celluloid fame in *The Third Man*, in the scene where Holly Martins finally confronts Harry Lime, and featured in the James Bond flick *The Living Daylights*.

Admission includes entry into the Panorama, a collection of disused wheel-cabins filled with models depicting scenes from the city's history, including Roman Vienna and the Turkish invasions. See also the Planetarium (p84) for joint tickets with the Riesenrad, and the Donauturm (p87) for an additional combination ticket.

Riesenrad in the Prater (see above)

WIENER KRIMINALMUSEUM
Map pp244-5

☎ 214 44 678; www.kriminalmuseum.at; 02, Grosse Sperlgasse 24; adult/concession/child €4.50/3.50/2.50; ☼ 10am-5pm Tue-Sun; tram N, 21, bus 5A

Adding to the Viennese obsession with death is the Wiener Kriminalmuseum (Vienna Crime Museum). It gives a prurient, tabloid-style look at crimes and criminals in Austria. It dwells on murders in the last 100 years or so with particularly grisly relish, though there are skulls of earlier criminals, and even an 18th-century head pickled in a jar. Displays include death masks of convicted murderers and weapons supposedly used to carry out the murders.

WIENER PORZELLANMANUFAKTUR AUGARTEN Map pp244-5

☎ 211 24-0; www.augarten.at; 02, Obere Augartenstrasse 1, Schloss Augarten; tours €4; ☼ 9.30am Mon-Fri; bus 5A

If you go gaga over a good tea set, take a tour of Vienna's Porcelain Factory, the second oldest of its kind in Europe, and learn how these exquisite pieces are created. The tour explains the process of turning white kaolin, feldspar and quartz into delicate creations through the process of moulding, casting, luting, glazing and painting. Tours generally last around an hour. There's also a shop on the premises (see p167).

ACROSS THE DANUBE

Eating p126

The districts of Floridsdorf and Donaustadt make up all that there is of Vienna on the eastern side of the Danube. Known locally as Transdanubia (a Hungarian term meaning 'across the Danube'), the area holds little interest to tourists and many locals who live west of the river. And it doesn't often make the cut in Vienna's tourist board's promotional glossies – an extensively flat geography and wide streets lined with 1950s residential blocks won't have many tourists rushing off to their local travel agency to book a flight.

But don't be too hasty about crossing this area off your itinerary completely. The Donauinsel and the Alte Donau, the area's two greatest features, are waterways the Viennese just can't get enough of. The Donauinsel, a long, slender island in the Danube created in 1970, which is constantly undergoing recreational improvements, is dotted with small beaches and frequented by cyclists, runners, walkers and in-line skaters. The Alte Donau, a loop of Danube long cut off from its original source, is almost 100 years older than the Donauinsel and therefore far more established in the hearts and minds of the Viennese. In summer, finding a quiet spot away from families grilling up a feast or friends enjoying the water and each other's company can sometimes be a lengthy task. In between these beloved summer playgrounds are the UNO City, home to the UN, and the Donaupark (Danube Park), dominated by Vienna's tallest structure, the Donauturm.

At the southern extremes of Donaustadt is the Lobau, an area of dense scrub and woodland home to the western extension of the Nationalpark Donau-Auen, a couple of industrial sights and an abundance of small lakes. Any way you look at it, it's a bizarre combination. In summer, Vienna's alternative crowd flock to the Lobau for a bit of skinny-dipping. To the very north of Floridsdorf is the neighbourhood of Stammersdorf, home to an oft-forgotten concentration of *Heurigen* (wine taverns). Topographically it's the only hilly area around; on a balmy summer evening it easily rivals Vienna's better-known *Heuriger* regions on the slopes of the Wienerwald.

Orientation

'Across the Danube' refers to Vienna's expansion to the east of the Danube. This massive land mass is made up of only two districts, Floridsdorf to the north and Donaustadt to the south. Donaustadt is easily Vienna's largest district, greater in size than the Innere Stadt and the districts inside the Gürtel combined. Five bridges cross the Danube, connecting the districts with the rest of Vienna. The A22, an autobahn running from the most southern bridge, Praterbrücke, north along the Neue Donau (New Danube) to just past Stockerau, creates an artificial border between the river and the residential expanse.

FLORIDSDORF

DONAUINSEL Map pp238-9
U1 Donauinsel, U6 Neue Donau

Dividing the Danube from the Neue Donau is the svelte Donauinsel, which stretches some 21½km from opposite Klosterneuburg in the north to the Nationalpark Donau-Auen in the south. It's Vienna's prime aqua playground, with long sections of beach (don't except much sand though) perfect for swimming, boating and even a bit of waterskiing. Either end of the island is devoted to one the Viennese's favourite pastimes: getting naked. These FKK (*Freikörperkultur*; free body culture) zones are reserved for nudist bathers who also like to dine, drink, walk, bike and in-line skate *au naturel*. It's quite a sight. Concrete paths run the entire length of the island, and there are bicycle and in-line skate rental stores. Restaurants and snack bars are dotted along the paths, but the highest concentration of bars – collectively known as Sunken City and Copa Cagrana – is near Reichsbrücke and the U1 Donauinsel stop. In late June the island hosts the Donauinselfest (Danube Island Festival) – see p9 for more details.

For more information on outdoor activities and nightlife on the island, see the Entertainment chapter (p137).

DONAUSTADT

ALTE DONAU
U1 Alte Donau, U6 Neue Donau

The Alte Donau is a landlocked arm of the Danube, a third of which lies in Floridsdorf. It carried the main flow of the river until 1875, when manmade flood precautions created the Danube's path you see today. Now the 160-hectare water expanse is a favourite of Viennese sailing and boating enthusiasts, and also attracts swimmers, walkers, fishermen and in winter (when it's cold enough), ice skaters. Alongside free access points to the Alte Donau are almost a dozen city-owned bathing complexes which are open (approximately) from May to September. The biggest of these is the Gänsehäufel complex, on an island jutting out into the Alte Donau. The island also has a nudist section, swimming pools and lake access. For more information see the Entertainment chapter (p137).

NATIONALPARK DONAU-AUEN
☎ 022 12-34 50; www.donauauen.at; bus 91A

The Donau-Auen national park is the most easterly section of Vienna. Established in 1996, the park currently covers around 9300 hectares and runs in a thin strip on both sides of the Danube, extending from the edge of Vienna to the Slovakian border. About 60% is forested and approximately 25% is lakes and waterways. It was created to try to protect an environment that was threatened by the building of a hydroelectric power station in Hainburg. You'll find plentiful flora and fauna, including 700 species of fern and flowering plants, and a high density of kingfishers (feeding off the 50 species of fish).

DONAUTURM Map pp238-9
☎ 263 35 72; www.donauturm.at; 22, Donauturmstrasse 4; adult/concession/child €5.20/4.10/3.70; ⏲ 10am-11.30pm; U1 Kaisermühlen Vienna International Centre, bus 20B

UNO City complex (p88)

At 252m, the Donauturm (Danube Tower) in Donaupark is Vienna's tallest structure – next highest is the newly constructed Millennium Tower at 202m. Its revolving restaurant at 170m allows fantastic panoramic views of the whole city and beyond – it's just a pity the food isn't that great. Tickets covering entrance to the Donauturm and Riesenrad cost €9.60/5/4 per adult/concession/child. The adventurous out there might consider bungee jumping off the side of the tower.

UNO CITY Map pp238-9
☎ 260 60-33 28; www.unvienna.org; 22, Wagramer

Strasse 5; adult/concession/child €4/2.50/1; ☒ 11am-2pm Mon-Fri; U1 Kaisermühlen Vienna International Centre

The UNO City is home to a plethora of international organisations, but mainly houses the UN's third-largest office in the world. Guided tours take you through conference rooms and exhibitions on UN activities and add insight into what goes on behind normally closed doors. The City probably looked the picture of modernism way back in 1979 when it was built, but now looks quite out of date. It has extraterritorial status, so take your passport when visiting.

INSIDE THE GÜRTEL

Eating p127; Shopping p167; Sleeping p177

The districts inside the Gürtel (a multilaned road following the contour of the Ringstrasse but further out from the city's centre) are a dense concentration of apartment blocks pocketed by leafy parks, with a couple of grand baroque palaces thrown in for good measure. Many of Vienna's more refined citizens call this area home, as do a large number of students, young go-getters and successful entrepreneurs. This mix of people creates a diverse atmosphere which is at times hard to fathom: one neighbourhood will be the epitome of repose while the next is laden down with

noisy, progressive bars and quality restaurants. While the area isn't overflowing with sights, its strange bedfellows make exploring these districts a life-sized treasure hunt: you never know what little gem you may find tucked away down one of the side streets or back alleys.

The Gürtel was originally the site of *Linienwall*, Vienna's first line of defence against invaders. These days, it still forms a kind of barrier, albeit an invisible one: many of the city's immigrants fail to penetrate the inner sanctum of the districts inside the Gürtel and invariably settle in the poorer areas just outside the big road. Lined with excellent bars and an ever-decreasing array of sex shops and divey strip bars, the Gürtel is one of Vienna's few areas of true urban grit.

Inside the Gürtel Top Sights

- Admiring the distinctive architecture of Friedensreich Hundertwasser at the **KunstHausWien** (p90) and **Hundertwasser Haus** (p90)
- Marvelling at the magnificent **Liechtenstein Museum** (p96) and its extensive private collection of art gems
- Being overawed by the baroque splendour of the **Belvedere** (p91)
- Discovering the often-forgotten military exploits of Austria at the **Heeresgeschichtliches Museum** (p89) in the Arsenal
- Seeing how much your stomach can take at the **Pathologisch-anatomische Bundesmuseum** (p96)

Landstrasse, the largest of the districts inside the Gürtel, contains some of the area's best attractions. This is where you'll find the Belvedere, arguably the finest baroque palace in Europe, the Hundertwasser Haus, an apartment block where straight lines and even surfaces are outlawed, and the Arsenal, home to the enthralling Museum of Military History. Even though Wieden is small for a district, it has plenty to offer. Karlsplatz is crowded with things to see and do, and its bar scene, which is centred on and around Schleifmühlgasse, is almost unrivalled. Forming a border between Wieden and its northern neighbour is the Naschmarkt, the prima donna of Vienna's markets. Its all here – Turkish kebabs, Greek feta, Austrian wines and Asian diners. Margareten is bereft of individual sights that would interest tourists, but its restaurant scene is fast catapulting it up the place-to-dine ladder.

Mariahilf is dominated by Mariahilfer Strasse, the city's boldest and brightest shopping street. This is one of the few places where Vienna (outside the Innere Stadt) can actually feel crowded. The Viennese literally flood the street on a Saturday morning looking for all sorts of electronic accessories and High St brands. Except for a couple of small parks and museums, and the not so small flak tower in Esterhazypark, the rest of Mariahilf is given over to residential apartment buildings. Neubau, the district to the north of Mariahilfer Strasse, is where many of Vienna's select shops have gone into hiding. Neubaugasse is a particularly good fix for shopaholics, as are the cobblestone alleys of Spittalberg, a quaint neighbourhood tucked in behind the MuseumsQuartier. Spittalberg is also famous for its Christmas market and concentration of bars and restaurants. Neubau as a whole is fast becoming the place to dine and party away the wee small hours.

To the north of Neubau is Josefstadt, where the close proximity to the Universität has traditionally attracted many students. It also has its fair share of noble residents and fine restaurants. Its main street, Josefstädter Strasse, is lined with shops, the majority of which are basically extensions of their owner's personality and ooze individual flair. Alsergrund is on the northern border of the districts inside the Gürtel. It is often forgotten by the Viennese, for one reason or another, and this is a mistake. Its quiet streets hide the beautiful Liechtenstein Palais, the Alte AKH, a university campus with shaded courtyards and garden bars.

Orientation

The Ringstrasse and the Gürtel, Vienna's busiest roads, cordon off seven of the city's districts, which together basically form a large 'U' around the Innere Stadt to the north, south and west. The open section of this 'U' is the Danube Canal. Running from east to west along the area's southern stretch are the districts of Landstrasse, Wieden and Margareten. Climbing north from Margareten to the Danube Canal are the districts Mariahilf, Neubau, Josefstadt and Alsergrund. The Wien Fluss (Vienna River), a shallow, channelled river flowing from the Wienerwald to the Danube Canal, is the border between Margareten and Mariahilf.

Each district has one or two major roads connecting the Gürtel and the Ringstrasse. Their names often follow the district: eg Wiedner Hauptstrasse in Wieden, Margareten Strasse in Margareten, Josefstädter Strasse in Josefstadt.

LANDSTRASSE
HEERESGESCHICHTLICHES MUSEUM
Map pp248-9

☎ /95 61-60420; www.bundesheer.at/hgm, German only; 03, Arsenal; adult/concession/child under 11/family €5.10/3.30/free/7.30; ۞ 9am-5pm Sat-Thu; tram 18, bus 69A

In the wake of the 1848 rebellion, Franz Josef I decided his defences needed strengthening and ordered the Arsenal built – the large barracks and munitions depot was completed in neo-Byzantine style in 1856. Its handsome façade belied the true purpose of the building: it was a fortress built to quash any further uprisings. At the same time Franz Josef established the Heeresgeschichtliches Museum (Museum of Military History) within the Arsenal, making it the oldest public museum in Vienna.

It's not a modern museum as museums go, but it packs some punch. The first sign of this is the vaulted entrance hall, which is lined with life-size marble statues of pre-1848 Austrian military leaders. The second is the Ruhmeshalle (Hall of Fame) at the top of the stairs on the 1st floor. Its heavily frescoed ceiling is spectacular, and beautifully complemented by Moorish columns.

If you wish to follow the exploits of the Austrians chronologically, your tour of the museum should start on the 1st floor. It works its way from the Thirty Years' War (1618–48) through to the Hungarian Uprising and the Austro-Prussian War (ending in 1866), taking the Napoleonic and Turkish Wars with it. Some of the booty from the Turkish invasions is impressive, but first prize goes to the Great Seal of Mustafa Pasha, which fell to Prince Eugene of Savoy in the Battle of Zenta in 1697.

The ground floor picks up where the 1st floor left off, with a show of the imperial army uniforms from 1867 onwards. However, the room on the assassination of Archduke Franz Ferdinand in Sarajevo in 1914 – which set off a chain of events culminating in the start of WWI – steals the show. The car he was shot in (complete with bullet holes), the sofa he bled to death on and his rather grisly blood-stained coat are on display. Suitably morbid and suitably Viennese. The next room moves onto the war itself; the star attraction here is a 1916 Haubitze, a colossal cannon of immense power. The eastern wing covers the Republic years after WWI up until the Anschluss in 1938. The excellent displays are peppered with propaganda posters and Nazi paraphernalia, plus video footage of Hitler hypnotising the masses. The last room is devoted to Austria's navy – yes, navy – when the Adriatic coastline fell within its territory.

The courtyard is filled with tanks frozen in motion; Eastern and Western tanks are equally represented.

HUNDERTWASSER HAUS Map pp248-9
03, Löwengasse/Kegelgasse; tram N

This residential block of flats was designed by none other than Friedensreich Hundertwasser himself. It is now one of Vienna's most prestigious addresses, even though it only provides rented accommodation and is owned by the city of Vienna – plus, the uneven floors, broken mirrors and circus of tourists must be hell to live with. It's not possible to see inside the house but you can visit the **Kalke Village** (Map pp248–9; ☉ 9am-5pm, until 7pm in summer), also the handiwork of Hundertwasser, created from an old Michelin factory. It contains over-priced cafés, souvenir shops and art shops, all in typical Hundertwasser fashion with uneven surfaces and colourful ceramics.

KUNSTHAUSWIEN Map pp244-5
☎ 712 04 91; www.kunsthauswien.at; 03, Untere Weissgerberstrasse 13; adult/concession €8/6, incl temporary exhibitions €14/10; ☉ 10am-7pm; tram N, O

It's easy to see the KunstHausWien (Art House Vienna) is another of Hundertwasser's inventive creations: the colourful exterior, with its bulging ceramics and lack of straight lines, is a dead giveaway.

The stroke of Hundertwasser's brush doesn't stop with the façade, however. Uneven floors, patchwork paintwork and irregular corners greet you upon opening the art gallery's heavy doors (and a sign pointing downwards to New Zealand, Hundertwasser's second home). The contents of the KunstHausWien are something of a paean in honour of Hundertwasser,

---

The Best of Bombastic Baroque

- **Belvedere** (p91) Arguably the finest baroque palace in Europe.
- **Karlskirche** (p93) A classic baroque church with touches of Byzantine thrown in.
- **Kunsthistorisches Museum** (p77) We're not talking about the building here, but the extensive baroque art collection it houses.
- **Liechtenstein** (p96) Gives Belvedere a run for its money for the city's top baroque palace title.
- **Schönbrunn** (p100) The palace may be over-shadowed by Belvedere and Liechtenstein, but its gardens outshine anything in Vienna with majesty and grace.

---

displaying his paintings, graphics, tapestry, philosophy, ecology and architecture. His vivid paintings are as distinctive as his diverse building projects. Hundertwasser's quotes are everywhere; some of his pronouncements are annoyingly didactic or smack of old hippy-dom ('each raindrop is a kiss from heaven'), but they're often thought-provoking. There are even a couple of films about him. The gallery also puts on quality temporary exhibitions featuring other artists. Be sure to wander to the rooftop where you'll find a shady patch of grass under the grove of trees.

Monday is half-price day (unless it's a holiday) and the gallery's café around the back is open 10am to midnight daily.

ST MARXER FRIEDHOF Map pp248-9
03, Leberstrasse 6-8; ☉ 7am-7pm Jun-Aug, 7am-6pm May & Sep, 7am-5pm Apr & Oct, 7am-dusk Nov-Mar; tram 71, bus 74A

Also known as the Biedermeier cemetery, after the period when all 6000 graves were laid out, St Marxer Friedhof (Cemetery of St Mark) is a pilgrimage site for Mozart aficionados. In December 1791 Mozart was buried in an un-marked grave with none of his family present. Over time the site was forgotten and his wife's search for the exact location went in vain. It did, however, bear one fruit: a poignant memorial (Mozartgrab) made from a broken pillar and a discarded stone angel was erected in the area where he was most likely buried.

STRASSENBAHN MUSEUM Map pp248-9
☎ 786 03 03; www.wiener-tramwaymuseum.org, German only; 03, Erdbergstrasse 109; adult/child €2/free; ☉ 9am-4pm Sat & Sun May-Oct; U3 Schlach-thausgasse, tram 18, bus 77A, 79A

The Viennese love their 'Bims' (the nickname for street trams, which comes from the sound of their bell) so much they've set up a museum dedicated to this great form of transport. Here you'll find some 80 trams – the oldest a horse-drawn trolley from 1871, and the newest, a Porsche-designed tram in use today – plus the odd bus or two. The museum also runs old-timer tours of the city (see Organised Tours p50).

SCHLOSS BELVEDERE Map pp248-9
www.belvedere.at; Tram D, 71
Belvedere is considered one of the finest baroque palaces in the world. Designed by Johann Lukas von Hildebrandt, it was built for the brilliant military strategist Prince Eugene of Savoy (see p92), conqueror of the Turks in 1718 and hero to a nation. The Unteres (Lower) Belvedere was built first (1714–16), with an orangery attached, and was the prince's summer residence. Connected to it by a long, landscaped garden is the Oberes (Upper) Belvedere (1721–23), the venue for the prince's banquets and other big bashes.

Considered together, the Belvedere residences were at the time almost more magnificent than the imperial residence, the Hofburg. This was something of an irritation to the Habsburgs, especially as the prince was able to look down onto the city from the elevated vantage point of the Oberes Belvedere. It was therefore with some satisfaction that Maria Theresia was able to purchase the Belvedere after the prince's death. It then became a Habsburg residence, most recently occupied by the Archduke Franz Ferdinand who started a court there to rival his uncle's (Franz Josef I) in the Hofburg. Ferdinand was assassinated in 1914, an event that sparked off WWI.

The Belvedere is now home to the **Österreichische Galerie** (Austrian Gallery), split between the Unteres Belvedere, which houses the baroque section, and the Oberes Belvedere, showcasing 19th- and 20th-century art. A combined ticket of €7.50/5 per adult/concession allows entry to the Unteres and Oberes Belvedere, plus the Atelier Augarten/Gustinus Ambrosi-Museum (see p84). Fortunately this ticket is valid for more than one day. Regular children's events are held in both the Oberes and Unteres Belvedere, usually on a Sunday. Pick up information from the palace itself or log on to the website.

GARDENS
03, Rennweg/Prinz-Eugen-Strasse; tram D, 71
The long garden between the two Belvederes was laid out in classical French style and has sphinxes and other mythical beasts along its borders. South of the Oberes Belvedere is a small **Alpine Garden** (Map pp248–9; adult/concession €4/3; ☺ 10am-6pm Apr-Jul), which has 3500 plant species and a bonsai section. North from here is the much larger **Botanic Gardens** (Map pp248–9; admission free; ☺ 9am-1 hr before dusk) belonging to the Vienna University.

OBERES BELVEDERE Map pp248-9
☎ 795 57 134; www.belvedere.at; 03, Prinz-Eugen-Strasse 27; adult/concession/child/family €7.50/5/3/15; ☺ 10am-6pm Tue-Sun; tram D
The Oberes Belvedere is a must for all visitors to Vienna, firstly for the collection it houses (which is easily the more important of the two in the Belvedere) and secondly for the sublime baroque palace itself. It's a mix of styles that strangely works: the baroque interior provides a diverting setting for the drift into modern art. Appropriately, Herculean figures supporting columns greet you in the entrance lobby and exploits of Alexander the Great flank the stairs climbing from the entrance way to the 1st floor.

The 1st floor has paintings from the turn of the 19th century, particularly the works of Hans Makart (1840–84) and Anton Romakos (1832–89); these artists both influenced the later Viennese Art-Nouveau artists. While you can't take anything away from these 19th-century painters, the 20th-century section of this floor has the gallery's best exhibits. The works of Austrian artists on display are simply breathtaking, and only the Leopold Museum's collection comes anywhere close to matching it.

The two most noteworthy artists are Gustav Klimt (1862–1918) and Egon Schiele (1890–1918). Klimt was one of the founders of the Secessionist Art-Nouveau school. His later pictures (such as the two portraits of Adele Bloch-Bauer) employ a harmonious but ostentatious use of background colour (with much metallic gold and silver) to evoke or symbolise the emotions of the main figures. One of the best known but also one of the most intriguing works here is Klimt's *The Kiss* (1908). It shows a couple embracing within what looks like a yellow overcoat, surrounded by the usual Klimt circles and rectangles. The man's neck is twisted unnaturally as he strains towards her; her face is half turned away and enclosed within her hands. Nobody knows quite how to interpret this scene: is she demurely and willingly proffering her cheek, or is she trying to avoid his advances? Some of Klimt's impressionist landscapes are also on display.

Schiele produced intense, melancholic works. Notice the hypnotic and bulging eyes on the portrait of his friend, *Eduard Kosmack* (1910). Schiele's bold, brooding colours and unforgiving outlines are in complete contrast to Klimt's golden tapestries and idealised forms. He lived with one of Klimt's models for a while – Schiele's portraits of her were very explicit, bordering on the pornographic. Some critics are fond of trying to explain his obsessions with sex and desperate subjects by looking at Schiele's upbringing: his father went insane from syphilis and destroyed the family's stocks and bonds in a fire. Schiele's last work is *The Family*. He added the child between the woman's legs when he found out his own wife was pregnant; however, she died of Egyptian flu before the child was born. Schiele died of the same illness before this painting was completely finished (look closely and you'll see the imprecision of the male's left hand).

Other artists represented include Herbert Boeckl, Anton Hanak, Arnulf Rainer and Fritz Wotruba. There are several examples of the output of Austria's third great modernist (after Klimt and Schiele; who comes first and second is still hotly debated), the influential expressionist Oskar Kokoschka (1886–1980). A smattering of international artists is also on display, including such greats as Munch, Monet, Van Gogh, Renoir and Cézanne.

The top (2nd) floor has a concentration of 19th-century paintings from the romantic, classical and Biedermeier periods. In particular, this section has work by the Biedermeier painter Georg Waldmüller (1793–1865), showing to good effect his very precise portraits and rural scenes. Other artists represented include Friedrich von Amerling (1803–1887), Casper David Friedrich (1774–1840) and Moritz von Schwind (1804–1871).

Headphones with a commentary in English can be rented for €4, and are certainly worth the cost.

UNTERES BELVEDERE Map pp248-9

☎ 795 57 134; www.belvedere.at; 03, Rennweg 6; adult/concession €6/3; ☼ 10am-6pm Tue-Sun; tram 71

The baroque section offers some good statuary, such as the originals from George Raphael Donner's (1693–1741) Neuer Markt fountain and the *Apotheosis of Prince Eugene*. Eugene was presumably suffering delusions of grandeur by this time, for he commissioned the latter work himself; the artist, not to be outdone, depicted himself at the prince's feet. Paintings include those of Maria Theresia and her husband, Franz Stephan. A room is devoted to the vibrant paintings by Franz Anton Maulbertsch (1724–96), and other notable Austrian baroque artists on display include Johann Michael Rottmayer (1654–1730) and 'Kremser' Schmidt (1728–1796).

The attached **Orangery** (Map pp248–9) houses a collection of Austrian medieval art, which, it's no real surprise to find, is comprised of religious scenes, altarpieces and statues. There are several impressive works by Michael Pacher (1440–98), a Tirolean artist who was influenced by both early Low Countries art and the early Renaissance of northern Italy.

WIEDEN

BESTATTUNGSMUSEUM Map pp248-9

☎ 501 95-42 27; 04, Goldeggasse 19; admission free; ☼ by prior arrangement noon-3pm Mon-Fri; tram D, bus 13A

Vienna is the perfect place to find a Bestattungsmuseum – a museum devoted to the art of undertaking. This museum isn't in the same league as the Pathologisch-anatomische Bundesmuseum (p96) or the Josephinum (p95), but the sheer fascination value of this bizarre museum makes a visit well worth it. You won't uncover wax models or gruesome remains here, but you'll see photos, documents and paraphernalia retelling the history of undertaking in this often macabre city. Donations are welcome.

Prince Eugene

One of Austria's greatest military heroes wasn't even a native of the country. Prince Eugene of Savoy (1663–1736) was born in Paris. After being informed he was too short to be accepted into the French army he left France in 1683 to join the Habsburg forces. Eugene was just in time to help beat off the Turkish forces besieging Vienna. He was given his own regiment and within 10 years was promoted to field marshal. His skills as a military strategist were evident in his victories against the Turks at Zenta in 1697 and during the campaign in the Balkans from 1714 to 1718, which finally drove the Turks out of all but a small corner of Europe. His capture of the fortress at Belgrade in 1718 was instrumental in ending that war. Prince Eugene's skills as a statesman were also employed in the War of the Spanish Succession, where he negotiated with his former homeland.

GENERALI FOUNDATION Map pp248-9

☎ 504 98 80; www.gfound.or.at; 04, Wiedner Haupt-strasse 15; adult/concession €6/4.50; ⏱ 11am-8pm Thu-Sun; tram 62, 65

The Generali Foundation is a fine gallery which picks and chooses exhibition pieces from its vast collection – which numbers around 1400 – with the utmost care. The majority of its ensemble covers conceptual and performance art from the latter half of the 20th century, with names like Dan Graham and Gordon Matta-Clark popping up on a regular basis. The entrance to the exhibition hall is towards the back of a residential passageway.

HISTORISCHES MUSEUM DER STADT WIEN Map pp240-3

☎ 505 87 47-0; www.museum.vienna.at, German only; 04, Karlsplatz 5; adult/concession €4/2; ⏱ 9am-6pm Tue-Sun; U1, U2, U4 Karlsplatz, Karlsplatz trams, bus 4A

This museum near Karlskirche is the biggest and best of those run by the city of Vienna (see the boxed text p94). It gives a detailed rundown on the development of Vienna from prehistory to the present day, and does a pretty good job of putting the city and its personalities in context, without needing words. Exhibits occupy three floors and include maps and plans, artefacts, many paintings – works by Klimt, Schiele and Biedermeier-painters like Waldmüller are worth the entrance fee alone – and reconstructed rooms from the homes of Adolf Loos and Franz Grillparzer. Two models (on the 1st and 2nd floors) of the Innere Stadt show the impact of the Ringstrasse developments, and there are some good period photographs. The spoils of the second Turkish siege (1683) make for fine viewing on the 1st floor.

KARLSKIRCHE Map pp240-3

☎ 712 44 56; www.karlskirche.at, German only; 04, Karlsplatz; adult/concession/child under 10 €4/2/free; ⏱ 9am-12.30pm & 1-6pm Mon-Sat, 1-6pm Sun; U1, U2, U4 Karlsplatz

At the southeast corner of Resselpark is Karlskirche (Church of St Charles Borromeo), the finest baroque church in Vienna. This imposing creation was built between 1716 and 1739, after a vow by Karl VI at the end of the 1713 plague. It was designed and commenced by Johann Bernhard Fischer von Erlach and completed by his son Joseph. Although predominantly baroque, it combines several architectural styles. The twin columns are modelled on Trajan's Column in Rome and

Karlskirche (below)

show scenes from the life of St Charles Borromeo (who helped plague victims in Italy), to whom the church is dedicated. The huge oval dome reaches 72m; in combination with the church's large windows, the dome's height creates a bright, open nave. The admission fee includes entrance to Museo Borromeo, a small museum with a handful of religious art and clothing purportedly from the saint himself, but what it doesn't cover is the lift to the dome for a close-up view of the frescoes during their restoration period – that's an extra €2. What you'll see is details of cloud-bound celestial beings painted by Johann Michael Rottmayr. The altar panel is by Sebastiano Ricci and shows the Assumption of the Virgin. In front of the church is a pond, complete with a Henry Moore sculpture from 1978.

KUNSTHALLE PROJECT SPACE
Map pp240-3

☎ 512 18 90 33; 04, Treitlstrasse 2; adult/concession €2/1; ⏱ 1-7pm; U1, U2, U4 Karlsplatz, Karlsplatz trams

The Kunsthalle Project Space was formerly the home of contemporary art in Vienna, but this has since moved to within the confines of the mighty MuseumsQuartier. It still plays a role, albeit a minor one, in the contemporary-art scene and hosts temporary exhibitions of

Municipal Museums

The City of Vienna runs some 20 **municipal museums** (www.museum.vienna.at, German only) scattered around the city, all of which are included in a free booklet available at the Rathaus.

The leader of the municipal pack is the Historisches Museum der Stadt Wien (see p93), which covers the history of Vienna. Many are based in the former residences of the great composers, and generally contain assorted memorabilia and furniture of their exalted former inhabitants. Others highlight the Roman ruins scattered around the Innere Stadt, or are one-offs, like the Uhren Museum (p65) and the Hermesvilla (p99). All municipal museums are free for visits before noon on Friday and all day Sunday, and close on 1 January, 1 May and 25 December.

In addition, each district has its own *Bezirksmuseum* (district museum), with free entry and limited opening times – check addresses in the telephone book.

up-and-coming artists. Its 'other half' is the Kunsthalle Café (see p142), a popular haunt of an upwardly mobile crowd with an eye for art.

SCHUBERT COMMEMORATIVE ROOMS Map pp246-7

☎ 581 67 30; 04, Kettenbrückengasse 6; adult/concession €2/1; ☺ 1.30-4.30pm Tue-Sun; U4 Kettenbrückengasse, bus 59A

This is another one of those municipal museums that doesn't have a lot going for it other than the fact a famous musician was born, lived or died at the address. In this case it was Schubert, and he spent his dying days in this, his brother's apartment – 1 September to 10 November 1828 to be precise. Even on his death bed (he either died of typhoid fever from drinking infected water, or syphilis) he still managed to compose a string of piano sonatas and his last work, *Der Hirt auf dem Felsen* (The Shepherd on the Rock).

STADTBAHN PAVILLONS Map pp240-3

☎ 505 87 47-84 059; 04, Karlsplatz; adult/concession €2/1; ☺ 1.30-4.30pm Tue-Sun; U1, U2, U4 Karlsplatz, Karlsplatz trams, bus 4A

Within Resselpark at Karlsplatz are Otto Wagner's Stadtbahn Pavillons. They were created for Vienna's first public transport system, which was built from 1893 to 1902; Wagner was in charge of the overall design for the metro lines, bridges and station buildings. The pavilions are suitably Jugendstil flavoured, with floral designs

and gold trim on a steel and marble structure. When the new U-Bahn transport system was put in place, the west pavilion was used as an exit for the U4 line of the Karlsplatz station, and now also houses a small municipal museum used for temporary exhibitions. The east pavilion has been taken over by Club U (see p141).

MARIAHILF

HAUS DES MEERES Map pp246-7

☎ 587 14 17; www.haus-des-meeres.at; 06 im Esterhazypark, Fritz-Grünbaumplatz 1; adult/concession/child 6-15/under 6 €8.40/6.40/4/2.70; ☺ 9am-6pm; U3 Neubaugasse, bus 13A, 14A

The house of seafood is a rather unspectacular collection of lizards, sharks, crocodiles and snakes, with a few fish and spiders thrown in. Saving graces include the shark and piranha feeding at 3pm Wednesday and Sunday and the reptile feeding at 10am Sunday, and a glass tropical house filled with lithe monkeys and a small rainforest. It occupies the inside of a *Flakturm* (flak tower), giving you a chance to see the inside of one of these giant monoliths up close and personal.

HAYDN MUSEUM Map pp246-7

☎ 596 13 07; 06, Haydngasse 19; adult/concession €2/1; ☺ 9am-12.15pm & 1-4.30pm Tue-Sun; U3 Zieglergasse, bus 57A

Hayden bought this house in 1793 and, obviously thinking it too small, added an extra floor. He didn't move in until the end of 1796 and then spent the remainder of his years here, dying in 1809. Within that time he composed *The Creation* and *The Seasons*. There's not much to see except a smattering of period furniture and the odd piece of memorabilia. The museum also has rooms devoted to Brahms, displaying some of his personal items. The Haydn museum is a municipal museum.

MAJOLIKAHAUS MAP pp246-7

06, Linke Wienzeile 40; U4 Kettenbrückengasse

This Art-Nouveau masterpiece was created by Otto Wagner in 1899 and is named for the majolica tiles used to create the flowing floral motifs on the façade. No 38 next door is another Wagner concoction; it features railings created from metal leaves and a brace of jester figures on the roof which look like they could be shouting abuse at the traditional Viennese buildings nearby. The golden medallions on the façade are by Kolo Moser. Both buildings overlook the open-air Naschmarkt.

NEUBAU

BÜCHEREI WIEN Map pp246-7

☎ 400 08 45 00; www.buechereien.wien.at; 07, Urban-Loritz-Platz; ✆ 10am-7pm Mon-Fri, 10am-2pm Sat; U6 Burggasse-Stadthalle, tram 6, 18

Straddling the U6 line at Burggasse is Vienna's newest addition to its long list of libraries, the Bücherei Wien. It's the City of Vienna's biggest library, which recently moved from its cramped premises on Laudongasse to these brand-spanking-new digs. The entrance way is not exactly conventional: pyramid-like steps lead up to the main doors, whose height is equivalent to a 2nd-storey floor. If you continue to climb the steps you'll soon reach Canetti (see p129) and be treated to far-reaching views to the south.

HOFMOBILIENDEPOT Map pp246-7

☎ 524 33 57-0; www.hofmobiliendepot.at; 07, Mariahilfer Strasse 88; adult/concession/child €6.90/4.50/3.50; ✆ 10am-6pm Tue-Sun; U3 Zieglergasse

If you've even the smallest drop of love for interiors then this impressive collection of imperial furniture and fittings will surely please. The Hofmobiliendepot is a storage space for any unwanted pieces from the Hofburg, Schönbrunn, Belvedere and other Habsburg residences, so you can imagine the quality on display. Highlights include the Egyptian Cabinet Room and Crown Prince Rudoph's Turkish Room/Opium Den.

JOSEFSTADT

MUSEUM FÜR VOLKSKUNDE

Map pp244-5

☎ 406 89 05; www.volkskundemuseum.at; 08, Laudongasse 15-19; adult/child/family €4.35/1.45/7.25; ✆ 10am-5pm Tue-Sun; tram 5, 33, bus 13A

This museum devoted to folk art is stocked with handcrafted sculptures, paintings and furniture from throughout Austria and its neighbouring countries. Many of the pieces have a religious or rural theme. Temporary exhibitions are a regular feature and of a high standard; the building itself is a vintage 17th-century palace – Schönborn Palace, to be exact.

PIARISTENKIRCHE Map pp244-5

08, Jodok-Fink-Platz; admission free; tram J, bus 13A

The Piaristenkirche (Church of the Piarist Order), or Maria Treu Church, is notable for two interior pieces: the ceiling frescoes and the organ. The stunning frescoes, completed by Franz Anton Maulbertsch in 1753, depict various stories from the bible, while the organ holds the distinction of being used by Anton Bruckner for his entry examination into the Music Academy. At the end of his exam one judge was heard to say 'he should be examining us!'. The church is normally only open for services. In summer, two restaurants opposite set up outdoor seating on Jodok-Fink-Platz; it's quite a wonderful setting with the church as a backdrop.

ALSERGRUND

FERNWÄRME Map pp244-5

☎ 313 26 20 30; 09, Spittelauer Lände 45; admission free; tours by appointment only; U4, U6 Spittelau, tram D

This absorbing creation of Hundertwasser hides the mundane waste incinerator of the city. Commissioned to revamp the façade of the incinerator in 1989, which was quite an eyesore on the landscape, Hundertwasser has created a visual bonanza, the highlight of which is the smoke stack crowned with a massive golden bulb. Tours are available on request.

JOSEPHINUM Map pp244-5

☎ 427 76 34 01; 09, Währinger Strasse 25; adult/concession €2/1; ✆ 9am-3pm Mon-Fri, 10am-2pm 1st Sat every month; tram 37, 38, 40, 41, 42

The Josephinum, on the 1st floor of the building, is also known as the Geschichte der Medizin (Museum of Medical History).

The prime exhibits of the museum are the ceroplastic and wax specimen models of the human frame, created over 200 years ago by Felice Fontana and Paolo Mascagni. They were used in the Academy of Medico-Surgery, instigated by Joseph II in 1785 to try to improve the skills of army surgeons who lacked medical qualifications. These models, showing the make-up of the body under the skin, were intended to give the students a three-dimensional understanding of the organs, bones, veins and muscles. Three rooms of this gory lot will make you feel like you've wandered onto the set of a tacky horror movie. If you can dismiss your queasiness, the models are, in fact, quite intriguing and their level of detail is a compliment to their creators.

The rest of the museum contains arcane medical instruments, photos of past practitioners, accounts of unpleasant-looking operations and ailments, and some texts (one book is thoughtfully left open on a page dealing with the dissection of eyeballs).

LIECHTENSTEIN MUSEUM Map pp244-5

☎ 319 57 67-0; www.liechtensteinmuseum.at;
09, Fürstengasse 1; adult/concession/child €10/8/5;
🕑 9am-8pm; tram D, bus 40A

Until 1938, the Royal family of Liechtenstein resided in Vienna, but after the Anschluss made a hasty retreat to their small country squeezed between Austria and Switzerland. They didn't, however, manage to take everything with them, and it was only near the end of WWII that they transferred their collection of baroque masterpieces to Vaduz.

After many years collecting dust in depot vaults, this private collection of one Prince Hans-Adam II of Liechtenstein is once again on display in Palais Liechtenstein. It's one of the largest private collections in the world, consisting of some 200 paintings and 50 sculptures, dating from 1500 to 1700.

The magnificent Palais Liechtenstein almost outshines the collection itself. Built between 1690 and 1712, it is a supreme example of audacious and extravagant baroque architecture that completely dazzles the eyes. Frescoes and ceiling paintings by the likes of Johann Michael Rottmayer and Marcantonio Franceschini decorate the halls and corridors of this sumptuous palace. Its **Herkulessaal** (Hercules Hall) – so named for the Hercules motifs in its ceiling frescoes by renowned Roman painter Andrea Pozzo – is an absolute highlight which extends over two storeys. The neoclassical **Gentlemen's Apartment Library**, on the ground floor, is not to be missed. It contains an astounding 100,000 volumes and just breathing the air in this room will raise your IQ by 10 points. It's also an impressive reminder of how money and power were once the only way to gather knowledge. The extensive **gardens**, originally baroque and transformed into an English landscape in the 19th century, are just made for both exploring and relaxing.

The collection, known as the Princely Collection, is displayed over two of the three floors of the palace. Think of names such as Rubens, Raphael, van Dyck and Rembrandt and you'll have a fair idea of what there is to see. Four galleries – one devoted to sculpture and the rest to paintings – are located on the ground floor. Gallery III contains celebrated Biedermeier works and the lion's share of highlights on this floor; Friedrich von Amerling's *Portrait of Maria Franziska of Liechtenstein at Age Two* (1836) is a sublime piece of art capturing the peaceful princess.

The big guns, however, are on the upper floor. Seven galleries intertwine to provide a trip through 200 years of art history, starting in 1500 with early Italian religious paintings in Gallery IV. Gallery V is dedicated to Renaissance portraits; Raphael's *Portrait of a Man* (1503) takes first prize for the intensity and depth of the subject's stare. Moving onto Gallery VI, you'll find Italian baroque paintings; Sebastiano Ricci and Pompeo Batoni are both heavily featured here.

Leaving the Herkulessaal aside, the focal point of the upper floor is Gallery VII, which is home to Peter Paul Rubens' *Decius Mus* cycle (1618). Consisting of eight almost life-sized paintings, the cycle depicts the life and death of Decius Mus, a Roman leader who sacrificed himself so that his army would be victorious on the battlefield. The vivid paintings are a powerful display of art, detail and action, and easily take hold of the viewer. Gallery VIII is totally devoted to Rubens, with over 30 of his Flemish baroque paintings. Myths and legends are the subjects of many of his paintings, including his coy *Venus at a Mirror* (1613–14). And even more of Rubens' works are on display in Gallery IX – this time his portraits – alongside Van Dyck and Fran Hals. The sheer exuberance and life captured by Rubens in his *Portrait of Clara Serena Rubens* (1616) is testament to the great artist's talent. Gallery X is lined with Dutch stills and landscapes.

Like the Kunsthistorisches Museum, the Belvedere and the Albertina, it's best to take your time at the Liechtenstein, otherwise you'll find yourself art-ed out. The gardens are the perfect place to take a breather.

Guided and audio tours are available, for €4 apiece, and are well worth the extra expense.

PATHOLOGISCH-ANATOMISCHE BUNDESMUSEUM Map pp244-5

☎ 406 86 72; www.pathomus.or.at, German only; 09, Spitalgasse 2; admission free; 🕑 3-6pm Wed, 8-11am Thu; tram 5, 33

If the Bestattungsmuseum (Undertakers' Museum; p92), Josephinum (p95) or Wiener Kriminalmuseum (p86) didn't finish you off, the Pathologisch-anatomische Bundesmuseum (Pathological Anatomy Museum) surely will. Housed in the Narrenturm (Fool's Tower), which served as an insane asylum from 1784 to 1866, the museum is filled with medical oddities and abnormalities preserved in jars of formaldehyde, and the odd wax model with one grisly disease or another. This is not a place for those with a weak stomach. The Narrenturm is a bit hard to find inside the confusing layout of the Altes AKH (see p140); once inside the Altes AKH just consult a map.

SERVITEN KIRCHE Map pp244-5

09, Servitenplatz 9; U4 Rossauer Lände, tram D

The façade of the Serviten Church dominates the Serviten neighbourhood – a small confluence of cobblestone streets lined with bars, restaurants and shops. The church's fine, baroque interior and oval nave were inspired by the Karlskirche, but unfortunately it's only open for Mass; otherwise you'll have to make do peering through iron railings. The adjoining monastery is an oasis of calm and tranquillity, in particular its inner courtyard, but it's a pity there are no seats to sit on.

SIGMUND FREUD MUSEUM Map pp244-5

☎ 319 15 96; www.freud-museum.at; 09, Berggasse 19; adult/concession/child €5/3/2; ☼ 9am-6pm Jul-Sep, 9am-5pm Oct-Jun; tram D

This small museum is devoted to one of Vienna's most famous sons, Sigmund Freud. It's housed in the apartments where he lived and psychoanalysed from 1891 until 1938, when he was forced to flee to London ahead of the advancing wave of Nazism. It contains furniture, Freud's possessions (such as his case embossed with the initials SF), letters, documents and photographs; very detailed notes (in English) illuminate the offerings and audio guides are available at the ticket desk. Freud enthusiasts and his students could spend a while here, but most casual observers would probably just saunter through the rooms. There's also a home movie of Freud from the 1930s, narrated by his daughter Anna.

SCHUBERT GEBURTHAUS Map pp244-5

☎ 317 36 01; 09, Nussdorfer Strasse 54; adult/concession €2/1; ☼ 9am-12.15pm & 1-4.30pm Tue-Sun; tram 37, 38

The house where Franz Schubert was born in 1797 was known at that time as *Zum roten Krebsen* (The Red Crab), but Schubert probably didn't remember much of it as he and his family moved on when he was five. There's not a lot to see, but you can hear some of his music and catch the occasional concert. Bizarrely, a couple of rooms of the house are given over to Adalbert Stifter (1805–68) and his Biedermeier paintings. The two men had absolutely nothing to do with each other.

The Schubert Geburthaus is a municipal museum.

OUTSIDE THE GÜRTEL

Eating p134; Shopping p170; Sleeping p181

The districts which fall outside the Gürtel are quite a mix. Parts are rather dull and forbidding (for Viennese standards) – in particular towards the south – while others are beautiful beyond belief and home to some of Vienna's greatest treasures. Apart from a few well-trodden routes, tourists rarely venture into these mostly residential outskirts of the Golden City, but if you want to experience the real heartbeat of Vienna, this is where it's to be found.

Simmering, the most easterly of the districts outside the Gürtel, and its closest neighbour, Favoriten, are working class through and through. Rather ugly residential and industrial estates are trademarks of the area and there's not much here to hold your interest. Zentralfriedhof, Vienna's largest and most picturesque cemetery by far is one major exception. Liesing is a fairly nondescript district; the *Heurigen* at its western end in Mauer are its saving grace tourist-wise. Meidling is another working-class neighbourhood where Tiefwienerisch (a thick, almost lazy dialect of German) is commonly spoken.

The environment quickly changes once you enter Hietzing, a district which bettered itself on the back of imperialism. Schönbrunn, the glorious summer palace of the Habsburgs, is the prime attraction of the district, if not of Vienna. Further west is Lainzer Tiergarten, an expansive parkland that's very much part of the Wienerwald and home to an abundance of wildlife.

Penzing, Rudolfsheim-Fünfhaus, Ottakring and Hernals are, when taken in context with the rest of Vienna's districts, fairly similar to each other. Their western extremes, which penetrate the Wienerwald (Rudolfsheim-Fünfhaus is an exception), are inhabited by the wealthy, ie those who can afford houses rather than apartments. Closer to the Gürtel, however, the atmosphere and population make-up changes. This is where many of Vienna's immigrants have settled; it's not uncommon to walk down one of the Gürtel's tributaries and hear Turkish, Serbian, Croatian, but no German. This is particularly notable in the colourful Brunnenmarkt (see p166) in Ottakring.

To the north of Hernals are Währing and Döbling, two of Vienna's wealthiest districts. Unsurprisingly, the streets seem cleaner, the air fresher, and the atmosphere a little stuffier. The outer reaches of Döbling are *Heuriger* country – rich hillsides smothered with vineyards and wine taverns. *Heurigen* (see p144) are an absolute Viennese institution, and any self-respecting tourist and culture-lover needs to spend at least a couple of hours sampling the special ambiance of such places.

Orientation

The section of Vienna outside the Gürtel consists of 11 districts: a large swath of suburbia that surrounds the rest of the city from the south and west. From east to west, Favoriten, Simmering, Meidling and Liesing make up the southern border, while running south to north Hietzing, Penzing, Rudolfsheim-Fünfhaus, Ottakring, Hernals, Währing and Döbling are the city's western extremes.

Vienna's two main-road connections to the rest of Austria, the A1 Westautobahn and the A2 Südautobahn, pierce the outer skin of Penzing from the west and Liesing from south respectively. Aside from the Gürtel, main thoroughfares crisscrossing the area include the A4, heading out to Schwechat airport; the A23, connecting the A2 with east Vienna; Triester Strasse, the main link between the Gürtel and the A2; Wienzeile, handling traffic between the A1 and the Gürtel; Höhenstrasse, skirting the western districts through the Wienerwald; and Heiligenstädter Strasse, cutting north along the Danube to Klosterneuburg.

> ### Outside the Gürtel Top Sights
>
> - Discovering the pure genius of Otto Wagner at his **Kirche am Steinhof** (p103)
> - Exploring one of Europe's greatest cemeteries, the **Zentralfriedhof** (p99)
> - Gazing over the urban expanse of Vienna from the **Kahlenberg** (p104)
> - Strolling through the imperial **Schloss Schönbrunn** (p101) and its **gardens** (p102)
> - Taking coffee and cake and appreciating the view at the **Gloriette** (p135)

FAVORITEN

BÖHMISCHE PRATER Map pp238-9

688 71 06; 10, Laaer Wald; bus 68A

The Böhmische (Bohemian) Prater is a tiny, old-fashioned version of the Wurstelprater (see p85). Riding the merry-go-rounds and testing your strength on 'strongman' machines here is like stepping back to Victorian times, and a quaint reminder of how complicated entertainment has become these days. To get there take the 68A bus from the U1 Reumannplatz stop to Urselbrunnen Gasse and walk to the junction of Urselbrunnen and Laaer Wald.

SIMMERING

GASOMETER Map pp248-9

www.gasometer-wien.at, German only; 11, Guglgasse 6-14; 10am-7.30pm Mon-Fri, 9am-5pm Sat; U3 Gasometer

The Gasometer is a collective name for four round, uniform brownstone gas containers on the northern edge of Simmering's industrial

zone. Long disused (except for the occasional rave party), these 75m-tall constructions, which are big enough to house the Riesenrad, finally attracted the attention of the city council who decided it was time to once again put them to use. Four architectural firms were commissioned to make the transformation, the result of which is 615 apartments, a students' hostel, an event hall, a cinema and a shopping complex. They demand the attention of anyone glancing in their direction, in particular the northern-most of the four which has a modern construction, which looks like a glass sheet with a slight bend in the middle, casting a shadow over its outer walls.

NAMENLOSEN FRIEDHOF

11, Alberner Hafen; bus 6A

If you're a cemetery connoisseur then a trip to the Namenlosen Friedhof (Cemetery of the Nameless) is a must. Unidentified bodies washed up on the shores of the Danube eventually make their way here, a poignant cemetery on the southeastern edge of town.

Some may recognise it from the movie *Before Sunrise*. Bus 6A connects with tram 71 at the tram end-station, but it doesn't always go as far as the cemetery.

ZENTRALFRIEDHOF Map pp238-9

☎ 760 41-0; 11, Simmeringer Hauptstrasse 232-244; admission free; ✆ information office 8am-3pm Mon-Sat, cemetery 7am-7pm May-Aug, 7am-6pm Mar, Apr, Sep & Oct, 8am-5pm Nov-Feb; tram 71

Opened in 1874, the Zentralfriedhof (Central Cemetery) has grown to become one of Europe's biggest cemeteries – larger than the Innere Stadt and, with 2½ million graves, far exceeding the population of Vienna itself. It contains the lion's share of tombs to Vienna's greats, including numerous famous composers – Beethoven, Schubert, Brahms, Schönberg and the whole Strauss clan are buried here. A monument to Mozart has also been erected, but he was actually buried in an unmarked mass grave in the St Marxer Friedhof (see p90).

The cemetery has three gates. The first is opposite Schloss Concordia (see p135) and leads to the old Jewish graves while the second, the main gate, directs you to the tombs of honour and the cemetery's church, Dr Karl Lueger Kirche. The third is closer to the Protestant and new Jewish graves. The information centre and map of the cemetery are at Gate Two.

The Ehrengräber (Tombs of Honour) are just beyond Gate Two and, besides the clump of famous composers, includes Hans Makart, sculptor Fritz Wotruba, architects Theophil Hansen and Adolf Loos, and *the* man of Austrian pop, Falco (Hans Hölzel).

Behind the Dr Karl Lueger Kirche, at the far end of the cemetery, are simple plaques devoted to those who fell in the world wars. These are in contrast to the ostentatious displays of wealth in the mausoleums of the rich (who couldn't take it with them although it seems like they certainly tried). Most graves are neat, well tended and adorned with fresh flowers. For a further contrast, wander around the old Jewish section, where the tangle of broken headstones and undergrowth is a reminder that few relatives are around to maintain these graves.

HIETZING

HIETZINGER FRIEDHOF Map pp246-7

13, Maxingstrasse 15; admission free; ✆ 8am-6pm May-Aug, 8am-5pm Mar, Apr, Sep & Oct, 9am-4pm Nov-Feb; bus 56B, 58B, 156B

Aficionados of Vienna's Secessionist movement will want to make the pilgrimage to the Hietzinger cemetery to pay homage to some of its greatest members. Gustav Klimt, Kolo Moser and Otto Wagner are all buried here, although Wagner's haughty tomb won't impress many. Others buried in the cemetery include Engel Dollfuss, leader of the Austro-Fascists assassinated in 1934, and composer Alban Berg.

HERMESVILLA Map pp238-9

☎ 804 13 24; 13, Lainzer Tiergarten; adult/child €4/2; ✆ 10am-6pm Tue-Sun Apr-Sep, 9am-4.30pm Tue-Sun Oct-Mar; bus 60B

The Hermesvilla was commissioned by Franz Josef I and presented to his wife as a gift in an attempt to patch up their failing marriage.

Districts – Outside the Gürtel

Corpse Disposal, Viennese Style

It is said that nowhere are people so obsessed with death than they are in Vienna. Songs performed in wine taverns often deal with the subject, and the city has a unique museum dealing with coffins and the undertakers' craft, the Bestattungsmuseum (see p92). The country as a whole has one of the highest suicide rates in the world.

Being able to afford a lavish funeral at death is a lifetime ambition for many Viennese. Joseph II caused outrage in the 1780s with his scheme to introduce false-bottomed, reusable coffins.

In 1784 the huge Zentralfriedhof (Central Cemetery) was opened as there was simply no more space in the city cemeteries. To try to persuade the populace that their future dear departed would rest better in this new location, they shipped out the coffins of the famous composers where they now rest together in group 32A. An unusual method was contemplated for transporting bodies to the suburban site: engineers drew up plans for a tube, many kilometres long, down which coffins would be fired using compressed air. However, the high cost of this scheme (one million florins) led to its abandonment.

At dawn, before the public are admitted to the Zentralfriedhof, special hunters are employed to shoot male pheasants, hares and wild rabbits. The reason is that these inconsiderate creatures have a tendency to eat or disturb the carefully arranged flowers around the graves. Meanwhile, you won't find any cemeteries for pets in Vienna. Animals are expressly forbidden from being buried in the soil, as the high water table might be contaminated by seepage of chemicals used in inoculations and putting the pets down. Pet cremations are now big business, although they are strictly controlled.

Built by Karl von Hasenauer between 1882 and 1886, with Klimt and Makart on board as interior decorators, the villa is suitably plush and has all the hallmarks of a mansion as opposed to a villa. Empress Elisabeth's bedroom is particularly over the top, with the walls and ceiling covered in motifs of Shakespeare's *A Midsummer Night's Dream*.

For all its opulence and comforts, the villa unfortunately did not have the desired effect: Elisabeth never really took to the place and rarely ventured back to Vienna. She did, however, name it after her favourite Greek God.

HOFPAVILLON HIETZING Map pp246-7
☎ 877 15 71; 13, Schönbrunner Strasse; adult/child €2/1; ⏰ 1.30-4.30pm; U4 Hietzing, Hietzing trams & buses

Built between 1898 and 1899 by Otto Wagner as part of the public transport system, the Hofpavillon Hietzing was originally designed as a private station for the imperial court. The elaborate wood-panelled interior is suitable regal, and was designed by Wagner in conjunction with Josef Olbrich. Its white façade, decorated with wrought ironwork, is easily spotted just east of the U4 Hietzing stop.

LAINZER TIERGARTEN Map pp238-9
13, Hermesstrasse; ⏰ 8am-dusk; bus 60B

At 25 sq km, the Lainzer Tiergarten (Lainzer Zoo) is the largest (and wildest) of Vienna's city parks. The 'zoo' refers to the plethora of wild boar, deer, woodpeckers and squirrels that freely roam the park, and the famous Lippizzaner horses which summer here. At 2pm every day these wild beasts (not the horses) are fed by park staff; check the notice board at the park's gate for the location. Apart from the extensive walking possibilities through lush woodland, attractions of the park include the Hermesvilla (see p99) and the Hubertuswarte (508m), a viewing platform on top of Kaltbründlberg.

SCHÖNBRUNN

The Schönbrunn complex is the highlight of many tourist trips to Vienna, which should come as no surprise. The palace and its adjoining garden are second only to Versailles in a show of imperial wealth and might. And while it may not look a modest dwelling, this baroque palace is a much-diminished version of the grandiose imperial centrepiece that was originally planned.

The name comes from the Schöner Brunnen (Beautiful Fountain), which was built around a spring that Emperor Matthias (1557–1619) found while hunting. A pleasure palace was built here by Ferdinand II in 1637, but this was razed by the Turks in 1683. Soon after, Leopold I commissioned Johann Bernhard Fischer von Erlach to build a more luxurious summer palace. Fischer von Erlach came up with hugely ambitious plans for a palace that would dwarf Versailles to be built on the hill where the Gloriette Monument now stands. However, the imperial purse felt unworthy of the venture and a 'less elaborate' building was constructed. It was finished in 1700.

Maria Theresia, upon her accession to the throne in 1740, chose Schönbrunn as the base for her family and her court. The young architect Nikolaus Pacassi was commissioned to renovate and extend the palace to meet the new requirements, and work was carried out from 1744 to 1749. The interior was fitted out in rococo style, and the palace then had some 2000 rooms, as well as a chapel and a theatre. Like most imperial buildings associated with Maria Theresia, the exterior was painted her favourite colour: *Schönbrunngelb* (Schönbrunn yellow).

The Habsburgs were not the only famous residents of Schönbrunn. Napoleon took the palace as his own in 1805 and 1809. The last in the Habsburg line, Karl I, was also the last to leave when he abdicated in the Blue Chinese Salon in 1918. After that the palace became the property of the new republic. Bomb damage was suffered during WWII, and restoration was completed in 1955. In 1992 the palace administration was transferred to private hands, whereupon further renovations commenced at a slow pace and admission prices soared.

If you plan to see quite a few sights at Schönbrunn, consider purchasing a Classic or Gold Pass. The Classic Pass (adult/concession/child/family €18/15/9/39) covers entry to the Grand Tour, Gloriette, Maze and the **Schönbrunn bakery** (admission to bakery only €6.40; ⏰ 10am-5pm mid-Mar–Oct), where you can see strudel made from scratch and get to taste the results. The Gold Pass (adult/child €36/18) includes the Grand Tour, Tiergarten, Palmenhaus, Wüstenhaus, Wagenburg, Gloriette, Maze and Schönbrunn bakery. A separate combined-ticket for the Tiergarten, Palmenhaus and Wüstenhaus costs €16/13/7.50/6 per adult/senior/student/child.

The palace can be reached by the U4 line; 'Schönbrunn' is the closest stop, though 'Hietzing' is better for the zoo and the western part of the gardens.

SCHLOSS SCHÖNBRUNN Map pp246-7

☎ 811 13-0; www.schoenbrunn.at; 13 Schloss Schönbrunn; Imperial Tour adult/concession/child €8/5.40/4.30, Grand Tour €10.50/6.80/5.40; ⏱ 8.30am-6pm Jul-Aug, 8.30am-5pm Apr-Jun & Sept-Oct, 8.30am-4.30pm Nov-Mar; U4 Schönbrunn, Hietzing, bus 10A

The regal rooms of Schloss Schönbrunn (Schönbrunn Palace) are in a league of their own in Vienna – the Kaiserappartements of the Hofburg hardly come close. The interior of the palace is a majestic mix of frescoed ceilings, crystal chandeliers and gilded ornaments. However, the endless stucco and gold twirls can seem overdone at times. Franz Josef I evidently thought so, too, for he had the rococo excesses stripped from his personal bedchamber in 1854.

Of the 1441 rooms within the palace, only 40 are open to the public. The full quota are viewed in the Grand Tour, which takes in the apartments of Franz Josef and Empress Elisabeth, the ceremonial and state rooms and the audience chambers of Maria Theresia and her husband Franz Stephan. The Imperial Tour excludes the chambers of Maria Theresia and Franz Stephan and only visits 22 rooms. Both include an audio guide in English if there are no tour guides available. It may be worth opting for an audio guide either way, as you can set your own pace and won't be dragged along on someone else's schedule. Because of the popularity of the palace, tickets are stamped with a departure time, and there may be a time-lag before you're allowed to set off in summer, so buy your ticket straight away and then explore the gardens.

Both tours start in the west wing at the bottom of the **Blauerstiege** (Blue Staircase) and climb to the private rooms of Franz Josef and Elisabeth. They're similar in style to the Hofburg and probably won't hold your interest for long, but the small **Breakfast Room** has fine views of the gardens and is decorated with embroideries made by Maria Theresia and her daughters.

The ceremonial and state rooms start with the **Spiegelsaal** (Hall of Mirrors) where Mozart (then six) played his first royal concert in the presence of Maria Theresia and the royal family in 1762. His father revealed in a letter that afterwards young Wolfgang leapt onto the lap of the empress and kissed her. The pinnacle of finery is reached in the **Grosse Galerie** (Great Gallery). Gilded scrolls, ceiling frescoes, chandeliers and huge crystal mirrors create the effect. Numerous sumptuous balls were held here, including one for the delegates at the Congress of Vienna (1814-15).

Near the Grosse Galerie is the **Round Chinese Room**, which is touched by governing genius. Maria Theresia held secret consultations here: a hidden doorway led to her adviser's apartments and a fully laden table could be drawn up through the floor so that dignitaries could dine without being disturbed by servants.

The Imperial Tour ends with the **Ceremonial Hall**, blessed with a fine set of paintings by Martin van Meytens of Joseph II's wedding to Isabella of Parma in 1760. The Grand Tour continues with the **Blue Chinese Room** where Karl I abdicated in 1918.

The next room of interest is the **Napoleon Room**, where the man himself is thought to have slept. The stuffed crested lark here was the favourite childhood bird of Napoleon's son, Duc de Reichstadt, who died in this room.

Following on from the Napoleon Room is the **Porcelain Room** and the **Miniatures Room**, with drawings by members of the imperial family. Both are overshadowed by the **Million Room**, named after the sum that Maria Theresia paid for the decorations, which are comprised of Persian miniatures set on rosewood panels and framed with gilded rocaille frames. The

The formal gardens of Schloss Schönbrunn (above)

Gobelin Salon features Belgian tapestries from the 18th century.

While not joined to the main set of rooms, the **Bergl Rooms** are worth visiting to see paintings by Johann Wenzl Bergl (1718–89); his exotic depictions of flora and fauna attempt to bring the ambience of the gardens inside, with some success.

GARDENS

13, Schloss Schönbrunn; admission free; 🕙 **6am-dusk; U4 Schönbrunn, Hietzing, bus 10A**

The beautifully tended formal gardens of the palace, arranged in the French style, are a symphony of colour in the summer and a combination of greys and browns in winter; both are appealing in their own right. The grounds hide a number of attractions in their tree-lined avenues, arranged according to a grid and star-shaped system between 1750 and 1755. From 1772 to 1780 Ferdinand Hetzendorf added some of the final touches to the park under the instructions of Joseph II: fake **Roman Ruins** (Map pp246–7) in 1778, the **Neptunbrunnen** (Neptune Fountain; Map pp246–7), a riotous ensemble from Greek mythology, in 1781, and the crowning glory, the **Gloriette** (Map pp246–7) in 1775, standing tall on the hill overlooking the gardens. The view from up here, looking back towards the palace with Vienna shimmering in the distance, ranks among the best in Vienna. It's possible to go on the roof of the Gloriette (🕙 Apr-Oct; admission €3), but the view is only marginally superior. The original **Schöner Brunnen** (Map pp246–7), from which the palace gained its name, now pours through the stone pitcher of a nymph near the Roman ruins. The latest addition to the gardens is a 630m-long **Maze** (🕙 mid-Mar–Nov; admission €3.50). The gates of the park were thrown open to the public by Joseph II in 1779.

KINDERMUSEUM Map pp246-7

☎ 811 13-239; www.schoenbrunn.at; 13, Schloss Schönbrunn; adult/child/family €6.50/4.50/17; 🕙 10am-5pm Sat & Sun, school holidays 10am-5pm daily; U4 Schönbrunn, Hietzing, bus 10A

Schönbrunn's Kindermuseum (Children's Museum) sticks to what it knows best: imperialism. Activities and displays help kids discover the day-to-day life of the Habsburg court, and once they've got an idea, they can don princely or princessly outfits and start ordering the serfs (parents) around. Other rooms devoted to toys, natural science and archaeology all help to keep them entertained. When guided tours are offered, they depart from the ticket desk at 11am, 2pm and 3.30pm.

PALMENHAUS Map pp246-7

☎ 877 50 87-406; 13, Maxingstrasse 13b; adult/senior/student/child under 5 €4/3/2.50/2; 🕙 9.30am-6pm May-Sep, 9.30am-5pm Oct-Apr; U4 Hietzing, Hietzing trams & buses

If you think you're experiencing *déjà vu* on sighting the Palmenhaus (Palm House), you are: it was built in 1882 by F Segenschmid as a replica of the one in London's Kew Gardens. The glorious glass and iron construction still houses palms and hothouse plants from around the world, and is particularly photogenic after a heavy fall of snow.

WAGENBURG Map pp246-7

☎ 877 32 44; 13; Schloss Schönbrunn; adult/concession/family €4.50/3/9; 🕙 9am-6pm Apr-Oct, 10am-4pm Tue-Sun Nov-Mar; U4 Schönbrunn, bus 10A

Fanatics of low-riders, spoilers and fluffy dice have nothing on the imperials, as a visit to the Wagenburg (Imperial Coach Collection) will verify. On display is a vast array of carriages, but nothing can compete with Emperor Franz Stephan's coronation carriage, with its ornate gold plating, Venetian glass panes and painted cherubs. The whole thing weighs an astonishing 4000kg. Also look for the dainty child's carriage built for Napoleon's son, with eagle-wing-shaped mudguards and bee motifs. Audio guides are available for €2, as are guided tours in German. Entry to the Wagenburg is included in the price of a Gold ticket (see p52).

WÜSTENHAUS Map pp246-7

☎ 877 50 87; 13, Maxingstrasse 13b; adult/senior/student/child under 5 €4/3/2.50/2; 🕙 9am-6pm May-Sep, 9am-5pm Oct-Apr; U4 Hietzing, Hietzing trams & buses

The small Wüstenhaus (Desert House) near the Palmenhaus makes good use of the once disused Sonnenuhrhaus (Sun Dial House) to recreate arid desert scenes. There are four sections – Northern Africa and the Middle East, Africa, the Americas, and Madagascar – with rare cactus and desert animals, such as the naked mole from East Africa, on display.

TIERGARTEN Map pp246-7

☎ 877 92 94; www.zoovienna.at; 13, Maxingstrasse 13b; adult/senior/student/child €12/10/5/4; 🕙 9am-6.30pm May-Sep, 9am-5.30pm Mar & Oct, 9am-5pm Feb, 9am-4.30pm Nov-Jan; U4 Hietzing, Hietzing trams & buses

In 2002 the Schönbrunn Tiergarten (Zoo) celebrated its 250th birthday, making it the oldest zoo in the world. Founded in 1752 as a menagerie by Franz Stephan, the zoo now houses some 750 animals of all shapes and sizes; the most recent arrivals to excite crowds were giant pandas in 2003. Thankfully most of the original cramped cages have been updated and improved, but the odd one still remains untouched. The zoo's layout is reminiscent of a bicycle wheel, with pathways as spokes and an octagonal pavilion at its centre. The pavilion dates from 1759 and was used as the imperial breakfast room; it now houses a fine restaurant (so you can feel regal, too). Feeding times are staggered throughout the day – maps on display tell you who's dining when.

PENZING

KIRCHE AM STEINHOF Map pp238-9
☎ 910 60-11 204; 14, Baumgartner Höhe 1; tours €4; ⏱ 3-4pm Sat; bus 47A, 48A

This distinctive Art-Nouveau creation was the work of Otto Wagner from 1904 to 1907; Kolo Moser chipped in with the mosaic windows. The roof is topped by a copper-covered dome that earned the nickname Limoniberg (lemon mountain) from its original golden colour. The design illustrates the victory of function over ornamentation prevalent in much of Wagner's work, even down to the sloping floor to allow good drainage. The church is on the grounds of the Psychiatric Hospital of the City of Vienna.

ERNST FUCHS PRIVAT MUSEUM
Map pp238-9
☎ 914 85 75; www.ernstfuchs-zentrum.com; 14, Hüttelbergstrasse 26; adult/concession €11/6; ⏱ 10am-4pm Mon-Fri; bus 148, 152

About 2km north of the U4 Hütteldorf stop is this small museum, devoted to Ernst Fuchs' fantastical paintings, etchings and sculptures. The works have a, shall we say, drug-induced look about them and what may be more inter-esting to the visitor is the villa housing the collection. Built by Otto Wagner in 1888, it was saved from ruin by Fuchs and restored to its former glory in 1972. In the gardens (visible from the road) are some interesting statues, ceramics and the ornate **Brunnenhaus** created by Fuchs, and at No 28 is another fine villa designed by Wagner.

TECHNISCHES MUSEUM Map pp246-7
☎ 899 98-0; www.technischesmuseum.at; 14, Mariahilfer Strasse 212; adult/senior/child/family €8/6.50/5/16; ⏱ 9am-6pm Mon-Fri, 10am-6pm Sat & Sun; tram 52, 58

The Technisches Museum (Technical Museum) has been around since 1918, but thankfully enjoyed a well-deserved overhaul in the past few years. Covering four floors, it's a shrine to man's advances in the field of science and technology. There are loads of hands-on displays and heavy industrial equipment, but even with all the updating the exhibits recently received, they still look and feel outdated.

The ground floor is devoted to Nature and Knowledge, while the second floor is given over to Heavy Industry and Energy. Nature and Knowledge is full of interactive scientific experiments with mostly German instructions. If you're into gazing at steam engines and mining models, then Heavy Industry is for you, but the museum's saving grace is its Energy section – it's full of fun and physical displays (the human-sized mouse wheel is particularly enjoyable). The top two floors host temporary exhibitions plus permanent displays on musical instruments and transport. The latter has some wonderfully restored old-timer trams and planes, but the museum unfortunately employs a 'look but don't touch' policy. While you won't be entertained for hours at the museum, your kids will be, and if you time it right, they can join in with the regular activities organised by the museum's staff. Das Mini, on the third floor, has loads of kids toys and activities and is specifically aimed at two- to six-year-olds.

From its vantage point on top of a grassy knoll, the museum looks down over **Auer-Welsbach-Park** towards the yellow of Schönbrunn.

OTTAKRING

JUBILÄUMSWARTE Map pp238-9
16, Pelzer Rennweg; bus 46B, 148

Close to the outskirts of the city is the Jubiläumswarte (449m), a tower rising above the Wienerwald's tree canopy. The sweeping views from the uppermost platform take in most of Vienna, and on a windy day the climb to the top can be quite an adrenaline rush. The end-station of bus No 148 (from U4 Hütteldorf) stops close to the tower; from bus No 46B, there's a short, sharp climb uphill to your goal.

DÖBLING

EROICA HAUS Map pp244-5
☎ 369 14 24; 19, Döblinger Hauptstrasse 92; adult/concession €2/1; ⏱ 9am-12.15pm & 1-4.30pm Tue-Sun; tram 37, bus 10A, 39A

For the brief time Beethoven spent at Eroica Haus (the summer of 1803 all up), his work production was grandiose: it was here that he wrote Symphony No 3, *Eroica*. There isn't

Worth the Trip

These sights are not within the confines of Vienna, but are located in the small village of Klosterneuburg just north of Döbling.

Sammlung Essl (☎ 0800-232 800; www.sammlung-essl.at; Kunst Der Gegenwart, An der Donau-Au 1, Klosterneuburg; adult/concession/child €6.50/5/4; ☺ 10am-7pm Tue-Sun, until 9pm Wed; Schnellbahn S40, bus 239 (Weidling stop) from U4 Heiligenstadt) This fine gallery is the brainchild of Agnes and Karlheinz Essl, collectors of contemporary art from the 20th and 21st centuries. They desired somewhere suitable to showcase their extensive collection, so they built the gallery. Expect to see a plethora of big names: Gerhad Richter, Hermann Nitsch, Georg Baselitz and Elke Krystufek are but a few of the artists on show. The construction itself is the work of Austrian architect Heinz Tesar and incorporates clean white lines, an abundance of natural light and plenty of open space. Entry is free from 7pm to 9pm on Wednesday.

Stift Klosterneuburg (☎ 022 43-41 12 12; www.stift-klosterneuburg.at; Stiftplatz 1, Klosterneuburg; adult/concession €5.50/3.20; ☺ 10am-5pm Tue-Sun May–mid-Nov; Schnellbahn S40, bus 239 (Klosterneuburg-Kierling stop) from U4 Heiligenstadt) This large Augustinian abbey dominates the small town of Klosterneuburg. Founded in 1114, the abbey's baroque face-lift didn't begin until 1730, and wasn't completed until 1842. The plans actually called for something much more grand, but fortunately these were not realised, leaving large sections in their original medieval style intact. The abbey's museum is an eclectic mix of religious art from the Middle Ages to the present day. If you've ventured this far, however, you're better off including a guided tour on your itinerary, which takes in the cloister and the church (tours in English require advanced notice). The tour's highlight is the *Verdun Altar* in St Leopold's Chapel, an annexe of the church. Made in 1181 by Nicholas of Verdun, it is an unsurpassed example of medieval enamel work and is gloriously adorned with 51 enamelled panels showing biblical scenes. Like Sammlung Essl, the abbey is only a short bus or train ride north of Vienna's border (or within hiking distance of Kahlenberg).

much to see, and no personal effects of the great composer are present, but you can listen to *Eroica* and gaze at a few watercolours and maps. The Eroica Haus is a municipal museum.

KAHLENBERG
19, Höhenstrasse; bus 38A

The high peak of Kahlenberg (484m) is a fantastic spot to take in the expanse of Vienna; on a good day you can see across to the Lesser Carpathians hills of Slovakia with ease. There's a small café, restaurant, St Josef church and an abandoned – and particularly ugly – hotel. A pleasant alternative to taking the bus back down is to set off by foot through the vineyards of Nussdorf and Grinzing to the urban sprawl of the city, taking in a *Heuriger* or two along the way.

KARL-MARX-HOF Map pp238-9
19, Heiligenstädter Strasse 82-92; U4 Heiligenstadt, tram D

Stretching for almost one kilometre along Heiligenstädter Stadt is the Karl Marx Housing Project, the symbol of Red Vienna. This massive pale pink and yellow goliath was built by Karl

Ehm, a student of Otto Wagner, between 1927 and 1930. It original contained some 1600 flats, community facilities and inner courtyards and in 1934 was the centre of the Social Democratic resistance during the civil war. It received heavy bombardment by the Austro-Fascists to break the resistance and underwent a full restoration in 1989.

LIESING
KIRCHE ZUR HEILIGSTEN DREIFALTIGKEIT Map pp238-9
☎ 888 50 03; 23, Georgsgasse/Rysergasse; admission free; ☺ 2-6pm Sat, 9am-4pm Sun; bus 60A

The remarkable Kirche zur Heiligsten Dreifaltigkeit (Holy Trinity Church), known more by the name 'Wotrubakirche' after its architect, looks like a collection of concrete blocks haphazardly stacked together. It was designed by Fritz Wotruba and completed in 1976. It's a long way south of the city centre, but with its close proximity to the Wienerwald and Mauer *Heurigen* (see p193), you could make it part of an excellent afternoon/evening excursion.

Walking & Cycling Tours

Kärntner Strasse Loop   106
Karlsplatz to Schottentor   108
Leopoldstadt   109
Stadtpark to Karlsplatz   110
Schwedenplatz Cycling Roundtrip via
Vienna's Parks & Waterways   112

Walking & Cycling Tours

Walking and cycling in Vienna is an absolute pleasure. The only hills of serious concern are in the Wienerwald, but these are far to the west of where the action is. The Innere Stadt, in particular, is best explored on foot, as much of it is a maze of narrow, cobblestoned one-way streets. Its surrounding districts are generally all flat and contain a smattering of small parks. Two things to watch out for, though, are drivers and jaywalking; Austrians are notoriously aggressive behind the wheel, often ignoring zebra crossings, and jaywalking is severely discouraged. Crossing a road within 25m of a zebra crossing or not waiting for the green man at a traffic light can result in an instant fine if you're caught by the police.

The first four tours below are walking tours, while the last is specifically a cycling tour. Of the walking tours, only the Kärntner Strasse Loop cannot be turned into a cycling tour; the rest can be tackled with a combination of cycling and walking (each trail passes through a park where cycling is not permitted). If an organised tour is more your style, see p50 for details.

KÄRNTNER STRASSE LOOP

This walk takes you through some of the most well-trodden tourist trails in Vienna, but there's a reason why so many visitors flock to the area. Instantly recognisable sights – Gothic Stephansdom and the Hofburg, the Habsburg's winter palace – dominate this quarter of the Innere Stadt, while Kärntner Strasse, Graben and Kohlmarkt attract shoppers by the bus load. The beauty of it all, however, is that you can duck down a cobblestoned side street and feel as though you have the city to yourself.

Walk Facts

Start Staatsoper; travel there on U1, U2 or U4 to Karlsplatz, or Karlsplatz trams
Finish Staatsoper
Distance 2.5km
Duration 1½/2 hours

Start your walk at the **Staatsoper 1** (p151) and head north along **Kärntner Strasse 2** (p55), Vienna's main street. It soon becomes a pedestrian-only walkway of plush shops, trees, café

Aida café (opposite)

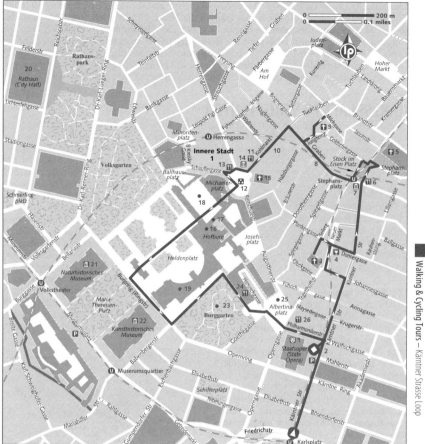

tables and street entertainers. The oldest building here is Esterházy Palace at No 41, dating from 1698. Detour left down Marco-d'Aviano-Gasse to Neuer Markt and the **Kaisergruft 3** (p56), final resting place of the Habsburg family. Continue north on Neue Markt before ducking down Kärntner Durchgang past the **American Bar 4** (p140), designed by Adolf Loos in 1908, and left onto Kärntner Strasse once more. A little north the pedestrianised street opens out into Stock-im-Eisen-Platz and eventually Stephansplatz. It will be impossible not to notice the glorious **Stephansdom 5** (p53), or its reflection in the glass façade of the opposing Haas Haus. If you're already in need of a coffee break, stop in at **Aida 6** (p119).

Take a peek inside the neo-Renaissance **Equitable Palais 7** (p56) and note the nail-studded stump on one of its outside corners, before heading west on **Graben 8** (p56). Wander down Graben and take a detour right onto Jungferngasse to admire **Peterskirche 9** (p57), one of the city's finest baroque churches. Retrace your steps before turning left onto **Kohlmarkt 10** (p57), so named for the charcoal once sold here. A coffee and cake break in **Demel 11** (p121) may be in order before heading to Michaelerplatz, and a plethora of architectural sights: the **Roman Ruins 12** (p65), **Café Griensteidl 13** (p121), the unusual **Loos Haus 14** (p62), **Michaelerkirche 15** (p62), and Michaelertor, gateway to the **Hofburg 16** (p58).

You could easily spend the entire day exploring the museums of the Hofburg, but since this is a walking tour, double-time it to Heldenplatz – with a brief pause to admire the

Schweizertor 17 (Swiss Gate; p58) and In der Burg 18 (p58) – and the impressive Neue Burg 19 (p58). The breathtaking view from the square takes in the Rathaus 20 (City Hall; p75), Naturhistorisches Museum 21 (p76) and Kunsthistorisches Museum 22 (p77). Exit Heldenplatz and turn left onto the Ringstrasse and duck around behind the Neue Burg to the quiet Burggarten 23 (p76) and its stunning Palmenhaus 24 (p102), now a bar/restaurant, before continuing on to Albertinaplatz 25 (p55). A quick stroll down Philharmonikerstrasse will bring you back to your starting point, but why not stop in at Café Sacher 26 (p120) for a well-deserved slice of *Sacher Torte*.

KARLSPLATZ TO SCHOTTENTOR

The architectural splendour stretching along the Ringstrasse from near Karlsplatz to Schottentor is head and shoulders above anything most European cities can muster up. It is simply astounding how so many visual delights can be crammed into such a small space.

Add to that the hustle and bustle of the Naschmarkt, the art space of the MuseumsQuartier and the golden dome of the Secession, and you have a walk to thrill even the most hardened and burnt-out tourist.

Instead of following the tempting course of the Ringstrasse, head west from Karlsplatz along Friedrichstrasse to the Secession 1 (p76) and admire its golden-leafed globe, before entering the tangle of the Naschmarkt 2 (p166), Vienna's biggest and brightest market. After a quick look around, retrace your steps to the Secession and continue west, then north, west again, and then south around the perimeter of the Akademie der bildenden Künste 3 (Academy of Fine Art; p75) and past Schillerplatz. Next, turn right onto Getreidemarkt heading northwest to the MuseumsQuartier 4 (p79). Enter from Mariahilfer Strasse and walk directly to the main square; here you're confronted with the black-and-white twin buildings of the Leopold Museum 5 (p80) and MUMOK 6 (p81). Exit via the central gates which lead onto Museumsplatz and cross the road to Maria-Theresien-Platz, where a proud statue of Maria Theresia resides over the Naturhistorisches Museum 7 (p76) and the Kunsthistorisches Museum 8 (p77), on either side of the square.

Drag yourself away from the square and turn left onto the leafy Ringstrasse. You'll soon see the Greek columns of the Parlament 9 (p75), after which the busts of great playwrights adorning the façade of the Burgtheater 10 (p152) come into view on your right. Towering above Rathauspark directly opposite the Burgtheater is the Rathaus 11 (City Hall; p75). Continue north along the Ringstrasse to the solid Universität 12 (p75) before veering off to the right up one of the last remnants of the old city walls, Mölker Bastei. Here you'll find the Pasqualati Haus 13 (p63), a former residence of Beethoven that's now a museum devoted to the great composer. Turn left up Schottengasse to Schottentor and the twin spires of the Votivkirche 14 (p66), and finish the walking tour with a bite to eat in Café Stein 15 (p141).

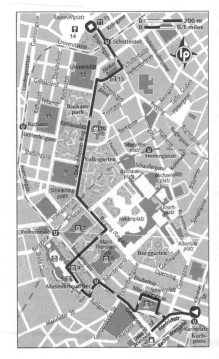

LEOPOLDSTADT

The absolute delight of this walk is the understated charm of the Leopoldstadt district. It's a mix of beautiful parks, lively markets and busy residential streets, all within striking distance of Praterstern, a gritty, urban transport hub.

From Schwedenplatz head north across the Danube Canal (Donaukanal) on Taborstrasse, past the striking façade of the **Odeon 1** (p150), until Haidgasse, where you

Walk Facts

Start Schwedenplatz; travel there on U1 or U4 to Schwedenplatz, or Schwedenplatz trams
Finish Prater
Distance 7.5km
Duration 3 hours

should turn left. Pass the quaint house which hides the **Weiner Kriminalmuseum 2** (p86) and head to **Karmelitermarkt 3** (p166), the district's central market. Be sure to start this walk around lunch time, so you can stop for a bite to eat at the **Schöne Perle 4** (p126), one block north of the market on Leopoldsgasse. Follow Leopoldsgasse north until it ends in a T-junction at Untere Augartenstrasse. Turn right and cross Obere Augartenstrasse, entering **Augarten 5** (p84) through the park's main gates. Directly in front of you is Augartenpalais, home to the **Wiener Porzellanmanufaktur 6** (p86), makers of fine porcelain ornaments.

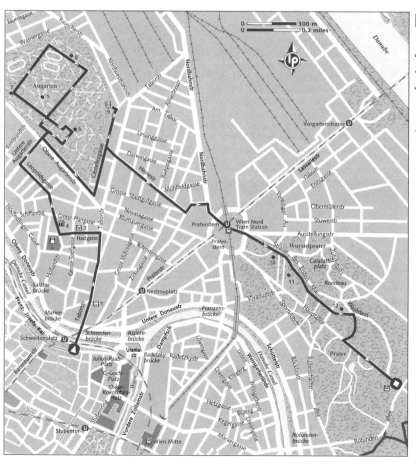

Circumnavigate the park to get an up-close-and-personal look at its two towering **Flak-türme** 7 & 8 (p84) before leaving by the gate from which you entered and heading southeast on Obere Augartenstrasse. At Castellezgasse turn left and head north. This street soon changes its name to Scherzergasse but that doesn't matter; what you're here for is the **Atelier Augarten** (p84), home to an excellent **coffee house** (p125) of the same name and the **Gustinus Ambrosi-Museum** 9 (p84). Retrace your steps back along Castellezgasse/Scherzergasse to Klanggasse, a short street that soon merges with Heinestrasse. Continue directly to the Praterstern, which won't hold your attention for long, then make a beeline for the **Prater** (p85) and the thrills and spills of the **Wurstelprater** 10 (an amusement park; p85). Take a spin on the **Riesenrad** 11 (p85) before recharging your batteries at the **Schweizerhaus** 12 (p126). Spend the rest of the day wandering around the Prater, or jump on the N Tram back to Schwedenplatz.

STADTPARK TO KARLSPLATZ

It's only a hop skip and a jump from Stadtpark to Karlsplatz using the Ringstrasse, but *not* if you go via Landstrasse. This long walk connects some of Vienna's better-known and lesser-known sights, following a path that winds its way through mainly residential districts. It's a fine combination of two faces of Vienna: the normal, everyday city where locals go about their daily business, and the stunning sights visitors come to see.

Begin by paying homage to some of Vienna's great composers, who are honoured with statues in the **Stadtpark** 1 (p83). At the northern end of the park join the Ringstrasse and head north, past **Museum für angewandte Kunst** 2 (MAK; p82) and Otto Wagner's celebrated **Postsparkasse** 3 (p82), to the **Urania** 4 (p144) on the banks of the Danube Canal. From Urania veer east on Uraniastrasse, which soon becomes Radetzkystrasse. Radetzkystrasse ends at Radetzkyplatz, where you'll find **Wild** 5 (p127), a perfect spot for a meal or just a drink. From here duck under the railway tracks and

Walk Facts

Start Stadtpark; travel there on U4 to Stadtpark, or tram 1 or 2
Finish Karlsplatz
Distance 6km
Duration 3 hours

Stadtbahn Pavillons (opposite)

follow Löwengasse southeast until you hit Krieglergasse, at which point turn left and head directly towards the **KunstHausWien** 6 (p90), one of Hundertwasser's eye-catching creations. Then turn right along Untere Weissgerberstrasse past another of Hundertwasser's works, the **Hundertwasser Haus** 7 (p90), and cut right at the end of the street onto Rasumofskygasse, which winds its way down to Landstrasser Hauptstrasse, the busy, commercial centre of Landstrasse. Turn left and follow Landstrasser Hauptstrasse southeast until you hit Neulinggasse on your right, which leads to Arenbergpark, home to two of the six goliath **Flaktürme** 8 & 9 (p84) in Vienna. One is currently being used as a temporary exhibition space by MAK.

Continue west along Neulinggasse until you arrive at Salesianergasse. Turn left and keep walking until you reach Rennweg and the gates of the **Unteres Belvedere** 10 (p92). Wander through the baroque palace's gardens to its second edifice, the **Oberes Belvedere** 11 (p83), before leaving by the southern gate and heading north along Prinz-Eugen-Strasse past **Hotel im Palais Schwarzenberg** 12 (p178). If you've brought your Sunday best, pop into the Palais' **bar** (p143) for a top-shelf whisky. At the southern end of **Schwarzenbergplatz** 13 (p82) veer left onto Technikerstrasse, which leads onto Karlsplatz and its ring of attractions – **Karlskirche** 14 (p93), **Historisches Museum der Stadt Wien** 15 (p93) and Otto Wagner's **Stadtbahn Pavillons** 16 (p94). At the far end of Karlsplatz is the **Kunsthalle Café** 17 (p142), where cold beer, hot coffees and refilling snacks await.

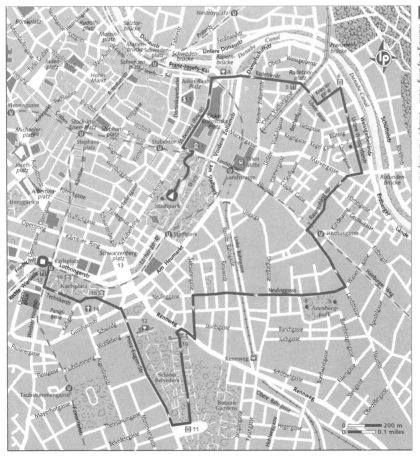

SCHWEDENPLATZ CYCLING ROUNDTRIP VIA VIENNA'S PARKS & WATERWAYS

With kilometres of bicycle paths to explore, a relatively flat topography and bike-rental racks scattered throughout the inner districts, Vienna is simply made for cycling. So it's highly appropriate to suggest at least one cycle tour of the city. This tour takes you east of the Innere Stadt to the waterways and parks the Viennese flock to over the summer months. There are no strenuous hills to test the legs, and for the most part the tour follows well-indicated cycle lanes, so pack your lunch and your swimming gear and you can easily make a day of it.

From Schwedenplatz head north along the western bank of the Danube Canal – not via the busy road, but down on the cycle and running path which hugs the canal. Glide past the **Summer Stage 1** (p132) near Rossauer Brücke, which, if it's summer, will be in full swing, and continue on your way until the **Fernwärme 2** (p95), the city's rubbish incinerator which has had a Hundertwasser make-over, comes into view. Just before the incinerator, take the cycle ramp on your left, which climbs above the canal and ducks behind Fernwärme. The path then makes a right turn (follow the sign 'Donauinsel') and crosses

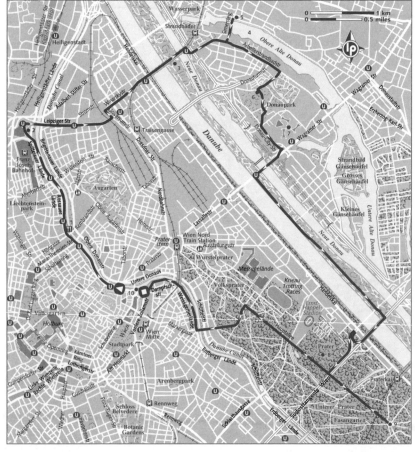

over the canal via the Gürtelbrücke to Leipziger Strasse and the district of Brigittenau. Stick to Leipziger until it hits Universumstrasse, at which point turn left and continue until it ends at Winarskystrasse. Turn right onto Winarskystrasse and follow the path to Nordbahnbrücke, which spans the mighty Danube (Donau), the Neue Donau (New Danube) and the **Donauinsel 3** (Danube Island; p87), a long island crisscrossed by paths and dotted with beaches.

At the eastern end of Nordbahnbrücke the path drops down onto Arbeiterstrandbadstrasse and the **Alte Donau 4** (p87). Stay on Arbeiterstrandbadstrasse until Birnersteig appears on your left: duck along this street to the northern side of the Alte Donau (Old Danube) for a much-needed pit stop at **Strandgasthaus Birner 5** (p126), a Viennese institution. Back on Arbeiterstrandbadstrasse, continue along the cycle path until it cuts right into the Donaupark (don't take the first sign to the Donauturm along Donauturmstrasse, take the second), directly to the base of the **Donauturm 6** (p87). Turn left and follow the path in the direction of

Cycle Facts

Start Schwedenplatz; travel there on U1 or U4 to Schwedenplatz, or Schwedenplatz trams
Finish Schwedenplatz
Distance 23km
Duration 4/5 hours

the **UNO City 7** (p88); your trail actually heads just west of the city itself. At the first street you come to, Leonard-Bernstein-Strasse, turn left, and then right into Donau-City-Strasse, a street that slices between the UNO City and Donau-City, Vienna's tallest apartment building. You'll soon find yourself at Reichsbrücke, where you want to turn right and cross the Neue Donau to the Donauinsel. Follow the bicycle path down onto the island itself and

Urania cinema complex (p114)

head southeast on any path that takes your fancy. This is a good place to stop and enjoy a refreshing dip.

Continue southeast until you hit Praterbrücke, and signs directing you to the **Prater 8** (p85), the city's favourite playground. Cross over the Danube once more and stick to the path leading into the Prater itself, which winds its way through the shipping centre Handelskai and onto Grünlandgasse before eventually hitting Hauptallee, the park's main thoroughfare. If you're peckish, turn left and stay on Hauptallee until you reach the **Lusthaus 9** (p126), a former hunting lodge. Back on Hauptallee, retrace your path northwest and continue until you reach the end station of the N Tram, and Rotunden Allee, a road off to the left leading to the Danube Canal. Cross over the canal on Rotundenbrücke and turn right until the **Urania 10** (p144) complex swings into view. This is your finishing point, and a perfect spot to reflect on the day's ride over a coffee or beer.

Innere Stadt   119
Stephansplatz   119
East of Stephansplatz   119
Kärntner Strasse, Graben & Kohlmarkt   120
Michaelerplatz to Mölker Bastei   121
Rotenturmstrasse to Schottenring   122
Cheap Eats   122

Ringstrasse   123
Schottentor to Parlament   124
Parlament to Schwarzenbergplatz   124
MuseumsQuartier   124
Schwarzenbergplatz to the Danube Canal   125
Cheap Eats   125

Between the Danube Canal & the Danube   125
Cheap Eat   126

Across the Danube   126

Inside the Gürtel   127
Landstrasse   127
Wieden   127
Margareten   128
Mariahilf   129
Neubau   129
Josefstadt   130
Alsergrund   131
Cheap Eats   132

Outside the Gürtel   134
Favoriten   134
Simmering   135
Hietzing   135
Rudolfsheim-Fünfhaus   135
Döbling   135
Cheap Eats   135

Eating

Eating

Eating out in Vienna is as much an attraction as seeing an opera at the stately Staatsoper or wandering the halls of Schönbrunn palace. It's a city where dining out doesn't equate to dining fast – here a meal is savoured, and the atmosphere is almost as important as the food.

The dining experience is not limited to restaurants, of which there are thousands to choose from. Vienna's legendary *Kaffeehäuser* (coffee houses) – esteemed cafés where pomp, ceremony and surly waiters are par for the course – are dotted across the city and are an absolute must for any visitor. Then there's the *Beisl*, Vienna's answer to the beer house or tavern: simple restaurants serving the best of Viennese cuisine in unhealthy portions. If you've no time to sit around and wait, a *Würstelstand* (sausage stand) will suffice; these stands are conveniently located on street corners and squares, ready with sausages, bread and beer. Last, but by no means least, is the *Heuriger*, an informal wine tavern with buffet-style food and an endless supply of new wine. *Heurigen* are covered in the Entertainment chapter (see p144).

Ten years ago in Vienna sushi was an exotic dish only the affluent, and experimental, would try. The mainstay was Viennese cuisine: hearty dishes of *Weiner Schnitzel*, *Schweinsbraten* (roast pork) and *Zwiebelrostbraten* (braised beefsteak with onions) washed down with a bitter *Krügerl* of beer. These days, however, the humble *Beisl* is fighting an invasion of Asian diners for custom. And the Asian diners are themselves competing with Spanish, Italian, Turkish, French, Persian and Indian eateries. The cuisine from these eateries might not have the bite of a true South Indian curry, or the sheer exuberance and gusto of a real Tuscan pasta, but it certainly comes close to the real thing and will most definitely tingle the taste buds.

Top Five Schnitzels

- **Figlmüller** (p120) Central and touristy, but the *Schnitzel* still wow the critics
- **Gasthaus Wickerl** (p131) *Schnitzel* like *Mutter* used to make, in relaxed surroundings
- **Schloss Concordia** (p135) Huge range, and a perfect stop after roaming the Zentralfriedhof
- **Zu den Zwei Liesln** (p134) In terms of *Schnitzel*, it doesn't get any bigger than this
- **Zum Alten Fassl** (p128) A touch of class, and a gorgeous garden to boot

Traditional Wiener Schnitzel served with salad

Areas with a high concentration of fine restaurants include bustling Naschmarkt, the MuseumsQuartier, cobblestoned Spittalberg, and the districts of Neubau and Josefstadt. It goes without saying that the Innere Stadt has its fair share of superlative restaurants (albeit pricier than the rest of Vienna).

Dogs, an integral part of many Viennese lives, are taken everywhere – including to restaurants, cafés and bars. Don't be surprised to see a wagging tail, occasional dogfight or canine tantrum under your next-door neighbour's table.

Opening Hours

Cafés operate seven days a week, as do most restaurants. A handful of restaurants, generally those in the upper echelons in price and within the Naschmarkt, will take Sunday off. Cafés open their doors early, often between 7am and 8am, and close anything between 7pm and 1am, depending on the market they are catering to. Restaurants open for lunch and dinner, and only a small percentage serves food in between these times. Odds-on your average *Beisl* will open around 11am and close near the midnight mark.

How Much?

Eating out in Vienna can set you back as little as €2.50 for a kebab or *Käsekrainer* (sausage infused with cheese) or €40 for a sumptuous banquet in palatial surroundings. The majority of restaurants are somewhere in between: main dishes on average range from €8 to €12, which makes eating out on a regular basis quite affordable for most Viennese.

Our Cheap Eats category, at the end of each district section, covers eateries with mains in the vicinity of €5 to €8. Note that price doesn't always equal quality in Vienna – some of the city's best eating options fall within Cheap Eats.

Booking Tables

Most restaurants take reservations, and if you're dead set on sampling the delights of a particularly popular eatery, it's advisable to book ahead. You'll generally strike it lucky, however, and the concierge will squeeze you in somewhere. If not, it won't be hard to find a bar close by to sit out the wait for a table. If a restaurant consistently requires a reservation, we've said so in the review.

Tipping

Tipping is an integral part of the Viennese culture that extends to restaurants and cafés. Even ordering a beer at the bar normally involves a tip. The general rule of thumb is to round up smaller bills (to the nearest 50 cents or euro) when buying coffee or beer, and to add 10% to the bill for full meals. In all but the most posh establishments, the tip is handed over when you pay – just tell the *Kellner* (waiter) or *Kellnerin* (waitress) the total amount you want to pay (bill and tip included) and they'll work it out for themselves.

If you think the service stinks, it's quite customary to voice your disapproval by not tipping.

Self-Catering

For a moderately sized city, Vienna has a surprisingly large selection of supermarkets. Hofer, Mondo, Penny Markt and Zielpunkt are acknowledged as the cheapest, while Billa, Spar and Merkur are slightly more up-market and often have well-stocked delis. These delis make sandwiches to order – a quick and inexpensive way to enjoy lunch on the run.

Supermarkets are a common sight throughout Vienna's districts, save the Innere Stadt; there you'll have to hunt around to find one, or ask a passer-by where the closest can be found. There is an Interspar (Map pp240-3) on the corner of Rotenturmstrasse and Fleischmarkt, and a Billa (Map pp240-3) on Singerstrasse. Typical opening hours are 7.30am or 8am to 7pm or 7.30pm Monday to Friday, and until 5pm on Saturday.

More than Just Coffee

Legend has it that coffee beans were left behind by the fleeing Turks in 1683, and it was this happy accident that resulted in today's plethora of coffee establishments in Vienna. The city's first coffee house opened in 1685, at 01, Rotenturmstrasse 14, but it could have been emulating successful establishments already opened in Venice (1647 – the first in Europe), Oxford (1650), London (1652), Paris (1660) and Hamburg (1677), rather than having anything to do with the Turks.

The popularity of the Viennese *Kaffeehaus* didn't take a firm hold on the city until the end of the 19th century; by this time there were a reputed 600 cafés in business. The tradition has waned over the years, but only slightly; the Viennese still love their coffee, their coffee rituals and, above all, their coffee houses.

When ordering a cup of the brown stuff in a traditional Viennese *Kaffeehaus*, a simple instruction of 'coffee, please' will not suffice. The list to choose from is as long as your arm, so it's best to know what you're ordering before making a random choice. It will generally be served on a silver platter accompanied by a glass of water and, if you're very lucky, with a small sweet.

Here's what you'll generally find on offer:

- *Brauner* – black but served with a tiny splash of milk; comes in *Gross* (large) or *Klein* (small)
- *Einspänner* – with whipped cream, served in a glass
- *Fiaker* – *Verlängerter* (see below) with rum and whipped cream
- *Kapuziner* – with a little milk and perhaps a sprinkling of grated chocolate
- *Maria Theresia* – with orange liqueur and whipped cream
- *Masagran* (or *Mazagran*) – cold coffee with ice and maraschino liqueur
- *Melange* – the Viennese classic; served with milk, and maybe whipped cream too, similar to the cappuccino
- *Mocca* (sometimes spelled *Mokka*) or *Schwarzer* – black coffee
- *Pharisäer* – strong *Mocca* topped with whipped cream, served with a glass of rum
- *Türkische* – comes in a copper pot with coffee grounds and sugar
- *Verlängerter* – *Brauner* weakened with hot water
- *Wiener Eiskaffee* – cold coffee with vanilla ice cream and whipped cream

Waiters generally speak English and can inform you on any specialities available. Expect them to be gruff and grumpy – anything less is just not Viennese. Don't feel obliged to finish your *Melange* in record time because of the waiters' rudeness, either: cafés are all about relaxing and taking your time. Cafés stock an astonishing range of newspapers and magazines, often including international titles, which patrons are encouraged to devour. And it's not uncommon to see regulars sit for hours ploughing through every publication while enjoying one measly cup of coffee.

Food markets abound. The best of the bunch are Naschmarkt, Brunnenmarkt, Freyungmarkt and Kamalietermarkt. See the Shopping chapter (p166) for information on these other markets.

Outside normal shopping hours it can be difficult to stock up on groceries. Westbahnhof has an Okay grocery store open 5.30am to 11pm daily, as does Südbahnhof, and petrol stations stock basic items but they're more expensive.

Meal Times

Most Viennese breakfast between 7am and 10am and generally do so at home. Otherwise you'll catch them at cafés ordering a *Melange* (cappuccino) and *Semmel* (bread roll) on the way to work. Weekends are the exception to the rule: many restaurants cater to a flood of people meeting over continental breakfasts or full fry-ups. The Naschmarkt is a prime spot for this on Saturday mornings.

Traditionally the main meal of the day is lunch, and restaurants are well attuned to their customers' needs; a large percentage offer set menus *(Mittag Menü)*, consisting of a salad or soup and a main dish, at a reduced price. Although many restaurants start serving at 6pm, Viennese don't commonly sit down to dinner until 8pm or later.

Throughout the chapter the term 'lunch' denotes opening hours from around 11am to 3pm; as a safe bet, expect a restaurant to open from 11.30am to 2.30pm. 'Dinner' is from 6pm until midnight, but some restaurants might close their kitchens at 11pm.

INNERE STADT

The Innere Stadt is full of surprises. You'd think that its small size would restrict the amount of top restaurants within its borders, but there seems to be one down every street. You'd also imagine that every eatery would suck the last euro from your wallet, yet you can still find budget options if you look hard enough. And you might also have assumed that only *Wiener Schnitzel* and *Schweinsbraten* would be on the menu, but this is not the case: the gastronomic range will satisfy the even the most hardened critic.

Prices on average are steeper than the rest of Vienna; however, that's to be expected in the heart of any big city.

STEPHANSPLATZ

AIDA Map pp240-3   *Café/Bakery*
☎ 512 29 77; 01, Stock-im-Eisen-Platz 2; cakes from €1.50; ☻ 7am-8pm Mon-Sat, 9am-8pm Sun; U1, U3 Stephansplatz

The Aida chain of cafés is an absolute icon in Vienna and a rival to the city's *Kaffeehäuser*, although at first glance it's hard to see why. Its pink and brown colour scheme – right down to the waitresses' socks – is a rather strange choice, the décor a retro collection from the '50s to the '70s and the majority of the clientele are well into retirement. Put it all together, however, and add fantastic cakes and pastries, and you have cafés with cult status. They're the perfect place for good coffee, people watching or eavesdropping on the latest colostomy bag story. Twenty-six such gems are scattered throughout Vienna.

DO & CO Map pp240-3   *International*
☎ 535 39 69; 01, Stephansplatz 12, Haas-Haus; mains around €20; ☻ lunch & dinner; U1, U3 Stephansplatz
☎ 532 96 69; 01, Albertinaplatz 1; mains €10-19; ☻ 10am-midnight; U1, U2, U4 Karlsplatz, Karlsplatz trams, bus 3A

DO & CO has managed to produce two of Vienna's finest restaurants in two of Vienna's most celebrated buildings. The first, taking pride of place in the Haas-Haus, offers views of Stephansdom and a menu with Asian creations and plenty of fish. The second, in the newly renovated Albertina, is a luxurious museum-café of the highest standard with the added bonus of an open terrace. Bookings are advisable.

Top Five Innere Stadt

- EN (p122)
- Expedit (p120)
- Meinl am Graben (p121)
- Trzesniewski (p123)
- Würstelstand am Hoher Markt (p123)

HAAS & HAAS Map pp240-3   *Tea House*
☎ 512 26 66; 01, Stephansplatz 4; cakes €3-15, breakfast €6-11; ☻ 8am-8pm Mon-Fri, 8am-6.30pm Sat; U1, U3 Stephansplatz, bus 1A

It might be a tea house, but the attraction here is the international range of breakfasts (served 8am to 11.30am), which will set you on the right track for the rest of the day. Oh, and the location ain't bad either: Stephansdom to your left, quiet inner courtyard to your right. With views like these, it's a wonder some people still come just to drink tea.

EAST OF STEPHANSPLATZ

BEIM CZAAK Map pp240-3   *Beisl*
☎ 513 72 15; 01, Postgasse 15; midday menus €6.40, mains €5.50-12.50; ☻ 11am-midnight Mon-Sat; U1, U4 Schwedenplatz, Schwedenplatz trams

Beim Czaak is a real local's *Beisl*, albeit more upmarket than average. Wood panels, boisterous bar-leaners and a hearty welcome greet you upon entering. The menu is solidly Viennese with splashes of Bohemian delights.

CAFÉ ENGLÄNDER Map pp240-3   *Café*
☎ 966 86 65; 01, Postgasse 2; midday menus €6.60-7, mains €10-15; ☻ 8am-1am Mon-Sat, 10am-1am Sun; U3 Stubentor

Engländer doesn't fall within the classic Viennese café genre, but it is nevertheless a classy café. With a discerning air, great coffee and a menu filled with modern Viennese standards, it attracts a regular troupe of city high-flyers.

COFFEESHOP COMPANY
Map pp240-3   *Café*
☎ 531 08 44; 01, Krugerstrasse 6; coffee from €3; ☻ 7am-11pm Mon-Sat, 10am-10pm Sun; U1, U2, U4 Karlsplatz, Karlsplatz trams

Long before Starbucks invaded the hallowed ground of 'Coffeedom' in Vienna, Coffeeshop Company was churning out American-style espresso-to-go. And it's still going strong – the cappuccinos in paper cups remain a hit with the younger, more mobile Viennese coffee drinker. It's now expanded to five locations around Vienna and has Internet access and web cams.

DIGLAS Map pp240-3 *Café*
☎ 512 57 65; 01, Wollzeile 10; light meals €8.50-12.50; ☺ 7am-midnight; U1, U3 Stephansplatz, bus 1A

This noble *Kaffeehaus* comes complete with swanky red velvet booths, stiff atmosphere and an extensive coffee range. Servings are delicate and more like snacks, but extend beyond the normal Viennese specialties to include a variety of Hungarian dishes. Live piano music can be heard from 8.30pm to 11.30pm every Tuesday, Friday and Saturday.

DREI HUSAREN Map pp240-3 *Viennese*
☎ 512 10 92; 01, Weihburggasse 4; mains €20-33; ☺ lunch & dinner; U1, U3 Stephansplatz

Drei Husaren is all about traditional Viennese cuisine of the highest standard in formal and elegant surroundings. There's a huge selection of excellent hors d'oeuvres, which are priced according to season and selection, and soothing live piano music to aid digestion.

EXPEDIT Map pp240-3 *Italian*
☎ 512 33 13-0; 01, Wiesingerstrasse 6; mains €8-18; ☺ noon-11pm Mon-Fri, 6-11pm Sat; tram 1, 2

With warehouse shelves, simple furniture and an open kitchen, the owners of Expedit have succeeded in creating a laid-back yet smart look. The only glitch is the television in the corner. The ever-changing menu offers a mix of Italian classics and creations from whatever is in season, all superbly prepared. Expedit also dabbles in retail; purchase a few of Italy's finest cooking ingredients from its well-stocked shelves before or after dining. Reservations recommended.

FIGLMÜLLER Map pp240-3 *Beisl*
☎ 512 61 77; 01, Wollzeile 5; mains €6.50-14; ☺ 11am-10.30pm (closed Aug); bus 1A

Figlmüller might be firmly on the tourist trail, but that doesn't detract from the huge schnitzels, which dwarf the plates they're served on. The interior has the look and feel of a rural *Heuriger* (see Entertainment, p144), and although it's generally packed and has a distinctly touristy feel, it's entertaining nonetheless.

GRIECHENBEISL Map pp240-3 *Beisl*
☎ 533 19 77; 01, Fleischmarkt 11; mains €14-18; ☺ 11am-1am; U1, U4 Schwedenplatz, Schwedenplatz trams

Griechenbeisl is almost more of a tourist attraction than a restaurant, and rightly so: it's been around since 1447 and was once frequented by the musical greats Beethoven, Schubert and Brahms. Choose to dine on Viennese standards in one of the vaulted rooms pierced by hanging antlers, or sit in the plant-fringed front garden.

IMMERVOLL
Map pp240-3 *Viennese & International*
☎ 513 52 88; 01, Weihburggasse 17; mains €7.20-15; ☺ noon-midnight; U1, U3 Stephansplatz

Thankfully Immervoll isn't always as its name suggests – 'always full' – so it's possible to find a table at this highly desirable Innere Stadt eatery. Vaulted ceilings, designer layout and a menu that offers something new each day keep diners coming back for more.

KÄRNTNER STRASSE, GRABEN & KOHLMARKT

CAFÉ BRÄUNERHOF Map pp240-3 *Café*
☎ 512 38 93; 01, Stallburggasse 2; snacks €3-6; ☺ 8am-9pm Mon-Fri, 8am-7pm Sat, 10am-7pm Sun; bus 2A, 3A

Not much has changed in this fine Viennese *Kaffeehaus* since the late great Thomas Bernhard once called it his *Stammlokal* (regular watering hole). There's classical music from 3pm to 6pm on Saturday, Sunday and holidays, and British newspapers are offered alongside Vienna's tabloids.

CAFÉ HAWELKA Map pp240-3 *Café*
☎ 512 82 30; 01, Dorotheergasse 6; snacks €3-6; ☺ 8am-2am Mon & Wed-Sat, 4pm-2am Sun; U1, U3 Stephansplatz

At first glance it's hard to see what all the fuss is about: scruffy pictures and posters, brown-stained walls, smoky air and cramped tables don't look too appealing. But a second glance explains it all – it's the perfect spot to people watch and chat to complete strangers. A traditional haunt for artists and writers, it attracts the gamut of Viennese society. You'll be constantly shunted up to accommodate new arrivals at the table. Be warned: the organising elderly Frau seizes any momentarily vacant chair (curtail your toilet visits!) to reassign elsewhere.

CAFÉ SACHER Map pp240-3 *Café*
☎ 541 56-661; 01, Philharmonikerstrasse 4; Sacher Torte around €3; ☺ 8am-11.30pm; U1, U2, U4 Karlsplatz, Karlsplatz trams

Sacher is the most celebrated café in all of Vienna, and almost every tourist to the city wants a slice of the action here – a slice of *Sacher Torte*, that is (see the boxed text p13). The café does have other redeeming features, such as opulent furnishings and a battalion of waiters.

CAFÉ TIROLERHOF Map pp240-3 *Café*
☎ 512 78 33; 01, Führichgasse 8; snacks €3-6;
🕑 7am-10pm Mon-Sat, 9am-8pm Sun; bus 3A

Looking for home-made strudel (around €3 to €4) in the heart of the World Capital of Strudeldom? Look no further than Tirolerhof, occupying a corner directly opposite the Albertina. This traditional Viennese café has another advantage: renovated Jugendstil décor from the 1920s.

DEMEL Map pp240-3 *Café*
☎ 535 17 17; 01, Kohlmarkt 14; mains €10-15;
🕑 10am-7pm; bus 2A, 3A

Demel is Café Sacher's *Torte* rival, and after an extended glimpse at the elaborate cakes in the front window, it's easy to see why. Naturally it's not the cheapest café in town, but you're paying for quality, location and elegance. The *Crème Schnitte* (cream slice) here is to die for.

KORSO Map pp240-3 *Viennese & International*
☎ 515 16-546; 01, Mahlerstrasse 2; mains €30-36;
🕑 lunch & 7pm-1am Sun-Fri, 7pm-1am Sat; U2, U4 Karlsplatz, Karlsplatz trams

Korso plays restaurant to the Bristol Hotel, and it shows: wood-panelled elegance and opulent chandeliers are just some of its stunning features. Add to that a vast wine cellar, live piano music (from 8pm to midnight) and delicate dishes, and you have a restaurant competing for Vienna's most luxurious prize. Without a suit and tie you'll feel out of place. Bookings advisable.

MEINL AM GRABEN
Map pp240-3 *International*
☎ 532 33 34; 01, Graben 19; mains €21-24;
🕑 8am-midnight Mon-Fri, from 8.30am Sat; bus U1, U3 Stephansplatz, bus 1A, 2A, 3A

Meinl am Graben carries the name of Julius Meinl – creator of Vienna's top, but now defunct, supermarket chain and a name synonymous with fine foods – to even greater heights. It's the best restaurant on the Graben, and possibly within the Innere Stadt, with cuisine of superlative quality, views of the Graben and a wine list to rival anything on this planet. It's above Vienna's most celebrated food store (see p164).

YOHM Map pp240-3 *Asian*
☎ 533 29 00; 01, Petersplatz 3; sushi brunch €18, mains €11.50-20.50; 🕑 lunch & dinner; U1, U3 Stephansplatz, bus 2A

Tucked away off Graben in the shadow of Peterskirche is Yohm, a modern restaurant of glass and steel with a contemporary Asian menu of high standard. Its sushi-brunch on weekends between 11.30am and 3.30pm is a must for sushi gluttons.

MICHAELERPLATZ TO MÖLKER BASTEI

CAFÉ CENTRAL Map pp240-3 *Café*
☎ 533 37 64-26; 01, Herrengasse 14; snacks €3-6;
🕑 8am-10pm Mon-Sat, 8am-7pm Sun; U3 Herrengasse

If you're looking for the typical Viennese café, look no further than Central, with its marble pillars, arched ceilings, glittering chandeliers, indifferent waiters and live classical music from 4pm to 7pm. Trotsky even came here to play chess. Say hello to the plaster patron with the walrus moustache near the door – a model of the poet Peter Altenberg.

CAFÉ GRIENSTEIDL Map pp240-3 *Café*
☎ 535 26 92; 01, Michaelerplatz 2; mains €6.60-17;
🕑 8am-11.30pm; U3 Herrengasse, bus 2A, 3A

Griensteidl holds a prestigious position between the splendour of the Hofburg and the

Café Central (above)

eyelash-less windows of the Loos Haus. It's a great place to people watch and flick through the large selection of international newspapers.

ROTENTURMSTRASSE TO SCHOTTENRING

BODEGA MARQUÉS Map pp240-3 *Spanish*
☎ 533 91 70; 01, Parisergasse 1; tapas €2.50-10; ☺ 6pm-1am Mon-Sat; bus 2A, 3A

Quiet, cobblestoned Parisergasse does a good job of concealing this lively, boisterous Spanish tapas bar. Choose from some 30-odd tapas and around 200 varieties of Spanish wine, which is perfectly complemented every Friday and Saturday night with live flamenco music.

É TRICAFFÉ Map pp240-3 *Italian*
☎ 535 32 22; 01, Wipplingerstrasse 34; coffee from €2.50; ☺ 8am-11pm; tram 1, 2

Slouching leather seats and Italian coffee at its best – that's what É Tricaffé is all about. Add to that high ceilings, a minimalist interior and the high-flyers from the *Börse* (stock exchange) next door, and you have a café of style and sophistication.

EN Map pp240-3 *Japanese*
☎ 532 44 90; 01, Werdertorgasse 8; midday menus €7.50-9.50, full meal €20; ☺ lunch & dinner; bus 3A

EN is definitely in the running for the 'best sushi' award in Vienna. But the whole gamut of Japanese specialities on the menu, including its delightful *gyoza* (dumplings), should be up for a medal, too. With shuffling kimono-clad waitresses, authentic décor, a demure atmosphere, and Japanese owners and managers, it's a small slice of Japan tucked away in the backstreets of the Innere Stadt. Reserve a table, or take a pew at the bar.

GELATERIA HOHER MARKT
Map pp240-3 *Ice Cream*
☎ 533 32 97-1; 01, Hoher Markt 4; ice cream €1.50; ☺ 9am-11.30pm; bus 1A, 2A, 3A

Forget Zanoni on Rotenturmstrasse and wander a few steps west to this supremely better ice-cream shop on Hoher Markt. Thirty varieties, a concoction of elaborate sundaes, outdoor seating and peaceful surroundings – need we say more?

LIVINGSTONE Map pp240-3 *Californian*
☎ 533 33 93; 01, Zelinkagasse 4; mains €13-20; ☺ 5pm-4am; tram 1, 2, bus 3A

There aren't many places in the Innere Stadt where, if you're peckish in the wee small hours of the morning, you can grab a bite to eat. Livingstone is one of them, which probably has something to do with its connection to Planter's Club next door. It calls itself a Californian restaurant, which means the menu swings from Japanese to Mexican and back again.

WRENKH Map pp240-3 *Vegetarian*
☎ 533 15 26; 01, Bauernmarkt 10; midday menus from €7.70, mains €8-15; ☺ lunch & dinner; U1, N Stephansplatz

This up-market restaurant in the heart of the Innere Stadt seems to have a split personality: the front section is a thoroughly modern affair with a vibrant feel, the rear a quiet, intimate room with booths. The food is the same in both, however – creative vegetarian dishes from around the world.

ZUM SCHWARZEN KAMEEL
Map pp240-3 *International*
☎ 533 81 25; 01, Bognergasse 5; sandwiches around €3, soups €6, mains from €20; ☺ 8.30am-midnight Mon-Sat; bus 1A, 2A

Zum Schwarzen Kameel is a strange combination of deli/sandwich shop and highbrow wine bar, which actually works. The high-society set who frequents the place normally nibble on sandwiches at the bar while pondering which *Achterl* (glass of wine) to select from the superb wine list. There are, however, sumptuous offerings in the wood-panelled dining area for lunch and dinner.

CHEAP EATS

EAST TO WEST Map pp240-3 *Chinese*
☎ 512 91 49; 01, Seilerstätte 14; midday menus €5-7, mains €5-7; ☺ lunch & 5.30-11pm; tram 1, 2

East to West is rated as above average for its clean and calm environment and its hefty selection of Chinese standards. In summer, the large, covered outdoor area is a major drawcard.

MASCHU MASCHU *Oriental/Israeli*
Map pp240-3; ☎ 533 29 04; 01, Rabensteig 8; mains €3-8; ☺ 11.30am-midnight Sun-Tue, 11.30-2am Wed, 11.30-3am Thu-Sat; U1, U4 Schwedenplatz, Schwedenplatz trams; Map pp246-7; ☎ 990 47 13; 07, Neubaugasse 20; mains €4-11; ☺ 11am-midnight; U3 Neubaugasse

Look no further than Maschu for the freshest falafels and hummus in the Innere Stadt. Informal and relaxed, it's basically a takeaway place with few seating options, which you'll have to fight for in the evening. The Neubaugasse premises are more of a sit-down venue, and the food is just as great as the Rabensteig location.

NUDEL & STRUDEL Map pp240-3 *Beisl*
☎ 533 61 28; 01, Schottenbastei 4; midday menus €6-10, mains €6-11; ☼ 9am-midnight Mon-Fri; U2 Schottentor, Schottentor trams

With a dark-wood interior, farm implements adorning the walls and solid Austrian fare, you'd expect to find Nudel & Strudel in some small village in Austria's countryside, not in the Innere Stadt. And that's what makes it so appealing. It's often full of students, due to the cheap student menu available (€3.80).

ROSENBERGER MARKT RESTAURANT
Map pp240-3 *Viennese Buffet*
☎ 512 34 58; 01, Maysedergasse 2; meals around €10; ☼ 6am-11pm; U1, U2, U4 Karlsplatz, Karlsplatz trams, bus 3A

This downstairs buffet place has a fine array of meats, drinks and desserts that enables you to compile a meal. Watch out for extras (like bread and butter) that can be pricey. If you really want to save some euros, concentrate on the salad or vegetable buffet.

SOUPKULTUR Map pp240-3 *Soups & Salads*
☎ 532 46 28; 01, Wipplingerstrasse 32; soups around €4, salads around €6; ☼ 11.30am-7pm Mon-Fri; bus 1A, 3A

With a selection of eight soups and six salads each week, it's no surprise Soupkultur is overrun with office workers looking for a healthy bite on the run. The range is imaginatively created, caters for vegetarians and meat lovers and always includes fresh ingredients. There is a token seating area, but this is a place designed more for takeaway.

TRZESNIEWSKI Map pp240-3 *Fast Food*
☎ 512 32 91; 01, Dorotheergasse 1; breads from €3; ☼ 8.30am-7.30pm Mon-Fri, 8am-5pm Sat; U1, U3 Stephansplatz

Trzesniewski is basically a deli bar, but it's also a Viennese institution and has had more than its fair share of famous patrons (Kafka was a regular here). You can either choose your bread, then select your spread, or pick from the ready-made sandwiches. They're quite tiny (two bites and they're gone), but they're also quite divine. This is one of seven to be found in Vienna.

Mensen

University cafeterias *(Mensen)* provide the cheapest sit-down meal in the Innere Stadt, and they're open to the general public. They normally only open Monday to Friday and have a limited range: two or three daily specials, including a vegetarian choice. Three of the bigger *Mensen* are:

Universität Mensa (Map pp240-3; ☎ 406 45 94; 01, Universitätsstrasse 7; full meals around €8; ☼ lunch Mon-Fri; U2 Schottentor, Schottentor trams) Take the doorless, continuous lift to the 6th floor (which is worth the trip in itself).

Katholisches Studenthaus Mensa (Map pp240-3; ☎ 408 35 85; 01, Ebendorferstrasse 8; mains €3-5.20; ☼ lunch Mon-Fri, closed Aug–mid-Sep; U2 Schottentor, Schottentor trams)

Music Academy Mensa (Map pp240-3; ☎ 512 94 70; 01, Johannesgasse 8; mains €3.80-4.80; ☼ lunch Mon-Fri, only to 1.30pm during summer holidays; tram 1, 2)

WÜRSTELSTAND AM HOHER MARKT
Map pp240-3 *Sausage Stand*
01, Hoher Markt; sausages from €3; ☼ 7am-5am; bus 1A, 2A, 3A

Possibly the best *Würstelstand* (sausage stand) in all of Vienna (which is really saying something), am Hoher Markt attracts people from all walks of life. It's the consistent quality of the sausages, the location and its incredible opening hours that maintain its top-dog status year after year. If you're going to eat one sausage while in town, make sure it's a *Käsekrainer*, a sausage infused with cheese. It's heavy, filling and can sometimes be a messy affair, but it's something you won't forget in a hurry. In their typically morose way, the Viennese have nicknamed a *Käsekrainer* served with the end of a bread loaf *'Eitrige mit an Buckl'*, which loosely translates as 'a hunchback full of pus'. To truly do it justice, wash it all down with a fine Austrian beer.

RINGSTRASSE
There isn't a plethora of eating options on the Ringstrasse: this prestigious street caters more to grand civic buildings, luxury hotels and expensive car dealerships. But what little there is, you can be sure it's of the highest standard.

Directly on the Ringstrasse is a collection of Vienna's finer cafés, not all of which fall into the traditional *Kaffeehaus* mould.

And close by in the new MuseumsQuartier is a bunch of innovative cafés and restaurants competing with the museums for attention.

SCHOTTENTOR TO PARLAMENT

CAFÉ LANDTMANN Map pp240-3   *Café*
☎ 241 00; 01, Dr-Karl-Lueger-Ring 4; midday menus €9.60, mains €7.80-19; ☺ 7.30am-midnight; U2 Schottentor, Schottentor trams

This elegant old dame has side-long views of the Burgtheater from its covered outdoor area, which could easily be the largest of any Viennese café. There's a huge selection of Austrian and international papers, and live piano music from 8pm to 10pm on Sunday.

VESTIBÜL Map pp240-3   *International*
☎ 532 49 99; 01, Dr-Karl-Lueger-Ring 2; evening menus €40, mains €20; ☺ 11am-midnight Mon-Fri, 6pm-midnight Sat; tram 1, 2, D

Vestibül takes pride of place in the southern wing of the Burgtheater and naturally attracts a thespian crowd. The rich interior – marble columns, chandeliers and sparkling mirrored bar – would have you believe you're dining in a palace, and the menu is a rich blend of Austria's finest and dishes from around the world. Reservations are recommended.

PARLAMENT TO SCHWARZENBERGPLATZ

EAT IT Map pp240-3   *Asian*
☎ 505 04 87; 01, Karlsplatz 2; mains €10-15; ☺ dinner Mon-Sat; U1, U2, U4 Karlsplatz, Karlsplatz trams

Eat It doesn't have the best location on busy Karlsplatz, but that's long forgotten once you enter the front door. Asian touches, attentive staff and dishes spiced with a deft touch are a perfect combination and create a relaxed, yet refined, eating experience.

MUSEUMSQUARTIER

HALLE Map pp240-3   *International*
☎ 523 70 01; 07, Museumsplatz 1; midday menus €7, mains from €7; ☺ 10am-2am; U2 Museumsquartier, U2, U3 Volkstheater

With excellent food, handsome waiters and a warm, gay-friendly atmosphere, it's no surprise Halle, the Kunsthalle's restaurant (see Entertainment, p142), is run by the same people who set Motto (p128) on its rise to fame. Antipastos, salads and pastas from the Italian kitchen are the mainstay of the menu, but there are other choices if that's not to your taste. Added bonuses include high, ornate ceilings and comfy benches.

UNA Map pp240-3   *Café*
☎ 523 65 66; 07, Museumsplatz 1; mains €6.20-15; ☺ 9am-midnight Mon-Fri, from 10am Sat, 10am-6pm Sun; U2 Museumsquartier, U2, U3 Volkstheater

Una is reputedly housed in what were once the imperial stables, and if this is indeed true, the horses had it better than most citizens. Striking tiled walls, arched ceilings and massive windows, along with an unpretentious atmosphere, complement an uncomplicated menu heavy on pasta and often offering seasonal specialities.

Una (above)

SCHWARZENBERGPLATZ TO THE DANUBE CANAL

CAFÉ PRÜCKEL Map pp240-3 *Café*

☎ 512 61 15; 01, Stubenring 24; coffee €1.80-3.60, mains €6-11; ⏰ 8.30am-10pm; U3 Stubentor, tram 1, 2

Prückel's unique mould is a little different from other Viennese cafés: instead of a sumptuous interior, you'll find a café where the 1950s still prevail. The coffee is superb, the cakes irresistible and the service as aloof as ever. Once again, live piano music is a feature of this true Viennese *Kaffeehaus*; catch a performance 7pm to 10pm Monday, Wednesday and Friday.

CAFÉ SCHWARZENBERG

Map pp240-3 *Café*

☎ 512 89 98; 01, Kärntner Ring 17; mains €10-23; ⏰ 7am-midnight Sun-Fri, from 9am Sat; tram 71, D, bus 3A

If the number of huge mirrors is anything to go by, then whoever designed the Schwarzenberg definitely felt it should look and feel a lot bigger. No matter, the result is a graceful café with a noble air that attracts coffee connoisseurs of all ages. Live piano can be heard on Wednesday and Friday between 7.30pm and 10pm, and Saturday and Sunday from 5pm to 7pm.

MAK CAFÉ Map pp240-3 *Café*

☎ 714 01 21; 01, Stubenring 3-5; midday menus €6.50-8, mains €7-18; ⏰ 10am-2am Tue-Sun; U3 Stubentor, tram 1, 2

The highlight of MAK Café, attached to the Museum für angewandte Kunst (see p82), isn't what's served in front of you but rather its 19th-century ornamental ceiling. This isn't meant to detract from the Viennese and international cuisine, however, which changes on a daily basis. The garden is a must in summer.

CHEAP EATS

KANTINE Map pp240-3 *Café*

☎ 523 82 39; 07, Museumsplatz 1; daily menus €5.50-6.50, pitta breads €4.50-9; ⏰ 10am-midnight Sun-Wed, until 2am Thu-Sat; U2 Museumsquartier, U2, U3 Volkstheater

This upbeat café-bar, complete with disco ball, is housed in the former stables of the emperor's personal horses. If the fresh daily menu – typically an Asian or Viennese dish with a vegetarian or fish choice thrown in – is sold out, you'll have to settle for salad-filled pitta bread. The cocktail list is quite extensive.

X-CELSIOR CAFFÉ-BAR Map pp240-3 *Café*

☎ 585 71 84; 01, Opernring 1; mains €3.90-9.90; ⏰ 7am-1am; U1, U2, U4 Karlsplatz, Karlsplatz trams

Don't come here looking for *Melange* and *Strudel*. This is the home of Italian coffee and cuisine – and excellent coffee and cuisine at that. The interior is all glass and steel, and the large windows are a voyeur's delight, providing views of the Opera House and all the comings-and-goings on busy Karlsplatz.

BETWEEN THE DANUBE CANAL & THE DANUBE

Leopoldstadt, Vienna's 2nd district, contains the lion's share of restaurants between the Danube Canal and the Danube. It's within easy striking distance by foot of the Innere Stadt, and has none of the pomp and ceremony of its larger and more illustrious neighbour. It's also a district slowly cultivating a cosmopolitan outlook, which is reflected in its restaurants.

ATELIER AUGARTEN

Map pp244-5 *International*

☎ 216 86 16-10; 02, Scherzergasse 1a; mains €9.50-16; ⏰ 10am-midnight Tue-Sun; tram 5, N

The Atelier is tucked away behind the museum of the same name (p84). Small, secluded and far removed from the hustle and bustle and tourist-trodden trails of the Innere Stadt, it serves good coffee and fine food in clean, white surroundings.

BAYOU Map pp244-5 *Creole & Cajun*

☎ 214 77 52; 02, Leopoldgasse 51; mains €8-15; ⏰ dinner; bus 5A

Bayou, Vienna's premiere Creole and Cajun restaurant, is *the* place to chow down on gumbos and jambalayas. There are other choices, but

---

Top Five Between the Danube Canal & the Danube

- **Bayou** (p125)
- **Contor** (p126)
- **Lusthaus** (p126)
- **Schöne Perle** (p126)
- **Schweizerhaus** (p126)

they're generally fish and seafood. Energetic staff and the occasional live band create a fun atmosphere.

CONTOR Map pp244-5 *Spanish*
☎ 219 63 16; 02, Leopoldgasse 51; tapas €3-8; ◷ 5pm-1am Mon-Thu, 5pm-2am Fri, 11am-2am Sat; bus 5A

Contor has a lot going for it: fine tapas, great wine and a smooth ambience. And with fresh cheese from Lower Austria, pastas and staff who know the superb wine list inside out, there's not much else you could ask for.

GESUNDES
Map pp240-3 *Organic/Vegetarian*
☎ 219 53 22; 02, Lilienbrunngasse 3; midday menus €7-8; ◷ 9am-6pm Mon, Tue, Thu & Fri, 9am-5.30pm Wed, 10am-2pm Sat; U1, U4 Schwedenplatz, tram N

Gesundes is the kind of place where just walking through the door makes you feel healthier. Only vegetarian/vegan organic dishes (made using the principles of the five elements, whatever that means) are on the menu, and it doubles as a shop for organic produce. With only two tables, it's more suited to takeaways.

LUSTHAUS Map pp248-9 *Austrian*
☎ 728 95 65; 02, Freudenau 254; mains €8.70-16.50; ◷ noon-11pm Mon-Fri, noon-6pm Sat & Sun May-Sep, noon-6pm Mon, Tue & Fri-Sun Oct & Apr, noon-6pm Sat-Tue Nov-Mar; bus 77A

Lusthaus harks back to the days when men wore silly bowler hats with pride and women squeezed into constricting corsets. It's an old hunting lodge with plenty of flair and a menu filled with Austrian specialities ready to satisfy even the hungriest stomachs. It's also a long way from anything – for Viennese standards – and not somewhere to drop in for a quick bite to eat.

SCHWEIZERHAUS Map pp244-5 *Austrian*
☎ 728 01 52; 02, Strasse des Ersten Mai 116; mains €10-15; ◷ 11am-11pm Mon-Fri, from 10am Sat & Sun mid-Mar–Oct; U1 Praterstern, tram 5, 21, 0

Every Viennese knows the Schweizerhaus, and probably every Viennese has eaten here at least once in their life. It's famous for its massive, tree-shaded garden, which is always full of tourists and locals alike. But it's also famous for what it serves: *Hintere Schweinsstelze* (roasted pork hocks). These gargantuan chunks of meat on the bone (€15 per kg, 750g minimum), best served with mustard and freshly grated horseradish, taste supremely better than they sound and are best shared between

two. Wash it all down with draught Budweiser (the Czech stuff) direct from the barrel.

ZUM INDER Map pp244-5 *Indian*
☎ 216 21 96; 02, Praterstrasse 57; midday buffet €6, mains €8-15; ◷ lunch & dinner; U1 Praterstern, tram 5, 0

The décor might look a little drab and there could be more lighting, but the curries at Zum Inder are solid and spicy (for Viennese standards) and the midday buffet is great value.

CHEAP EAT
SCHÖNE PERLE Map pp244-5 *Beisl*
☎ 243 35 93; 02, Grosse Pfarrgasse 2; midday menus €7, mains €5-12; ◷ noon-11pm Mon-Sat, until 10pm Sun; bus 5A

Schöne Perle has the look and feel of a student cafeteria, but the food is by no means as basic or as bland. Classic Austrian dishes are created with organic produce only and complemented by a fine list of Austrian wines and juices.

ACROSS THE DANUBE
East of the Danube, lining the banks of the Alte Donau, are traditional *Gasthäuser* (guesthouses), the perfect respite from a hard day boating, swimming or simply lounging in the sun.

STRANDGASTHAUS BIRNER
Map pp238-9 *Viennese*
☎ 271 53 63; 21, An der Oberen Alten Donau 47; midday menus €5, mains €5-12; ◷ 9am-10pm Thu-Tue summer, 9am-9pm Thu-Tue winter; U6 Floridsdorf, tram 26

Birner is an institution in these parts – like the Schweizerhaus (see p126), all Viennese know of its existence and it seems to have been in existence since time immemorial. Supreme fish soups and fish specialities and a sunbathed terrace with views of the Alte Donau attract herds of Viennese here in summer. Be aware that summer and winter opening times aren't date-specific but rather weather determined.

ZUR ALTEN KAISERMÜHLE
Map pp238-9 *Viennese*
☎ 263 35 29; 22, Fischerstrand 21a; mains €5.50-12.40; ◷ 11.30am-11pm mid-Apr–Sep, 11.30am-11pm Thu-Sun Oct–mid-Apr; U1 Alte Donau

This old *Gasthaus* is best appreciated in summer when its garden, a willow-tree haven right beside the Alte Donau, comes into its own. Go for spareribs (the menu is overflowing with grilled meat and fish dishes) and bring some insect repellent.

INSIDE THE GÜRTEL

The last few years have seen a surge in the variety and number of restaurants in Vienna, and the districts within the confines of the Gürtel have been at the forefront of this development in Vienna's eating scene. Persian, Chinese, Japanese, Italian, French, Bohemian and of course a healthy dose of Austrian – it's all here to sample, scintillate and satisfy. Plus, you're not always going to be bowled over by the outrageous prices the Innere Stadt can throw at you.

A number of restaurants here are a little stiff under the collar, but more often than not they're relaxed, young and flexible. They need to be: this part of the city is hungry to sample new food delights.

LANDSTRASSE
PALAIS SCHWARZENBERG
Map pp248-9 *Austrian*
☎ 798 45 15-600; 03, Schwarzenbergplatz 9; breakfast €25.50, lunch menus €33, dinner menus €55; ☺ 6.30-10.30am, noon-2pm, dinner; tram D
The restaurant of the hotel of the same name (see p178) is as opulent as anything you're likely to lay eyes on in Vienna. Its grand baroque dining room is only just overshadowed by the terrace, which enjoys sweeping views of the palace's 18-acre garden. The cuisine – Austrian with a splash of Mediterranean flair – is a fitting match for such rich surroundings.

PAN E WIEN
Map pp248-9 *Italian*
☎ 710 38 70; 03, Salesianergasse 25; midday menus €8.40, mains €17-20; ☺ lunch & dinner; tram 71
Pan e Wien belongs in the upper echelon of Italian restaurants in Vienna. The food, made with care and class, attracts the city's movers and shakers, and the dark-wood interior is a dignified touch. Wine buffs will not be disappointed by the selection. Reservations are recommended.

STEIRERECK
Map pp248-9 *Austrian*
☎ 713 31 68; 03, Rasumofskygasse 2; midday menus €35, evening menus €70; ☺ 10.30am-2pm & 7-11pm Mon-Sat

Top Five Inside the Gürtel
- Aromat (p132)
- Gaumenspiel (p130)
- Motto (p128)
- ON (p131)
- Stomach (p132)

Steirereck is gourmet territory. In fact, it's consistently rated as one of the best restaurants in Austria and leads the way in classic dishes from around the country. Formality prevails throughout the premises, but it will be interesting to see what effect the transition to new digs in the Stadtpark (formerly home to nightclub Meierei) will have. Menus are a minimum of three courses and, needless to say, reservations are essential.

WILD
Map pp240-3 *Viennese*
☎ 920 94 77; 03, Radetzkyplatz 1; midday menus €7, mains €7-15; ☺ 10am-1am Tue-Sun; tram N, O
Unassuming Radetzkyplatz is a strange place to hide such a sensational restaurant as Wild, but that's the way it is. The dark, wood-panelled interior is the first sign of class when you walk through the doors, the quiet ambience the second. The menu is Viennese through and through, ranging from *Gulasch* (goulash) to the ever-present *Schnitzel mit Erdäpfelsalat* (schnitzel with potato salad). Reservations for dinner are recommended.

WIEDEN
INDIAN PAVILLON
Map pp240-3 *Indian*
☎ 587 85 61; 04, Naschmarkt 74-75; mains €7-10; ☺ 11am-6.30pm Mon-Fri, until 5pm Sat; U1, U2, U4 Karlsplatz
Near the Innere Stadt end of the Naschmarkt is this tiny eatery serving dishes laden with spices from the Indian subcontinent. Here you can snack on kebabs and samosa (€3 to €6), munch on poppadums and rogan josh or down a Cobra beer to the beat of Indian music. Don't expect to find a table on Saturday mornings, however.

MR LEE
Map pp240-3 *Asian*
☎ 581 45 60; 04, Naschmarkt 278; mains €6-10; ☺ 10.30am-10pm Mon-Sat; U1, U2, U4 Karlsplatz
This Asian diner is one link in a chain of Asian eateries in the Naschmarkt. What makes it stand out are its consistently top-quality

dishes (many with a little extra spice), service so friendly it almost seems fake and an open kitchen that hides no secrets.

NASCHMARKT DELI

Map pp240-3 *American*
☎ 585 08 23; 04, Naschmarkt 421; sandwiches €4-7, mains €6-9; 🕑 7am-10pm Mon-Fri, 7am-midnight Sat; U4 Kettenbrückengasse

Like Do-An (p134) next door, Deli is a fish bowl and great for people-watching on a Saturday morning. But it's also a place to 'see and be seen', which often equates with overcrowding and a snooty air. Nevertheless, the wraps, baguettes and sandwiches are fine, and the breakfasts worth fighting over a table for. Just don't turn up at 10am on Saturday expecting to find a seat.

TANCREDI Map pp246-7 *International*
☎ 941 00 48; 04, Grosse Neugasse 5; midday menus €7, mains €7-16; 🕑 lunch & dinner Tue-Fri, dinner Sat; tram 62, 65

This ex-*Beisl* attracts a more affluent clientele with lovingly prepared regional and fish specialities, bio-products and an extensive range of Austrian wines. The harmonious surroundings are the icing on the cake: stripped-back wooden floors, warm, pastel-yellow walls, fittings from yesteryear and a tree-shaded garden that fills up quickly in summer. The entrance is on Rubengasse.

TOKO RI Map pp240-3 *Japanese*
☎ 587 26 16; 04, Naschmarkt 261-263; midday box €7-9, sushi, sashimi & maki €5-9; 🕑 11am-11pm Mon-Sat; U1, U2, U4 Karlsplatz

Toko Ri was one of the first Asian restaurants to move into the Naschmarkt, and its popularity hasn't waned even though a flood of similar places has hit its surroundings. Sit down to fresh sushi, sashimi or maki, or pick up a midday box and wander through busy Naschmarkt.

UBL Map pp246-7 *Beisl*
☎ 587 64 37; 04, Pressgasse 26; mains €8-12; 🕑 lunch & dinner; bus 59A

Once again, *riesige* (huge) schnitzels are the standard at another Viennese *Beisl*. Fortunately, however, the quiet, relaxed atmosphere and tree-shaded summer terrace helps to appease your groaning stomach. *Schnitzel* is not the only choice on the menu: old favourites like *Schinkenfleckerl* (pasta with ham) and *Schweinsbraten* (roast pork) are here to be had.

MARGARETEN
AMACORD

Map pp240-3 *Viennese & International*
☎ 587 47 09; 05, Rechte Wienzeile 15; breakfast €4.60-6, mains €6.40-10.80; 🕑 10am-2am; U1, U2, U4 Karlsplatz, bus 59A

Shoppers on a Saturday morning fill Amacord to bursting point with their bodies and bulging grocery bags, all fighting for a table and a chance to enjoy breakfast. At other times, the pace is more sedate, but the food – a mix of Viennese classics and Italian pastas – is of the highest quality and the atmosphere convivial.

KRAMER & GUTIERREZ

Map pp246-7 *Oriental*
☎ 585 49 00; 05, Wehrgasse 8; mains €7-12; 🕑 dinner Tue-Sun; bus 59A

Antipastos, pastas, vegetarian specialities and tapas with a Moroccan twist are the mainstays of Kramer's menu. If that isn't inviting enough, then the pared-down and refined décor, with plenty of dark wood, and a warm and social atmosphere, should hopefully tip the scales in favour of a visit.

MOTTO Map pp246-7 *International*
☎ 587 06 72; 05, Schönbrunner Strasse 30; mains €8-19; 🕑 6pm-4am; U4 Pilgramgasse, bus 59A

Motto is one place that justifies its status as a favourite of the current 'in-crowd'. The food, a fusion of Asian, Austrian and Italian, is a work of art, the wine list selective and the décor, well, caters to a gay clientele. Dressed in her house-cleaning frock, Frau Helena is the Yin to the young, handsome, well-groomed male waiters' Yang, but her steaks are legendary (Monday, Tuesday and Thursday only). Entrance is through the forbidding chrome door on Rüdigergasse. Reservations are recommended.

ZU DEN 3 BUCHTELN

Map pp246-7 *Bohemian*
☎ 587 83 65; 05, Wehrgasse 9; mains €8-12; 🕑 dinner Mon-Sat; bus 59A

If you've never had the opportunity to sample true Bohemian cuisine, then take the opportunity to make time for dinner at this place. Expect to find goulash, blood sausage, roast pork with dumplings, piles of sauerkraut and barrels of Czech beer.

ZUM ALTEN FASSL Map pp246-7 *Beisl*
☎ 544 42 98; 05, Ziegelofengasse 37; midday menus €5.70-6.40, mains €6-14.50; 🕑 lunch & dinner Sun-Fri, dinner Sat; bus 13A

An unassuming façade on a residential street hides this esteemed *Beisl* from many casual passers-by. Inside is a traditional *Beisl* setting, a convivial atmosphere and an inviting menu. Try the desserts – any of them – they're worth crossing town for. The rear garden is an absolute joy; overgrown with vines, it provides a sample of the hidden gardens of residential Vienna.

MARIAHILF

CAFÉ SPERL Map pp240-3 *Café*
☎ 586 41 58; 06, Gumpendorfer Strasse 11; mains €5-10; ☽ 7am-11pm Mon-Sat, 11am-8pm Sun (closed Sun in summer); bus 57A

Café Sperl is still popular and going strong despite its one-time infamous patron, Hitler. In fact, it's one of Vienna's top cafés, with a reputable menu (every dish comes with a salad) and excellent desserts, the highlight of which is the Sperl *Torte*, a mouthwatering mix of almonds and chocolate cream. Its Jugendstil fittings, grand dimensions and overall cosy appearance are a film-maker's dream, which has resulted in Sperl appearing in a number of movies.

PICCINI PICCOLO GOURMET
Map pp240-3 *Italian*
☎ 587 52 54; 06, Linke Wienzeile 4; mains €8-19; ☽ 11am-7.30pm Mon-Fri, 9.30am-2pm Sat; U1, U2, U4 Karlsplatz

'Gourmet' is a term used all too frequently these days and often used inappropriately with the likes of gourmet pizzas, gourmet burgers, and even gourmet sandwiches. But 'gourmet' fits perfectly to Piccini Piccolo. Here is a restaurant that knows its *pici* from its *tortelli*, its *Brunello* from its *Vino Nobile* (it needs to with some 60 varieties of wine). It's also a top spot for purchasing Italian produce (see p168).

RA'MIEN Map pp240-3 *Asian*
☎ 585 47 98; 06, Gumpendorfer Strasse 9; mains €6-15; ☽ 11am-midnight Tue-Sun; U2 Museumsquartier, bus 57A

Picture a greyish white room, with an open, simple look, full of bright, hip young things bent over bowls of piping hot noodles, and you have Ra'mien. The menu not only includes noodles but also covers the spectrum of Asian delights, from Thai to Japanese. It's best to book for evening dining, but it's no problem to wait for a table either; the lounge bar downstairs has regular DJs and opens until at least 2am.

SAIGON *Vietnamese*
Map pp240-3; ☎ 585 63 95; 06, Getreidemarkt 7; midday menus €5.30-6.80, mains €7.30-16; ☽ 11.30am-10.30pm Tue-Sun; U1, U2, U4 Karlsplatz
Map pp244-5; ☎ 408 74 36; 16, Neulerchenfelder Strasse 37; mains €7.30-16; ☽ 11.30am-10.30pm Tue-Sun; U6 Josefstädterstrasse, tram J

Five years ago it would have been highly unlikely to find authentic Vietnamese in the heart of Vienna, but these days it's nothing out of the ordinary, and Saigon is to be thanked for that. Bamboo screens, Asian art and an incredible selection of dishes (the soups are the highlight) are all inviting touches to this popular restaurant. The original Saigon has made its fortune from the patronage of Ottakringer residents.

VINISSIMO Map pp240-3 *Italian*
☎ 586 48 88; 06, Windmühlgasse 20; midday menus €6.40, mains €8.50-17; ☽ 11am-11pm Mon-Sat; bus 57A

Vinissimo is half wine shop, half bistro, and all tied together with Italian pizzazz. The menu is solidly Italian – a good portion of which is vegetarian – and changes daily. It's also the perfect place to sample some fine drops of Italian *vino*.

YOGA Map pp246-7 *Indian*
☎ 595 61 27; 06, Webgasse 3; midday menus €5-8, mains €6.50-10.40; ☽ lunch & dinner; bus 57A

Yoga is one of the few restaurants in Vienna to specialise in South Indian cuisine. It has a menu crowded with curries and heavily laden with vegetarian dishes. The dim lighting and soft background Indian music lend the place an intimate atmosphere.

NEUBAU

CANETTI Map pp246-7 *Café*
☎ 522 06 88; 07, Urban-Loritz-Platz 2A; midday menus €6, mains €7-18; ☽ 9am-midnight; U6 Burggasse/Stadthalle, tram 6, 18

Canetti is one of only a handful of eateries in Vienna with rooftop views. Perched on top of the new Bücherei Wien (p95), its vantage point provides a sweeping vista of Vienna to the south. The Viennese dishes can be hit-or-miss unfortunately, but it's a fine place for a quiet coffee or something stronger.

CHRINOR Map pp246-7 *International*
☎ 522 32 36; 07, Kirchengasse 21; midday menus €7, mains €8-15; ☽ 11.30am-midnight Tue-Fri, dinner Sat; tram 49, bus 13A

The soft lighting, high ceilings and huge mirrors here perform two tasks simultaneously: they create intimate, calm surroundings while tricking you into thinking Chrinor is a lot bigger than it actually is. The changing menu is certainly creative and often eclectic; expect to find anything from Asian to Italian to local recipes. Reservations are advisable for evening dining.

GAUMENSPIEL Map pp246-7 *Italian*
☎ 526 11 08; 07, Zieglergasse 54; midday menus €7, mains €8-15; ☺ lunch & dinner Tue-Fri, dinner Sat, lunch Sun; tram 49, bus 48A

Gaumenspiel keeps its regulars coming back time and time again, and with good reason. The food, an international mix with heavy Mediterranean influence, is cooked with professionalism and care, the service is attentive and friendly without being annoying and overbearing, and the whole eating experience is focused on enjoyment. The setup helps to instil a sense of calm and informality; the menu is written on chalkboards, the décor is light in detail and in summer there are a handful of streetside tables. Reservations for dinner are recommended.

PLUTZER BRAÜ Map pp240-3 *Pub*
☎ 526 12 15; 07, Schrankgasse 2; midday menus €6, mains from €5; ☺ 11am-2am Mon-Sat; U2, U3 Volkstheater, bus 48A

This basement brewery in the heart of Spittalberg is a haunt for a cross-section of society, and it offers a menu that swings from Asian creations to juicy, sauce-laden spareribs and back again. Its outdoor seating area is at the height of popularity in summer while indoors it's fairly subdued during the day. However, things do pick up indoors in the evening, helped along by a smattering of happy hours.

PODIUM Map pp246-7 *International*
☎ 522 15 87; 07, Westbahnstrasse 33; midday menus €6-7, mains €9-12; ☺ 11am-1am Mon-Fri, 5pm-1am Sat & Sun; tram 49

Podium goes heavy on the designer look and feel, but not at the expense of practicality and comfort. Take your pick of upright and correct chairs and tables by the windows or lazy couches in hidden corners to the rear. The menu, filled with strudel and pasta, changes on a regular basis. The crowd, which often just drops in for a drink and a chat, is arty and cultured.

ST JOSEF Map pp246-7 *Organic/Vegetarian*
☎ 526 68 18; 07, Mondscheingasse 10; small/large menus €4.80/5.80; ☺ 8am-6pm Mon-Wed & Fri, 8am-11.30pm Thu, 8am-4pm Sat; tram 49, bus 13A

It's hard to find a more laid-back and welcoming eatery than St Josef in all of Vienna. The creative menus, which roll out of the open kitchen all day, are 100% vegetarian and made from wholly organic produce. Take a seat upstairs or downstairs, or get something to go.

SCHILLING Map pp246-7 *Beisl*
☎ 524 17 75; 07, Burggasse 103; midday menus €6, mains €6-14; ☺ 11am-1am; bus 48A

With its all-wood décor and solid Viennese fare, Schilling definitely falls within the *Beisl* category. But its brightly lit interior, bubbly staff and upbeat atmosphere provide a modern twist. The midday menu attracts a plethora of workers from the surrounding neighbourhood.

JOSEFSTADT

CAFÉ DER PROVINZ Map pp244-5 *French*
☎ 0699 11 17 21 56; 08, Maria Treu Gasse 3; crepes €1.70-5.50, mains €6.50-9; ☺ 9am-11pm Mon-Sat, 9am-3pm Sun; tram J

This charming little café has plenty of atmosphere and great crepes ready made to order. If crepes aren't your thing, don't let that stop you dropping by – bring a friend for an intimate chat, kick back with your favourite book or surf the Internet in peace and quiet.

CAFÉ FLORIANIHOF Map pp244-5 *Café*
☎ 402 48 42; 08, Florianigasse 45; midday menus €7, mains € 7-12.20; ☺ 8am-midnight Mon-Fri, from 10am Sat & Sun; tram 5, 33

This child-friendly café is a Josefstadt institution. Food is heavily laden with bio ingredients, and the variety of juices available is quite remarkable. Paintings by local artists, which change on a regular basis, are also a drawcard. There's free Internet access but you must at least buy a drink. Note that the midday menu is offered only Monday to Friday.

CAFÉ HUMMEL Map pp244-5 *Café*
☎ 405 53 14; 08, Josefstädter Strasse 66; midday menus €5, mains from €5; ☺ 7am-2am Mon-Sat, 8am-2am Sun; tram 5, 33, J

Unpretentious Hummel is a locals' *Kaffeehaus*, with aloof waiters, a huge range of Viennese dishes, top coffee and home-made cakes to die for. The massive streetside seating area

Eating – Inside the Gürtel

is perfect for people-watching or browsing through the extensive collection of foreign-language papers.

FROMME HELENE
Map pp244-5 *International*

☎ 406 91 44; 08, Josefstädter Strasse 15; midday menus €5.50-7, mains €6-18; ⏰ 11.30am-1am; tram J, bus 13A

Fromme Helene attracts a more sedate diner with its cosy benches, soft lighting and altogether refined air. The menu does have its fair share of international flavours, but mainly sticks to a fine collection of Viennese cuisine.

KIANG IM ACHTEN Map pp244-5 *Asian*

☎ 405 31 97; 08, Lederergasse 14; mains €7-10; ⏰ lunch & dinner Sun-Fri, dinner Sat; bus 13A

Kiang is a bright, bustling and lively place with quick service and an open, informal feel. The menu is heavily Chinese-based, but the Sunday brunch is all about sushi. As brunches go, it's not cheap (€20), but it comes highly recommended. If it's full, ask for the location of its four sister restaurants scattered throughout Vienna.

KONOBA Map pp246-7 *Dalmatian*

☎ 929 41 11; 08, Lerchenfelder Strasse 66-68; mains €6-18; ⏰ lunch & dinner Sun-Fri, dinner Sat; tram 46

An open plan and a bustling atmosphere make this a convivial place despite the stuffy crowd. Fish and seafood specialities from the Dalmatian coast are the mainstay of the menu, and the only grumble here is slow service, which is probably due to the restaurant's popularity. Reservations are recommended.

ON Map pp244-5 *Asian*

☎ 402 63 33; 08, Lederergasse 16; midday menus €6, mains from €5; ⏰ lunch & dinner Wed-Fri, 5.30pm-11pm Sat & Sun; bus 13A

ON is another in a long list of spartan Asian restaurants to grace the Viennese restaurant scene in recent years. But what makes ON stand out from the crowd is a combination of creative, gluten-free Chinese, Thai and Malaysian dishes, superb spices, an open kitchen and a friendly atmosphere. With only a handful of tables, reservations are highly recommended.

PARS Map pp246-7 *Persian*

☎ 405 82 45; 08, Lerchenfelder Strasse 148; midday menus €6.40, mains €5.60-13.50; ⏰ 11am-midnight Mon-Sat; tram 46

Pars carries the sign of authenticity: Vienna's Persian community flock here to indulge in lamb specialities on beds of fluffy rice, or just to chat and smoke tobacco in water pipes.

SAMRAT Map pp244-5 *Indian*

☎ 408 47 41; 08, Florianigasse 20; midday buffet €7, mains €8-12; ⏰ lunch & dinner Mon-Sat; U2 Rathaus

It's hard to walk past Samrat without being drawn in by the mixture of spices wafting from the kitchen. It might also have something to do with the animated owner standing outside the entrance beckoning you with both arms. Either way, it's a good idea to head inside, sit yourself down among the trappings from the subcontinent and dig into a delectable curry.

SIDE STEP Map pp244-5 *Spanish*

☎ 0676 782 02 30; 08, Langegasse 52; tapas €3-6; ⏰ 6pm-2am Mon-Sat, 6pm-1am Sun; U2 Rathaus, bus 13A

With a selection of 40 tapas and 45 open wines, do you need any other reason to stop by Side Step? If you require more convincing, note that there are also cobblestone floors, cool brick walls and excellent grappa.

ALSERGRUND
GASTHAUS WICKERL

Map pp244-5 *Viennese*

☎ 317 74 89; 09, Porzellangasse 24a; mains €6-12; ⏰ 9am-midnight Mon-Fri, from 10am Sat; tram D

Wickerl is a real favourite of Viennese who are looking for some home cooking with all the trimmings. In addition the bare wooden floors, simple furniture, summer streetside seating and a relaxed, warm environment make this one of the better eateries in Alsergrund. Also worth swinging by is Wickerl's small pavilion on Naschmarkt (Map pp240-3; Stand 528–529).

KIM KOCHT Map pp244-5 *Asian*

☎ 319 02 42; 09, Lustkandlgasse 6; mains €10.50-27; ⏰ dinner Mon-Fri; U6 Währinger Strasse, tram 40, 41, 42

This wholesome, up-market Asian restaurant, hidden behind the Volksoper, has a selective menu that thankfully doesn't offer every Asian dish under the sun. It does, however, have a heavy Japanese slant (despite being Korean owned and run), and its tuna dishes are the talk of the town. Reservations are highly recommended.

LA PASTERIA Map pp244-5 *Italian*
☎ 310 27 36; 09, Servitengasse 10; mains €7-18;
🕐 10am-11pm Mon-Fri, 10am-2pm & dinner Sat; U4
Rossauer Lände, tram D

Small, classy and stylish, La Pasteria is the highlight of Servitengasse, a street lined with restaurants and boutique shops. The speciality here is pasta, which is made on the premises. Imported Italian products are available at the shop of the same name next door (see p170). Reservations are highly recommended.

RA'AN Map pp240-3 *Asian*
☎ 319 35 90; 09, Währinger Strasse 6-8; mains €6-10;
🕐 8am-1am; U2 Schottentor, Schottentor trams

Ra'mien's (p129) new sister has made a big splash in Vienna's restaurant scene since its recent opening. This is probably due to its older sister's reputation, but the food stands up for itself: a small but excellent selection of modern Asian dishes complemented by a discerning wine list. The service – grumpy and sarcastic to begin with, warm and amusing at the end – is typically Viennese, however. Try for a window seat for views of Votiv Kirche. There's also a dark bar downstairs. Reservations recommended.

RUBEN'S BRASSERIE Map pp244-5 *Austrian*
☎ 319 23 96; 09, Fürstengasse 1; mains €10-20;
🕐 11am-midnight Wed-Sun; tram D, bus 40A

In the shadow of the rejuvenated Palais Liechtenstein is Ruben's, a small brasserie with style and grace to match the palace itself. Modern Austrian is the flavour of the menu, which equates with chefs adding their own masterful touches to old favourites such as *Schnitzel* and *Nockerl* (home-made pasta). The wine list reads like an encyclopaedia of Austrian wines. Reservations are recommended.

S-BAR Map pp244-5 *American*
☎ 319 17 17; 09, Porzellangasse 13; midday menus €5.40-7, mains €5-10; 🕐 9am-2am Sun-Fri, 5pm-2am Sat; tram D

S-Bar is run by the Naschmarkt Deli owners, and it has a similar atmosphere and standing among the movers and shakers, minus the masses. The simple décor, with its low stools and sky-high windows, is highly appealing, and the international and vegetarian menu will satisfy most punters. It's connected with the Schauspielhaus (see p152) and so attracts a theatrical crowd.

STOMACH Map pp244-5 *Austrian*
☎ 310 20 99; 09, Seegasse 26; mains €10-17;
🕐 4pm-midnight Wed-Sat, 10am-10pm Sun;
U4 Rossauer Lände

Stomach has been serving seriously good food for years, and it only seems to gets better with age. The menu is a healthy mix of meat and vegetarian dishes and features plenty of game when it's in season. The interior is straight out of rural Austria, and its garden, with its overgrown look and uneven cobblestones, has more character than some districts. The name 'Stomach' comes from the rearrangement of the word Tomaschek, the butcher's shop originally located here. Reservations are highly recommended.

SUMMER STAGE
Map pp244-5 *International*
☎ 315 52 02; 09, Rossauer Lände; mains €5-20;
🕐 5pm-1am Mon-Sat, 2pm-1am Sun May-Sep;
U4 Rossauer Lände

A diverse range of restaurants set up shop over the summer months at Summer Stage, a covered area overlooking the Danube Canal near the Rossauer Lände U4 stop. The food ranges from Viennese to Mexican, and the atmosphere is festive. There's a volleyball court and trampolines for use, and regular jazz and classical concerts in the evening.

VEGI RANT Map pp244-5 *Vegetarian*
☎ 407 82 87; 09, Währinger Strasse 57; midday menus €5.50-8, mains €6-10; 🕐 11.30am-9pm Mon-Fri, lunch Sun; U6 Währinger Strasse, tram 40, 41, 42

You get the feeling meals at Vegi Rant are not only nutritional for the body but also good for the soul. The salad buffet is a health-food buff's heaven, and the food shop next door is well stocked with natural remedies and all sorts of goodies.

CHEAP EATS
AMERLINGBEISL Map pp244-5 *Beisl*
☎ 526 16 60; 07, Stiftgasse 8; midday menus from €5, mains €4.50-8; 🕐 9am-2am; U2, U3 Volkstheater, bus 48A

Amerlingbeisl is one of the better restaurants in cobblestoned Spittalberg. It attracts a young crowd, eager to take advantage of the cheap menu and relatively cheap beer. On balmy nights the roof slides back for those able to cram into the rear courtyard.

AROMAT Map pp246-7 *Beisl*
☎ 913 24 53; 04, Margareten Strasse 52; menus €5-7, mains around €5; 🕐 11am-midnight Mon-Sat; bus 59A

There are so many good things about Aromat it's hard to know where to start. OK, we'll try

Eating – Inside the Gürtel

Aromat (opposite)

After a hard night drinking or dancing, greet the dawn at Café Drechsler where you'll rub shoulders with traders at the Naschmarkt. It's no surprise that the breakfasts here are among the best in the business, but the *Gulasch* also gives other cafés a run for their money.

CAFÉ RÜDIGERHOF Map pp246-7 · *Café*
☎ 586 31 38; 05, Hamburgerstrasse 20; menus €4.60-5.70, mains €4.40-6.60; ⏲ 10am-2am; U4 Kettenbrückengasse

If you're into Jugendstil and 1950s retro, then Rüdigerhof will suit you to a T. The façade is a glorious example of Jugendstil architecture, and the furniture and fittings inside could be straight out of an *I Love Lucy* set. The atmosphere is homely and familiar, the terrace open and sunny (on a good day), and the meals hearty.

CENTIMETRE II Map pp240-3 · *Viennese*
☎ 524 33 29; 07, Stiftgasse 4; all-day menus €4.30-5, mains €3.50-6; ⏲ 10am-2am Mon-Fri, 11am-2am Sat, 11am-midnight Sun; tram 49

Centimetre restaurants (there are five in Vienna; the original is at Lenaugasse 11 in Josef Stadt) have a unique ordering system for their breads with spreads: €0.10 per centimetre for cold toppings and 0.15€ for warm. The menu is also full of *Schnitzel* and *Eier-knockerl* (egg noodles), which generally come in portions too large to finish. Centimetre II backs onto Spittalberg, a small confluence of cobblestone streets lined with art shops, bars and restaurants.

CHANG · *Asian*
Map pp248-9; ☎ 961 92 12; 04, Waaggasse 1; mains €5.70-7; ⏲ lunch & dinner Mon-Sat; tram 62, 65
Map pp238-9; ☎ 269 83 82; 22, Donau-City Strasse 6; mains €5.70-7; ⏲ lunch & dinner Mon-Sat; U1 Kaisermühlen-Vienna International Centre

If you've craving Asian noodles, don't plan on dining anywhere else but Chang. The selection is simply great, the noodles are cooked with expertise and flair, and everything on the menu is also available to take away. Chang's setup sticks to the school of modern Asian diners in Vienna: bright, uncomplicated, open and highly relaxed. The Donau-City location is often full to bursting point with UN staff.

DIE GROSSMUTTER KOCHT
Map pp240-3 · *African*
☎ 523 55 28; 07, Fasszziehergasse 1; midday menus €4, mains around €5; ⏲ lunch & dinner; U2, U3 Volkstheater, bus 48A

the food first: going with whatever's fresh at the Naschmarkt that day, the chefs will concoct a menu of imaginative dishes that will easily please. Next comes atmosphere: dining here is like attending your best friend's dinner party. Staff members are so friendly and relaxed you could join them in the kitchen and they probably wouldn't bat an eyelid. They don't take reservations so it's first come first served, and with seating for around 30 people, don't be surprised to find it full.

BAGEL STATION Map pp240-3 · *Fast Food*
☎ 208 08 94; 06, Capistrangasse 10; bagels €1.50-4; ⏲ 7am-9pm Mon-Fri, 9am-9pm Sat, 10am-6pm Sun; U3 Neubaugasse
☎ 276 30 88; 09, Währinger Strasse 2-4; bagels €1.50-4; ⏲ 7am-9pm Mon-Fri, 9am-9pm Sat, 10am-6pm Sun; U2 Schottentor

It's been a long time coming, but finally the bagel has made a comeback in Vienna (it was invented here in 1683 after the second Turkish siege). These bright, bold bagel stations deal in bagel-and-coffee combos to go, and have plenty of weekly specials. Bagels range from classic cream cheese to the New Yorker, a bagel jammed with almost every conceivable filling. Or you could just create your own combination. Coffee with soy milk is also available.

CAFÉ DRECHSLER Map pp240-3 · *Café*
☎ 587 85 80; 06, Linke Wienzeile 22; mains €4.70-5.50; ⏲ 3am-8pm Mon-Fri, 3am-6pm Sat; U4 Kettenbrückengasse

'Grandmother Cooks' is unlike any other place in Vienna. For starters, it serves African cuisine (42 different choices to be exact), diners sit on the floor, tables and cutlery are optional, and the wait can long or short. But you can be assured the atmosphere will be lively and buzzing.

DO-AN Map pp240-3 *Café*
☎ 585 82 53; 04, Naschmarkt 412; breakfast €4-6, salads €4.60-6.60; ☽ 8am-10pm; U4 Kettenbrückengasse

Of all the places to breakfast on a Saturday morning in the Naschmarkt, Do-An is among the best. The range available is extensive and encompasses the globe, except for the English feast, which is glaringly absent (some would argue the American version makes up for it, however). Like Deli Naschmarkt (see p128), it's a fish bowl, with huge windows and not much else holding up the ceiling. Great for people watching but hellish if you're a shy diner. Occasional DJs spin tunes in the evenings.

GOVINDA Map pp240-3 *Indian/Vegetarian*
☎ 522 28 17; 07, Lindengasse 2a; all-day menus €5; ☽ 10am-6.30pm Mon-Fri, 10am-2pm Sat; tram 49

Discuss the meaning of life and the existence of God at Govinda, a Hare-Krishna-run restaurant-cum-esoteric shop one street north of Mariahilfer Strasse. It specialises in heavenly meatless Indian curries just right for the Viennese palate: not too spicy, not too bland. Takeaway meals are also available.

LA GONDOLA Map pp240-3 *Italian*
☎ 526 40 02; 07, Burggasse 15; pizza €4.50-8; ☽ 11.30am-midnight; U2, U3 Volkstheater; bus 48A

If you're looking for a pizza – any kind of pizza – in the Spittalberg area then La Gondola is your place. The range is quite extensive, and doesn't stick to Italian classics – you won't find too many curry or Hawaiian toppings on pizzas in Naples. The interior décor, a colourful, cheerful and uneven work reminiscent of Hundertwasser, makes great use of broken and discarded tiles.

BREAKFAST CLUB
Map pp240-3 *International*
☎ 581 26 92; 05, Schleifmühlgasse 12-14; breakfasts €3.40-5; ☽ 6am-2pm Wed-Fri, 6am-3pm Sat & Sun; bus 59A

Mix and match from an international range of breakfasts at the Breakfast Club, a compact New York–style breakfast joint on lively Schleifmühlgasse. Kids will love it: there's a small bar especially designed for the little ones, and a separate menu too.

WEGENSTEIN Map pp246-7 *Beisl*
☎ 526 78 82; 07, Lerchenfelder Strasse 73; daily menus €4.45, mains €5-10; ☽ 8am-midnight Mon-Fri; tram 46

Photos from yesteryear, well-used farming tools on wood-panelled walls and wrought-iron touches help make Wegenstein a special *Beisl* in city full of them. The authenticity extends to the menu: *Schnitzel*, *Schweinsbraten*, *Knödel*, it's all here. The only thing that seems out of place is the Guinness on tap.

ZU DEN ZWEI LIESLN Map pp246-7 *Beisl*
☎ 523 32 82; 07, Burggasse 63; mains €4.40-8; ☽ 10am-10pm Mon-Sat; bus 48A

Legend has it that some customers at Zu den Zwei Liesln, who range from students to celebrities, have been consumed by their *Wiener Schnitzel* rather than the other way around. And when you receive the *riesige* (huge) portions it's half-believable. This thoroughly authentic *Beisl* is among the best in the business, and its courtyard is a popular spot on warm summer days and evenings.

OUTSIDE THE GÜRTEL

While the outer districts do not have the wealth of quality restaurants that you'll find in the Innere Stadt or the variety of places that exist just outside this region, the area we've classed as 'Outside the Gürtel' is by no means a culinary wasteland. Little gems are scattered throughout the expanse of Vienna's largest districts, and hunting them down can prove to be a highly rewarding experience. Worthy of special note is not one restaurant but an entire neighbourhood – 'Little Turkey' – which is centred on the bustling Brunnenmarkt (see the boxed text on p166) in the 16th district. Here Turkish bakeries and restaurants flourish through the patronage of Vienna's Turkish community and the many Viennese who flock here to sample the authentic cuisine.

FAVORITEN

TICHY Map pp248-9 *Ice-cream Parlour*
☎ 604 44 46; 10, Reumannplatz 13; ice cream from €1.50; ☽ 10am-11pm mid-Mar–Sep; U1 Reumannplatz

Viennese migrate from every district just to get their hands on Tichy's ice cream, in particular its strawberry variety. That's saying something considering ice-cream parlours are everywhere and the Viennese are notoriously lazy.

SIMMERING

SCHLOSS CONCORDIA

Map pp238-9   *Austrian*

☎ 769 88 88; 11, Simmeringer Hauptstrasse 283;
mains around €10; ⏱ 10am-1am; tram 71, 72

Concordia hasn't much in common with your
classic palace, but its overgrown garden, bare
wooden floors, gargantuan mirrors and stained-
glass roof do exude a substantial air of regality.
The large stone Jesus statue that greets prospect-
ive diners only adds to its ambience. *Schnitzel* is
the name of the game here, and although the
menu reads like a list from the abattoir, there is
a smattering of vegetarian options.

HIETZING

CAFÉ DOMMAYER Map pp246-7   *Café*

☎ 877 73 70-26; 13, Auhofstrasse 2; mains €6-13;
⏱ 7am-midnight; U4 Hietzing, tram 58

It was here in Dommayer that Johann Strauss
Junior first performed in 1844, and classical
music continues to fill this noble café: live
piano music or ensemble can be heard every
Saturday from 2pm to 4pm. The arts don't stop
there, however – at 5pm every third Sunday
of the month from May to September various
theatre companies perform on stage in the
café's large garden.

Like any respectable Viennese *Kaffeehaus*,
the selection of international and local newspapers is quite outstanding.

CAFÉ GLORIETTE Map pp246-7   *Café*

☎ 879 13 11; 13, Gloriette; snacks €6-8;
⏱ 9am-1am; U4 Schönbrunn, Hietzing

Café Gloriette occupies the Gloriette, a neoclassical construction high on a hill behind
Schloss Schönbrunn, built for the pleasure of
Maria Theresia in 1775. With sweeping views
of the Schloss, its magnificent gardens and the
districts to the north, Gloriette has arguably
one of the best vistas in all of Vienna. And it's
a welcome pit stop after the short but sharp
climb up the hill.

RUDOLFSHEIM-FÜNFHAUS

HAPPY BUDDHA Map pp246-7   *Chinese*

☎ 893 42 17; 15, Mariahilfer Gürtel 9; midday buffets
€5.70, mains €5-12; ⏱ lunch & dinner; U6 Gumpendorfer Strasse, tram 6, 18

Happy Buddha doesn't have the most appealing location on a busy corner on the Gürtel, but
it's what's inside that counts. The kitchen churns
out excellent Cantonese dishes, but the highlight of the menu is its dim sum, which is legendary in Vienna. Kids will love it here too: there's a
room set aside as a children's play room.

DÖBLING

SALETTL Map pp244-5   *Austrian*

☎ 479 22 22; 19, Hartäckerstrasse, 80; mains €6.40-8;
⏱ 6.30am-1.30am; bus 40A

Salettl has one of the most appealing gardens
in the outer districts, with views of the Wienerwald northwest of Vienna. It's the perfect place
for breakfast – the diverse range is served from
6.30am to 2pm – but it's just as fine for a quiet
drink on a hot summer evening.

CHEAP EATS

ETAP Map pp244-5   *Turkish*

☎ 406 04 78; 16, Neulerchenfelder Strasse 13-15;
midday menus €5-6.50, mains €3.50-11; ⏱ 10.30am-
midnight Sun-Thu, until 2am Fri & Sat; U6 Josefstädterstrasse, tram J

Etap might not have Kent's (see below) garden or its popularity, but it certainly has its
authenticity and heavenly Turkish cuisine. The
open buffet (€9), on Friday and Saturday, will
have you spending all day inside, sampling
the fresh dishes and sweet desserts one after
the other.

KENT Map pp244-5   *Turkish*

☎ 405 91 73; 16, Brunnengasse 67; mains €3-9;
⏱ 6am-2am; U6 Josefstädterstrasse, tram J

Kent has been leading the Turkish restaurant
pack for years, but has only recently dropped
off the pace slightly, probably due to its incredible popularity. Still, it's a wonderful eatery with
plenty of plus points, such as a huge summer
garden, excellent kebabs, pizzas and breakfasts Turkish-style and a plethora of takeaway
meals. On a Friday night you'd think half of
Vienna's Turkish population comes to play cards
in the back room.

For late-night desserts (or indeed midday
ones), try the bakery next door, which has

135

highly practical opening times for sweet-tooth affiliates: 24-hours a day, seven days a week.

QUELL Map pp246-7 *Beisl*
☎ 893 24 07; 15, Reindorfgasse 19; mains €5-11; 🕑 11am-midnight Mon-Fri; bus 12A, 57A

Quell is very much a locals' haunt, situated in a neighbourhood far removed from the open-air museum that is the Innere Stadt. A smattering of German would be helpful in this typically Viennese *Beisl*: the menu is full to the brim with Viennese specialities.

WORLD RESTAURANT
Map pp246-7 *International*
☎ 0699 11 30 28 07; 16, Hofferplatz 5; midday menus from €4.40, mains €5-12; 🕑 lunch & dinner Mon-Fri, dinner Sat; tram 46

Tucked away in an unassuming, residential area of the 16th district is the superb World Restaurant. Most dishes on the menu are a harmonious mix of Sri Lankan and Caribbean cuisine, but you'll also find Austrian offerings. Sri Lankan and Caribbean, you ask? That equates to curries, fish specialities and plenty of vegetarian choices.

Entertainment

Bars & Pubs	139
Heurigen	144
Clubs	146
Live Music	147
Opera & Classical Music	149
Theatre & Dance	152
Cinema	153
Sports	155
Football	155
Horse Racing	155
Health & Fitness	155
Boating	156
Climbing	156
Cycling	156
Golf	156
Gyms	156
Hiking	156
Ice Skating	156
In-line Skating	157
Skiing	157
Swimming	157

Entertainment

Vienna's reputation as a classical music mecca is without equal. The streets, rather than the hills, are alive with the sound of music: it's not uncommon to hear classically trained singers, or even harp players, busking on Kärntner Strasse and Graben. The program of musical events is unceasing, and Mozart lookalikes roam the streets, accosting tourists in the main thoroughfares of the Innere Stadt with tickets to all manner of concerts.

But Vienna's entertainment options are by no means limited to classical music and opera. The Viennese have a penchant for first-rate jazz, rock and ethnic sounds, and world-class DJs are frequent guests at the more progressive clubs. They also don't mind sinking a few brews; the bar scene has seen a much-needed injection of hip, stylish *Lokale* (pubs or bars) in the past 10 years. OK, so the scene isn't massive, but what it lacks in size it certainly makes up in quality. Sports-wise, the Viennese are more into relaxing than exerting the body too much. Swimming is by far the favourite sporting pastime; pools are scattered throughout the city and, come the heat of summer, the Donauinsel and Alte Donau are crawling with locals vying for the best shade and the flattest ground to spread their towel on.

The distinction between bar and restaurant, and bar and club, is quite often blurred in Vienna. Don't dismiss a place because of the label above the door: many restaurants are just as good for a night out as the bars listed

Busker on Kärntner Strasse (p57)

here, and more and more bars are catering for a crowd wanting to push back the tables and dance the night away. This also applies to coffee houses, which feature in the Eating chapter (see p115). These very Viennese institutions aren't bursting at the seams with energy, but they are fine places to relax and share a drink and a chat.

The best source of information for what's on when is the weekly *Falter*. It's your one-stop rag for everything in the city, with music listings covering every genre, cinema schedules, clubbing, children's and sporting events. Its website, www.falter.at, is just as informative. Both are in German only, but the listings are fairly simple to decipher. *City*, which is basically the *Falter* on a diet, is another weekly events paper, but nowhere near as comprehensive. FM4 (103.8FM), a local radio station, has the lowdown on events in English at various times throughout the day. The tourist office produces a monthly listing of events covering theatre, concerts, film festivals, spectator sports, exhibitions and more; see also its seasonal magazine, *Vienna Scene*.

Vienna is one of the safest cities in the world, so if you have the urge to walk home after a night out don't think twice about it. To be on the safe side, however, avoid the Prater at night, along with Mexikoplatz, which are well known for their drug trade.

Tickets & Reservations

BUNDESTHEATERKASSEN Map pp240-3

☎ 514 44-7880; www.bundestheater.at, German only; 01, Hanuschgasse 3; ⏰ 8am-6pm Mon-Fri, 9am-noon Sat & Sun; U1, U2, U4 Karlsplatz, Karlsplatz trams

The state ticket office only sells tickets to federal venues: Akademietheater, Burgtheater, Schauspielhaus, Staatsoper and Volksoper. The office charges no commission, and tickets for the Staatsoper and Volksoper are available here one month prior to the performance. Credit cards are accepted and credit-card purchases can be made by telephone (☎ 513 15 13; 10am-9pm; English spoken). Alternatively, you can book your tickets over the Internet.

JIRSA THEATER KARTEN BÜRO
Map pp246-7

☎ 400 600; http://viennaticket.at; 08, Lerchenfelder Strasse 12; ⏰ 9.30am-5.30pm Mon-Fri; tram 46, bus 13A

Jirsa is one of the larger ticketing offices in the city (there are around 20 in total). Tickets for a range of performances and venues are sold here, but you might be charged commission (some places add 20% to 30%).

WIEN-TICKET PAVILLON Map pp240-3

01, Herbert-von-Karajan-Platz; ⏰ 10am-7pm; U1, U2, U4 Karlsplatz

This ticket booth, housed in the hut by the Oper, is linked to the city government and charges either no commission or up to 6%. Tickets for all venues are sold here.

WEBSITES

Ticketline (www.ticketline.cc) Extensive online ticketing agent, covering the whole entertainment spectrum; in German only.

ClubTicket (www.clubticket.at) Another comprehensive online ticket agent, also with last-minute deals; in German only.

BARS & PUBS

Despite its rather old-fashioned image, Vienna is a place where you can party all night. And unlike some other capital cities, you don't have to spend a lot of money in bars and pubs to stay up until the early morning hours. Venues are by no means limited to the Innere Stadt; in fact, many of the city's best bars are located in the outer districts, in areas that have taken off in the past few

Top Five Drinking Places

- **Café Stein** (p141) Just one of those bars that everyone can agree to meet at
- **Kleines Café** (p142) A tiny *Lokal* (bar) with lots of heart and a reminder of Vienna's heady, bohemian *fin-de-siècle* days
- **Palmenhaus** (p143) The most gorgeous location in town: inside a Jugendstil (Art-Nouveau) palm house
- **rhiz** (p143) How a bar should be: relaxed, welcoming and cool without even trying
- **Schikaneder** (p143) An unpretentious student haunt and a favourite of the arty crowd, plus movies to boot

years. In particular, you'll find a concentration of trendsetting bars to the north and south of the Naschmarkt, around Spittalberg (many of these double as restaurants) and along the Gürtel (mainly around the U6 stops of Josefstädter Strasse and Nussdorfer Strasse). The Bermuda Dreieck (Bermuda Triangle), near the Danube Canal in the Innere Stadt, was for a long time the heart of Vienna's nightlife scene. It has recently fallen on hard times, and although there are still a few bars in the area, the atmosphere is more often than not quite flat.

Keeping cool in the summer heat is a major consideration, and fortunately the majority of bars have outdoor seating. The area around the U1 Donauinsel U-Bahn station, known as Copa Kagrana and Sunken City, comes alive with outdoor bars and clubs over the summer months. It's quite a tacky affair, but it can be a lot of fun. Summer Stage (see p132) and the Alte AKH (see p140) also wage war against the threat of melting indoors.

Getting home after a night out is not a major hassle; see the Public Transport section in the Directory chapter (p200) for details on the city's night buses.

A BAR SHABU Map pp244-5

☎ 0664 460 24 41; 02, Rotensterngasse 8; ⏰ 9pm-until late Tue-Sat, 1pm-11pm Sun; bus 5A

Shabu is the highlight of Leopoldstadt's nightlife scene – a bar outfitted in '70s retro. Regular DJs provide an excellent backdrop of calming tunes, and the absinthe selection from around Europe is extensive. Don't miss the Japanese room, or should we say closet.

Entertainment – Bars & Pubs

ALT WIEN Map pp240-3

☎ 512 52 22; 01, Bäckerstrasse 9; ☺ 10am-2am Sun-Thu, 10am-4am Fri & Sat; U1, U3 Stephansplatz, bus 1A, 2A

Alt Wien is a rather dark coffee house, attracting students and arty types. At night it becomes a lively drinking venue, partially due to the cheap *Krügerl* (500mL of beer). Food is available; the *Gulasch* (goulash) is particularly good.

ALTE AKH Map pp244-5

09, Alser Strasse/Spitalgasse; Tram 5, 33, 43, 44

The Alte AKH, the city's original hospital, now houses a university campus. In summer, the main tree-shaded courtyard hosts a number of bars, which are a welcome alternative to staying in the hot and stuffy indoors. A few remain open year-round, and in December a small *Christkindlmarkt* (Christmas market) takes pride of place in the courtyard; expect kitschy stalls and plenty of *Glühwein* (mulled wine).

AMERICAN BAR Map pp240-3

☎ 512 32 83; 01, Kärntner Durchgang 10; ☺ noon-4am summer, noon-4am Sun-Wed, noon-5am Thu-Sat winter; U1, U3 Stephansplatz

The American Bar also goes by the name Loos-Bar, as it was designed by the one-and-only Adolf Loos in 1908. It's basically a small box with enough room to fit about 20 people in comfortably, but the mirrored walls help to trick you into thinking it's much larger. The cocktails on offer are some of the city's best.

B72 Map pp244-5

☎ 409 21 28; www.b72.at, German only; 08, Hernalser Gürtel 72; ☺ 8pm-4am; U6 Alser Strasse, tram 43, 44

B72 is a classic Gürtel bar, with large glass walls, arched brickwork and an alternative audience. Live bands feature three to four times a month, and a wide spectrum of music is selected by regular DJs. Expect to pay an entrance fee when bands are playing or events are staged; otherwise there's no charge to prop up the bar.

BAR ITALIA LOUNGE Map pp240-3

☎ 585 28 38; 06, Mariahilfer Strasse 19-21; ☺ noon-2.30pm & 6.30pm-3am Mon-Fri, 6.30pm-3am Sat & Sun; U2 Museumsquartier

This place is two bars in one: on the ground floor is Bar Italia, the perfect place for an evening glass of wine or a quick espresso; down in the basement is the Lounge, where a mix of folk drink, dance and party the night away.

BLAUSTERN Map pp244-5

☎ 369 65 64; 19, Döblinger Gürtel 2; ☺ 7am-1am Mon-Thu, 7am-2am Fri, 8am-2am Sat, 9am-1am Sun; U6 Nussdorfer Strasse, tram 37, 38

Blaustern comes from the same mould as Café Stein, attracting a student base during the day and white-collar workers in the evening. The difference here, however, is the two groups mix together without a hitch. The students are invariably from the nearby Economics University. During the day it's quiet, but come night-time it fills up quickly with chattering people. Try the Blaustern coffee, roasted on the premises.

BLUE BOX Map pp246-7

☎ 523 26 82; 07, Richtergasse 8; ☺ 6pm-2am Mon, 10am-2am Tue-Thu & Sun, 10am-4am Fri & Sat; U3 Neubaugasse, bus 13A

Don't let the smoke and the run-down appearance of Blue Box put you off. These trademarks, which seem to have been around for generations, are an integral part of the Blue Box experience. It's too small to afford dance-floor space, and most guests groove to the regular DJ beats in their seats. Superb breakfasts are available from 10am to 5pm Tuesday to Sunday.

BRICKS Map pp244-5

☎ 216 37 01; 02, Taborstrasse 38; ☺ 8pm-4am; tram N, 21

Bricks calls itself a 'lazy dance-bar' – which conjures up images of elderly couples circling to easy-listening standards – but that's probably one of the most inaccurate descriptions imaginable. This unpretentious cellar-bar is well known for its loud sounds, late-night/early-morning drinking and mixed crowd. DJs and dancing are regular sights at Bricks.

CAFÉ ANZENGRUBER Map pp240-3

☎ 587 82 97; 04, Schleifmühlgasse 19; ☺ 11am-2am Mon-Sat; bus 59A

This corner café attracts an arty crowd and many of Vienna's jazz musicians. Both the décor and atmosphere are laid-back, and the food, which has a distinct Croatian slant, is highly recommended. There's also a pool table.

CAFÉ BERG Map pp244-5

☎ 319 57 20; 09, Berggasse 8; ☺ 10am-1am; U2 Schottentor, Schottentor trams, bus 40A

With some of the nicest staff in Vienna, a lovely, open layout and all-round friendly vibe, it's no wonder Café Berg is often full with a gay and straight crowd. Its bookshop, **Löwenherz** (☺ 10am-7pm Mon-Fri, 10am-5pm Sat), stocks a grand collection of gay magazines and books.

CAFÉ SAVOY Map pp246-7

☎ 586 73 48; 06, Linke Wienzeile 36; 5pm-2am Mon-Fri, 9am-2am Sat; U4 Kettenbrückengasse

Café Savoy is an old gay haunt that has a more traditional café feel to it, except for the feathers everywhere. The clientele is generally very mixed on a Saturday – mainly due to the proximity of the Naschmarkt – but at other times it's full of men of all ages.

CAFÉ STEIN Map pp240-3

☎ 319 72 41; 09, Währinger Strasse 6-8; ☉ 7am-1am Mon-Sat, 9am-1am Sun; U2 Schottentor, Schottentor trams

During the day this three-level café is a popular haunt of students from the nearby university; come evening the clientele metamorphoses into city workers with a lot more money to spend. DJs control the decks in the evenings, and the all-day menu is extensive. During the summer there is outside seating, which allows you to enjoy superb views of the Votivkirche.

CAFÉ WILLENDORF Map pp246-7

☎ 587 17 89; 06, Linke Wienzeile 102; ☉ 6pm-2am; U4 Pilgramgasse, bus 13A

This is one of Vienna's seminal gay and lesbian bars. Housed in the pink Rosa Lila Villa (see p205), it's a very popular place to meet for a chat, a drink or a meal. The lovely garden/inner courtyard opens for the summer months.

CHELSEA Map pp244-5

☎ 407 93 09; www.chelsea.co.at, German only; 08, Lerchenfelder Gürtel 29-31; ☉ 6pm-4am Mon-Sat, 4pm-3am Sun; U6 Thaliastrasse, tram 46

Chelsea is the old dog of the Gürtel scene and very much an alternative haunt. There's a DJ spinning loud sounds (usually indie, sometimes techno) and live bands weekly, attracting a crowd usually dressed to blend into the dark surroundings. On Sunday and one other time during the week (more if the Champions league is under way) you can sit and sip your Guinness or Kilkenny and watch TV coverage of English premier league football with expats and locals alike.

CLUB U Map pp240-3

☎ 505 99 04; 04, Künstlerhauspassage; ☉ 10pm-2am Thu & Sun, 10pm-4am Fri & Sat; U1, U2, U4 Karlsplatz

Gay & Lesbian Options

- **Café Berg** (p140) It's hard to find a friendlier place in town than this open café
- **Café Savoy** (p141) All the atmosphere of a traditional Viennese café, with a little pizzazz thrown into the mix
- **Café Willendorf** (p141) One of the most frequented bars in Vienna, inside the Rosa Lila Villa
- **Orlando** (p143) Lesbian-owned and -run restaurant-bar with excellent food and loads of ambience
- **Frauencafé** (p142) Strictly women-only and a peaceful sanctuary

Club U occupies one of Otto Wagner's Stadtbahn Pavillons on Karlsplatz (see p94). It's a small, student-infested place with top DJs and a wonderful outdoor seating area in the summer months.

DAS MÖBEL Map pp240-3

☎ 524 94 97; 08, Burggasse 10; ☉ 10am-1am; U2, U3 Volkstheater, bus 48A

Das Möbel is the place to pick up something a little unusual for the sitting room or kitchen – it stocks furniture produced by local designers, and it's all for sale (check out their funky bags near the door, too). It's frequented by a relaxed crowd who tend to spend the evening chatting over a couple of drinks. One hint: avoid the food.

DONAU Map pp240-3

☎ 523 81 05; 07, Karl-Schweighofer-Gasse 10; 8pm-4am Mon-Sat, 8pm-2am Sun; U2 Museumsquartier, tram 49

The arched hall of a former synagogue now houses Donau, a bar devoted to the dance movement. Techno, hip-hop, drum n' bass, house – it's all here to be had on various nights of the week. It's not well marked, however – look for an inconspicuous blue door on the Museums-Quartier side of Karl-Schweighofer-Gasse.

EUROPA Map pp246-7

☎ 526 33 83; 07, Zollergasse 8; ☉ 9am-5am; U3 Neubaugasse, bus 13A

Europa is a place to spend all day entertaining yourself: enjoy a meal during the day, a drink in the evening and then dance all night until the early morning. It's also a fine place to kick back and read the papers, and it serves up a mean hangover breakfast between 9am and 3pm on weekends.

Entertainment – Bars & Pubs

FIRST FLOOR Map pp240-3
☎ 533 78 66; 01, Seitenstettengasse 5; ⏰ 7pm-4am Mon-Sat, 8pm-3am Sun; U1, U4 Schwedenplatz, Schwedenplatz trams

Choose from more than 100 cocktails and enjoy the 1930s interior, aquarium and eclectic crowd at First Floor, one of the few bars in the Bermuda Dreieck with any semblance of style.

FRAUENCAFÉ Map pp240-3
☎ 406 37 54; 05, Lange Gasse 8; ⏰ 6.30pm-2am Tue-Sat, tram 46

This long-established café/bar is a popular place in the lesbian scene and is strictly women-only. It has a homely, relaxed feel and is located away from the hub of gay and lesbian bars around the Rosa Lila Villa.

FUTUREGARDEN BAR & ART CLUB
Map pp246-7
☎ 585 26 13; 06, Schadekgasse 6; ⏰ 7pm-2am Mon-Sat, 9pm-2am Sun; U3 Neubaugasse, bus 13A, 14A

With white walls, an open bar and basic furniture, it's hard to find a simpler place in Vienna. Its one piece of decoration – apart from the occasional art exhibition by local artists – is its rectangular disco 'ball', which swings from the ceiling. Futuregarden attracts a 30s to 40s crowd eager to soak up the buzzing atmosphere and listen to DJs spinning soothing sounds.

HOLD Map pp244-5
☎ 405 1198; 08, Josefstädter Strasse 50; ⏰ 8am-11pm Mon-Fri, 9am-11pm Sat; tram J

This narrow wine bar is a little slice of Italy in Josefstadt. The wine selection is heavily Italian-influenced, as are the sandwiches and snacks that so many of the clientele nibble away on. The breakfast is also highly regarded.

KLEINES CAFÉ Map pp240-3
01, Franziskanerplatz 3; ⏰ 10am-2am Mon-Sat, 1pm-2am Sun; U1, U3 Stephansplatz

As the German name suggests, Kleines (small) Café is indeed tiny. But what it lacks in size it makes up for with oodles of bohemian atmosphere, excellent midday menus and wonderful summer outdoor seating on Franziskanerplatz. It also featured in the movie *Before Sunrise*.

KUNSTHALLE CAFÉ Map pp240-3
☎ 586 98 64; 04, Treitlstrasse 2; mains €6-10; ⏰ 10am-2am; U1, U2, U4 Karlsplatz

It might be a little subdued at times, but the Kunsthalle Café certainly carries plenty of 'cool' clout, especially considering it shares its glass-

Kunsthalle Café (below)

box premises with the Kunsthalle Project Space (see p93). In summer, its large wooden terrace is packed to overflowing with all manner of creatures from Vienna's art scene, and hopefully one day soon the billboards surrounding the café will be pulled down to let in the sights and sounds of the city.

LO:SCH Map pp246-7
☎ 895 99 79; 15, Fünfhausgasse 1; ⏰ 10pm-2am Fri & Sat; U6 Gumpendorfer Strasse, bus 57A

This leather-fetish bar is normally strictly men only, but occasionally it hosts unisex parties on Saturday nights. Lo:sch sometimes opens during the week for special events.

MANGO BAR Map pp240-3
☎ 587 44 48; 06, Laimgrubengasse 3; ⏰ 9pm-4am; U4 Kettenbrückengasse, bus 57A

Mango attracts a young, often men-only gay crowd with good music, friendly staff and plenty of mirrors to check the hair. It usually serves as a kick-start for a big night out on the town.

MÁS! Map pp244-5
☎ 403 83 24; 08, Laudongasse 36; ⏰ 6pm-2am; tram 5, 33

This stylish cocktail bar is comfortable and cosy, with large helpings of 'cool'. It's frequented by an affluent set keen to sample the fine cocktails, which are half-price between 6pm and 8pm daily. Its Sunday brunch – a mix of Cajun, English and American breakfasts – is legendary. Beware the bar stools: they can be deceptively wobbly.

ONYX-BAR Map pp240-3
☎ 535 39 69; 01, Stephansplatz 12, Haas-Haus; ☽ 9am-2am Mon-Sat; U1, U3 Stephansplatz
The Onyx-Bar is a favourite haunt of the upper echelons of Vienna's society and, although the atmosphere can be stifling, the location – right on Stephansplatz with superb views of Stephansdom – is a big selling point.

ORLANDO Map pp246-7
☎ 967 35 50; 06, Mollardgasse 3; ☽ 5pm-1am Sun-Thu, 6pm-2am Fri & Sat; U4 Pilgramgasse, bus 13A, 14A
The lesbian-owned and -run Orlando is a great little bar-restaurant that welcomes all walks of life. Many just come for the food, while others love to lounge in the bar's soft ambience and either partake of a bit of people-watching or pursue a more active night out.

PALAIS BAR Map pp248-9
☎ 798 45 15; www.palais-schwarzenberg.com; 03, Schwarzenbergplatz 9; ☽ 10am-1pm; tram D
Stop in at the Hotel im Palais Schwarzenberg's sophisticated bar for a cool martini before or after the opera. It'll make you feel like you're living in the lap of luxury. Guys will feel more at home wearing a tie.

PALMENHAUS Map pp240-3
☎ 533 10 33; Burggarten; ☽ 10am-2am, closed Mon & Tue Nov-Mar; U1, U2, U4 Karlsplatz, bus 3A
The Palmenhaus occupies one of the most attractive locations in Vienna. It's housed in a beautifully renovated palm house, complete with high arched ceilings, glass walls and steel beams. The crowd is generally well-to-do, but the ambience is often relaxed and welcoming to all walks of life. The outdoor seating in summer is a must, and there are occasional club nights. Unfortunately the food is overpriced and often under par.

RHIZ Map pp244-5
☎ 409 25 05; www.rhiz.org; 08, Lerchenfelder Gürtel 37-38; ☽ 6pm-4am Mon-Sat, 6pm-2am Sun; U6 Josefstädter Strasse, tram J, 33
The best of the Gürtel's bunch of bars is rhiz, a bar favouring invariably loud electronic music and guest DJs, and frequented by a large crowd of regulars. Like other bars inhabiting the *Bögen* (arches) of the U6 line, rhiz is all brick and glass. Its outdoor seating is extremely popular in summer; however, be prepared to compete with the noise of Gürtel traffic and U-Bahn overhead. The staff couldn't be friendlier and there's Internet access.

SANTO SPIRITO Map pp240-3
☎ 512 99 98; 01, Kumpfgasse 7; ☽ 6pm-2am Mon-Thu, 6pm-3am Fri, 11am-3pm Sat, 10am-2am Sun; U3 Stubentor, tram 1, 2
It's quite a surprise to walk into a bar and hear classical music, but that's what you get at Santo Spirito. The music, which seems to increase in volume as the night progresses, helps to create a lively atmosphere and attracts a musical and artistic crowd, both straight and gay. In summer, customers spill out onto the cobbled street to take a break from the noise.

SCHIKANEDER Map pp246-7
☎ 585 58 88; 05, Margareten Strasse 22-24; ☽ 6pm-4am; bus 59A
Most of the colour in Schikaneder comes from the regularly projected movies splayed across one of its white walls – the students and arty crowd who frequent this grungy bar dress predominantly in black. But that's not to detract from the bar's atmosphere, which exudes energy well into the wee small hours of the morning. Schikaneder also hosts movies most nights (see p154).

SHEBEEN Map pp246-7
☎ 524 79 00; 07, Lerchenfelder Strasse 45; ☽ 5pm-2am Mon, 5pm-4am Tue-Fri, 1pm-4am Sat, 10am-2am Sun; tram 46
Shebeen is one of the better expat pubs in Vienna, and more often than not it's crowded with Austrians eager to practise their English. The dark wood-panelling and high ceilings are vaguely reminiscent of an English pub, while the boisterous clientele and lashings of beer are undisputedly English. International football and rugby games are regularly shown in the back room.

SHULTZ Map pp246-7
☎ 522 91 20; 07, Siebensterngasse 31; ☽ 9am-2am Mon-Thu, 9am-3am Fri & Sat, 5pm-2am Sun; tram 49
This lovely '60s-style bar mixes wonderful cocktails and attracts a laid-back and unpretentious crowd. During the day the glass walls allow daylight to flood the bar, while at night they provide ample room to watch the world roll on by outside.

SPARK Map pp244-5

☎ 968 57 02; 18, Währinger Gürtel 107; ⊙ 6pm-4am Mon-Fri, 7pm-4am Sat; U6 Währinger Strasse, tram 40, 41
This highly chilled bar is a bit of a trek from the centre of town, but it's well worth the effort. The '70s retro décor and low couches add to the relaxed feel, and its daily dose of DJs is supplemented with monthly live concerts.

TANZCAFÉ JENSEITS Map pp246-7

☎ 587 12 33; 06, Nelkengasse 3; ⊙ 9pm-4am Mon-Sat; U3 Neubaugasse, bus 13A, 14A
Rumour has it Jenseits was formerly a brothel, which is highly plausible considering the kitschy red-velvet interior. It attracts a mainly alternative and arty crowd, and DJs, who perform most nights, quickly fill the tiny dance floor.

TOP KINO BAR Map pp240-3

☎ 585 58 88; 06, Rahlgasse 1; ⊙ 4pm-4am Mon-Sat, 3pm-4am Sun; U2 Museumsquartier, bus 57A
Occupying the foyer of the Top Kino (see p154) is the Top Kino Bar, a pleasantly relaxed place that attracts an alternative crowd. The décor is highly retro, and there are tunes to match the furniture. Kozel, one of the Czech Republic's better Pilsners, is lined up against Austria's finest lagers.

URANIA Map pp240-3

☎ 713 30 66; 01, Uraniastrasse 1; ⊙ 9am-2am Mon-Wed, 9am-3am Thu-Sat, 9am-midnight Sun; tram 1, 2
It seems like an age since renovations of the old Urania cinema began, but they're finally finished. The result is a rejuvenated cinema and this bar-café-restaurant, a glass-and-steel construction occupying a grand spot on the banks of the Danube Canal. Stop by for a coffee during the day, and come back at night for a cocktail from its extensive range.

VOLKSGARTEN PAVILLON Map pp240-3

☎ 532 09 07; 01, Burgring 1; ⊙ 11am-4am Jun-Sep, 10pm-2am Mar-May & Oct; U2, U3 Volkstheater, Volkstheater trams
The second Volksgarten venue (after the Volksgarten club p147) is this 1950s-style pavilion. Its large garden is incredibly popular on a warm evening, with views of the Hofburg and DJs providing a chilled-out atmosphere. Entry is normally free, except for occasional unplugged concerts or garden barbecues.

WIRR Map pp246-7

☎ 929 40 50; 07, Burggasse 70; ⊙ 10am-2am; bus 48A
On weekends it's often hard to find seat – especially on the comfy sofas – at this colourful,

alternative bar. Its rooms are spacious and open, the walls are covered in local artists' work and downstairs is home to one of Vienna's more crowded dance floors. Its small menu reads like a list of international fast-food dishes: burgers, sandwiches, samosas and goulash.

HEURIGEN

The *Heuriger* (wine tavern) tradition in Vienna dates back to the Middle Ages, but it was Joseph II in 1784 who first officially granted producers the right to sell their wine directly from their own premises. It proved to be one of his more enduring reforms. These taverns are now one of Vienna's most popular institutions with visitors.

Heurigen can normally be identified by a green wreath or branch (the *Busch'n*) hanging over the door. Inside you'll find a rustic look you'd expect to see in rural parts of Austria, and outside most *Heurigen* have a large garden or inner courtyard with grapevine shade and picnic tables. *Heurigen* almost invariably serve food: Viennese standards, such as roast pork and dumplings, are the norm. Some also feature traditional live music, perhaps ranging from a solo accordion player to a fully fledged oompah band.

The large majority of *Heurigen* are concentrated around the wine-growing areas to the north, west, northwest and south of the city, but a few are dotted around the inner districts. Grinzing, in the northwest, is the best-known area and a favourite of tour groups and their guides. If you're up for a rowdy night with live music and large crowds, this is the place for you. Most of the *Heurigen* are concentrated along Cobenzlgasse and Sandgasse. Far more rewarding are the *Heurigen* in Nussdorf and on Kahlenberg: the atmosphere is more relaxed and traditional, and the views of the city stupendous. Other *Heuriger* areas in the northwest include Sievering and Neustift am Walde, and further south in the western extremes of Ottakring. To the north across the Danube the neighbourhoods of Strebersdorf and Stammeersdorf produce around 30% of the city's wine, making it Vienna's largest wine-growing district. The *Heurigen* here are far more traditional, and less frequented by tourists. Mauer, a small suburb in the southwest corner of the Liesing district, has another pocket of traditional *Heurigen* that receives few tourists.

ECKERT

☎ 292 25 96; 21, Strebersdorfer Strasse 158; ⌚ from 10am daily every odd month; tram 32

Located in the very northern outskirts of Vienna, Eckert is a *Heuriger* with a difference. Paintings by local artists are regularly featured, and there's live music once a month (anything from jazz to rock and roll).

ESTERHÁZYKELLER Map pp240-3

☎ 533 34 82; 01, Haarhof 1; ⌚ 11am-11pm Mon-Fri, 4-11pm Sat & Sun; U3 Herrengasse, bus 1A

Esterházykeller is one of the few city *Heurigen* to grace the Innere Stadt. Low ceilings and rural decorations create a beautiful interior, and the wine, from the Esterházy Palace cellar in Eisenstadt, is above par. Alongside the usual buffet is a midday menu for €9.50 to €14.50. Unusually for a *Heuriger*, there is beer on tap.

GÖBEL

☎ 294 84 20; 21, Stammersdorfer Kellergasse 151; ⌚ 3-10pm Mon, 11am-10pm Sat & Sun, for other days, call ahead; bus 228, 233

Peter Göbel has managed to combine two of his exceptional talents in this outstanding *Heuriger*: wine making and architectural design. His reds are probably the best in the Vienna area, and his modern take on the traditional *Heuriger* has created a stylish establishment. It's also perfectly located in the vineyards themselves.

HIRT Map pp238-9

☎ 318 96 41; 19, Eisernenhandgasse 165; ⌚ 3pm until late Wed-Fri, from noon Sat & Sun Apr-Oct, noon until late Fri-Sun Nov-Mar; bus 38A

Hirt is a fantastic little *Heuriger* well hidden among the vineyards of Kahlenberg. It has everything going for it: superb views, great food, friendly service and plenty of wine. Hirt is best approached from the top of Kahlenberg; any other way and you're faced with a steep and exhausting uphill climb.

MAYER AM PFARRPLATZ Map pp238-9

☎ 370 12 87; 19, Pfarrplatz 2; ⌚ 4pm-midnight Mon-Sat, from 11am Sun; bus 38A

Mayer is not only a quaint *Heuriger* but it also has a place in the history annals: in 1817 Beethoven called it home. Its large garden is particularly pleasant, and there's live music from 7pm to midnight daily.

REINPRECHT Map pp238-9

☎ 320 14 71; 19, Cobenzlgasse 22; ⌚ 3pm-midnight Mar–mid-Dec; bus 38A

Situated in the heart of the Grinzig *Heuriger* overkill is Reinprecht. It stands out among a rather tacky collection of bushel-bearing establishments for its premiere wines, lively, singalong environment and its massive garden, which is large enough to cope with the bus loads of tourists.

SCHMIDT

☎ 292 66 88; 21, Stammersdorfer Strasse 105; ⌚ 3pm-midnight Thu-Sun, closed Jul; tram 31, bus 30A

Schmidt is another of Stammersdorf's well-established *Heurigen* along Stammersdorfer Strasse. Highlights here include its wonderful Muskateller and Grüner Veltliner, wine tastings of local vintages and, in November, its goose specialities.

SCHREIBERHAUS Map pp238-9

☎ 440 38 44; 19, Rathstrasse 54; ⌚ 11am-1am; bus 35A

To the west of Grinzing (and a few degrees below it in the tacky-tourist levels) is the small wine-growing area of Neustift am Walde and the *Heuriger* Schreiberhaus. It's quite a large place with a fine garden, friendly staff and lively atmosphere.

SIRBU Map pp238-9

☎ 320 59 28; 19, Kahlenberger Strasse 210; ⌚ 3pm-midnight Mon-Sat, Apr–mid-Oct; bus 38A

Like Hirt, Sirbu has far-reaching views across Vienna's urban expanse and a quiet spot in among the vineyards of Kahlenberg. Its wines have reached the pinnacle of Austrian success in recent years, and its garden is the perfect place to while away a sunny afternoon. Because of its lofty location, Sirbu is best approached from the vantage point of Kahlenberg rather than from the neighbourhood of Grinzing.

WEINGUT AM REISENBERG Map pp238-9

☎ 320 93 93; 19, Oberer Reisenbergweg 15; ⌚ 4pm-midnight Mon-Fri, noon-midnight Sat & Sun May-Sep, 6pm-midnight Wed-Sat Oct-Dec, 4pm-midnight Thu & Fri, noon-midnight Sat & Sun Apr; bus 38A

Weingut am Reisenberg offers supreme views over Vienna and a place to escape the busloads of Grinzing. Don't expect to find a rustic *Heuriger*, however – the place and its patrons ooze money. It's a good 10-minute walk up a steep hill just north of Grinzing village; another 20 minutes further up Obere Reisenbergweg is Cobenzl, where you'll find a café and even better views of Vienna.

WEINGUT SCHILLING

☎ 292 41 89; 21, Langenzersdorferstrasse 54;
🕐 4pm–midnight Mon–Fri, from 3pm Sat & Sun even months; tram 32

Wiengut Schilling is located in the small neighbourhood of Strebersdorf, about a 30-minute walk west of Stammersdorf. It has a good reputation for wine and an exceptionally large garden that backs onto its vineyard on the slopes of Bisamberg hill. If you ask nicely, tours of the cellar are available.

WIENINGER

☎ 292 41 06; 21, Stammersdorfer Strasse 78;
🕐 3pm–midnight Wed–Fri, from noon Sat & Sun Mar–mid-Jul & mid-Aug–Dec; tram 31, bus 30A

Of the many *Heurigen* in the Stammersdorf area, Wieninger is classed as one of the finest. This is for several reasons: a lovely, rustic setting, consistently great food and Weingut Wieninger, its own wine label, which is considered among Austria's best.

ZAHEL Map pp238-9

☎ 889 13 18; 23, Maurer Hauptplatz 9;
🕐 3pm–midnight Tue–Sun; tram 60, bus 60A

Zahel is classed as one of the oldest *Heurigen* in Vienna and rates among the best the Mauer area has to offer. It's not situated within the vineyards like some of its Döbling counterparts, but its 250-year-old premises exudes enough traditional ambience to easily make up for that. The wine is of an above-average quality to boot.

ZWÖLF APOSTELKELLER Map pp240-3

☎ 512 67 77; 01, Sonnenfelsgasse 3; 🕐 4.30pm–midnight; U1, U3 Stephansplatz, bus 1A

Even though Zwölf Apostelkeller (Twelve Apostle Cellar) plays it up for the tourists, it still retains plenty of charm, dignity and authenticity. This is mostly due to the premises themselves: a vast, dimly lit multilevel cellar. The atmosphere is often lively and rowdy, helped along by traditional *Heuriger* music from 7pm Wednesday to Friday.

CLUBS

Like the bar scene in Vienna, the club scene has come along in leaps and bounds in the past few years. No longer are night owls restricted to a handful of clubs to keep them occupied until the wee small hours. As most local folk detest queuing, crowded dance

---

Top Five Clubs

- **Flex** (p147) If you visit only one club in town, make it this one
- **Goodmann** (p147) Where hardcore clubbers congregate when the lame clubs close
- **Roxy** (p147) Progressive sounds, fine DJs and not big enough to lose your friends
- **U4** (p147) It might be past its peak, but it still manages to wow the crowds
- **Volksgarten** (p147) One of the larger clubs in town, churning out dance anthems in a superb setting

---

floors and hefty entry prices, clubs are invariably small and fairly intimate, and the massive, bombastic variety is rare.

The dividing line between a club and bar in Vienna is often quite blurred and hard to pick. The following are certainly clubs – places where people congregate to sweat it out on the dance floor – but they're also just as good for a drink, a chat or an ogle. The same rule applies to bars and pubs; some, for instance Europa, Jenseits and Wirr, have small, well-used dance floors. Even rhiz even been known to push back the tables for a bit of a boogie. Entry prices vary wildly – from nothing to €20 – and depend on what's on the decks or, more importantly, who's on the decks.

AUX GAZELLES Map pp240-3

☎ 585 66 45; www.auxgazelles.at; 06, Rahlgasse 5;
🕐 8am–2am Mon–Thu, until 4am Fri & Sat, 10am–9pm Sun; U2 Museumsquartier, bus 57A

This is one of the newest instalments in Vienna's nightlife scene. It's a bizarre mix of restaurant-bar-club that has the punters coming back for more. The theme is thoroughly North African, with a plethora of low, comfy couches, dim lighting, ethnic sounds and even animal skins. Don't turn up in ripped jeans and an AC/DC T-shirt – this place is all about style.

BACH Map pp238-9

☎ 480 19 70; www.bach.co.at; 16, Bachgasse 21;
🕐 9pm–3am Thu–Sat; tram 9, 46

Bach is an underground club located on an unassuming residential street in the far-flung reaches of Ottakring. You'll find the crowd relaxed, the music a mix of fine techno sounds with the occasional live band, and the dance floor small and intimate.

FLEX Map pp244-5

☎ 533 75 25; www.flex.at; 01, Donaukanal, Augartenbrücke; ⏱ 6pm-4am; U2, U4 Schottenring, tram 1, 2, 31

So it looks like a complete dive, the stairwell leading from the U-Bahn stop to its doors constantly reeks of urine, and the circling dealers are an annoyance, but Flex is still the finest club in town. Time after time this uninhibited shrine to music on the Danube Canal puts on great shows and features top DJs from Vienna and abroad. Live bands are also commonly featured. Each night is a different theme, with Dub Club on Monday and London Calling (alternative and indie) on Wednesday among the most popular.

GOODMANN Map pp240-3

☎ 967 44 15; www.goodmann.at; 04, Rechte Wienzeile 23; ⏱ 4am-10am Mon-Sat; U4 Kettenbrückengasse, bus 59A

Goodmann must keep the strangest opening hours of any establishment in Vienna, but no-one seems to care. This is where clubbers go when the clubs close; most come for a snack (food is served until 8am) before heading downstairs to dance until closing.

ROXY Map pp240-3

☎ 961 88 00; www.sunshine.at; 04, Operngasse 24; ⏱ 10pm-until late Tue-Sat; U1, U2, U4 Karlsplatz, bus 59A

Roxy is one of those places that manages to keep pace with Vienna's progressive clubbing scene and often leads the way. Its tiny dance floor is regularly bursting at the seams, and the sounds can be a bit of a lucky dip (ranging from garage to jazz and Brazilian). Unfortunately rumours of an imminent closure are circulating, but let's hope for the best.

SUBZERO Map pp246-7

☎ 0676 544 18 04; www.subzero.at; 07, Siebensterngasse 27/1; ⏱ 9pm-4am Thu, 10pm-4am Fri & Sat; tram 49, bus 13A

This underground club in an old brick cellar is reminiscent of a rabbit's warren. The DJs spin loud, brash drum n' bass, hip-hop, techno and reggae, but there's enough space, and plenty of comfy couches, if you need to escape the noise. It often attracts a very young crowd, however.

TITANIC Map pp240-3

☎ 587 47 58; www.titanicbar.at; 06, Theobaldgasse 11; ⏱ 10pm-4am Wed, until 6am Thu-Sat; U2 Museumsquartier, bus 57A

If you make it past Titanic's random door-check, you'll join a heaving mass of party people in this popular club. Two dance floors compete for your attention, one pumping out Latin grooves and the other mixing it up with funk and hip-hop from the '70s to the present-day.

U4 Map pp246-7

☎ 815 83 07; www.u4club.at; 12, Schönbrunner Strasse 222; ⏱ 10pm-until late; U4 Meidling Hauptstrasse, bus 10A

U4 set the club standard in Vienna for decades, and although it's fallen behind the likes of Flex and Roxy, it still manages to pull loads of eager club-goers. Its two dance floors host an ever-changing mix of music genres, which in turn attracts a diverse range of clientele. 'Heaven', every Thursday night, is an extremely popular night for the gay and lesbian scene, but it's frequented by all walks of life.

VOLKSGARTEN Map pp240-3

☎ 532 42 41; 01, Burgring 1; ⏱ 8pm-5am; U2, U3 Volkstheater, tram D, J, 1, 2

Located in the Volksgarten, it doesn't matter how loud the volume gets at this club – it's never going to disturb the neighbours. It attracts a well-dressed crowd, keen to strut their stuff and scan for talent from the long bar. The quality sound system pumps out an array of music styles, which changes from night to night.

WHY NOT? Map pp240-3

☎ 535 11 58; www.why-not.at; 01, Tiefer Graben 22; ⏱ 10pm-6am Fri-Sat; bus 1A, 3A

Why Not? is one of the few clubs that focuses its attention towards the gay scene. The small club quickly fills up with mainly young guys out for a boogie and as much fun as possible.

LIVE MUSIC

Vienna manages to attract both big-name and new bands, mainly over summer. The yearly repertoire is a healthy mix of jazz, rock (both alternative and mainstream) and ethnic sounds. Posters advertising future concerts are plastered all over the city, so it's easy to pick up on who's in town. And like clubbing advertising, flyers are commonly used to herald up-and-coming concerts. Venues are invariably small and the crowds fairly subdued, making it easy to push your way to the front and not end the night with the wind squeezed out of you. Concerts can cost as little as €5 for local performers (sometimes they're free of charge) or €50 for an internationally acclaimed act. In general, however, most international names will set you back €15 to €25.

Aside from the venues listed below, Flex (p147), rhiz (p143), Chelsea (p141) and B72 (p140) regularly host touring bands. Festivals such as the Donauinsel Fest, JazzFest Wien and Wiesen are also excellent places to catch local and international talent (see p9).

ARENA Map pp248-9
☎ 798 85 95; www.arena.co.at; 03, Baumgasse 80; 🕒 2pm until late summer, from 4pm winter; U3 Erdberg

The music Arena normally hosts – hard rock, metal, rock and a small mix of reggae and soul – is well suited to the industrial zone it's located in. From May to September this former slaughterhouse opens up its outdoor stage to acts, while the rest of the year bands play in one of its two indoor halls. When there are no concerts, Arena often plays films or holds once-a-month all-night parties; 'Iceberg', a German-British 1970s new wave bash, is particularly popular.

CAFÉ CARINA Map pp244-5
☎ 406 43 22; 08, Josefstädter Strasse 84; 🕒 5pm-2am; U6 Josefstädter Strasse, tram J, 33

This small, dingy bar is a surprisingly good venue for live music. Bands don't perform every night, but when they do the crowd is generally enthusiastic and the music, often slanting towards jazz or folk, is powerful and uplifting.

CAFÉ CONCERTO Map pp244-5
☎ 406 47 95; 16, Lerchenfelder Gürtel 53; 🕒 4pm until late Tue-Sat; U6 Josefstädter Strasse, tram J, 33

Directly opposite Café Carina is Concerto, which hosts a plethora of music styles in its basement. It's not the best location for live performances, and the music can sometimes leave a lot to be desired, but it can be fun and chilled.

JAZZLAND Map pp240-3
☎ 533 25 75; www.jazzland.at; 01, Franz-Josefs-Kai 29; 🕒 7pm-2am Mon-Sat; U1, U4 Schwedenplatz, Schwedenplatz trams

Jazzland has been an institution of Vienna's jazz scene for the past 30 years. The music covers the whole jazz spectrum, and the brick venue features a grand mixture of local and international acts.

METROPOL Map pp244-5
☎ 407 77 40; www.wiener-metropol.at, German only; 17, Hernalser Hauptstrasse 55; box office 🕒 10am-8pm Mon-Sat; tram 43

The Metropol is a bit of a musical chameleon: one week might see performances by rock bands, while the next it's Broadway shows, cabaret and folk music. Either way, the shows are often top quality and there's plenty of tables.

MILES SMILES Map pp244-5
☎ 405 95 17; 08, Langegasse 51; 🕒 8pm-2am Sun-Thu, 8pm-4am Fri & Sat; tram J, bus 13A

Taking its name from the one and only Miles Davis, Miles Smiles is a small club with a big heart and plenty of great live jazz acts. Its cosy dance floor is regularly crowded with an audience blissfully lost in the rhythmical music.

PLANET MUSIC Map pp244-5
☎ 332 46 41-0; www.planet.tt; 20, Adalbert-Stifter-Strasse 73; tram N, 31, 33

This strictly rock and thrash music venue is rather dark and divey, but the acoustics aren't bad and the program features some international acts just sliding off the popularity wagon. Located in the northern reaches of Brigittenau, it's not the easiest place to get to.

PORGY & BESS Map pp240-3
☎ 512 88 11; www.porgy.at; 01, Riemergasse 11; 🕒 8pm-4am Mon-Sat, 7pm-4am Sun; U3 Stubentor, bus 1A

Porgy & Bess has finally given up its wanderings and settled down in Riemergasse, which is superb news for jazz aficionados. This is the prime location for modern local and international jazz acts, and the atmosphere and interior are very relaxed and grown-up. DJs are a regular feature on weekends, and Wednesday night sees impromptu jam sessions.

STADTHALLE Map pp246-7
☎ 981 00; www.stadthalle.com; 15, Vogelweidplatz 14; U6 Burggasse/Stadthalle, tram 6, 18

This is the biggest hall for rock concerts, and it usually caters for large, mainstream rock bands and local heroes. Check the posters around town for upcoming shows or check the website.

SZENE WIEN Map pp248-9
☎ 749 33 41; www.szenewien.com; 11, Hauffgasse 26; U3 Zipperstrasse

Szene Wien is an intimate venue that allows you to get up close and personal with whoever's on stage. Concerts cover a broad spectrum of musical tastes, including rock, reggae, funk, jazz and world music. It's a superb place to catch international bands without fighting off the crowds.

TUNNEL Map pp244-5
☎ 405 34 65; www.tunnelvienna.at; 08, Florianigasse 39; ⏰ 9am-2am; tram 5, 33, bus 13A
This established student haunt has been around for donkey's years. Most come for the cheap beer and excellent, inexpensive breakfasts, but its cellar is given over to live music acts and, depending on the day, you'll catch anything from jazz to rock. In November Tunnel hosts the Vienna Blues Festival, which features local and international acts.

WUK Map pp244-5
☎ 40 121-0; www.wuk.at; 09, Währinger Strasse 59; U6 Währinger Strasse, tram 40, 41, 41
WUK (Werkstätten- und Kulturhaus; Workshop and Culture House) is many things to many people. It's basically a space for art (government subsidised but free to pursue an independent course) and hosts a huge array of events in its concert hall. International and local rock acts vie with clubbing nights, classical concerts, film evenings, theatre and even children's shows. H.A.P.P.Y., a regular gay clubbing event, takes place here every second or fourth Friday of the month.

Women's groups, temporary exhibitions and practical skills workshops are also on site, along with a smoky café with a fabulous cobbled courtyard.

OPERA & CLASSICAL MUSIC

There's no doubting Vienna is the world capital of opera and classical music. The rich musical legacy that flows through the city is evident everywhere: the plethora of monuments to its greatest composers and its princely music venues easily outnumber those of some countries, let alone other capital cities. A quick walk down Kärntner Strasse from the Staatsoper to Stephansplatz will turn up more Mozart lookalikes than you care to shake a baton at.

With such a presence in the city, it should be no problem to catch a concert or two on your visit. The only stumbling block might be in obtaining tickets in the more salubrious venues, such as the Staatsoper

and Musikverein; with these, it's advisable to book well ahead. Otherwise just turn up and soak up the atmosphere.

Churches and coffee houses are some of the best, and cheapest, places to hear classical music. Such churches as the Augustinkirche, Minoritenkirche and Burgkapelle often complement Mass on Sunday morning with a full choir and orchestra, and some have regular evening concerts; see the Districts chapter (p47) for more details. Coffee houses featuring live music are mentioned throughout the Eating chapter (p115), otherwise pick up the handy *Wiener Konzert Cafés* (Vienna's Concert Cafés) brochure from the tourist office.

Festivals should also not be overlooked. The KlangBogen Festival and Vienna Festival are highlights on the music calendar, and the Rathausplatz plays host to a film festival of opera and classical concerts in July and August (see p10 for information). Organised performances by amateur music and choir groups are constantly held in various locations throughout city; contact Marketing Tourismus Synergie (☎ 817 41 65-0; mts@mts.co.at; 13, Schloss Schönbrunn) for more information, or check out www.vienna.info/voices-e.html.

Ticket costs vary greatly. Standing room tickets can go for as little as €1, whereas a prime spot at a gala performance in the Staatsoper will set you back €254. Most venues produce a handy map of the seating layout, which is invaluable in choosing the perfect seat to match your budget.

If you're around in 2006 then you're in for a treat. Vienna will celebrate the 250th anniversary of Mozart's birth with a lavish agenda of concerts and performances, which should prove to be quite a spectacle.

HOFBURG Map pp240-3
www.hofburgorchester.at; 01, Heldenplatz; U3 Herrengasse, tram D, J, 1, 2
The Neue Hofburg's sumptuous Festsaal and Redoutensaal are regularly used for Mozart and Strauss concerts, featuring the Hofburg Orchestra and soloists from the Staatsoper and Volksoper. Performances usually start at 8.30pm, and tickets are available from travel agents, hotels and Mozart lookalikes.

KAMMEROPER Map pp240-3
☎ 512 01 0077; www.wienerkammeroper.at; 01, Fleischmarkt 24; box office ⏰ noon-6pm Mon-Fri; U1, U4 Schwedenplatz, Schwedenplatz trams

Vienna Boys' Choir

The Vienna Boys' Choir (Wiener Sängerknaben) is an institution of the city. It is actually four separate choirs; duties are rotated between singing in Vienna, touring the world, resting and perhaps even occasionally going to school. The choir dates back to 1498 when it was instigated by Maximilian I, and at one time it numbered Haydn and Schubert in its ranks. The choir sings every Sunday (except during July and August) at 9.15am in the Burgkapelle (Royal Chapel) in the Hofburg (see p59).

Tickets for seats are €5 to €29 and should be booked around eight weeks in advance (☎ 533 99 27; www.bmbwk. gv.at/hmk, German only). Otherwise try your luck for a last-minute ticket at the Burgkapelle box office from 11am to 1pm and 3pm to 5pm Friday for the following Sunday or immediately before Mass between 8.15am and 8.45am. Standing room is free, and you need to queue by 8.30am to find a place inside the open doors, but you can get a flavour of what's going on from the TV in the foyer.

The choir also sings a mixed program of music in the Musikverein at 4 pm on Friday in May, June, September and October. Tickets range from €35 to €48, and can be purchased from Reisebüro Mondial (Map pp240-3; ☎ 588 04 141, www.mondial.at; 04, Faulmanngasse 4) and hotels in Vienna.

Entertainment – Opera & Classical Music

The Kammeroper ranks as Vienna's third opera house after the Staatsoper and Volksoper. Its small venue is perfect for the lesser-known operas it produces, and over summer the entire company is transported to the Schlosstheater Schönbrunn to continue productions in more opulent surroundings. Standing room tickets go for €5, and students receive a 30% discount on all tickets.

KONZERTHAUS Map pp240-3
☎ 242 002; www.konzerthaus.at; 03, Lothringer-strasse 20; box office ☺ 9am-7.45pm Mon-Fri, 9am-1pm Sat; U4 Stadtpark, bus 4A

The Konzerthaus is a major venue in classical music circles, but throughout the year ethnic music, rock, pop or jazz can also be heard in its hallowed halls. Up to three simultaneous performances, in the Grosser Saal, the Mozart Saal and the Schubert Saal, can be staged. Student tickets are half-price, and it's closed in July and August except when it hosts one-off summer events.

KURSALON Map pp240-3
☎ 512 57 90; www.strauss-konzerte.at; 01, Johannes-gasse 33; U4 Stadtpark, tram 1, 2

The Renaissance Kursalon recently underwent much-needed refurbishment and is once again back to hosting Strauss performances, including a repertoire of ballet and operetta. If you can't afford the time for an evening concert, stop by for coffee, cake and quartet waltz performance in the garden.

MUSIKVEREIN Map pp240-3
☎ 505 81 90; www.musikverein.at; 01, Bösendorfer-strasse 12; box office ☺ 9am-7.30pm Mon-Fri, 9am-5pm Sat; U1, U2, U4 Karlsplatz, Karlsplatz trams

The famous Vienna Philharmonic Orchestra performs in the Grosser Saal (large hall) in the Musikverein, which is said to have the best acoustics of any concert hall in Austria. The interior is suitably lavish and can be visited on the occasional guided tour. Standing-room tickets in the main hall cost €5 to €7; there are no student tickets. Smaller-scale performances are held in the Brahms Saal. The Musikverein closes in July and August.

ODEON Map pp240-3
☎ 216 51 27; www.odeon-theater.at, German only; 02, Taborstrasse 10; box office ☺ 10am-6pm Mon-Fri; U1, U4 Schwedenplatz, Schwedenplatz trams

This oft-forgotten performance venue looks suitably grand from the outside but unfortunately doesn't quite live up to expectations inside. Anything from classical concerts to raves are held within its walls.

ORANGERY Map pp246-7
☎ 812 50 04; 13, Schloss Schönbrunn; box office ☺ 9am-7pm; U4 Schönbrunn, bus 10A

Year-round Mozart and Strauss concerts take place in the lovely Orangery, Schönbrunn's former imperial greenhouse. Performances last around two hours and begin at 8.30pm daily.

PALAIS PALFFY Map pp240-3
☎ 513 21 76; www.palais-palffy.com; 01, Josefsplatz 6; box office ☺ 9am-10pm; U3 Herrengasse

Performances of Mozart, Beethoven, Strauss and Schubert are held in Palais Palffy's stunning baroque Figarosaal (Figaro Hall). Mozart himself performed here as a child in 1762, and although the music isn't of the same quality as that of the Philharmonic, it's lively and enthusiastic.

RAIMUND THEATER Map pp246-7

☎ 599 77; www.musicalvienna.at; 06, Wallgasse 18-20; box office ⏲ 10am-1pm & 2-6pm; U6 Gumpendorfer Strasse, tram 6, 18

The Raimund Theater hosts big, Broadway-style musicals these days, but when it opened its doors in 1893 it produced only spoken dramas. With a seating capacity of more than 1000, it should be no problem getting a ticket.

STAATSOPER Map pp240-3

☎ 514 44 7880; www.wiener-staatsoper.at; 01, Opernring 2; tours adult/child €4.50/1.50; box office ⏲ 9am until 2hr before performance Mon-Fri, 9am-noon Sat; U1, U2, U3 Karlsplatz, Karlsplatz trams

The premiere opera and classical music venue in Vienna, and possibly the world, is the Staatsoper. Built between 1861 and 1869 by August Siccardsburg and Eduard van der Null, it initially didn't go down well with the Viennese public and Habsburg royalty alike. It was quickly nicknamed the 'stone turtle'. Both architects took it the worst possible way: van der Null hung himself and Siccardsburg died of a heart attack two months later. Neither saw the Staatsoper's first staged production. This shocked Franz Josef to such an extent that he kept his official comments from then on to: 'It was very nice. I enjoyed it very much.'

Productions are lavish affairs and should not be missed. The Viennese take their opera very seriously and dress up accordingly. Wander around the foyer and refreshment rooms in the interval to fully appreciate the gold and crystal interior. Opera is not performed here in July and August, but its repertoire still includes more than 70 different productions.

Standing-room tickets, which go for €2 to €3.50, can be purchased only 80 minutes before the beginning of performances and any unsold tickets are available for €30 one day before a performance (call ☎ 514 44 2950 for more information). For information and times of year-round tours of the Staatsoper, call ☎ 514 44 2606.

THEATER AN DER WIEN Map pp240-3

☎ 588 30 265; www.musicalvienna.at; 06, Linke Wienzeile 6; box office ⏲ 10am-7pm; U1, U2, U4 Karlsplatz

The Theater an der Wien has hosted some monumental premiere performances, such as Beethoven's *Fidelo*, Mozart's *Die Zauberflöte* and Strauss Jnr's *Die Fledermaus*. These days the theatre is more attuned to popular culture and features musicals such as *Elisabeth* and *Mozart*. Standing tickets go on sale one hour before performances, and while they're cheap (€2.50), you probably won't see much.

VOLKSOPER Map pp244-5

☎ 514 44 3670; www.volksoper.at; 09, Währinger Strasse 78; box office ⏲ 8am-6pm Mon-Fri, 9am-noon Sat; U6 Währinger Strasse, tram 40, 41, 42

Vienna's second venue for opera is the Volksoper (People's Opera), a large opera house near

Staatsoper (above)

Entertainment – Opera & Classical Music

the Gürtel. Its heavy schedule is filled with kitsch operettas, dance performances and musicals, and is peppered with operas. Standing tickets go for as little as €1 and, like many venues, there are a plethora of discounts and reduced tickets 30 minutes before performances.

THEATRE & DANCE

Theatre is often overshadowed by Vienna's grand opera and classical music history, but the city enjoys a rich tradition in all things theatrical. It all started around 220 years ago with the creation of the Burgtheater, the oldest theatre in the German-speaking world. Today some 50 theatres are thriving in this theatre-loving city, but invariably performances are in German only. However, you can always count on the English and International Theatres to provide shows in English. Ticket costs vary greatly; at the low end of the scale are standing tickets, which normally go for around €2. Seated tickets start at €4 and top out at €62, but almost every venue has one form of discount or another, and sell bargain tickets 30 minutes to an hour before performances.

Considering the cultural bonanza that is Vienna, it comes as quite a surprise that the city has only recently established a centre for contemporary dance, the Tanzquartier Wien. Opened in 2001, it is a pleasure to see it go from strength to strength. Traditional ballet features at both the Staatsoper and the Volksoper during the opera season. ImPulsTanz (see p10), a quality dance festival from mid-July to mid-August, is about the only other option for catching dance performances in Vienna.

BURGTHEATER Map pp240-3
☎ 514 44-4140; www.burgtheater.at; 01, Dr-Karl-Lueger-Ring; tours adult/concession/child €4.50/2/1; box office ⊗ 8am-6pm Mon-Fri, 9am-noon Sat & Sun; tram D, 1, 2

Opposite the Rathaus is the Burgtheater (National Theatre), one of the prime theatre venues in the German-speaking world. It was built in Renaissance style to designs by Gottfried Semper and Karl von Hasenauer, and had to be rebuilt after sustaining severe damage in WWII. The interior is equally grand and has stairway frescoes painted by the Klimt brothers, Gustav and Ernst. Tours of the theatre are conducted daily at 2pm and 3pm in July and August and at 3pm daily for the remainder of the year. The Burgtheater also runs the small

Kasino am Schwarzenbergplatz (Map pp240-3; 03, Schwarzenbergplatz 1; tram D, 1, 2, 71) theatre and the 500-seater Akademietheater (Map pp240-3; 03, Lisztstrasse 1; U4 Stadtpark, bus 4A), which was built between 1911 and 1913.

Tickets at the Burgtheater and Akademietheater sell for 50% of their face-value price an hour before performances, and students can purchase tickets for €7 half an hour before performances. Standing places are €1.50.

INTERNATIONAL THEATRE Map pp244-5
☎ 319 62 72; www.internationaltheatre.at; 09, Porzellangasse 8; box office ⊗ 11am-3pm Mon-Fri, 6-7.30pm on performance days; tram D

The small International Theatre, with its entrance on Müllnergasse, has a mainly American company living locally. Discounted tickets are available to students and senior citizens. It closes for around five weeks at the beginning of August, and has a linked venue, Fundus, at 09, Müllnergasse 6A.

MARIONETTENTHEATER Map pp246-7
☎ 817 32 47-0; www.marionettentheater.at; 13, Schloss Schönbrunn; box office ⊗ 2-5pm Thu-Mon; U4 Schönbrunn, bus 10A

This small theatre in the confines of Schloss Schönbrunn puts on marionette performances of much-loved productions such as *The Magic Flute* and *Aladdin*. Shows can last up to 2½ hours, but fortunately the theatre also puts on 30-minute shows (adult/child €7/5) that might be better suited to children.

SCHAUSPIELHAUS Map pp244-5
☎ 317 01 01-18; www.schauspielhaus.at; 09, Porzellangasse 19; box office ⊗ 3-6pm Mon-Fri, 2 hr before performances; tram D

The Schauspielhaus pushes the boundaries of theatre in Vienna with unconventional productions, ranging from ethnic dance performances to political satires. Whatever the theme, you can guarantee it will be thought-provoking. After the show stop in the theatre's fine bar, the S-Bar (see p132).

TANZQUARTIER WIEN Map pp240-3
☎ 581 35 91; www.tqw.at; 07, Museumsplatz 1; box office ⊗ 10am-7pm Mon-Sat; U2 Museumsquartier, U2, U3 Volkstheater, bus 2A

In 2001 Vienna opened its first dance institution, the Tanzquartier Wien. Located in the newly completed MuseumsQuartier, it hosts an array of local and international performances with a strong experimental nature.

THEATER IN DER JOSEFSTADT
Map pp244-5

☎ 427 00 300; www.josefstadt.org, German only; 08, Josefstädter Strasse 26; box office ☺ 10am performance time Mon-Fri, 1pm performance time Sat & Sun; tram J, bus 13A

Theater in der Josefstadt is another theatre in the Volkstheater mould, with an ornate interior and traditional German productions. One hour before performances tickets are available to students and school children for €4; disabled persons and children can purchase tickets for €11 at any time. From 3pm Tuesday tickets go on sale for half-price for the evening performance.

VIENNA'S ENGLISH THEATRE
Map pp246-7

☎ 402 12 60; www.englishtheatre.at; 08, Josefsgasse 12; box office ☺ 10am-5pm Mon-Fri; U2 Rathaus, tram J

Founded in 1963, Vienna's English Theatre is the oldest foreign-language theatre in Vienna (the occasional French or Italian production is also shown). Productions range from timeless pieces, such as Shakespeare, through to contemporary works. Students, children and the disabled receive a 20% discount on all tickets, and standby tickets for €9 go on sale 15 minutes before the performance starts.

VOLKSTHEATER Map pp240-3

☎ 524 72 63/4; www.volkstheater.at, German only; 07, Neustiftgasse 1; box office ☺ 10am-6pm Mon-Fri Jul & Aug, 10am-performance Mon-Sat Sep-Jun; U2, U3 Volkstheater, tram 49

With a seating capacity close to 1000, the Volkstheater is one of Vienna's largest theatre venues. It was built in 1889 so it's no surprise that the interior is suitably grand. Only German-language shows are produced, and unsold tickets go on sale one hour before performances start for €3.60, but only to students.

CINEMA

The Viennese love their *Kino* (cinema) and attend in droves. And being a traditionally thoughtful bunch, independent art-house films are just as sought after as big Hollywood blockbusters. Unlike television, where almost 100% of movies screened are dubbed in German, there are plenty of opportunities to catch films on the celluloid screen in their original language. The

weekly *Falter* and daily *Der Standard* papers are the best sources of listings. Look out for small letters following the film title that indicate which language it will be screened in: *OF* or *OV* means in the original language; *OmU* means in the original language with German subtitles; and *OmenglU* and *OmeU* indicates it's in the original language with English subtitles. Monday is known as *Kinomontag*, when all cinema seats go for around €5.50; a normal screening costs anything from €6.50 to €10.

In mid-October Vienna is home to the Viennale, an international film festival. By no means as prestigious as Cannes, it still attracts top-quality films from all over the world and is geared to the viewer rather than the film-makers. For two weeks a number of cinemas continuously play screenings that could broadly be described as fringe, ranging from documentaries to short and feature films, and tickets for the more popular screenings can be hard to come by. Tickets can be bought two weeks before the first films are screened from a number of stands around town. For more information, and a list of the current festival screenings, call ☎ 0800 664 003 or check www.viennale.at.

ARTIS INTERNATIONAL Map pp240-3

☎ 535 65 70; www.cineplexx.at; 01, Schultergasse 5; bus 1A, 2A, 3A

Artis has six small cinemas in the heart of the Innere Stadt. It only shows English-language films, which are invariably straight out of Hollywood's larger studios.

BREITENSEER LICHTSPIELE Map pp246-7

☎ 982 21 73; 14, Breitenseer Strasse 21; bus 51A

This delightful Art-Nouveau cinema is an absolute gem, and if you're into cinemas, a special trip to the outer districts is required. Opened in 1909, the Breitenseer still retains its original wooden seats and carries the atmosphere of a bygone era in cinema history. Films are usually in English with German subtitles.

BURG KINO Map pp240-3

☎ 587 84 06; www.burgkino.at; 01, Opernring 19; U1, U2, U4 Karlsplatz, Karlsplatz trams

The Burg Kino is a central cinema that shows only English films, and it has regular screenings of the *The Third Man*, Orson Welles' timeless classic set in post-WWII Vienna, at 11pm Friday and 3pm Sunday.

CINEMAGIC Map pp240-3

☎ 586 43 03; www.cinemagic.at, German only;
01, Friedrichstrasse 4; admission €4.70; U1, U2, U4
Karlsplatz, Karlsplatz trams

An initiative of the City of Vienna aimed at entertainment for children, Cinemagic is a cinema totally devoted to the little 'uns. Films come from around the globe, and screen every Saturday and Sunday at 3pm. In mid-November the cinema, along with three others, hosts a Children's Film Festival, showcasing the best of international children's film. For more information go to www.kinderfilmfestival.at, German only.

DE FRANCE Map pp240-3

☎ 317 52 36; www.defrance.at; 01, Schottenring 5;
U2 Schottentor, Schottentor trams

De France recently reopened after renovation, and dived straight back into its screening schedule: original-language films with subtitles, with a healthy dose of English-language films.

ENGLISH CINEMA HAYDN Map pp246-7

☎ 587 22 62; www.haydnkino.at; 06, Mariahilfer
Strasse 57; U3 Neubaugasse, bus 13A

The Haydn cinema is a comfortable cinema that screens only mainstream Hollywood-style films in their original language.

FILMCASINO Map pp246-7

☎ 587 90 62; www.filmcasino.at; 05, Margareten
Strasse 78; U4 Pilgramgasse, bus 13A, 59A

An art-house cinema of some distinction, the Filmcasino screens an excellent mix of Asian and European docos and avant-garde short films, along with independent full-length films from around the world. Its '50s-style foyer is particularly impressive.

GARTENBAUKINO Map pp240-3

☎ 512 23 54; www.gartenbaukino.at, German only;
01, Parkring 12; U3 Stubentor, U4 Stadpark, tram 1, 2

Fortunately the interior of the Gartenbaukino has survived since the 1960s, making a trip to the flicks here all the more appealing. The actual cinema seats a whopping 750 people, which is often packed during Viennale screenings. Its regular screening schedule is full to overflowing with art-house films, normally with subtitles.

IMAX WIEN Map pp246-7

☎ 894 01 01; www.imax.at, German only; 14, Mariahilfer Strasse 212; ⊗ 9.30am-9pm Mon-Wed & Sun,
9.30am-10pm Thu-Sat; U4 Schönbrunn, tram 52, 58

IMAX Wien is appropriately situated next to the Technisches Museum. Its giant screen, which takes up a massive 600 sq metres, shows all sorts of weird and wonderful films, ranging from outer space voyages to trips through the Serengeti.

ÖSTERREICHISCHE FILMMUSEUM
Map pp240-3

☎ 533 70 54; www.filmmuseum.at; 01, Augustinerstrasse 1; ⊗ Oct-Jun; U1, U2, U4 Karlsplatz, Karlsplatz
trams

Finally the Filmmuseum has benefited from a much-needed overhaul, and the original arse-numbing seats have been replaced with posterior-friendly chairs. The range of films on show is quite extensive; each month features a retrospective on a group of directors or a certain theme from around the world. Tickets costs €9; with a year's membership (€10.90) this drops to €5.

SCHIKANEDER Map pp246-7

☎ 585 28 67; www.schikaneder.at, German only;
04, Margareten Strasse 24; bus 59A

Located in the bar of the same name (see p143), Schikaneder is the darling of the alternative cinema scene in Vienna. The film subject range is quite broad but also highly selective, and art house through and through. Schikaneder only seats 80, and all screenings are €6.

TOP KINO Map pp240-3

☎ 585 58 88; www.topkino.at, German only; 06,
Rahlgasse 1; U2 Museumsquartier, bus 57A

Open-Air Cinema

With the Viennese love of sitting out under the stars on a balmy evening, it didn't take long for people to combine cinema and the outdoors. **Kino Unter Sternen** (Cinema Under the Stars; ☎ 585 23 24-25; www.kinountersternen.at, German only; 02, Augarten; tram 31, bus 5A) is a popular outdoor cinema in the shadow of one of Augarten's Flaktürme that shows films from mid-July to mid-August. The selection is an eclectic mix of classics, and films in English are often shown. Kino Unter Sternen's main competitor is **Krieau** (Map pp248-9; ☎ 524 68 02; www.krieau.com, German only; 02, Norportalstrasse 247; tram 21, bus 80B), but the range of English films isn't so great. It's situated in the Prater and runs from July to August.

Entertainment – Cinema

Top is another cinema to open recently after an extended hibernation period. It is associated with Schikaneder, which gives you an idea of the type of films shown. Movies are generally in original language with German subtitles. Its bar is a fine place for a drink after the screening (see p144).

VOTIVKINO Map pp244-5
☎ 317 35 71; www.votivkino.at, German only; 09, Währinger Strasse 12; tram 37, 38, 40, 41, 42
Built in 1912, the Votiv is one of the oldest cinemas in Vienna. It's been extensively updated since then and is now among the best cinemas in the city. Its three screens feature a mix of Hollywood and art-house films in their original language.

SPORTS

In general, the Viennese aren't a particularly sporty bunch. The only exercise many partake of is a bit of splashing about in the water during the summer months, the occasional hike in the Wienerwald or getting from A to B on their bicycle. In Vienna itself, the only spectator sport of note that gains regular audiences is football. The Viennese, like the rest of their compatriots, are fanatical about skiing but with no mountains close at hand, it's hard to catch any live races.

FOOTBALL
AUSTRIA MEMPHIS FRANZ-HORR-STADION Map pp238-9
☎ 688 01 50; 10, Fischhofgasse 12; tram 67, bus 15A
Austria Memphis is one of two national league teams residing in Vienna (the other is Rapid Vienna). They are supported by the city's more affluent set, and have in recent years enjoyed some success over their arch rivals Rapid. Games, played in the Horr Stadium, hardly ever sell out so obtaining a ticket won't be a hard task.

ERNST-HAPPEL-STADION Map pp248-9
☎ 728 08 54; 02, Meiereistrasse 7; tram 21, bus 80B
With a seating capacity nearing 50,000, the Ernst-Happel stadium is the largest sporting venue in Vienna. It mainly hosts international and domestic football matches and the occasional concert. It's named after the Austrian player and coach who died in 1992.

RAPID VIENNA GERHARD-HANAPPI-STADION Map pp238-9
☎ 914 55 19; 14, Keisslergasse 6; U4 Hütteldorf, bus 147
The Hanappi stadium hosts Rapid Vienna, a team favoured by Vienna's working class. Of the city's two national league teams, Rapid has been the most successful internationally, fighting their way through to the European Cup finals on two occasions. Like Austria Memphis games, Rapid fixtures rarely sell out so it should be no problem obtaining a ticket.

STADTHALLE Map pp246-7
☎ 981 00-0; 15, Vogelweidplatz 15; U6 Burggasse/Stadthalle, tram 6, 18, bus 48A
The Stadthalle hosts a national football tournament at the end of December and other events as diverse as tennis tournaments, horse shows and ice hockey events. The swimming pool here is a major venue for aquatic events like races, water polo and synchronised swimming.

HORSE RACING
FREUDENAU Map pp238-9
☎ 728 95 17; 02, Rennbahnstrasse 65; bus 77A
In the southern extremes of the Prater is Freudenau, Vienna's premiere horse-racing track and one of the oldest in Europe. Bus 77A doesn't always go as far as the track so you might have to walk from the Lusthaus (see Eating p126).

KRIEAU Map pp238-9
☎ 728 00 46; 02, Nordportalstrasse 274; tram 21, bus 80B
Sidling up to the Ernst-Happel-Stadion in the Prater is Krieau, the track where Vienna's trotting meets are held. It's normally only open on Sunday afternoons from September to June.

HEALTH & FITNESS

With its abundance of parks, waterways and woodlands, Vienna is a great city for a bit of exercise and some fresh air. There are plenty of opportunities for visitors to participate in activities such as horse riding, basketball, tennis, squash, sailing, swimming, bowling etc, and the main culprits are covered below. For more contacts and locations check the *Gelbe Seiten* (Yellow Pages) or pick up a copy of *Sports & Nature in Vienna*, a brochure produced by the Vienna tourist board. It can also be downloaded from their website www.wien.info.

BOATING

The Alte Donau is the main boating and sailing centre in Vienna, but the Neue Donau also provides opportunities for boating, windsurfing and water-skiing.

HOFBAUER Map pp238-9

☎ 203 86 80; www.hofbauer.at, German only; 22, Wagramer Strasse 49; ☺ May–mid-Oct; U1 Alte Donau
Hofbauer rents electric boats for €12.60 for a full day or €14 after 8pm, rudder boats (basically dinghies) for €6.40/7, and pedal boats for €9.40/10.50. There are another couple of boat rental places close at hand if Hofbauer has nothing to rent.

SAILING SCHOOL HOFBAUER
Map pp238-9

☎ 204 34 35; www.hofbauer.at; 22, An der Obere Alte Donau 191; ☺ Apr-Oct; U1 Alte Donau
The sailing arm of Hofbauer is on the eastern bank of the Alte Donau and has sailing boats and windsurfers for hire, along with lessons for both in English.

CLIMBING

Vienna has a few climbing walls scattered throughout its districts. Most are indoors.

KLETTERANLAGE FLAKTURM
Map pp246-7

☎ 585 47 48; 06, Esterhazypark; around €15 for 2 hr; ☺ 2pm-dusk Mon-Fri, 1pm-dusk Sat & Sun Apr-Oct; U3 Neubaugasse, bus 13A, 14A
The stark outside walls of the Flakturm (flak tower) in Esterhazypark are used for climbing exercises organised by the Österreichischer Alpenverein. Twenty routes (gradients four to eight) climb to a maximum height of 34m.

CYCLING

Vienna's layout and well-marked cycle lanes make cycling a pleasant and popular activity, especially along the banks of the Danube, in the Prater and around the Ringstrasse. The Wienerwald is also popular for mountain biking; check the websites www.mbike.at (German only) and www.mtbwienerwald.at (German only) for ideas and trails.

The Directory chapter (p198) has information on bicycle hire and taking bicycles on public transport, and the Walking & Cycling Tours chapter (p105) provides two cycle-tour suggestions.

GOLF

GOLF CLUB WIEN Map pp238-9

☎ 728 18 08; 02, Freudenau 65A; green fees €60; bus 77A
This 18-hole course in the Prater cuts through part of the Freudenau race course. It belongs to Golf Club Vienna, which is the oldest club in the country. You need to be a member of a golf club to play here.

GYMS

Most large hotels have their own fitness centre open to guests, but there are plenty of independent centres that provide day passes to visitors.

CLUB DANUBE Map pp248-9

☎ 798 84 00; www.clubdanube.at, German only; 03, Franzosengraben; day membership €14.20; ☺ 8am-10pm Mon-Fri, 8am-9pm Sat & Sun; U3 Erdberg
Club Danube has a range of sports and activities alongside its well-appointed gym. There are more than 10 such Club Danube gyms in the city; this one is in the same building as the U3 Erdberg station.

HIKING

To the west of the city, the rolling hills and marked trails of the Wienerwald (see p193) are perfect for walkers. The Prater (see p85) also has a wood with walking trails.

A good trail to try starts in Nussdorf (take tram D from the Ring) and climbs Kahlenberg (see p104). On your return to Nussdorf you can undo all that exercise with a few wines at a *Heuriger*. The round trip is around 11km, or you can save your legs by taking the Nussdorf-Kahlenberg 38A bus in one or both directions.

Another place to roam around is the Lainzer Tiergarten (see p100) animal reserve, a wild park in the west of Vienna.

ICE SKATING

Come winter time one of the most popular activities in Vienna is ice skating. Along with specialised ice-skating rinks, a number of outdoor basketball courts are turned into rinks during the winter months. For as little as €1 you can spend the whole day floating around on these temporary rinks; look for them at 08, Buchfeldgasse 7A (Map pp240-3), 16, Gallitzinstrasse 4 (Map pp238-9) and 19, Osterleitengasse 14 (Map pp244–5). When it's cold enough, the Alte Donau is transformed into an ice-skater's paradise, with miles of natural ice.

WIENER EISLAUFVEREIN Map pp240-3
☎ 713 63 53; 03, Lothringerstrasse 22; entry €7, boot rental €5.50; ⏰ 9am-8pm Mon, Sat & Sun, 9am-9pm Tue, Thu, Fri, 9am-10pm Wed Nov–mid-Mar; U4 Stadtpark
At 6000 sq metres, the Wiener Eislaufverein is the world's largest open-air skating rink. It's close to the Ringstrasse and Stadtpark. Remember to bring mittens and a hat.

WIENER EISTRAUM Map pp240-3
☎ 409 00 40; 01, Rathausplatz; ⏰ 9am-11pm Feb-Mar; U2 Rathaus, tram D, 1, 2
In February and March the Rathausplatz is home to an 1800-sq-metre ice rink. It's a bit of a mecca for the city's ice-skaters, and the rink is complemented by food stands, special events and punch bars.

IN-LINE SKATING
With wide, smooth tar-sealed paths, the Donauinsel and Prater are just made for in-line skating. Skates can be rented from a number of places on the island, particularly around the Copa Cagrana area. If you'd like to hook up with like-minded skaters, roll along to Heldenplatz at 9pm on Friday from May to September and join the **Friday Night Skating** team on a tour of the city. Participation is free.

SKATELAB Map pp238-9
☎ 214 9565; www.skatelab.at, German only; 02, Engerthstrasse 160-178; entry €6.75; ⏰ 2pm-9pm Tue-Fri, 10am-8pm Sat & Sun Nov-Apr; U1 Vorgartenstrasse, bus 11A
Skatelab is Austria's largest indoor skating rink. There are plenty of obstacles, ramps and even a street course to keep you entertained. Unfortunately in-line skates are not available for rent.

SKIING
Yes, there is skiing in Vienna. Only a handful of places offer skiing within the city limits, but if you've come this far and want to go skiing you're much better off heading west and taking advantage of Austria's stunning Alps.

SKIANLAGE DOLLWIESE Map pp238-9
☎ 812 12 01; 13, Ghelengasse 44; day pass €13; ⏰ 9am-9.30pm Mon-Fri, 9am-10pm Sat & Sun; bus 54B, 55B
Edging up to the Lainzer Tiergarten is Dollwiese, supposedly one of Austria's oldest ski slopes. At only 400m long, it's quite short.

SKIANLAGE HOHE WAND Map pp238-9
☎ 979 10 57; 14, Mauerbachstrasse 172-174; day pass €13; ⏰ noon-dusk Mon-Fri, 10am-dusk Sat & Sun; bus 249, 250, 449
The Hohe Wand ski slopes can be used only when there is enough natural snow to cope with daily layerings of artificial snow. It's quite a way from the city centre, in the Wienerwald.

SWIMMING
Swimming is a favourite summer pastime of the Viennese. The Donauinsel, Alte Donau and Lobau are often swamped with citizens eager to cool off on steamy hot summer days. Topless sunbathing is quite the norm, as is nude sunbathing but only in designated areas; much of Lobau and both tips of the Donauinsel are FKK (*Freikörperkultur*; free body culture) areas.

Alongside natural swimming areas are a large number of swimming pools owned and run by the city. In general, entry to these pools costs €4/2 per adult/child, €3.50/2.50 after noon and €2.50 after 4pm. For a full list of pools call ☎ 60112 8044 between 7.30am and 3.30pm Monday to Friday, or log on to www.wien.at/baeder.

AMALIENBAD Map pp248-9
☎ 607 47 47; 10, Reumannplatz 23; U1 Reumannplatz
This stunning Jugendstil bath has a range of facilities, including a solarium, steam room, massage, cosmetic treatments and a restaurant. There are separate saunas for men and women, and a unisex one.

KRAPFENWALDBAD Map pp238-9
☎ 320 15 01; 19, Krapfenwaldgasse 65-73; bus 38A
Krapfenwaldbad is possibly Vienna's highest bath, and it certainly has the best views of the city. Even though there's a kids' playground, football playing area, volleyball court and loads of sun-bathing chairs, it still gets crowded in summer.

STRANDBAD ALTE DONAU Map pp238-9
☎ 263 65 38; 22, Arbeiterstrandbadstrasse 91; U1 Alte Donau, bus 91A

Amalienbad (p157)

This bathing area makes great use of the Alte Donau during the summer months. It's a favourite of the working class and gets extremely crowded on weekends during summer. Facilities include a restaurant, beach volleyball court, playing field, slides and plenty of tree shade.

STRANDBAD GÄNSEHÄUFEL
Map pp238-9
☎ 269 90 16; 22, Moissigasse 21; bus 90A, 91A, 92A
Gänsehäufel is another swimming area on the Alte Donau – actually in the Alte Donau as it occupies a section of a small island. It does get crowded in summer, but there's normally enough space to escape the mob. There's a swimming pool and FKK area.

THERMALBAD OBERLAA Map pp238-9
☎ 6800 996 00; 10, Kurbadstrasse 14; tram 67
In the southern reaches of Vienna is Oberlaa, a large thermal complex with both indoor and outdoor pools. It often stages concerts and theatrical performances and runs a wellness centre.

Innere Stadt — 161
Stephansplatz — 161
East of Stephansplatz — 161
Kärntner Strasse, Graben & Kohlmarkt — 162
Michaelerplatz to Mölker Bastei — 165
Rotenturmstrasse to Schottenring — 165

Ringstrasse — 167
Parlament to Schwarzenbergplatz — 167
MuseumsQuartier — 167

Between the Danube Canal & the Danube — 167

Inside the Gürtel — 167
Wieden — 167
Margareten — 167
Mariahilf — 167
Neubau — 169
Josefstadt — 170
Alsergrund — 170

Outside the Gürtel — 170
Simmering — 170
Rudolfsheim-Fünfhaus — 170
Ottakring — 170
Hernals — 170

Shopping

Shopping

Mariahilfer Strasse (p89)

The Viennese love to shop, and they don't mind spending a bit of cash to get exactly what they want. Therefore, although Vienna is not a place for cheap shopping, it does offer numerous elegant shops and quality products. Local specialities include porcelain, ceramics, handmade dolls, wrought-iron work and leather goods. Many shops sell collectable stamps *(Briefmarken)*, coins *(Münze)* and second-hand odds and ends *(Altwaren)*. Like many cities around the world however, Vienna is being infiltrated by global High St stores, with such big names as H&M, Zara, New Yorker, Mango and Diesel popping up all over town. This is great for the average shopper, but it is slowly forcing individual shops out of business. Little gems do exist, but you need to leave the main avenues and shopping thoroughfares and explore the hidden alleyways and back streets to find them. A bit of legwork can bring great rewards.

It seems everywhere you look in Vienna there will be at least one shop trading in one product or another. There are, however, particular streets with a high concentration of shops. In the Innere Stadt, pedestrian-only Kärntner Strasse, Graben and Kohlmarkt are your best options. Mainly upmarket and specialist shops are featured here, but big brands are slowly forcing their way in. Generally speaking, outside the Ring is where you'll find shops catering for those with shallower pockets. Mariahilfer Strasse is regarded as the best shopping street, particularly the stretch between Ringstrasse and Westbahnhof. Most districts have their own shopping street, such as Landstrasser Hauptstrasse in Landstrasse and Meidlinger Hauptstrasse in Meidling. Look out for Josefstädter Strasse and Neubaugasse; both are lined with speciality shops, and the latter enjoys a line of second-hand stores stocked with unusual delights.

For major shopping expeditions, the Viennese head south of the city to Shopping City Süd, marketed simply as SCS. It's said to be the biggest shopping centre in Europe. Parking places are difficult to find here after about 10am on Saturday, so a good alternative is to take the IKEA bus departing from opposite the Staatsoper (near the tram No 2 stop) to the IKEA furniture shop. The Lokalbahn tram service to Baden, departing opposite the Hotel Bristol, also stops at SCS. SCS is just south of the city precincts at Vösendorf, near the junction of the A21 and A2.

Many of Vienna's finest shops are listed in the free *Shopping, Wining & Dining* booklet, produced by the tourist office. Most of these are within the Innere Stadt or on Mariahilfer Strasse. *Best of Vienna*, a quarterly magazine, has a large and typically idiosyncratic section devoted to shopping (in German). For special reductions, look out for *Aktion* signs. The Viennese advertise their second-hand goods in *Bazar*, a thrice-weekly magazine available from pavement newsstands. If you plan to do a bit of shopping, consider purchasing the 'Vienna Card' (see the Directory chapter, p204, for more details).

Opening Hours

Most shops are open between 9am and 6pm on Monday to Friday and until 5pm on Saturday. Some have extended hours on Thursday or Friday till around 7.30pm. Shops don't open on Sunday, and the city looks like a cemetery on the last day of the week. If a shop's opening hours deviate from the above by more than 30 minutes, we've included their hours in the review.

Consumer Taxes

Value-added tax (*Mehrwertsteuer*, or MWST) is set at 20% for most goods. Prices are displayed inclusive of all taxes, even (usually) service charges in hotels and restaurants.

All non-EU visitors are entitled to a refund of the MWST on purchases over €75. To claim the tax, a tax-refund cheque must be filled out by the shop at the time of purchase (show your passport), which must then be stamped by border officials when you leave the EU. No stamp, no refund. Vienna airport has a counter for payment of instant refunds. Counters are also at Westbahnhof and Südbahnhof, and at major border crossings. The refund is best claimed upon departing the EU, as otherwise you'll have to track down an international refund office or make a claim by post. After a handling fee is deducted, refunds normally amount to 13% of the purchase price.

Bargaining

Bargaining is basically a no-no in shops, although you can certainly haggle when buying second-hand. It's also well worth a try at the *Flohmarkt* (flea market) on Naschmarkt every Saturday morning (see p166), and you could possibly haggle for a better price at the food markets around town.

Top Five Shopping Strips

- **Josefstädter Strasse** – an old-fashioned shopping street filled with quaint shops selling anything from flowers to tea
- **Kärntner Strasse** – it might have lost its shopping sparkle, but it's still the Innere Stadt's main shopping street and a real crowd-puller
- **Mariahilfer Strasse** – Vienna's largest shopping street, with plenty of High St names and masses of people
- **Neubaugasse** – a second-hand hunter's paradise and lined with unusual shops
- **Shopping City Süd (SCS)** – not a strip as such but Vienna's equivalent of a mall, south of the city

---

INNERE STADT

STEPHANSPLATZ

AIDA Map pp240-3   *Café/Bakery*
☎ 512 29 77; 01, Stock-im-Eisen-Platz 2; 🕙 7am-8pm Mon-Sat, 9am-8pm Sun; U1, U3 Stephansplatz
This fabulous coffee-house chain (see p119) not only serves fine coffee but also churns out sublime cakes. All their goodies can be taken away, and forget about those calories – you're on holiday. There are 26 Aida in Vienna.

EAST OF STEPHANSPLATZ

ART DECO Map pp240-3   *Jewellery*
☎ 513 30 76; www.artdeco.at; 01, Riemergasse 13/1; U3 Stubentor, bus 1A
Art Deco creates quite exquisite jewellery in the Art-Deco style. Pieces are generally made from 925 sterling silver, and embedded with semiprecious stones and pearls.

BRITISH BOOKSHOP Map pp240-3   *Books*
☎ 512 19 45; www.britishbookshop.at; 01, Weihburggasse 24; tram 1, 2
The British Bookshop has the largest selection of English reference and teaching books in Vienna. Sharing equal space with the teaching

---

Top Five Chocolate & Cakes

- **Aida** (p161) Retro interiors and fabulous cakes and sweets
- **Altmann & Kühne** (p162) World-famous bonbons made using a hundred-year-old recipe
- **Café Sacher** (p162) It's only a cake, but some tourists list it in their 'must-dos' in Vienna
- **Demel** (p162) Sugar, flour and icing turned into works of art
- **Manner Fabriksverkauf** (p170) Manner Schnitten in a multitude of flavours and bargain seconds to boot

reference books is a vast collection of mainstream novels, kids' books and history books. There's a second branch on **Mariahilfer Strasse** (Map pp240-3; ☎ 522 67 30; 07, Mariahilfer Strasse 4).

DOMINICI Map pp240-3 *Shoes*
☎ 513 45 411; 01, Singerstrasse 2; ⏰ 9.30am-7pm Mon-Fri, 9.30am-5pm Sat; U1, U3 Stephansplatz
Dominici specialises in Italian designer footwear, ranging from sneakers to ankle-breaking high heels. They don't come cheap, but they're of the highest quality.

PRADA Map pp240-3 *Fashion*
☎ 513 61 65; 01, Weihburggasse 9; ⏰ 10am-6.30pm Mon-Fri, 10am-6pm Sat; U1, U3 Stephansplatz
The world-famous label has a shop here in Vienna, selling all its latest styles and designs.

WOKA Map pp240-3 *Lighting*
☎ 513 29 12; www.woka.at; 01, Singerstrasse 16; 10am-6pm Mon-Fri, 10am-5pm Sat; U1, U3 Karlsplatz
Accurate re-creations of Wiener Werkstätte lamps are the hallmark of Woka. In operation since 1977, the firm has faithfully stuck to designs by the likes of Adolf Loos, Kolo Moser and Josef Hoffmann. The collection on show is quite remarkable.

KÄRNTNER STRASSE, GRABEN & KOHLMARKT

ALTMANN & KÜHNE
Map pp240-3 *Confectionery*
☎ 533 09 27; 01, Graben 30; ⏰ 9am-6.30pm Mon-Fri, 10am-5pm Sat; U1, U3 Stephansplatz
Altmann & Kühne have been producing handmade bonbons for more than 100 years using a well-kept secret recipe. They not only taste divine, they also look great: the packaging is designed by Wiener Werkstätte.

Top Five Vienna Made

- Eva Blut bags (p169)
- Manner Schnitten (p170)
- Perzy Snow Globes (p168)
- Porzellanmanufaktur Augarten porcelain (p167)
- Woka lamps (p162)

BOUTIQUE CHARME
Map pp240-3 *Lingerie*
☎ 512 91 39; 01, Operngasse 2; ⏰ 11am-7pm Mon-Fri, 11am-5pm Sat; U1, U2, U4 Karlsplatz, Karlsplatz trams
Well placed between the Staatsoper and the Albertina is this shrine to the delicate creations of La Perla. Lacy bras, stockings, nighties, suspenders, accessories – it's all here. It's worth a peek inside just for the shop's ornate, arched ceiling.

BRAUN & CO Map pp240-3 *Clothing*
☎ 512 55 05-0; 01, Graben 8; ⏰ 10am-6.30pm Mon-Fri, 10am-6pm Sat; U1, U3 Stephansplatz, bus 2A, 3A
Braun & Co is possibly the noblest of all the fashion and designer shops in this fair city; in 1911 Franz Josef himself granted the shop the famous KuK (*Kaiserlich und Königlich*; Imperial and Kingly) seal of approval. Five generations on, the quality and prices are still fit for a king.

CAFÉ SACHER Map pp240-3 *Confectionery*
☎ 541 56-661; www.sacher.at; 01, Philharmonikerstrasse 4; ⏰ 8am-11.30pm; U1, U2, U4 Karlsplatz, Karlsplatz trams
The legendary *Sacher Torte* can only be purchased at Café Sacher (see p120), or over the Internet if you'd like it delivered to your door. This tantalising mix of jam, chocolate and icing has been wowing Viennese and tourists alike since it was first invented for Franz Josef.

DEMEL Map pp240-3 *Confectionery*
☎ 535 17 17; www.demel.at; 01, Kohlmarkt 14; ⏰ 10am-7pm; bus 2A, 3A
It's amazing what some people will fight about. Demel and Sacher (see above) have been embroiled in a battle over the right to claim their torte as the original *Sacher Torte* for years, but it seems Sacher has come out on top, for the time being. This, however, takes nothing away from the stunning cakes Demel produces, all of which are lovingly prepared – and lovingly devoured. Cakes can also be ordered over the Internet.

DOROTHEUM Map pp240-3 *Auction House*
☎ 515 60-0; www.dorotheum.com; 01, Dorotheergasse 17; bus 2A, 3A
Founded in 1707 by Joseph I, the Dorotheum ranks among the largest auction houses in Europe. The range of objects up for sale is quite extraordinary, but stick to the categories of art, antiques and collectables. Expect to find glass, porcelain, contemporary art, furniture, photography, jewellery, coins, posters…the list

goes on. Not everything is priced out of most people's budgets – there are also affordable household ornaments up for grabs. On the 2nd floor are Austria's largest jewellery store and the 'Freier Verkauf' section, a massive antique gallery where you can buy on the spot at marked prices. There are some great items here (jewellery, ornaments, oil paintings etc) and it's fun just to wander around, and look, and dream…

It's interesting to watch auction proceedings even if you don't intend to buy anything. Plenty of items can be inspected in advance with the opening prices marked. If you don't have the confidence to bid yourself you can commission an agent to do it for you. The hammer price usually excludes VAT; you'll have to pay this but you may be able to claim it back later. The Dorotheum is housed in Palais Dorotheum, a neobaroque palace from the 1890s.

DOUGLAS Map pp240-3   Cosmetics
☎ 533 09 78; 01, Graben 29a; 9am-7pm Mon-Fri, 9am-5pm Sat; U1, U3 Stephansplatz, bus 2A, 3A
Douglas is your one-stop shop for all things associated with make-up. There's also a small range of accessories, and you'll find branches scattered throughout the city.

FREYTAG & BERNDT
Map pp240-3   Books & Maps
☎ 533 86 85; www.freytagberndt.at; 01, Kohlmarkt 9; 9am-7pm Mon-Fri, 9am-6pm Sat; U3 Herrengasse, bus 2A, 3A
There is no better place for maps and travel guides than Freytag & Berndt. Maps and guides are not only restricted to Austria (of which there are some superbly detailed walking maps) but also cover the whole globe. Freytag & Berndt stock many of their competitors' maps.

GLASFABRIK Map pp240-3   Antiques
☎ 533 60 26; 01, Habsburgergasse 9; 10am-6.30pm Mon-Fri, 10am-5pm Sat; U1, U3 Stephansplatz, bus 2A, 3A
Glasfabrik specialises in antiques and old wares dating from 1670 to 1970, so the range on offer is eclectic to say the least. Books, furniture, pictures, lamps, ornaments – anything and everything is here to be had.

HELMUT LANG Map pp240-3   Fashion
☎ 586 07 73; 01, Seilergasse 6; U1, U3 Stephansplatz
The premiere store of Austria's top designer (there are only six worldwide), Helmut Lang stocks fantastic clothes that will empty your wallet. See p15 for a lowdown on the rise and rise of the man.

Clothing Sizes
Measurements approximate only, try before you buy

Women's Clothing

Aus/UK	8	10	12	14	16	18
Europe	36	38	40	42	44	46
Japan	5	7	9	11	13	15
USA	6	8	10	12	14	16

Women's Shoes

Aus/USA	5	6	7	8	9	10
Europe	35	36	37	38	39	40
France only	35	36	38	39	40	42
Japan	22	23	24	25	26	27
UK	3½	4½	5½	6½	7½	8½

Men's Clothing

Aus	92	96	100	104	108	112
Europe	46	48	50	52	54	56
Japan	S		M	M		L
UK/USA	35	36	37	38	39	40

Men's Shirts (Collar Sizes)

Aus/Japan	38	39	40	41	42	43
Europe	38	39	40	41	42	43
UK/USA	15	15½	16	16½	17	17½

Men's Shoes

Aus/UK	7	8	9	10	11	12
Europe	41	42	43	44½	46	47
Japan	26	27	27½	28	29	30
USA	7½	8½	9½	10½	11½	12½

HUMANIC Map pp240-3   Shoes
☎ 513 89 22; 01, Kärntner Strasse 1; 10am-7pm Mon-Fri, to 9pm Thu, 10am-6pm Sat; U1, U3 Stephansplatz
Humanic is the stock shoe store of Vienna (there are Humanic shops all over the city), where many go to buy their daily footwear. The styles on offer aren't particularly adventurous, but the price is right and on the odd occasion you may just come across something special.

J & L LOBMEYR Map pp240-3   Glassware
☎ 512 05 08; www.lobmeyr.com; 01, Kärntner Strasse 26; U1, U3 Stephansplatz
Most of Kärntner Strasse's up-market stores have been replaced by High St names and souvenir shops, but Lobmeyr is one of the few left. The firm has been in business since the beginning of the 19th century when it exclusively supplied the imperial court with glassware. These days, the production is more focused towards Werkstätte pieces, but the quality still remains.

MEINL AM GRABEN Map pp240-3 *Food*

☎ 532 33 34; www.meinlamgraben.at, German only; 01, Graben 19; ⏲ 8am-6.30pm Mon-Fri, 8.30am-5pm Sat; bus 1A, 2A, 3A

It's hard to beat the local and international selection at Meinl am Graben, Vienna's prestigious supermarket. The only drawback is the vegetable and fruit section, which leaves a lot to be desired.

NIEDERMEYER Map pp240-3 *Electronics*

☎ 512 33 61; 01, Graben 11; ⏲ 9am-7pm Mon-Fri, 9am-5pm Sat; U1, U3 Stephansplatz, bus 2A, 3A

The Niedermeyer chain store is one of the cheapest places to buy electronic gear, including cameras and film. The chain has more than 50 branches in Vienna, so it won't be hard to locate one while wandering around town.

ÖSTERREICHISCHE WERKSTÄTTEN

Map pp240-3 *Ornaments*

☎ 512 24 18; www.oew.at; 01, Kärntner Strasse 6; U1, U3 Stephansplatz

The result of a collaboration of art groups in 1948, the Österreichische Werkstätten supports and creates the production of quality handmade craftworks, including jewellery, glassware and ornaments. The emphasis is on achieving a balance between form and function.

PALMERS Map pp240-3 *Lingerie*

☎ 512 57 72; 01, Kärntner Strasse 53-55; ⏲ 9am-6.30pm Mon-Fri, 9am-5pm Sat; U1, U3 Stephansplatz

Palmers is easily the Queen of Lingerie in Austria. This home-grown company seems to have a store (or three) on every major shopping street, which makes you wonder how big the average Viennese top drawer is. Their billboard ad campaign is one of the most beloved – and anticipated – by the male population.

STEFFL Map pp240-3 *Department Store*

☎ 514 31; 01, Kärntner Strasse 19; ⏲ 9.30am-7pm Mon-Fri, to 9pm Thu, 9.30am-6pm Sat; U1, U3 Stephansplatz

Steffl is the classiest of Vienna's department stores. It's filled with designer labels – cosmetics on the ground floor, clothes on the first. Down in the basement is Don Gil, another label-packed clothing store, and sharing the first floor is Amadeus (see p167).

SWAROVSKI Map pp240-3 *Crystal*

☎ 512 90 32-33; www.swarovski.com; 01, Kärntner Strasse 8; ⏲ 9am-7pm Mon-Fri, to 9pm Thu, 9am-6pm Sat; U1, U3 Stephansplatz

Named after the inventor of the unique machine used to cut the beautiful crystal, Swarovski showcases some of the finest crystal jewellery and ornaments you're ever likely

Entrance to exclusive Meinl am Graben supermarket (above)

to see. And you wouldn't be alone in thinking you've seen a few of the pieces before; Audrey Hepburn wore Swarovski in *My Fair Lady* and Grace Kelly wore it in *High Society*.

WOLFORD Map pp240-3 *Lingerie*
☎ 513 16 20; 01, Kärntner Strasse 19; ✆ 9.30am-7pm Mon-Fri, to 9pm Thu, 9.30am-6pm Sat; U1, U3 Stephansplatz

Austria's world-famous lingerie maker (its headquarters are in Bregenz, Vorarlberg) has set up shop in a couple of locations around town, with the Kärntner Strasse branch as its largest. Filled mainly with bodies and stockings, for which it gained its reputation, there's also a small corner for men's underwear.

MICHAELERPLATZ TO MÖLKER BASTEI

KAUFHAUS SCHIEPEK
Map pp240-3 *Jewellery/Accessories*
☎ 533 15 75; 01, Teinfaltstrasse 3; ✆ 10am-7pm Mon-Fri, 10am-6pm Sat; bus 1A

If you're looking for cheap, colourful jewellery or beads to create your own, look no further than Kaufhaus Schiepek. The range is extensive, and includes glittering bags and purses.

LODEN-PLANKL Map pp240-3 *Clothing*
☎ 533 80 32; 01, Michaelerplatz 6; ✆ 9am-6pm Mon-Fri, 10am-5pm Sat; U3 Herrengasse, bus 2A, 3A

Loden-Plankl specialises in *Trachten*, traditional Austrian wear. It's been in operation for more than 170 years, which is probably why its *Lederhosen* (leather trousers) and *Dirndl* (traditional women's dress) aren't exactly 'budget' prices.

SHIPPING Map pp240-3 *Knick-Knacks*
☎ 533 15 75; 01, Teinfaltstrasse 4; ✆ 1-6pm Mon-Fri, 10am-5pm Sat; bus 1A

Owned and run by Kaufhaus Schiepek (and directly opposite its owners), Shipping specialises in colourful plastic objects – bowls, plates, lamps etc. They also stock an intriguing range of Asian dishes and kitchen ware.

XOCOLAT Map pp240-3 *Confectionery*
☎ 535 43 63; 01, Freyung 2; ✆ 10am-6pm Mon-Sat, noon-5pm Sun; U3 Herrengasse, bus 1A

Tucked away down the mosaic-covered Freyung Passage is this small but incredibly delicious chocolate shop. Its 200 varieties of chocolate, sourced from across the globe, are almost too artfully designed to eat.

ROTENTURMSTRASSE TO SCHOTTENRING

BLACK MARKET Map pp240-3 *Music*
☎ 533 76 17-0; 01, Gonzagagasse 9; ✆ 10am-7.30pm Mon-Fri, 10am-5pm Sat; tram 1, 2, bus 2A

Black Market is Vienna's house, techno and electronic specialist. The vinyl selection is enormous and the staff highly knowledgeable. You'll also find a small lounge with coffee, and T-shirts and sweats that are cooler than cool.

ES BRENNT Map pp240-3 *Furniture*
☎ 532 09 00; 01, Freisingergasse 1; ✆ 3-6.30pm Mon-Fri, 11am-4pm Sat; U1, U3 Stephansplatz

Es Brennt specialises in furniture from 1900 to 1970, but focuses much of its attention on the 50s, 60s and 70s. Don't expect to find much that would fall under 'ordinary' or 'bland' labels.

FEINER NATURKOSTLADEN
Map pp240-3 *Organic*
01, Judengasse 4; ✆ 10am-7.30pm Mon-Fri, 10am-5pm Sat; bus 1A, 2A

It's hard to beat an organic-product shop that sells Bert and Ernie biscuits! This small place, tucked away in the back streets of the Innere Stadt, has fine assortment of great bio biscuits, bread and produce, and makes fresh pancakes for lunch from Monday to Friday.

LUCKY STAR ORGANIX
Map pp240-3 *Organic Clothing*
01, Rubengasse 1; ✆ 11am-7pm Mon-Fri, 11am-6pm Sat; bus 1A, 2A, 3A

Lucky Star Organix's motto is 'non-toxic fashion and lifestyle', which in practical terms means it sells only clothing made from 100% organic cotton or hemp. Clothes are generally a mix of earthy browns and greens, but there is also a fine selection of bright colours. Prices aren't out of this world.

SHAKESPEARE & CO Map pp240-3 *Books*
☎ 535 50 53; www.shakespeare.co.at; 01, Sterngasse 2; ✆ 9am-7pm Mon-Wed & Sat, 9am-9pm Thu & Fri; bus 2A, 3A

The Shakespeare is the place to go for literary and hard-to-find titles in English. Staff members are incredibly friendly and are only too eager to help with any queries. Its ceiling-high shelves are overloaded with books, and the slightly cluttered look of the shop only adds to its charm.

Shopping – Innere Stadt

SONG Map pp240-3   *Clothes & Accessories*

☎ 532 28 58; 01, Landskrongasse 2; 🕐 10am-7pm Mon-Fri, 10am-5pm Sat; U1, U3 Stephansplatz, bus 1A

For the latest, and often most experimental, clothing from young designers across the globe, head to Song. Many pieces are strongly colourful and almost have a life of their own, which is a much-needed break-away from the drab blacks and greys many Viennese don. Hats, shoes and bags complement the racks of outfits.

UNGER UND KLEIN Map pp240-3   *Wine*

☎ 532 13 23; 01, Gölsdorfgasse 2; 🕐 3pm-midnight Mon-Fri, 5-11pm Sat; tram 1, 2, bus 2A, 3A

Unger und Klein's wine collection spans the entire globe, but the majority of its labels come from Europe. Of course Austria makes a great show, and the best the country has to offer – whether expensive boutique varieties or bargain-bin bottles – is available. At night, the place moonlights as a crowded bar.

WEIN & CO Map pp240-3   *Wine*

☎ 535 09 16; www.weinco.at, German only; 01, Jasomirgottstrasse 3-5; 🕐 10am-midnight Mon-Sat, 11am-midnight Sun; U1, U3 Stephansplatz

Wein & Co is arguably the best place to buy wine in Vienna. Prices are extremely competitive, the selection is hard to beat and the concentration of New World wines is impressive. On top of this five wines chosen for special attention every month are free to taste. Five other Wine & Co shops are scattered around town.

Markets

With globalisation storming the world, multinational companies gobbling up local chains and small shop-owners being forced into early retirement, it's so refreshing to know that the traditional market is still alive and kicking in Vienna. Almost every district has at least one, if not more, markets selling fresh produce from Monday to Saturday. Many reflect the ethnic diversity of their neighbourhood. Some host *Bauernmärkte* (farmers markets) on Saturday mornings, where growers from the surrounding countryside travel to the big city to sell their wares. Fresh vegetables, tree-ripened fruit, cured hams, free-range eggs, home-made schnapps and bunches of flowers are some of the products for sale.

The following are the best of the bunch:

Brunnenmarkt (Map pp244-5; 16, Brunnengasse; 🕐 6am-6.30pm Mon-Fri, 6am-2pm Sat; U6 Josefstädter Strasse, tram J) Brunnenmarkt is the largest street-market in Vienna and reflects its ethnic neighbourhood – most stallholders are of Turkish or Balkan descent. The majority of produce sold is vegetables and fruit, but there are a few places selling unbelievably tacky clothes – this is the place to pick up that Hulk Hogan T-shirt you've always wanted. The kebab houses here are truly superb (see Kent, p135, and Etap, p135, in the Eating chapter). On Saturday nearby Yppenplatz features the best Bauernmarkt in the city.

Flohmarkt (Map pp246-7; 05, Kettenbrückengasse; 🕐 dawn-5pm Sat; U4 Kettenbrückengasse) On Saturday this flea market is tacked onto the southwestern end of the Naschmarkt, extending for several blocks. It's very atmospheric – more like the markets of Eastern Europe – and shouldn't be missed, with goods piled up in apparent chaos on the walkway. You can find anything you want (and everything you don't want): books, clothes, records, ancient electrical goods, old postcards, ornaments, carpets…you name it. Bargain for prices here.

Freyung (Map pp240-3; 01, Freyung; 🕐 8am-7.30pm Fri & Sat; U2 Schottentor, bus 1A) The Freyung market exclusively sells organic produce from farmers. The atmosphere here is quite sedate compared to the markets mentioned above.

Karmelitermarkt (Map pp244-5; 02, Im Werd; 🕐 6am-6.30pm Mon-Fri, 6am-2pm Sat; bus 5A) A market with a long tradition, the Karmelitermarkt is another which reflects the ethnic diversity of the neighbourhood in which it is set. Fruit and vegetables stalls share the marketplace with butchers selling kosher and halal meats. On Saturday the square features a Bauernmarkt.

Naschmarkt (Map pp246-7; 06, Linke & Rechte Wienzeile; 🕐 6am-6.30pm Mon-Fri, 6am-5pm Sat; U1, U2, U4 Karlsplatz, U4 Kettenbrückengasse) *The* market in Vienna. This massive market extends for more than 500m along Linke Wienzeile between the U4 stops of Kettenbrückengasse and Karlsplatz. It mainly consists of stalls selling meats, fruit and vegetables (this is the place for that hard-to-find exotic variety), spices, cheeses and olives, but there are some stalls selling clothes and curios. It's also a great place for food and drink; its kebab and falafel stalls are among the best in the business, and on either side of the main thoroughfare are Asian, Indian and Austrian restaurants.

RINGSTRASSE

PARLAMENT TO SCHWARZENBERGPLATZ

PACHISI Map pp240-3 _Toys_
☎ 512 71 50; 01, Kärntner Ring 5-13, Ringstrassen Gallerien; ◷ 10am-7pm Mon-Fri, 10am-6pm Sat; U1, U2, U4 Karlsplatz, Karlsplatz trams
If you're looking for unusual but beautiful toys, Pachisi is the place for you. The range of wooden toys is quite astounding (you won't find much plastic here), and great big cuddly animals are utterly huggable.

RINGSTRASSEN GALERIEN
Map pp240-3 _Shopping Centre_
www.ringstrassen-galerien.at; 01, Kärntner Ring 5-13; ◷ 10am-7pm Mon-Wed & Fri, 10am-9pm Thu, 10am-6pm Sat; U1, U2, U4 Karlsplatz, Karlsplatz trams
This large shopping complex on the Ringstrasse covers three floors and houses 70 shops. It's mainly filled with boutique fashion shops, which aren't the cheapest in town. Apart from the excellent Billa in the basement, the entire place lacks a bit of spark.

MUSEUMSQUARTIER

LOMOSHOP Map pp240-3 _Photography_
☎ 523 70 16; 07, Museumsplatz 1; ◷ 10am-7pm, to 10pm Thu; U2, U3 Volkstheater, bus 48A
What began in the '80s as a bit of fun for a few Lomo fanatics has now turned into a worldwide cult, and the Lomoshop is considered the heart of the Lomo movement. There's all manner of Lomo cameras, gadgets and accessories for sale; an original Russian-made Lomo will set you back around €150, newer ones around €50.

BETWEEN THE DANUBE CANAL & THE DANUBE

GESUNDES
Map pp240-3 _Organic/Vegetarian_
☎ 219 53 22; 02, Lilienbrunngasse 3; ◷ 9am-6pm Mon, Tue, Thu, Fri, 9am-5.30pm Wed, 10am-2pm Sat; U1, U4 Schwedenplatz, tram N
This small, organic foodstuffs store has a variety of products from around Austria, and an excellent menu of vegetarian dishes (see p126).

WIENER PORZELLANMANUFAKTUR AUGARTEN Map pp244-5 _Porcelain_
☎ 211 24-0; www.augarten.at; 02, Obere Augartenstrasse 1, Schloss Augarten; ◷ 9.30am-5pm Mon-Fri; tram 31, bus 5A
Exquisite, albeit very traditional, porcelain ornaments and gifts are produced at this well-established factory. Prices start at around €35 and just keep on going. The Augarten porcelain factory has outlets in the **Innere Stadt** (Map pp240-3; ☎ 512 14 94; 01, Stock-im-Eisen-Platz 3), **Mariahilf** (Map pp240-3; ☎ 587 92 18; 06, Mariahilfer Strasse 31) and at the **airport** (☎ 7007 31 63). Tours of the factory are available.

INSIDE THE GÜRTEL

WIEDEN

BABETTES Map pp246-7 _Cooking_
☎ 585 51 65; 04 Schleifmühlgasse 17; ◷ 10am-7pm Mon-Fri, 10am-5pm Sat; bus 59A
Babettes is a unique concept in Vienna. Part eatery, part cookbook and spice store, it caters to a growing market of Viennese willing to experiment with their home cuisine. With more than a thousand cookbooks from around the world, you should be able to find something to match your tastes. Cooking courses are also available.

BOBBY'S FOOD STORE
Map pp248-9 _Food_
☎ 586 75 34; 04, Schleifmühlgasse 8; ◷ 10am-6.30pm Mon-Fri, 10am-2pm Sat; tram 62, 65, bus 59A
Have a craving for Vegemite or Marmite? Heinz baked beans? Boddingtons? Salt-and-vinegar crisps? Bobby's is a one-stop food store for brands from the US and UK that are hard to find anywhere else in Vienna.

MARGARETEN

M. FREY WILLE Map pp246-7 _Jewellery_
☎ 599 25; www.m-frey.com; 06, Gumpendorfer Strasse 81; U4 Pilgramgasse, bus 57A
Elaborate bracelets, watches, rings and pendants are the work of this fine jeweller. The colourful styles decorating the pieces pay homage to the likes of Klimt and ancient Egypt.

MARIAHILF

AMADEUS Map pp246-7 _Books & Music_
☎ 595 45 50; 06, Mariahilfer Strasse 99; ◷ 9.30am-7pm Mon-Fri, 9.30am-6pm Sat; U3 Zieglergasse

Snow Globes

There are many impersonators but only one true snow-globe original – the Perzy Snow Globe. Back in 1900 in his workshop in Vienna, Erwin Perzy I had the idea of designing a globe containing a church and filled with liquid and rice, which, when shaken, produced the effect of snow falling. It became an instant hit, even with Emperor Franz Josef.

More than a hundred years on the company is still going strong, and is still in family hands; Erwin Perzy III, the grandson of the snow globe creator, is current head of the company. Their products have travelled the globe, and have landed in some illustrious paws – a Perzy snow globe was produced for Bill Clinton's inauguration and contains the actual confetti from the event. One-off pieces have also been produced for the films *Citizen Kane*, *Heidi* and *True Lies*.

In a world of cheap-and-cheerful products, churned out in their thousands by automated production lines, its surprising, and refreshing, to learn that every snow globe is still handmade. The Perzy factory contains a small **museum** (Map pp244-5; ☎ 486 43 41; www.viennasnowglobe.at; 17, Schumanngasse 87; ☽ 8am-noon & 1-3pm Mon-Thu; tram 9, 42), which stocks their snow globes and can be visited by appointment.

One of the largest book stores in Vienna, Amadeus has a wide range of travel books and fiction in English and there's a mass of CDs on the top floor. Amadeus has branches in **Landstrasse** (Map pp240–3; 03, Landstrasser Hauptstrasse 2a) and in the Steffl department store (p164).

GENERALLI CENTER

Map pp246-7 *Shopping Centre*
☎ 586 30 24; 06, Mariahilfer Strasse 77; ☽ 10am-9pm Mon-Thu, 10am-7pm Fri, 10am-6pm Sat; U3 Neubaugasse, bus 13A
The Generalli Center is a relatively small shopping centre, but what it lacks in quantity it certainly makes up in quality. Prestigious shops within its halls include Swarovski, Nike and Pan, a clothes store stocking last year's top designer labels at half price.

MÖRTZ Map pp240-3 *Shoes*
☎ 587 57 87; 06, Windmühlgasse 9; ☽ 8.30am-1pm & 2-6pm Mon-Fri, 8.30am-noon Sat; bus 57A
On any given weekend, elderly Viennese can be seen riding the buses and trams to the Wienerwald for a bit of *wandern* (hiking). Their boots look as though they've survived both world wars and they'd easily survive another couple – and they're probably from Mörtz. Here you can find superb hand-made hiking boots sturdy enough for any hike you care to undertake, and they're comfortable to boot.

PICCINI PICCOLO GOURMET

Map pp240-3 *Food*
☎ 587 52 54; 06, Linke Wienzeile 4; ☽ 11am-7.30pm Mon-Fri, 9.30am-2pm Sat; U1, U2, U4 Karlsplatz
You might be on holiday in Vienna, but it's worth taking some Italian food products home with you. Piccini stocks only the finest and freshest from Italy, all of which are handled with love and care. It's also a superb restaurant (see p129).

POLYKLAMOTT

Map pp246-7 *Second-Hand Clothes*
☎ 969 03 37; 06, Hofmühlgasse 6; ☽ 11am-7.30pm Mon-Fri, 11am-5pm Sat; U4 Pilgramgasse, bus 13A
Looking for that special shirt for a 'Bad Shirt Night', but all the shops are closed? Polyklamott has the answer – an automatic clothes dispenser. All items in its *Automat* are €5, and it's open for business 24 hours a day. During normal opening hours, the full range of Polyklamott's fine second-hand clothes can be sifted through.

RAVE UP Map pp246-7 *Music*
☎ 596 96 50; 06, Hofmühlgasse 1; 10am-6.30pm Mon-Fri, 10am-5pm Sat; U4 Pilgramgasse, bus 13A
Friendly staff, loads of vinyl and a massive collection covering every genre of world music makes a trip to Rave Up a real pleasure. The store specialises in indie and alternative imports from the UK and US, but you'll find plenty of electronica, hip-hop and retro tunes, too.

SHU! Map pp246-7 *Shoes*
☎ 523 14 49; 07, Neubaugasse 34; ☽ 10am-6.30pm Mon-Fri, 10am-5pm Sat; tram 49, bus 13A
Shoe fanatics flock to this store in droves, not only for the latest designer styles but also for the accompanying easy-on-the-wallet price. Shu! stocks both men's and women's shoes.

VIRGIN MEGASTORE Map pp240-3 *Music*
☎ 588 37; 06, Mariahilfer Strasse 37-39; ☽ 9am-7pm Mon-Fri, 9am-6pm Sat; U3 Neubaugasse
As the name suggests, this is an excessively large store. Two floors are crammed with CDs, DVDs, records, tapes and videos, and although most fall within the mainstream category, you can find some unusual titles if you look hard enough. There's a small section of English videos and DVDs.

NEUBAU

DAS MÖBEL
Map pp240-3   *Furniture & Accessories*

☎ 524 94 97; 07, Burggasse 10; ☺ 10-1am; U2, U3 Volkstheater, bus 48A

Das Möbel is more of a bar than a shop (see p141), but it showcases some of the funkiest and most original furniture in Vienna. Local artists and designers fill the place with their latest creations, and it's all for sale. The bags hanging just inside the door are also locally designed and produced, and are truly special creations.

EVA BLUT
Map pp246-7   *Bags & Accessories*

☎ 524 05 95; www.evablut.org; 07, Schottenfeldgasse 41-43/28a; ☺ by appointment only; tram 49

Need a bag and a jacket but have room for only one? Never fear, Eva Blut is here. This creative young designer produces funky bags that fold out into jackets or skirts, or vice versa. Her wares have reportedly gained cult status in Japan. Phone ahead to make an appointment.

GERNGOSS
Map pp240-3   *Shopping Centre*

☎ 521 80; 07, Mariahilfer Strasse 38-40; ☺ 9.30am-7pm Mon-Fri, 9am-6pm Sat; U3 Neubaugasse, bus 13A

Gerngoss is a truly one-stop shopping experience. Five floors of shops cover most shopping genres, but the selection is very mainstream. The top floor is devoted to Cosmos, a massive electronic store with a sea of CD-ROMs, DVDs and CDs. Sports Experts takes up the fourth floor, while Merkur supermarket fills the basement.

LOLLIPOP
Map pp246-7   *Confectionery*

☎ 526 33 38; 07, Burggasse 57; ☺ 7.30am-8pm Mon-Fri, 8am-8pm Sat, 10am-8pm Sun; bus 13A, 48A

Like alcohol and cigarettes, everyone knows too much sugar's bad for you. But why does it taste so good? Lollipop will satisfy the most ardent sweet fan, with a selection too good to resist.

ORATOR
Map pp246-7   *Photography*

☎ 526 10 10-0; 07, Westbahnstrasse 23; ☺ 9.30am-6pm Mon-Thu, 9.30am-7pm; tram 5, 49

Orator is one of a handful of specialist photography shops at the western end of Westbahnstrasse. The range of digital and SLR cameras and lenses is quite impressive, and the second-hand stock is worth browsing through.

SUBSTANCE
Map pp246-7   *Music*

☎ 523 67 57; 07, Westbahnstrasse 16; ☺ 11am-7.30pm Mon-Fri, 11am-6pm Sat; tram 49, bus 13A

Substance stocks the weird, the wild, the wicked and the wonderful of the music industry. There's a decent section devoted to second-hand records as well as a handful of T-shirts, books and DVDs.

Christmas Markets

From around the middle of November, *Christkindlmärkte* (Christmas markets) start to pop up all over Vienna. Ranging from kitsch to quaint in style and atmosphere, they all have a few things in common: plenty of people, loads of Christmas gifts to purchase, mugs of *Glühwein* (mulled wine) and hot-plates loaded down with *Kartoffelpuffer* (hot potato patties) and *Maroni* (roasted chestnuts). Most close a day or two before Christmas day.

Some of the best include:

Alte AKH (Map pp244-5; tram 43, 44) A favourite of students, this small market occupies a corner of the Alte AKH's largest courtyard. There are farm animals and a horse-drawn sleigh for the kids.

Freyung (Map pp240-3; U2 Schottentor, bus 1A) Freyung's stalls devote themselves to Austrian arts and crafts, and the entire market attempts, with some success, to emit an old-worldy feel.

Heiligenkreuzerhof (Map pp240-3; U1, U4 Schwedenplatz, Schwedenplatz trams) This oft-forgotten market is arguably the most authentic and quaint of all the *Christkindlmärkte*. It's off Schönlaterngasse, hidden within a residential courtyard.

Karlsplatz (Map pp240-3; U1, U2 U4 Karlsplatz) The Karlsplatz market mainly has stalls selling arty gifts and is situated close to the Karlskirche. People flock here to crowd around flaming metal barrels, clutching their cup of *Glühwein*.

Rathausplatz (Map pp240-3; tram 1, 2) This is easily the biggest and most touristy Christmas market in Vienna, held on the square in front of the Rathaus (City Hall). Most of the Christmas gifts on sale are kitschy beyond belief, but the atmosphere is lively and the *Glühwein* just keeps on flowing.

Schönbrunn (Map pp246-7; U4 Schönbrunn, bus 10A) Directly in front of the palace, the circle of stalls are generally quite upmarket, but there's loads of events for the kids and daily classical concerts at 6pm (more on weekends).

Spittalberg (Map pp240-3; U2, U3 Volkstheater, tram 49, bus 48A) Occupying the charming cobblestoned streets of the Spittalberg quarter, this market is traditionally the most beloved of the Viennese. Stalls sell quality arts and crafts, but they're not cheap. No matter what the temperature, people crowd around *Glühwein* stalls, especially outside Lux and Plutzerbräu.

JOSEFSTADT
KRÄUTERDROGERIE

Map pp244-5   *Health Foods*

☎ 405 45 22; 08, Kochgasse 34; ☺ 8.30am-6pm
Mon-Fri, 8.30am-1pm Sat; tram 43, 44, bus 13A
The Kräuterdrogerie is a shop for those on a
health kick, or for people who feel it's time to
treat the body right. It stocks a huge array of
health food and Ayurvedic remedies, and also
has good vegetarian lunches.

SZAAL Map pp244-5   *Furniture*
☎ 406 63 30; www.szaal.at; 08, Josefstädter Strasse
74; ☺ 10am-6pm Mon-Fri, 10am-noon Sat; U6 Josefstädter Strasse, tram J, 33
Szaal is a specialist in Biedermeier and baroque
furniture, dating from around 1700 to 1840.
You'll also find a few pieces from the late-19th
and 20th centuries. The store can arrange ship-
ment back to your home country.

TEUCHTLER Map pp240-3   *Music*
☎ 586 21 33; 08, Windmühlgasse 10; ☺ 1-6pm Mon-
Fri, 10am-1pm Sat; bus 57A
This second-hand shop buys, sells and exchanges records and CDs, including rare and
deleted titles. It's one of the best of its kind
in Vienna, and has classical, jazz, rock, pop,
electronic and world/folk sections.

ALSERGRUND
LA PASTERIA Map pp244-5   *Food*
☎ 310 27 36; 09, Servitengasse 10; ☺ 10am-7pm
Mon-Fri, 9am-1pm Sat; U4 Rossauer Lände, tram D
La Pasteria stocks a selective array of the best
that Italy produces – wine, cheese, ham, pasta,
sweets and breads. It's not cheap, but it's damn
fine. It's connected to a restaurant by the same
name next door (see p132).

OUTSIDE THE GÜRTEL
SIMMERING
PISCHINGER FABRIKSVERKAUF
Map pp238-9   *Confectionery*
☎ 523 25 71-22; 10, Himberger Strasse 2; ☺ 9am-
6pm Mon-Fri, 9am-5pm Sat; tram 67

Not as well known as Manner but still famous
in Vienna, Pischinger makes fine chocolate and
sweets. Its factory store sells giant packets of
chocolate at discounted rates and has a range
of seconds.

RUDOLFSHEIM-FÜNFHAUS
LUGNER CITY
Map pp246-7   *Shopping Centre*
☎ 981 50; 15, Gablenzgasse 5-13; ☺ 9am-7pm
Mon-Thu, 9am-9pm Fri, 9am-6pm Sat; U6 Burggasse/
Stadthalle, tram 6, 18, bus 48A
Lugner City isn't the most illustrious shopping
centre in Vienna, but it's cheap and cheerful. It
contains most of the main chain stores as well
as restaurants, cafés and supermarkets.

OTTAKRING
STAUD Map pp244-5   *Jams & Pickles*
☎ 406 88 050; 16, Yppenplatz; ☺ 8am-12.30pm Tue-
Thu, 2.30-6pm Fri, 8am-1.30pm Sat; U6 Josefstädter
Strasse, tram J, 44
The family business Staud has been making
jams and pickled vegetables and fruit for more
than 30 years. Prices are more than you'd pay for
other brands in supermarkets, but the quality
here is by far the best in Vienna. Saturday morning is a great time to visit, when the nearby
Brunnenmarkt (see p166) is in full swing.

HERNALS
MANNER FABRIKSVERKAUF
Map pp238-9   *Confectionery*
☎ 488 22; 17, Wilhelminenstrasse 6; ☺ 9am-5pm
Mon-Thu, 9am-2pm Fri; tram 9, 44
If you only try one sweet or confectionery
item while in Vienna, then it *has* to be Manner
Schnitten. This glorious collaboration of wafers
and hazelnut cream has been around since
1898 and just gets better with time. Most Viennese glaze over and start to dribble at their
very mention; even Arnie loves the little things
and featured them in *Terminator 3*.

The Manner factory is in the far reaches of
Hernals. Its factory shop sells the whole Manner confectionery range, and stocks piles and
piles of seconds; look for the massive bags of
Mozart Kügeln (Mozart Balls) for only €2.

Innere Stadt	173
Stephansplatz	173
East of Stephansplatz	173
Kärntner Strasse, Graben & Kohlmarkt	174
Rotenturmstrasse to Schottenring	175
Cheap Sleeps	175

Ringstrasse	176
Schottentor to Parlament	176
Parlament to Schwarzenbergplatz	176
Schwarzenbergplatz to the Danube Canal	176

Between the Danube Canal & the Danube	177
Cheap Sleeps	177

Inside the Gürtel	177
Landstrasse	178
Wieden	178
Mariahilf	178
Neubau	178
Josefstadt	179
Alsergrund	179
Cheap Sleeps	179

Outside the Gürtel	181
Favoriten	181
Hietzing	181
Rudolfsheim-Fünfhaus	181
Hernals	181
Während	181
Döbling	182
Cheap Sleeps	182

Sleeping

Sleeping

Vienna's sleeping options cover the full spectrum, from basic youth hostels and student residences to hotels where chandeliers, antique furniture and original 19th-century oil paintings are the norm rather than the exception. In between are homely *Pensionen* (guesthouses) and less ostentatious hotels, plus a small but smart range of apartments for longer-term rentals.

Standards remain high, and so do prices; accommodation will probably be the most expensive item on your budget, unless you're a shopaholic. High season – June to September and over the Christmas and New Year period – means high prices and often a lack of availability at popular choices. At this time it's best to book ahead. Note that reservations are binding and compensation may be claimed by the hotel if you do not take a reserved room, or by you if the room is unavailable.

Over winter, rates can drop substantially and many places offer discounts and specials for longer stays. Some, especially the five-star hotels, offer special weekend rates, or 'two nights for the price of one' packages. It's definitely worth inquiring about cheaper rates before signing on the dotted line.

> ## Top Five Sleeps
> - **Best Design** Das Triest (p178)
> - **Best Extras** Hotel im Palais Schwarzenberg (p178)
> - **Best Just Plain Viennese** Auer (p179)
> - **Best Cheap Night** Wombat's (p182)
> - **Best View** Hotel am Stephansplatz (p173)

As a general guideline, breakfast is included in the price at hostels, *Pensionen* and hotels. It usually consists of a continental buffet, but you'll often find that the more the room costs, the more substantial the breakfast will be. Parking is extra and can be anything from €6 to €26.

Prices quoted here are basic rates in high season. We've classed anything under €70 for a double room as budget and listed them under the Cheap Sleeps headings at the end of each section.

Accommodation Styles
HOSTELS & STUDENT RESIDENCES
Vienna has a smattering of *Jugendherberge*, private hostels or hostels affiliated with Hostelling International (HI). In the former, no membership is required. Dorm beds, singles and doubles are generally available in both; expect to pay around €15 to €20 for a dorm bed in high season.

Austria has two youth hostel organisations affiliated with the worldwide HI network: **Österreichischer Jugendherbergsverband** (ÖJHN; Map pp244–5; ☎ 533 53 53; www.oejhv.or.at; 01, Schottenring 28; ☺ 9am-5pm Mon-Thu, 9am-3pm Fri; U2, U4 Schottenring, tram 1, 2) and **Österreichischer Jugendherbergswerk** (ÖJHW; Map pp240–3; ☎ 533 18 33; www.oejhw.at; 01, Helferstorferstrasse 4; ☺ 9.30am-6pm Mon-Fri; tram 1, 2). Either can provide information on all of Vienna's HI hostels.

While university students are on holiday from July to September, their student halls of residences are available to tourists. Rooms are perfectly OK but nothing fancy; expect single beds (perhaps placed together in doubles), a work desk and a wardrobe. Cheaper places have institutional-style ablutions blocks while pricier places offer private shower and toilet and are all but indistinguishable from conventional hotels. Most are outside the Innere Stadt, but are still reasonably convenient for the centre.

HOTELS & PENSIONEN
As hotels and *Pensionen* (B&B guesthouses) make up the bulk of accommodation options in Vienna, a huge variation in styles and tastes exist. Leaving aside five-star hotels, which are in a league of their own, hotels tend to be larger than *Pensionen*, have more facilities

(on-site parking, bars and restaurants) and come with more extras (room service, laundry service etc). *Pensionen*, however, are often located in apartment blocks, and can be far more personable and less standardised, with larger rooms. Prices start from around €50 to €60 for a basic double room with shared bath and top out at approximately €200 to €250 for an upmarket ensuite double in a four-star hotel. On average, expect to pay €90 to €100 for a decent double room in a hotel or *Pension*.

Many of the older hotels and *Pensionen* have a range of rooms and facilities, the cheapest of which share a toilet and shower with other guests. Others come with a shower and/or toilet, while others go the whole hog and come complete with shower and toilet, and possibly bath.

LONGER-TERM RENTALS
Viennese looking for apartments rely on word of mouth or turn to *Bazar* magazine. It's *the* magazine if you're looking to buy, sell or rent anything, including apartments or rooms. The time scale of places on offer may range from indefinite rental to occupation of a flat for a month or so while the resident is on holiday. *Falter*, *Kurier* and *Der Standard* also carry accommodation ads.

A couple of short-term apartment rentals are listed in this chapter.

INNERE STADT

The Innere Stadt is easily Vienna's prime accommodation location and, with the lion's share of attractions and an excellent selection of restaurants, bars and music venues, it's not hard to see why. Comparatively, prices tend to outdo the rest of Vienna (except the Ringstrasse) and reservations are more often than not a prerequisite.

STEPHANSPLATZ
HOTEL AM STEPHANSPLATZ
Map pp240-3   *Hotel*
☎ 534 05-0; www.hotelamstephansplatz.at; 01, Stephansplatz 9; s/d from €105/130; U1, U3 Stephansplatz

Want to wake up with the Stephansdom's glorious Gothic-ness towering above you every morning? Then this is your place: directly opposite the cathedral, you can't get any closer than this. Rooms are genuinely comfy and sizable and, of course, those fronting Stephansplatz are the most sought after.

EAST OF STEPHANSPLATZ
APPARTEMENT PENSION
RIEMERGASSE Map pp240-3   *Apartments*
☎ 512 72 200; www.riemergasse.at; 01, Riemergasse 8; apt per night/month from €91/2355; U3 Stubentor, tram 1, 2

Apartments in Riemergasse all come with a kitchenette, telephone, cable TV, toilet and bath or shower, are recently renovated and about five minutes by foot from Stephansdom.

Breakfast and parking can be arranged for an extra €5 and €15 respectively.

HOTEL AUSTRIA Map pp240-3   *Hotel*
☎ 515 23; office@hotelaustria-wien.at; 01, Am Fleischmarkt 20; s/d €63/90; U1, U4 Schwedenplatz, Schwedenplatz trams

This three-star hotel has the advantage of close proximity to the Innere Stadt's action while maintaining a quiet, genteel atmosphere due to its hidden location on a low-key, cobblestone cul-de-sac. Accommodating staff and finely furnished rooms add to Austria's charm.

HOTEL KAISERIN ELISABETH
Map pp240-3   *Hotel*
☎ 515 26; www.kaiserinelisabeth.at; 01, Weihburggasse 3; s/d €75/200; U1, U3 Stephansplatz

The relatively plain frontage of the Hotel Kaiserin Elisabeth belies its pleasant interior and long history: the likes of Mozart, Wagner and Liszt all graced the hotel with their presence at one time. Rooms have a late-19th-century look and feel, which comes across as demure yet highly appealing.

HOTEL KÄRNTNERHOF Map pp240-3 *Hotel*
☎ 512 19 23; www.karntnerhof.com; 01, Grashofgasse 4; s/d €92/120; U1, U4 Schwedenplatz, Schwedenplatz trams

The hidden cul-de-sacs of the Innere Stadt are full of surprises, and Grashofgasse is no exception. Here you'll find the demure Kärntnerhof, a central yet quiet hotel run by staff with an eye for detail and a knack for quality service. You certainly won't lose yourself in the rooms, but they're highly appealing and modern to boot.

HOTEL-PENSION SUZANNE

Map pp240-3   *Pension*

☎ 513 25 07; www.pension-suzanne.at; 01, Walfisch-
gasse 4; s/d €72/90; U1, U2, U4 Karlsplatz, Karlsplatz
trams

The name may say 'hotel', but Suzanne's look
and feel easily puts it in the *Pension* category.
Antique furniture distracts you from the smallish
size of the rooms (many with kitchenettes) and
adds a noble touch, while family management
makes you feel relaxed and quite at home.

HOTEL ZUR WIENER STAATSOPER

Map pp240-3   *Hotel*

☎ 513 12 74; www.zurwienerstaatsoper.at; 01,
Krugerstrasse 11; s/d from €77/109; U1, U2, U4 Karlsplatz, Karlsplatz trams

Zur Wiener Staatsoper was closed for renovation at the time of research, but you can rest
assured that its rooms will be of the highest
standard, if a little compact.

KÖNIG VON HUNGARN

Map pp240-3   *Hotel*

☎ 515 84-0; www.kvu.at; 01, Schulerstrasse 10; s/d
€133/153; U1, U3 Stephansplatz

The 'King of Hungary' pulls off a hard task: bal-
ancing class with informality. The wonderful
inner courtyard, with its glass roof, quiet ambience, leather furniture and attentive bar staff, is
its first accomplishment in achieving this combination. The rooms are next to impress: each
is individually decorated in antique furniture
and displays plenty of stripped wood, yet still
manages to convey a homely appeal.

SCHLOSSHOTEL RÖMISCHER KAISER

Map pp240-3   *Hotel*

☎ 512 77 51; www.hotel-romischer-kaiser.at; 01,
Annagasse 16; r from €159; U1, U2, U4 Karlsplatz,
Karlsplatz trams

The 'Roman Emperor' is on a quiet street off Vienna's *Hauptstrasse* (High St), Kärntner Strasse.
Rooms are a little small, but they're quite comfortable and all individually decorated. Children up to the age of six stay for free.

SINGERSTRASSE APARTMENTS

Map pp240-3   *Apartments*

☎ 514 49-0; www.singerstrasse2125.at; 01,
Singerstrasse 21-25; apt per week/month from
€616/2161; U1, U3 Stephansplatz

Singerstrasse apartments are normally
snapped up by people on business in Vienna.
They range in size from studios to large one-

bed apartments and come complete with
telephone, satellite TV, Internet facilities for
laptops, a kitchenette and the all-important
cleaning service. All bills – except phone – are
included in the price and the office is open
from 8am to 8pm Monday to Friday.

KÄRNTNER STRASSE, GRABEN & KOHLMARKT

HOTEL AMBASSADOR Map pp240-3   *Hotel*

☎ 961 61-0; www.ambassador.at; 01, Kärntner
Strasse 22/Neuer Markt 5; s/d from €218/277; U1, U3
Stephansplatz

Recently reopened after extensive renovations, this lavish hotel looks and feels more
like a palace and whoever redesigned it sure
had a thing for chandeliers. Rooms still manage to capture the Ambassador's century-old
history while meeting every requirement of a
thoroughly modern hotel.

HOTEL SACHER Map pp240-3   *Hotel*

☎ 514 56-0; www.sacher.com; 01, Philharmonikerstrasse 4; s/d from €215/312; U1, U2, U4 Karlsplatz,
Karlsplatz trams

There is absolutely no coincidence Hotel Sacher
has the same name as the famous *Sacher Torte*:
the chocolate delight's original creator, Eduard
Sacher, opened the hotel in 1876. It's almost a
reflection of the Innere Stadt: elegant, dignified,
historic, and often teeming with tourists. Rooms
are styled in baroque and are complemented
by genuine 19th-century oil paintings.

HOTEL WANDL Map pp240-3   *Hotel*

☎ 534 55-0; www.hotel-wandl.com; 01, Petersplatz
9; s/d from €58/100; U1, U3 Stephansplatz

Built as a residence in 1700, this house changed
hands, and names (it was originally known as
the Four Seasons), in the mid-1850s and reinvented itself as Hotel Wandl. Rooms, many of
which face inner courtyards, have been fitted
with mod cons, but still manage to retain an
air of elegance.

PENSION AM OPERNECK

Map pp240-3   *Pension*

☎ 512 93 10; fax 512 93 10-20; 01 Kärntner Strasse
47; s/d €53/75; U1, U2, U4 Karlsplatz, Karlsplatz trams

Like Nossek (see p175), Am Operneck's massive draw card is its proximity to the heart of
Vienna. Rooms are large, basic and comfy, and
since there are only six of them, you'll usually
need to reserve at least a month ahead.

Porter outside Hotel Sacher (opposite)

PENSION NOSSEK Map pp240-3 *Pension*
☎ 533 70 41-0; www.pension-nossek.at, German only;
01, Graben 17; s/d from €54/105; U1, U3 Stephansplatz
When it comes to real estate, it's all about location, location, location. And Nossek has oodles of all three. With a front door facing grand Graben and Stephansdom within sight, plus spotless baroque-style rooms, it's no wonder you need to book this fine *Pension* weeks in advance during high season.

PENSION PERTSCHY Map pp240-3 *Pension*
☎ 534 49-0; www.pertschy.com; 01, Habsburgergasse 5; s/d €77/122; U1, U3 Stephansplatz
This gem of a *Pension* is worth overnighting in for its location alone. But it also has the advantage of a peaceful inner courtyard, expansive rooms and toys for the toddlers. Room furnishings are a little dated, but that only adds to Pertschy's charm. Breakfast is included in the price.

ROTENTURMSTRASSE TO SCHOTTENRING

HOTEL AMADEUS Map pp240-3 *Hotel*
☎ 533 87 38; www.hotel-amadeus.at; 01, Wildpretmarkt 5; s/d from €80/142; U1, U3 Stephansplatz
The first indication that this hotel is something special is the completely carpeted lift. The sec-

ond is the rooms: colourful and warm, they are filled with period furniture, except for the bathrooms, which are thankfully modern. Accommodating staff make the stay here all the more enjoyable.

HOTEL ORIENT Map pp240-3 *Love Hotel*
☎ 533 73 07; 01, Tiefer Graben 30; r per hr €52-77; U1, U3 Stephansplatz
This is not a place to spend a night (rooms are only rented for the night on Saturday and Sunday), but rather an hour or more, depending on your energy and lust levels. Hotel Orient rents out its incredibly ornate rooms, in a variety of themes, by the hour for those wishing to spice up their sex life, or keep it discreet. It's a high-class joint, and by no means seedy. Even if it's not your kind of thing, it's worth stopping by to gaze at the *fin-de-siècle* hallway and façade (scenes from *The Third Man* were shot here).

MERCURE WIEN ZENTRUM
Map pp240-3 *Hotel*
☎ 534 60-0; www.accorhotels.com; 01, Fleischmarkt 1A; s/d from €125/145; U1, U4 Schwedenplatz, Schwedenplatz trams
Mercure's position is quite inviting – in the heart of the old cobblestone Jewish quarter and literally a hop, skip and a jump from the nightspots of the Bermuda Dreieck (Bermuda Triangle). Rooms are what you'd expect from most Mercure hotels around the world: orderly and appealing.

STARLIGHT Map pp240-3 *Hotel*
☎ 535 92 22; www.starlighthotels.com; 01, am Salzgries 12; s/d €135/165; tram 1, 2
The only fault that could be picked with the Starlight is a slight lack of light in rooms; apart from that, there are large, modern accommodation facilities with spacious bathrooms and minimal cooking facilities. Staff couldn't be more helpful and organised.

CHEAP SLEEPS

HOTEL POST Map pp240-3 *Hotel*
☎ 515 83-0; www.hotel-post-wien.at; 01, Fleischmarkt 24; s/d from €36/62; U1, U4 Schwedenplatz, Schwedenplatz trams
If you're addicted to sending postcards while on holiday, then Post is your best option – Vienna's main post office is directly across the street. Rooms are bright, spartan and great value for the Innere Stadt. Expect to pay a third extra for rooms with shower and toilet.

SCHWEIZER PENSION

Map pp240-3 *Pension*

☎ 533 81 56; www.schweizerpension.com; 01, Heinrichsgasse 2; s/d from €40/60; tram 1, 2

This super-clean *Pension* has bright, modern rooms with homely touches such as ornamental ceramic stoves. With only 11 rooms, a central location and low price (rooms with private showers are more expensive than those quoted above), it's advisable to reserve well in advance.

RINGSTRASSE

With glorious architecture lining almost its every inch, it's no surprise the Ringstrasse is home to some of Vienna's most luxurious hotels. It's a boulevard where the saying 'If you have to ask, you can't afford it' truly applies. There are, however, one or two hotels where affordability comes before grandeur.

SCHOTTENTOR TO PARLAMENT

RATHAUSPARK Map pp240-3 *Hotel*

☎ 404 12-0; rathauspark@austria-trend.at; 01, Rathausstrasse 17; s/d from €103/165; tram 43, 44

Undergoing renovation at the time of writing, this noble hotel was once the home of writer Stefan Zweig and is close to the university, Rathaus and the 8th district. Room highlights include ornate ceilings and calming colours. The buffet breakfast will keep you on the go for hours.

PARLAMENT TO SCHWARZENBERGPLATZ

GRAND HOTEL Map pp240-3 *Hotel*

☎ 515 80-0; www.grandhotelwien.com; 01, Kärntner Ring 9; s/d from €300/370; U2, U4 Karlsplatz, Karlsplatz trams

Lavish rooms, attention to detail and a superb location on the Ringstrasse are what you pay for at the Grand. Built in 1870, it was completely overhauled in the 1990s to bring it into the modern age, but its original charm – the richness of the foyer and banquet rooms are testament to this – hasn't been compromised.

HOTEL BRISTOL Map pp240-3 *Hotel*

☎ 515 16-536; www.westin.com/bristol; 01, Kärntner Ring 1; r from €385; U2, U4 Karlsplatz, Karlsplatz trams

The Bristol is a Vienna landmark with impressive views of the Staatsoper. It's saturated with Art-Nouveau furnishings – deep armchairs, sumptuously brocaded beds and marble-lined bathrooms – and has every conceivable service and modern amenity. Its Korso restaurant is Michelin-starred (see p121).

HOTEL IMPERIAL Map pp240-3 *Hotel*

☎ 501 10-333; www.luxurycollection.com/imperial; 01 Kärntner Ring 16; s/d from €446/535, royal ste from €3950; U2, U4 Karlsplatz, Karlsplatz trams

Originally the palace of the Prince of Württemberg, the Imperial reinvented itself as a hotel for the World Fair in 1873, but retained all the glory and majesty of its former status. It is a truly remarkable hotel (some, however, would say 'over the top'); marble bathrooms, precious antiques, original paintings and silver service all help to re-create 19th-century Vienna.

LE MERIDIEN Map pp240-3 *Hotel*

☎ 0800-295 390; www.lemeridien.com; 01, Opernring 13; r from €305; U1, U2, U4 Karlsplatz, Karlsplatz trams

The newly built Le Meridien all but overshadows anything on offer in Vienna. Modern is not the right word to describe the rooms – impeccably furnished, most have a touch of interior-design genius about them and make the rooms in the grand old dames scattered around the Ringstrasse seem like ageing dinosaurs. Power showers, mammoth flat-screen plasma TVs and Vienna-motif glass headboards make you feel special, while small touches, like real coffee and an ironing board and iron, make you feel right at home.

SCHWARZENBERGPLATZ TO THE DANUBE CANAL

HOTEL AM SCHUBERTRING

Map pp240-3 *Hotel*

☎ 717 02-0; www.schubertring.at; 01, Schubertring 11; s/d from €106/135; U4 Stadtpark, tram 1, 2

Of the highly sought after hotels on the Ringstrasse, Am Schubertring is one of the cheaper options. Mazelike corridors, Biedermeier or Art-Nouveau furnished rooms (some with rooftop views) and a welcoming atmosphere top the list of attractions here.

HOTEL MARRIOTT Map pp240-3 *Hotel*

☎ 515 18-0; www.marriotthotels.com/vieat; 01, Parkring 12a; r from €270; U3 Stubentor, tram 1, 2; Ⓟ

Sleeping – Ringstrasse

The Marriot has one advantage over many of the other Ringstrasse luxury hotels: views of the city park (Stadtpark) rather than another posh hotel. Rooms are large and modern in appearance, but lack a touch of grandness. The fitness room, sauna and 13m swimming pool are free for hotel guests, and the galleried lobby is lined with shops and cafés.

INTERCONTINENTAL Map pp240-3   *Hotel*
☎ 711 22-0; www.vienna.intercontinental.com; 03, Johannesgasse 28; r from €260; U4 Stadtpark
The InterContinental is a modern multistorey monolith that seems out of place compared with the architectural treasure trove that is the Ringstrasse (the hotel is not directly on the Ringstrasse, but with its price tag it might as well be). The inside makes up for it though: a huge lobby, stylish ballroom, and plush rooms with traditional furnishings.

RADISSON SAS PALAIS HOTEL
Map pp240-3   *Hotel*
☎ 515 17-0; www.radissonsas.com; 01, Parkring 16; r from €260; tram 1, 2
This 247-room hotel is the combination of two refurbished and renovated extravagant town houses. Rooms are fitted with highly modern amenities yet still contain an old-world feel, and the atrium inner courtyard is a tranquil setting for a rejuvenating *Melange* (cappuccino). And like the Marriot, the Radisson enjoys views over green Stadtpark.

BETWEEN THE DANUBE CANAL & THE DANUBE

There aren't a lot of options in Vienna's eastern districts and quite often they are far from the action. But one or two places are worth the trek across the Danube Canal (Donaukanal) into this residential neighbourhood little visited by tourists and locals alike. Plus, you can lose yourself in the nearby Prater and Donauinsel (Danube Island), outdoor play areas for both adults and kids, and the bubbling Karmelitermarkt, a food market with a massive Jewish presence.

ACCORDIA Map pp240-3   *Student Residence*
☎ 212 16 68; www.albertina-hotels.at; 02, Grosse Schiffgasse 12; s/d €52/78; bus 5A

Top Five for Luxury

- **Hotel Bristol** (p176) The perfect mix of old-world extravagance and state-of-the-art amenities
- **Hotel im Palais Schwarzenberg** (p178) The opulence of a palace, because that's what it is
- **Hotel Imperial** (p176) When royalty visit Vienna, this is where they stay
- **Hotel Sacher** (p174) A baroque gem with modern conveniences
- **Le Meridien** (p176) A thoroughly modern affair, and the newest of the bunch

This modern, multifloored high-rise is normally a student residence, but moonlights as a hotel from July to September. Pluses include private bathrooms, a bike storage room and a buffet breakfast. And it's only a short walk across the Danube Canal to the Innere Stadt.

HOTEL ADLON Map pp240-3   *Hotel*
☎ 216 67 88; www.adlon-wien.at; 02, Hofenedergasse 4; s/d €62/92; U1 Praterstern, tram 0
Hotel Adlon's location isn't the best but its rooms have a relaxing ambience and the neighbourhood is quiet. Soft shoe soles are a must if you don't want to disturb the fish in the floor aquarium at reception.

CHEAP SLEEPS
JUGENDGÄSTHAUS WIEN-BRIGITTENAU Map pp244-5   *Hostel*
☎ 332 82 94; jgh1200@chello.at; 20, Friedrich Engels Platz 24; dm from €14.50; tram 31, 33, N
Wien-Brigittenau is one of five HI hostels in Vienna and, with 410 beds, is by far the largest. It's modern, multistoreyed and just a couple of minutes' walk from the Danube (Donau) and the Donauinsel, but not particularly handy to the Innere Stadt. There are buffet meals, a garden and the reception stays open 24 hours.

INSIDE THE GÜRTEL

Inside the Gürtel encompasses the 3rd to the 9th district, a basic L-shape which borders the Innere Stadt to the north, south and west. Many of Vienna's best and boldest restaurants and bars are within its confines, which attract hordes of Vienna's bright young things who live, work and play here. And it has the added bonus of the Innere Stadt within easy striking distance by foot and public transport.

LANDSTRASSE

HOTEL IM PALAIS SCHWARZENBERG

Map pp248-9 *Hotel*

☎ 798 45 15; www.palais-schwarzenberg.com; 03, Schwarzenbergplatz 9; s/d from €255/330; tram D
Combining history, luxury and decorum, Im Palais Schwarzenberg is arguably the best address to stay at in Vienna. While this exclusive hotel opened its doors in the early '60s, the baroque palace's history goes back to the 17th century when Prince Heinrich commissioned its construction. Rooms are all about opulence and style, but it's the extras that are truly extravagant: seven hectares acres of private grounds, which sidle up to Belvedere, include a swimming pool and five clay tennis courts which are out-of-bounds to the general public. And to top it all off, the hotel bar and restaurant are of the utmost sophistication (see Palais Bar p143 and Palais Schwarzenberg p127 respectively).

WIEDEN

ATTACHÉ

Map pp248-9 *Pension*

☎ 505 18 18; www.bestviennahotels.at; 04, Wiedner Hauptstrasse 71; s/d from €72/102; tram 62, 65, bus 13A
This clean, neat *Pension* is small and homely, and many of its 26 rooms are furnished with period or antique fittings, including the celebrated Art-Nouveau style.

DAS TRIEST

Map pp248-9 *Hotel*

☎ 589 18-0; www.dastriest.at; 04, Wiedner Hauptstrasse 12; s/d €190/245; tram 62, 65
Das Triest is a refreshing change from the luxury and regality many of Vienna's top hotels so adamantly love to flaunt. Stylish in its simplicity and bathed in pastel warmth, it's an interior designer's dream; everything, from the rooms to the lobby to the stairwells, seems to fit effortlessly together in a mix of modern Italian and Viennese.

MARIAHILF

DAS TYROL

Map pp240-3 *Hotel*

☎ 587 54 15; www.das-tyrol.at; 06, Mariahilfer Strasse 15; s/d from €110/140; U2 Museumsquartier
This intimate hotel has smallish, cosy rooms and is staffed by a friendly bunch. The greatest advantage here though is location: a plethora of the city's finest museums, the food delights of the Naschmarkt, the quaintness of Spittalberg and the High St shops of Mariahilfer Strasse are all within an easy stroll. The entrance is around the side on Königsklostergasse.

PENSION KRAML

Map pp246-7 *Pension*

☎ 587 85 88; www.pensionkraml.at; 06, Brauergasse 5; s/d €28/48, apt from €85; U4 Pilgramgasse, bus 13A, 57A
This little gem of a *Pension* is small, friendly and family-run. Rooms are cosy indeed, and private

Palais Schwarzenberg (above)

facilities will cost a little more than the rates quoted (buffet breakfast is included). While it's not handy to blockbuster sights in the Innere Stadt, it's only two U-Bahn stops from Karlsplatz and within easy striking distance of Mariahilfer Strasse and a concentration of fine nightspots.

QUISISANA Map pp240-3 *Hotel*
☎ 587 71 55; www.quisisana-wien.co.at; 06, Windmühlgasse 6; s/d from €30/44; U2 Museumsquartier
Like Das Tyrol, Quisisana's big draw card is its proximity to museums, shopping and eating options. Rooms, with both shared and private bathrooms, are small and simple, but perfectly adequate for a weekend break.

NEUBAU

ALLA LENZ Map pp246-7 *Pension*
☎ 523 69 89-0; www.allalenz.com; 07, Halbgasse 3-5; s/d from €60/72; U3 Burggasse-Stadthalle
This fine *Pension* has the novelty of a rooftop swimming pool, which comes in very handy on scorching summer days. Rooms have aircon and a private bathroom, and breakfast is included in the price.

HOTEL AM SCHOTTENFELD
Map pp246-7 *Hotel*
☎ 526 51 81; www.falkensteiner.com; 07, Schottenfeldgasse 74; s/d €129/164; bus 48A
Don't let the garish reception and bar put you off – the highly modern rooms at the Schottenfeld are more than fine. Built in 2003, this hotel is definitely slanted towards business clientele but caters well to individual travellers and has a fitness room with sauna, steam room and solarium add-ons.

HOTEL-PENSION CONTINENTAL
Map pp246-7 *Hotel*
☎ 523 24 18; www.hotel-continental.at; 07, Kirchengasse 1; s/d from 50/70; U3 Neubaugasse
Depending on how you look at it, this hotel's location is either an advantage or a disadvantage: it's handy to Mariahilfer Strasse and the U3, but Vienna's main shopping street can throw up a lot of noise. Rooms facing the inner courtyard are cheapest but don't attract much sun.

K+K MARIA THERESIA Map pp240-3 *Hotel*
☎ 521 23; www.kkhotels.com; 07, Kirchberggasse 6; s/d €155/205; U2, U3 Volkstheater
The only markings of royalty on the 'Kaiser und König' Maria Theresia is the Schönbrunn yellow façade. Inside is a thoroughly modern hotel serviced by highly professional staff that seems used to tour groups. The neatness and order doesn't leave a lot of room for character though.

PENSION ATRIUM Map pp246-7 *Pension*
☎ 523 31 14; pension.atrium@chello.at; 07, Burggasse 118; s/d €51/73; U6 Burggasse-Stadthalle
You won't be blown away by the plush interior at the Atrium, but rooms are clean, roomy and come complete with balcony. Plus breakfast can be enjoyed in the privacy of your room. Burggasse is a main thoroughfare so it may be worth asking for something at the back.

PENSION CARANTANIA
Map pp246-7 *Pension*
☎ 526 73 40; www.carantania.at; 07, Kandlgasse 35; s/d €55/80; U6 Burggasse-Stadthalle
It's easy to tell this is a family-run *Pension*: convivial staff, old-style furnishings and characterful rooms are dead giveaways. The breakfast room, with a big bay window overlooking Kandlgasse, is bright and welcoming. Carantania has only six rooms, so it's advisable to book ahead.

JOSEFSTADT

LAUDON COURT Map pp244-5 *Apartments*
☎ 407 13 70; laudoncourt@chello.at; 08, Laudongasse 8; apt per day/month from €69/1350; tram 43, 44
Stay as long as a year or as little as a day at Laudon Court, an apartment building used for short-term rentals. The modern, fully furnished apartments (washing machines and dryers are in the basement) range in size from 35 sq metres to 50 sq metres and are cleaned on a daily basis. Rates include gas, water and electricity but not telephone calls.

THEATER-HOTEL Map pp244-5 *Hotel*
☎ 405 36 48; www.theaterhotelwien.at; 08, Josefstädter Strasse 22; s/d €140/183; tram J
Art-Nouveau touches and friendly staff make this hotel one of the better 8th-district choices. Rooms are small, but have an attached kitchen unit. Unfortunately, you don't receive brownie points with Theater in der Josefstadt next door for staying here.

ALSERGRUND

ALBATROS Map pp244-5 *Hotel*
☎ 317 35 08; www.austria-trend.at/alb; 09, Liechtensteinstrasse 89; s/d €110/120; tram 37, 38
The Albatros won't have you taking snaps of the grand reception or oohing and ahing the

antique furniture, but what it will do is provide you with highly adequate rooms. There's a sauna and solarium on site (charge payable), and free tea and coffee in the lobby.

HOTEL ARKADENHOF Map pp244-5 *Hotel*
☎ 310 08 37; www.arkadenhof.com; 09, Viriotgasse 5; s/d €115/151; U6 Nussdorferstrasse, tram 37, 38
Small Arkadenhof has seen better days, but it does occupy a quiet corner of the 9th district and both rooms and bathrooms offer more space than most. Breakfast is included in the price.

HOTEL ATLANTA Map pp244-5 *Hotel*
☎ 405 12 30; www.icnet.at/hotelatlanta; 09, Währinger Strasse 33; s/d €91/128; tram 37, 38, 40, 41, 42
Built in 1895, the Atlanta has lost its sparkle of once-held grandeur, but still exudes an air of nobility. Chandeliers, creaky floors, ornate stained-glass windows and spacious rooms all add up to a charming, albeit over-the-hill, hotel.

HOTEL BOLTZMANN Map pp244-5 *Hotel*
☎ 316 12-0; boltzmann@arcotel.at; 09, Boltzmanngasse 8; s/d from €115/145; tram 37, 38, 40, 41, 42
Cheerful rooms and cheerful staff make this four-star hotel, half-way between the Ringstrasse and the Gürtel, a solid bet. Breakfast is not included, but a summer garden is thrown in for free.

CHEAP SLEEPS

ACADEMIA Map pp246-7 *Student Residence*
☎ 401 76 55; www.academia-hotels.co.at; 08, Pfeilgasse 3a; s/d €48/64; tram 46, J
Academia is a massive 498-bed student residence (with a lift, thankfully), which opens its doors to visitors over the summer months. Rooms are quite spacious and have en-suite bathrooms but no TV. A buffet breakfast is included in the price and there's a coffee bar on site.

AUER Map pp244-5 *Pension*
☎ 406 21 21; auer.pension@chello.at; 09, Lazarettgasse 3; s/d €29/44; tram 5, 33
Homely, personable, friendly, cluttered – if that sounds good to you then you'll love Auer. The rooms aren't modern, but there is something wonderfully eclectic and very Viennese about them. Some rooms have private facilities (an extra €6) and breakfast is included in the price; reception is on the 1st floor and there's no lift.

AVIS Map pp246-7 *Student Residence*
☎ 401 76 55; www.academia-hotels.co.at; 08, Pfeilgasse 4; s/d €48/64; tram 46, J
Avis is directly opposite Academia (see p179) and run by the same company. It offers similar facilities minus the bar and breakfast room, which it shares with its larger cousin. The building itself looks less institutional and more residential than Academia.

HOTEL FÜRSTENHOF Map pp246-7 *Hotel*
☎ 523 32 67; www.hotel-fuerstenhof.com; 07, Neubaugürtel 4; s/d from €44/62; U3, U6 Westbahnhof
Fürstenhof is a family-run hotel that's more than handy to Westbahnhof and only five U-Bahn stops from Stephansplatz. Unfortunately the rooms don't match the elegance of the entrance way and stairwell, but they're a decent size, and have a homely feel and refurbished bathrooms.

JUGENDHERBERGE MYRTHENGASSE
Map pp246-7 *Hostel*
☎ 523 63 16; hostel@chello.at; 07, Myrthengasse 7; dm €15.50, tw €35; bus 48A
This well-organised HI hostel on a quiet side street has all the trappings you'd expect. Based in two buildings, it's convenient, busy and offers daytime check-in. All rooms have a private shower and bedside lights. Telephone reservations are accepted and strongly advised.

KOLPING WIEN-ZENTRAL
Map pp240-3 *Hotel/Student Residence*
☎ 587 56 31; www.wien-zentral.kolping.at; 06, Gumpendorfer Strasse 39; s/d €52/80, student s&d €44, student tr €66; U4 Kettenbrückengasse
This bold, brash and colourful student residence has a combination of hotel-style accommodation year-round and student dorms in July and August. Rooms come with shower and toilet but are a tad soulless. Enter via Stiegengasse.

PENSION FALSTAFF Map pp244-5 *Pension*
☎ 317 91 27; www.pension-falstaff.cjb.net; 09, Müllnergasse 5; s/d from €33/51; tram D
The rooms and furniture at this friendly *Pension* could do with an overhaul, but they're comfy and roomy enough to satisfy. Cheaper rooms (quoted above) share toilet and shower with other guests but there's the option to pay a little extra for private facilities. The price includes breakfast.

PENSION HARGITA Map pp246-7 *Pension*
☎ 526 19 28; www.hargita.at; 07, Andreasgasse 1; s/d from €31/45; U3 Zieglergasse

Sleeping – Inside the Gürtel

Hargita is a tiny part of Magyarország (Hungary) transferred across the border to Vienna. Hungarian owned and run, the walls of this *Pension* are lined with maps, pictures and folk art from the land of the Great Plain. Rooms are clean, quaint and old-fashioned.

PENSION WILD Map pp240-3 *Pension*
☎ 406 51 74; www.pension-wild.com; 08, Lange Gasse 10; s/d from €37/45; tram 46
When a *Pension* brands itself 'Vienna's friendly guesthouse', it generally starts warning bells ringing. But Wild is actually a very friendly place, both to straights and gays. Standard rooms are clean but on the basic side and have shared facilities, while its top-floor *Luxuszimmer* (luxury rooms) come complete with bathroom and are substantially more appealing. Note 'Wild' is the family name, not a description of the atmosphere.

WESTEND CITY HOSTEL
Map pp246-7 *Hostel*
☎ 597 67 29; www.westendhostel.at; 06, Fügergasse 3; s/d €40.50/44.40, dm in 4-/12-bed r €16.80/19; U3, U6 Westbahnhof
Westend is more than handy to Westbahnhof and caters to backpackers and travellers looking for a cheap place to rest their weary bodies. By no stretch of the imagination is this a party hostel, but it's very well organised and has a 24-hour reception, lockers, bathrooms and toilets in every room, Internet access (€4.40 per hour) and a complete laundry service (€6).

OUTSIDE THE GÜRTEL
You won't be in the thick of things if you stay in these heavily residential outlying suburbs, but you will be amongst the Viennese, whether it is in the predominantly rich 13th and 19th districts, the working class neighbourhoods of the 10th to 12th, or the Turkish and Balkan influenced 15th and 16th.

You'll also have the advantage of close proximity to some of Vienna's larger natural attractions, the Wienerwald (Vienna Woods) and Lainzer Tiergarten, and easy escape by car to excursion destinations.

FAVORITEN
FAVORITA Map pp248-9 *Hotel*
☎ 601 46-0; www.austria-trend.at/fav; 10, Laxenburger Strasse 8-10; s/d €112/138; U1 Keplerplatz, tram O

The first thing you notice about Favorita is its striking yet simple façade, in almost Jugendstil style. Rooms are modern and bright and there's a free sauna and steam bath for guests to relax those weary bones in.

HIETZING
HOTEL VIKTORIA Map pp246-7 *Hotel*
☎ 877 11 50; hotel.viktoria@magnet.at; 13, Eduard Klein Gasse 9; s/d €50/90; U4 Hietzing
This three-star hotel is handy to Schloss Schönbrunn and the U4 U-Bahn line. It has a mixture of renovated and unrenovated rooms, some of which have views of busy Hietzing junction.

PARKHOTEL SCHÖNBRUNN
Map pp246-7 *Hotel*
☎ 878 04-0; parkhotel.schoenbrunn@austria-trend.at; 13, Hietzinger Hauptstrasse 10-20; s/d from €125/170; U4 Hietzing
Partially built with money from Emperor Franz Josef I, who considered it his guesthouse, Parkhotel Schönbrunn still exudes an air of regality. The façade is, of course, painted Schönbrunn yellow, the lobby and grand ballroom all have the majesty of a five-star place, and many rooms surround a large garden with sun lounges, trees and grass. There's also a 12m swimming pool, fitness room and sauna (all free for guests).

RUDOLFSHEIM-FÜNFHAUS
ALTWIENERHOF Map pp246-7 *Hotel*
☎ 892 60 00; www.altwienerhof.at; 15, Herklotzgasse 6; s/d €57/90; U6 Gumpendorfer Strasse, tram 6, 18
Altwienerhof, a small, family-run three-star hotel only a stone's throw from the Gürtel, offers an air of sophistication without the price tag. Rooms aren't overly plush, but they're stylish and well cared for by friendly and welcoming staff.

HERNALS
HOTEL DONAUWALZER
Map pp244-5 *Hotel*
☎ 405 76 45; www.donauwalzer.at; 17, Ottakringer Strasse 5; r from €70; U6 Alser Strasse
Donauwalzer may be on the busy Gürtel, but that makes it all that much closer to the vibrant nightlife and bar scene in these parts. Its characterful rooms vary in quality and style, which could be anything from baroque to oriental.

WÄHRING

THÜRINGER HOF Map pp244-5 — *Hotel*
☎ 401 79-0; www.thueringerhof.at; 18, Jörgerstrasse 4-8; s/d €75.60/99.60; U6 Alser Strasse; Ⓟ

While Thüringer Hof's rooms could do with an update, they have the advantage of being particularly spacious (ones facing the inner courtyard are quietest). Children aged six to 12 gain a 50% discount and those under six stay for free.

DÖBLING

CELTES Map pp238-9 — *Hotel*
☎ 440 41 51; www.hotelceltes.at; 19, Celtesgasse 1; s/d €70/109; bus 35A

Celtes is perfectly located if you're into wine and walks: it's in the heart of the Neustift am Walde *Heuriger* (wine tavern) and vineyard area and convenient to the Wienerwald. There's also a bar and a garden on the premises.

CHEAP SLEEPS

DO STEP INN Map pp246-7 — *Hostel*
☎ 923 27 69; www.dostepinn.at; 15, Felberstrasse 22/6; s/d €29/35; U3, U6 Westbahnhof

Newly opened Do Step Inn, a hop, step and a jump from Westbahnhof, has bright, colourful rooms decked out in Ikea-like simplicity. Facilities, which include a better-than-average kitchen, are shared with other guests. Helpful staff give the place a decidedly relaxed air. Ten percent is added to the price if you're only staying one night.

FÜNFHAUS Map pp246-7 — *Pension*
☎ 892 35 45; fax 892 04 60; 15, Sperrgasse 12; s/d from €30/44; tram 52, 58

Fünfhaus is well situated in a quiet residential area so there's no threat of excessive road noise. Rooms come with a range of amenities and in various sizes, but all are clean and fresh. Be aware that this place closes from mid-November through February.

SCHLOSSHERBERGE AM WILHELMINENBERG Map pp238-9 — *Hostel*
☎ 485 85 03-700; shb@verkehrsbuero.at; 16, Savoyenstrasse 2; dm €18; bus 46B, 146B

This HI hostel, in the grounds of Schloss Wilhelminenberg, may be a long way from the city centre but it has glorious views of the city and easy access to the Wienerwald. Plus, it's only a quick stroll to a concentration of *Heurigen* near the Ottakringer cemetery. The four-bed dorms have an attached shower and toilet.

SOPHIENALPE Map pp238-9 — *Hotel*
☎ 486 24 32; www.sophienalpe.at; 14, Sophienalpestrasse 13; s/d €41/60; bus 243, 443

The address may officially be within Vienna's borders, but Sophienalpe's location is in reality outside of the city's urban development and in the middle of the Wienerwald. Depending on your tastes though, this may not be a bad thing: walks abound in all directions and Sophienalpe has a distinct retreat feel to it. Rooms are comfy and there's an indoor swimming pool and a restaurant. Disadvantages are you really need a car to get around and it's closed from 1 November to 31 March.

WOMBAT'S Map pp246-7 — *Hostel*
☎ 897 23 36; www.wombats.at; 15, Grangasse 6; dm from €16, r €42; tram 52, 58, bus 12A

It's hard to find a more relaxed hostel than Wombat's in Vienna – the atmosphere is more like the Gold Coast, Australia than the Capital of Culture. The staff is friendly, there's Internet access, bike rental, a pub, pool and garden, and it's about a 10-minute walk from Westbahnhof.

Excursions

Wine	186
Towns	186
Nature	186
Driving	186
Melk	186
Dürnstein	188
Krems	189
Neusiedler See	190
Eisenstadt	191
Wienerwald	193
Bratislava	194
Baden	195

To Horn (19km)

To Prague (275km)

37

34

303
E59

Gföhl

35

Langenlois

34

Kirchberg am Wagram

4

KREMS

19

Stockerau

Weissenkirchen

3

Dürnstein

Mautern an der Donau

3

Tulln

14

Spitz

Wachau

S33

Traismauer

Danube

Naturp Kirchen

Willendorf

Herzogenburg

1

To Melk (4.8km)

1

19

Böheim-kirchen

Neulengbach

Purkersdorf

Pressbaum

A1

Loosdorf

1

ST PÖLTEN

Lainz Tiergar

E5

A1

Wienerwald (Vienna Woods)

13

To Schloss Schallaburg
(2.5km); Linz (75km);
Salzburg (183km)

Ober-Grafendorf

Naturpar Föhrenber

29

20

Wilhelmsburg

A21

E60

Traisen

Gölsen

Heiligenkreuz

Mayerling

210

39

Traisen

St Veit

18

Hainfeld

Baden

Kirchberg an der Pielach

Lilienfeld

18

Pottenstein

Bad Vöslau

LOWER AUSTRIA
(NIEDERÖSTERREICH)

Berndorf

212

214

20

Pernitz

E59
A2

21

Markt-Piesting

21

27

Naturpark
Hohe Wand

Schneeberg
(2076m)

Naturpark
Sierningtal

17

STYRIA
(STEINMARK)

Ternitz

Neunkirchen

54

S6

A2
E7

To Leoben
(72km)

To Graz
(112km)

Excursions

As if there isn't enough to do in Vienna, the surrounding countryside holds a multitude of sights which make for tempting excursions out of the city. You'll discover a stunning stretch of the Danube and the gentle hills of the Wienerwald to the west, ancient spa towns to the south and a large lake made for water enthusiasts to the east. And that's not even including Hungary, Slovakia and the Czech Republic, which are all within a few hours of the city.

The excursions mentioned here are an easy day trip from the city by public transport, but because of their close proximity to one another, the freedom of a car will allow you to tick off a number of destinations in one day. Note that many attractions are only open between April and October, and places like Baden all but close down over the winter months.

WINE

Wine has been fighting a war of attrition on Vienna and the surrounding countryside for thousands of years, a war that the local populace has happily lost from day one. If you're willing to show the locals a bit of solidarity, the Wachau region, in particular the towns of Krems (p189) and Dürnstein (p188), is a perfect place to start. If you still want more, head for Baden (p195), Eisenstadt (p191) and, on the banks of the Neusiedler See, the quiet town of Rust (p191).

TOWNS

Many of the towns in the region are full of history. Baden (p195), a quiet spa town, can trace its past back to Roman days, while Eisenstadt (p191), provincial capital of Burgenland, is the traditional stronghold of the powerful Esterházy family and was once home to Haydn for more than 30 years. Bratislava (p194), the capital of Slovakia, was for many centuries the centre of the Hungarian empire and today is a bustling, vibrant metropolis.

NATURE

The Viennese love to get out of their city and experience the best nature has to offer. Virtually on the city borders is the Wienerwald (Vienna Woods; p193), a dense forest covering the last of the Alps' foothills and a favourite of walkers and cyclists alike. For those with an eye for bird life and water sports, the shallow, watery expanse of the Neusiedler See (p190) is the perfect option.

DRIVING

The Wachau section of the Danube, between Krems (p189) and Melk (below), is a scenic extravaganza. Wine-growing villages, forested slopes, vineyards and imposing fortresses appear around nearly every bend. It's no wonder the region's been a Unesco site since 2000.

MELK

Lying in the lee of its imposing monastery-fortress, Melk is arguably the most essential excursion destination from Vienna.

Bottles of Viennese wine

The **Stift Melk**, perched on a hill, dominates the town and provides an excellent view of the surrounding area. It was once the residence of the Babenberg family, but the Benedic-tine monks transformed it into a monastery in 1089 and it has stayed that way ever since. Receiving a major overhaul in the 18th century, it's an example of baroque gone mad, with endless prancing angels and gold twirls, but is very impressive nonetheless. The absolute highlights are the library and the mirror room, both of which have an extra tier painted on the ceiling (by Paul Troger) to give the illusion of greater height. The ceilings are also slightly curved to aid the effect. Imperial rooms, where various dignitaries (including Napoleon) stayed, contain museum exhibits. Guided tours (often in English, but phone ahead to be sure) of this Benedictine abbey explain its historical importance and are well worth the extra money.

The countryside surrounding Melk is home to some fine palaces. **Schloss Schallaburg**, 5km south of Melk, is a 16th-century Renaissance palace with magnificent terracotta arches and prestigious temporary exhibitions. There's also a permanent exhibition of toys through history. A reduced combination ticket with Stift Melk monastery is available. Just under 5km northeast is **Schloss Schönbühel**, on the southern bank of the Danube, along with a 17th-century Servite monastery (the Servites were a mendicant order of friars), and the ruins of the 12th-century **Burg Aggstein**.

Sights & Information

Melk Tourist Office (☎ 02752-523 07-410; www .tiscover.com/melk; Babenbergerstrasse 1; ☼ 9am-7pm Mon-Sat, 10am-2pm Sun Apr-Oct, 9am-noon & 2-6pm Mon-Fri, 10am-2pm Sat Nov-Mar) Provides information on all the big attractions.

Schloss Schallaburg (☎ 02754-6317; www.schal laburg.at; Anzendorf; adult/child €7/3, combined ticket with Stift Melk €11.50; ☼ 9am-5pm Mon-Fri, until 6pm Sat)

Stift Melk (☎ 02752-555 232; www.stiftmelk.at; adult/child €6.90/4.10, with guided tour €8.50/5.70; ☼ 9am-6pm May-Sep, 9am-5pm Apr & Oct, guided tours only Nov-Mar) Reservations for tours in English are advisable (call ahead). The last admission is one hour before closing.

Eating

Tom's Restaurant (☎ 02752-524 75; Hauptplatz 1; mains €10-20; ☼ noon-3pm & 6.30-10pm) An excellent restaurant in the heart of the town.

Sleeping

HI Jugendherberge (☎ 02752-526 81; melk@noejhw .at; Abt Karl Strasse 42; dm €16; ☼ mid-Mar–Oct) Hostel with sports and games facilities and parking spaces.

Stadt Melk (☎ 02752-525 47; hotel.stadtmelk@netway.at; Hauptplatz 1; s/d from €55/80) Small *Pension*/hotel above Tom's Restaurant.

Zur Post (☎ 02752-523 45; Linzer Strasse 1; s/d from €50/80) A four-star hotel built in the late 1920s, but with all the modern amenities.

DÜRNSTEIN

Dürnstein achieved 12th-century notoriety for its imprisonment of King Richard the Lion-Heart of England. Today, this compact, picturesque village is one of the prime destinations in the Wachau region.

High on the hill, commanding a marvellous view of the curve of the Danube, stand the ruins of **Kuenringerburg**, where Richard was incarcerated from 1192 to 1193. His crime was insulting Leopold V; his misfortune was being recognised despite his disguise when journeying through Austria on his way home from the crusades. His liberty was achieved only upon the payment of a huge ransom which funded the building of Wiener Neustadt. The hike up from the village takes 15 to 20 minutes.

In the village, Hauptstrasse is a cobbled street with some picturesque 16th-century houses, wrought-iron signs and floral displays. The town's **Chorherrenstift** (Abbey church) has been meticulously restored. The baroque interior effectively combines white stucco and dark wood and the balcony overlooking the blue Danube is perfect for that holiday snap.

Travelling west from Dürnstein along the banks of the Danube, the steep hills are densely covered with vineyards. Riesling and Veltliners, two of Austria's top wines, are grown in these parts, and served in traditional *Heurigen* (wine taverns). Six kilometres on from Dürnstein is **Weissenkirchen**, a peaceful town that hasn't changed much in the last 100 years. Its centrepiece is a fortified **parish church** rising from a hill, with a labyrinth of covered pathways leading to its front doors. This Gothic church was built in the 15th century and has an impressive baroque altar. Directly below the church is the **Wachau Museum**, which showcases artists of the Danube School. A further 5km west and **Spitz** swings into view, a village surrounded by vineyards and lined with quiet, cobblestoned streets. Its **parish church** is noteworthy for its unusual chancel, which is out of line with the main body of the church. Also note the 15th-century statues of the 12 apostles lining the organ loft. Continuing on another 5km towards Melk and **Willendorf** soon appears, where the 25,000-year-old Venus sandstone statuette was discovered.

Sights & Information

Chorherrenstift (☎ 02711-375; Stiftshof; admission €2.20; ⏰ 9am-6pm Apr-Oct)

Dürnstein Information Office (☎ 02711-200; Dürnstein Bahnhof; ⏰ 1-7pm Mon, Thu, Fri, 11am-7pm Sat & Sun mid-Apr–Oct) Near the train station.

Rathaus Information Office (☎ 02711-219; Hauptstrasse 25; ⏰ 8am-noon & 1.30-4pm Mon-Fri)

Wachau Museum (☎ 02715-2268; Weissenkirchen 32; adult/child €2.20/1.10; ⏰ 10am-5pm Tue-Sun Apr-Oct)

Eating

Alter Klosterkeller (☎ 02711-378; Anzuggasse; mains €5-15; ⏰ 3-11pm Wed-Mon Apr-Nov) An attractive *Heuriger*.

Loibnerhof (☎ 02732-828 90; Unterloiben 7; mains €7-15; ⏰ 11.30am-9.30pm Wed-Sun) Large restaurant with an attractive garden, 1km east of Dürnstein in Unterloiben.

Sleeping

Gasthof Sänger Blondel (☎ 02711-253; www.saenger blondel.at; Klosterplatz; s/d €59/82) Right in the heart of Dürnstein.

Pension Böhmer (☎ 02711-239; pension.boehmer@ i-one.at; Hauptstrasse 22; s/d €30/40) Small *Pension* that doubles as a wine shop.

Transport

Distance from Vienna to Dürnstein 73km
Direction West
Bicycle See Melk (p186) for details.
Boat Only one boat links Vienna and Dürnstein: DDSG (see p199, for details) operates a Sunday service from May to September at 8.45am, returning at 4.30pm (one-way/return €19/25, 5¾ hours).
Car There are two options by car. From just east of the Danube take the A22 north out of Vienna towards Stockerau; when it ends turn onto the Bundesbahn 304, which heads west to Krems. From Krems follow Bundesbahn 3, which keeps heading west and runs directly to Dürnstein, Weissenkirchen and Spitz. The second option is to head west out of Vienna via Penzing on Bundesbahn 1. At Purkersdorf the road forks; take the right-hand fork, which passes through Gablitz, Ried-am-Riederberg and Sieghartskirchen. At Mitterndorf, turn right onto Bundesbahn 43, which takes you through Traismauer and connects with S33, which in-turn leads directly to Krems. Once again, from Krems take Bundesbahn 3.
Train From Franz-Josef-Bahnhof, one change is required for Dürnstein (the station is called Dürnstein-Oberloiben) at Krems. With a good connection, the trip will take around 1¼ hours.

KREMS

Krems is one of the larger towns in the Wachau region and has a historical core which dates back over a 1000 years. It's on the northern bank of the Danube, surrounded by terraced vineyards, and has been a centre of the wine trade for most of its history.

The town is comprised of three parts: Krems to the east, the smaller settlement of Stein 2km to the west, and the connecting suburb of Und – an unusual name which inspires an example of Austrian humour: 'Krems and (*und* in German) Stein are three towns'. The best thing to do here is relax and enjoy the peaceful ambience. Take your time and wander around the cobbled streets, quiet courtyards and ancient city walls; the Austropa travel office in Kloster Und can supply you with a map pinpointing all the architectural and cultural attractions around town.

Transport

Distance from Vienna 64km
Direction West
Bicycle See Melk (p186) for details.
Boat DDSG (see Directory p199 for details) operates a boat from Vienna at 8.45am, returning at 4.50pm, every Sunday between May and September (one-way/return €17/22, one hour 10 minutes).
Car See Dürnstein (p188) for details.
Train Eight direct trains daily travel between Franz-Josefs-Bahnhof and Krems (one hour).

Krems has several churches worth poking around in. The **Pfarrkirche St Veit** on the hill at Pfarrplatz is baroque in style, with frescoes by Martin Johann Schmidt, an 18th-century local artist. **Piaristenkirche**, up behind St Veit's on Frauenbergplatz, has Gothic vaulting, huge windows and baroque altars, while **Dominikanerkirche** contains collections of religious and modern art and the Weinstadt museum with wine-making artefacts. Offering something quite different is the **Karikaturmuseum**, which has a large collection of humorous caricatures and is the only museum of its kind in Austria. The town's arts centre, the **Kunsthalle**, is also located here.

Much of Krems' economic strength comes from its wine culture, and it's a perfect venue for wine tasting; both **Kloster Und** and **Weingut der Stadt Krems** have many wines to sample and buy.

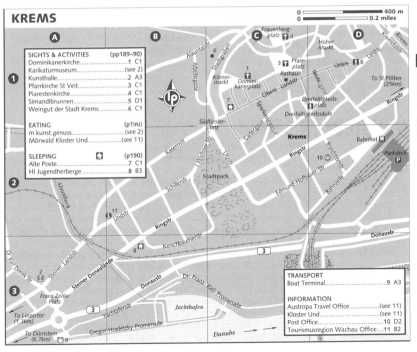

KREMS

0 — 400 m
0 — 0.2 miles

SIGHTS & ACTIVITIES	(pp189–90)
Dominikanerkirche	1 C1
Karikaturmuseum	(see 2)
Kunsthalle	2 A3
Pfarrkirche St Veit	3 C1
Piarestenkirche	4 C1
Simandlbrunnen	5 D1
Weingut der Stadt Krems	6 C1

EATING	(p190)
m.kunst.genuss	(see 2)
Mörwald Kloster Und	(see 11)

SLEEPING	(p190)
Alte Poste	7 C1
HI Jugendherberge	8 B3

TRANSPORT	
Boat Terminal	9 A3

INFORMATION	
Austropa Travel Office	(see 11)
Kloster Und	(see 11)
Post Office	10 D2
Tourismusregion Wachau Office	11 B2

Excursions – Krems

Detour: Tulln

The township of Tulln, on the southern banks of the Danube some 30km west of Vienna, makes for a pleasant detour on the way to Krems. Formerly a Roman camp called Comagena, and named as a town settlement in 791, Tulln trumpets itself as the 'Birthplace of Austria', and was in effect the nation's first capital.

These days Tulln is a busy town with a couple of fine museums. Egon Schiele was born here, and is suitably immortalised in the **Egon Schiele Museum** (☎ 02272-645 70; Donaulände 28; adult/child €3.50/2; ☺ 10am-6pm Tue-Sun Feb-Nov), housed in the former jail in which he was imprisoned for his provocative nudes of pubescent girls. There is of course a **Römermuseum** (Roman Museum; ☎ 02272-659 22; Marc Aurel-Park 1b; adult/child €3/2; ☺ 10am-6pm Tue-Sun Mar-Nov) and a museum devoted to the history of the town, the **Tullner Museen** (☎ 02272-619 15; Minoritenplatz 1; adult/child €3/2; ☺ 10am-6pm Tue-Sun May-Sep). The oldest Roman ruin is the **Römerturm** (Donaulände), a watchtower built in 360 under the direction of Emperor Diocletian.

For more information contact the **Tulln Stadt Information Office** (☎ 02272-658 36; www.tulln.at; Minoritenplatz 2; ☺ 9am-7pm Apr-Oct, 8am-3pm Mon-Fri Nov-Mar), which is next to the immaculate **Minoritenkirche**.

Sights & Information

Austropa Travel Office (☎ 02732-826 76; www.tiscover .com/krems; Undstrasse 6; ☺ 8.30am-6.30pm Mon-Fri, 10am-noon & 1-6pm Sat, 10am-noon & 1-4pm Sun May-Oct, 8.30am-5pm Mon-Fri Nov-Apr)

Dominikanerkirche (Dominikanerplatz; adult/child €4/3; ☺ 9am-6pm Tue, 1-6pm Wed-Sun Mar-Nov)

Karikaturmuseum (☎ 02732-908 020; www.karikatur museum.at, German only; Steiner Landstrasse 3a; adult/child €7.50/3.50; ☺ 10am-6pm)

Kloster Und (☎ 02732-704 493; Undstrasse 6; ☺ 1-7pm Wed-Sun)

Kunsthalle (☎ 02732-908 010-19; Steiner Landstrasse 3; admission €5; ☺ 9am-5pm Mon-Fri)

Tourismusregion Wachau Office (☎ 02732-856 20; Undstrasse 6; ☺ 9am-6pm Mon-Fri, 10am-noon & 1-7pm Sat)

Weingut der Stadt Krems (☎ 02732-801 441; Stadtgraben 11; ☺ 9am-noon & 1-5pm Mon-Sat)

Eating

Mörwald Kloster Und (☎ 02732-704 930; Undstrasse 6; mains €17-20; ☺ 10am-10pm Wed-Sun) European cuisine, stone floors, stylish interior and an amazing selection of wine.

m.kunst.genuss (☎ 02732-908 010-21; Steiner Landstrasse 3; mains €10-20; ☺ 10am-10pm) Stylish interior and creative regional cuisine.

Sleeping

Alte Poste (☎ 02732-822 76; www.altepost-krems.at, German only; Obere Landstrasse 32; s/d €42/70) Guesthouse located in a historic 500-year-old house with an enchanting courtyard.

HI Jugendherberge (☎ 02732-834 52; oejhv.noe .krems@aon.at; Ringstrasse 77; dm €15; ☺ Apr-Oct) Excellent hostel with facilities for cyclists.

NEUSIEDLER SEE

This, the only steppe lake in Central Europe, is not only a popular summer holiday getaway for many Viennese and a top wine growing region, but it's also a favourite breeding ground for nearly 300 species of birds.

Neusiedler See is a shallow lake (1.8m at its deepest) that has no natural outlet, giving the water a slightly saline quality. It's ringed by a wetland area of reed beds, particularly thick on the western bank, which provides an ideal breeding ground for birds. Bird-watchers flock to the area to catch a glimpse of the multitude of species; the national park **Seewinkel**, on the east shore, is a grassland interspersed with a myriad of smaller lakes and a popular spot for birds and bird-voyeurs.

Water sports are big here, with boats and windsurfers for hire at various resorts around the lake. The area's main town is **Neusiedl am See**, at the lake's northern end, but the best spot to propel yourself across the lake under wind power is **Podersdorf**, 12km southeast of Neusiedl, which has the best access to the water. Cycling is another popular outdoor activity in these parts; a cycle track winds all the way around the reed beds, making it possible to complete a circuit of the lake, but remember to take your passport as the southern section is in Hungary. Pick up a copy of *Radtouren*, a handy map of the lake with cycle paths and distances marked, from any of the tourist offices listed on p191.

Much of the western side of Neusiedler is given over to vineyards. **Rust**, 30km southwest of Neusiedl, has some 60 wine growers nearby, though its name derives from Rüster (German for 'elm tree'). The town's prosperity has been based on wine for centuries. In 1524 the emperor granted local vintners the exclusive right to display the letter 'R' on their wine barrels; corks today bear the same insignia. From the end of March to late August storks descend on Rust to rear their young. If you stroll around town during this time, you'll see twig-nests perched precariously on chimney tops and, if you're quiet, hear the clicking of expectant beaks. A good vantage point is attained from the tower of the **Katholische Kirche** on Rathausplatz. The **Fischerkirche** at the opposite end of Rathausplatz is the oldest church in Rust (12th to 16th centuries).

Six kilometres further south from Rust is **Mörbisch**. It's worth spending an hour or so here, enjoying the relaxed atmosphere and the quaint whitewashed houses with hanging corn and flower-strewn balconies. The town hosts **Seefestspiele** (www.seefestspiele-moerbisch.at), a summer operetta festival which runs from mid-July to late August. It attracts some 200,000 people each year. Its biggest competition is **Opern Festspiele** (www.ofs.at), an opera festival held in an old Roman quarry near St Margareten, also from mid-July to August.

Sights & Information

Fischerkirche (Rathausplatz, Rust; admission €1; ☾ summer only)

Katholische Kirche (Haydngasse, Rust; admission €1; ☾ summer only)

Nationalpark Neusiedler See-Seewinkel (☎ 02175-344 20; www.nationalpark-neusiedlersee.org, German only; Illmitz; ☾ 8am-5pm Mon-Fri, 9am-5pm Sat, 9am-noon Sun Jul-Aug, 8am-4pm Mon-Sat, 9am-noon Sun Apr-Jun & Sep-Oct)

Neusiedler See Tourismus (☎ 02167-86 00-0; www.neusiedlersee.com; Obere Hauptstrasse 24; ☾ 8am-5pm Mon-Fri, 9am-5pm Sat, 9am-noon Sun Jul-Aug, 8am-4pm Mon-Sat, 9am-noon Sun Apr-Jun & Sep-Oct)

Rust Tourismus (☎ 02685-505; www.rust.or.at, German only; Conradplatz 1, Rathaus; ☾ 9am-6pm Mon-Fri, 9am-4pm Sat, 9am-noon Sun Jul-Aug, 9am-5pm Mon-Fri, 9am-noon Sat & Sun Apr-Jun & Sep, 9am-4pm Mon-Thu, 9am-noon Fri Oct-Mar) Has a list of wine growers offering tastings.

Eating

Inamera (☎ 02685-64 73; Oggauer Strasse 29, Rust; mains €9-21; ☾ 11.30am-2.30pm & 6-10pm Wed-Fri, 11.30am-10pm Sat & Sun) Upmarket restaurant with fantastic tree-shaded garden.

Zur Dankbarkeit (☎ 02177-22 23; Hauptstrasse 39, Podersdorf; mains €6.50-19; ☾ 11.30am-2pm & 5.30-9pm Mon, Tue, Fri, 11.30am-9pm Sat & Sun) Lovely old guesthouse with regional cooking.

Transport

Distance from Vienna to Neusiedl am See 50km

Direction Southeast

Bus Buses run approximately hourly to and from Eisenstadt (30 minutes) for Rust, and then on to Mörbisch (an extra 10 minutes).

Car For Neusiedl and Podersdorf, take the A4 southeast out of Vienna till the Neusiedl am See exit; signposts can direct you from there. For Rust and Mörbisch, head south out of Vienna on the A2 and exit onto the A3 at the Guntramsdorf junction. When the A3 ends, follow the signs to Eisenstadt (east), exit the road at Eisenstadt Süd and continue east, passing through Trausdorf and St Margareten before arriving in Rust.

Ferries During the summer months ferries link Rust with Podersdorf, Podersdorf with Breitenbrunn, and Mörbish with Illmitz.

Train Neusiedl is the only town on the lake reachable by train. Seven direct trains (45 minutes) leave from Südbahnhof daily.

Sleeping

Hotel Sifkovits (☎ 02685-276; Am Seekanal 8, Rust; s/d €67/102) A quiet hotel with a decent restaurant and wine selection.

Hotel Wende (☎ 02167-81 81 11; www.hotel-wende.at; Seestrasse 40-42, Neusiedl am See; s/d €80/140) Modern hotel.

EISENSTADT

Tourism in Eisenstadt is primarily centred on one factor – the town's association with Josef Haydn.

Josef Haydn revealed that Eisenstadt was 'where I wish to live and to die'. He achieved the former, being a resident for 31 years, but it was in Vienna that he finally tinkled his last tune. He also rather carelessly omitted any directive about his preferred residency after

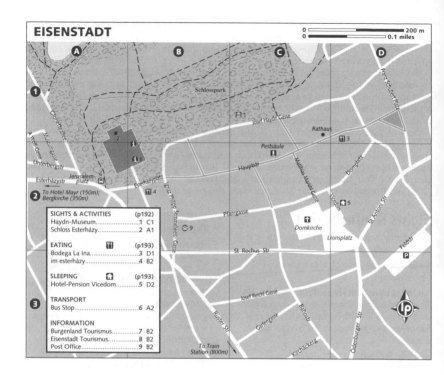

EISENSTADT

0 ——— 200 m
0 ——— 0.1 miles

A B C D

1

Schlosspark

Josef Haydn Gasse

🗷 1

Rathaus ●

🏛 3

Pestsäule
ℹ

Hauptstr

Matthias-Mariahöfer Gasse

Dompl atz

Franz-Schubert-Platz

St-Antoni-Str

2

2 🏠
8 🏠

Unterbergstr

Jerusalem-
platz 6
Esterházystr

To Hotel Mayr (150m);
Bergkirche (350m)

Esterházyplatz

🏠 4

Pfarrgasse

⊗ 9

🏠 5

Viccolo

Feldstr

Ignaz-Philipp-Semmelweis-Gasse

Domkirche

Lionsplatz

St-Rochus-Str

P

SIGHTS & ACTIVITIES	(p192)
Haydn-Museum	1 C1
Schloss Esterházy	2 A1
EATING 🍴	(p193)
Bodega La Ina	3 D1
im esterházy	4 B2
SLEEPING 🛏	(p193)
Hotel-Pension Vicedom	5 D2
TRANSPORT	
Bus Stop	6 A2
INFORMATION	
Burgenland Tourismus	7 B2
Eisenstadt Tourismus	8 B2
Post Office	9 B2

3

Josef Reichl Gasse

Ruster Str

Gartengasse

Bahndr

Oldenburger Str

Kirchäckerl

To Train
Station (800m)

LP

---

death. His skull was stolen from a temporary grave shortly after he died in 1809, and later became a museum exhibit in Vienna. The headless cadaver was subsequently returned to Eisenstadt (in 1932), but it wasn't until 1954 that the skull joined it.

Haydn's white marble tomb can now be seen in the **Bergkirche**. The church itself is remarkable for the Kalvarienberg, a unique Calvary display; access is via a separate entrance to the rear of the church. Life-sized figures depict the Stations of the Cross in a series of suitably austere, dungeon-like rooms.

You can't miss the baroque, 14th-century **Schloss Esterházy**, which dominates the town. Still owned by the powerful – and rich – Hungarian family Esterházy, the highlight of the palace is the frescoed Haydn Hall, which has the second-best acoustics of any concert hall in Austria (after Vienna's Musikverein). The **International Haydn Festival** (☎ 02682-618 66; www .haydnfestival.at, German only) is staged here around the middle of September.

Not far from the palace, Haydn's former residence has been turned into the **Haydn-Museum** and contains a few of his personal belongings. Behind the palace is a large, relaxing park, the **Schlosspark**, the setting for the Fest der 1000 Weine (Festival of 1000 Wines) in late August.

Sights & Information

Bergkirche (☎ 02682-626 38; www.haydnkirche.at, German only; Joseph Haydn Platz 1; adult/child €2.50/2; ⏰ 9am-noon & 1-5pm mid-Apr–Oct)

Burgenland Tourismus (☎ 02682-633 84-0; www.burgen land.info; Schoss Esterházy; ⏰ 9am-5pm daily Apr-Oct, 9am-2pm Mon-Fri Nov-Mar) A regional tourist office.

Eisenstadt Tourismus (☎ 02682-673 90; www.eisen stadt.at, German only; Schloss Esterházy; ⏰ 9am-5pm daily Apr-Oct, 9am-2pm Mon-Fri Nov-Mar) Can organise a guided tour of the town.

Haydn-Museum (☎ 02682-719 3900; www.haydnmu seum.at; Joseph Haydn-Gasse 19-21; adult/child €3/2; ⏰ 9am-5pm Apr-Oct, by appointment only Nov-Mar)

Schloss Esterházy (☎ 02682-719 3000; www.schloss -esterhazy.at; Schloss Esterházy; adult/child €4.50/3, grand tours €7/5.50; ⏰ 9am-6pm Apr-Oct, 9am-5pm Mon-Fri Nov-Mar) Grand tours are available only at 10am and 2pm daily July and August.

Eating

Bodega La Ina (☎ 02682-623 05; Hauptstrasse 48; tapas
€3-8; ⏱ 8am-midnight Tue-Thu, 8am-1am Fri & Sat)
Modern tapas and wine bar occupying a quiet courtyard off
the main street.

im esterházy (☎ 02682-628 19; Esterházyplatz; mains
€8-20; ⏱ 8am-midnight Mon-Thu, 8am-2am Fri & Sat,
9am-midnight Sun) Located opposite the Schloss Esterházy, this restaurant offers fine dining in cool, cellar-like
surroundings.

Sleeping

Hotel Mayr (☎ 02682-627 51; www.tiscover.com/hotel
.mayr; Kalvarienbergplatz 1; s/d €30/55) Simple hotel with
decent rooms.

Transport
Distance from Vienna 60km
Direction Southeast
Bus Frequent direct buses depart from Südtiroler
Platz (70 minutes).
Car Head south out of Vienna on the A2 and exit
onto the A3 at the Guntramsdorf junction. When the
A3 ends, follow the signs to Eisenstadt (east).
Train There are no direct trains from Vienna to Eisen-
stadt; change at Neusiedl am See (1 hr 35 mins; trains
connect with those heading to and from Südbahnhof).

Hotel-Pension Vicedom (☎ 02682-642 22; www.krato
.at; Vicedom 5; s/d from €36/62) Comfortable hotel-
Pension in the heart of the town.

WIENERWALD

The Wienerwald, west of Vienna, is a place to get off the tourist track and enjoy nature. Attractive settlements, such as the wine-growing centres of Perchtoldsdorf, Mödling and Gumpoldskirchen, speckle the area. **Mayerling** has little to see now, but the bloody event that occurred there still brings people to the site (see the boxed text below). The area is also crisscrossed with mountain-bike tracks; for more information see the website www.mtbwienerwald.at (German only).

About 6km northeast of Mayerling is **Heiligenkreuz**, where Marie Vetsera's (see the boxed text below) grave can be seen. The 12th-century **Cistercian Abbey** here is the final resting place of most of the Babenberg dynasty who ruled Austria until 1246. The church and cloister are a combination of Romanesque and Gothic styles and the abbey museum contains models by Giovanni Giuliani, who also created the trinity column in the courtyard.

Between Mödling and Heiligenkreuz, is the **Seegrotte Hinterbrühl**, Europe's largest underground lake. The site was used by the Nazis in WWII to build aircraft.

Mystery at Mayerling

It's the stuff of lurid pulp fiction: the heir to the throne found dead in a hunting lodge with his teenage mistress. It became fact in Mayerling on 30 January 1889, yet for years the details of the case were shrouded in secrecy and denial.

The heir was Archduke Rudolf, 30-year-old son of Emperor Franz Josef, husband of Stephanie of Coburg, and something of a liberal who was fond of drinking and womanising. Rudolf's marriage was little more than a public façade
by the time he met 17-year-old Baroness Marie Vetsera in the autumn of 1888. The attraction was immediate, but it
wasn't until 13 January the following year that the affair was consummated, an event commemorated by an inscribed
cigarette case, a gift from Marie to Rudolf.

On 28 January Rudolf secretly took Marie with him on a trip to his hunting lodge in Mayerling. His other guests arrived
a day later; Marie's presence, however, remained unknown to them. On the night of the 29th, the valet, Loschek, heard
the couple talking until the early hours, and at about 5.30am a fully dressed Rudolf appeared and instructed him to
prepare a horse and carriage. As Loschek was doing his master's bidding, two gunshots resounded through the air.
He raced back to find Rudolf lifeless on his bed, a revolver by his side. Marie was on her bed, also fully clothed, also dead.
Just two days earlier Rudolf had discussed a suicide pact with a former mistress. Apparently he hadn't been joking.

Almost immediately the cover-up began. Count Hoyos, a guest at the lodge, told Marie's mother that it was Marie who
killed both herself and the archduke with the aid of poison. The official line from Empress Elisabeth was that Rudolf died
of heart failure. There was no hint of suicide or a mistress. The newspapers ran with the heart-failure story, though a few
speculated about a hunting accident. It was only much later that Rudolf's suicide letter to his wife was published in her
memoirs, in which he talked of going calmly to his death. Even now a definitive picture has yet to be established. As late as
1989 – the 100th anniversary of the tragedy – Empress Zita claimed publicly that the heir had actually been murdered.

Sights & Information

Cistercian Abbey (☎ 02258-870 3-0; www.stift
-heiligenkreuz.at, German only; Heiligenkreuz 1; tours
adult/child €6/2.90; tours 10am, 11am, 2pm, 3pm & 4pm
Mon-Sat, 11am, 2pm, 3pm & 4pm Sun)

Seegrotte Hinterbrühl (☎ 02236-263 64; Grutschgasse
2; tours adult/child €6/4; ⏱ 9am-noon & 1-5pm Apr-Oct,
9am-noon & 1-3pm Nov-Mar)

Wienerwald Tourismus (☎ 02231-621 76 12; tourismus
.region.wienerwald@netway.at; Hauptplatz 11, Purkersdorf; ⏱ 9am-5pm Mon-Fri)

Transport

Distance from Vienna to Heiligenkreuz 27km
Direction Southwest
Bus Services are patchy. The Baden–Alland
Bundesbus stops at Heiligenkreuz and Mayerling but
it's fairly infrequent. From Mödling (reached on the
Vienna Südbahnhof–Baden train route) there are
frequent buses to Hinterbrühl (17 minutes).
Car It's best to explore this region by car. Take the
A2 south out of Vienna and exit onto the A21 at
the Vösendorf junction; the A21 leads directly to
Hinterbrühl and Heiligenkreuz (Mayerling is a short
drive southwest of Heiligenkreuz).

BRATISLAVA

First impressions of Bratislava, with its bland castle, rather small old town and plethora of
Communist-era architecture, may disappoint. However, the Slovak Republic capital, and far
and away its largest city, is in fact a vibrant, pulsing city. Its historical centre is small, easy to
explore on foot and crammed with historical buildings, which have received a well-earned
makeover in recent years. The currency is Slovak koruna (crowns), which are easily changed at
banks and bus, boat and train stations. Nationals of most EU countries, Australia, Canada and
New Zealand do not need a visa for tourist visits of up to 90 days. UK citizens can stay up to 180
days without a visa; US, Italian and South African citizens only 30 days. In theory EU citizens
only require an identity card to visit Slovakia, but in practice it's still best to carry a passport.

Bratislava Castle is the city's most prominent sight, and while it doesn't have much aesthetic
appeal (it looks like an upturned bed), gems lie within. On the ground floor is the Treasury of
Slovakia, containing a small but important collection of archaeological finds dating from 5000
BC and earlier – the *Venus of Moravany*, a 25,000-year-old fertility statue of a naked woman,
is a highlight. The top floors of the castle are taken up by the Slovak National Museum, which covers
folk crafts, furniture, modern art and history and also includes the all-important ice-hockey
hall of fame. Views from the castle take in the vastness of the Petržalka housing estate.

Down in the old town St Martin Cathedral, the city's finest gothic structure, dominates. Of the
museums here, the best is the Municipal Museum, located in the 14th-century town hall. It now
comes complete with Renaissance courtyard and green-roofed neogothic annexe. Next door
is the Primatial Palace, where Napoleon signed a peace treaty with Austria's Franz I in 1805.

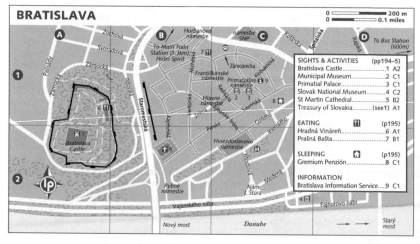

Also worth noting is the **Nový most**, (Nový Bridge) a modernist lopsided structure (1972) with what looks like a 1970s B-grade-film flying saucer hovering above it. Collectively Michalská and Ventúrska make up the main street of Bratislava while the main shopping area (and hub for trams) is Kamenné námestie (Kamenné square).

Sights & Information

Bratislava Castle (☺ 9am-8pm Apr-Sep, 9am-6pm Oct-Mar)

Bratislava Information Service (☎ 00421-2-54 43 37 15; www.bratislava.sk; Klobučnícka 2; ☺ 8.30am-6pm Mon-Fri, 9am-6pm Sat & Sun May-mid–Oct, 8am-6pm Mon-Fri, 9am-2pm Sat mid-Oct–Apr)

Municipal Museum (☎ 00421-2-54 43 47 42; Primaciálne námestie 3; adult/child 30/10Sk; ☺ 10am-5pm Tue-Fri, 11am-6pm Sat & Sun)

Primatial Palace (☎ 00421-2-54 43 14 73; Primaciálne námestie 1; adult/child 30Sk/free; ☺ 10am-5pm Tue-Sun)

Slovak National Museum (☎ 00421-2-54 41 14 44; adult/child 60/30Sk; ☺ 9am-5pm Tue-Sun)

Slowakische Zentrale für Tourismus (☎ 513 95 69; www.slovakiatourism.sk; 06, Fillgradergasse 7, 4. Stock; ☺ 9am-1pm & 2-5pm Mon-Fri) Slovak Tourism Board's representative in Vienna; hard-working and informative.

St Martin Cathedral (Rudnayovo námestie; admission free; ☺ 10am-4.45pm Mon-Sat, 2-4.45pm Sun)

Treasury of Slovakia (☎ 00421-2-54 41 14 44; Bratislava Castle; adult/child 10/5Sk; ☺ 10am-noon & 1-4pm Tue-Sun)

Eating

Hradná Vináreň (☎ 00421-2-59 34 13 58; Námestie A Dubčeka 1; mains around 200Sk) Located within the castle grounds, this quality wine tavern is the perfect spot for a romantic dinner overlooking the old town.

Prašná Bašta (☎ 00421-2-54 43 49 57; Zámočnícka 11; mains 100-200Sk) An excellent Slovakian menu and appealing settings; choose from its quiet garden or cellar-like interior.

Sleeping

Gremium Penzión (☎ 00421-2-54 13 10 26; www .gremium.sk; Gorkého 11; s/d 920/1650Sk) With its prime location, fine rooms and busy bar, you'll have to book ahead to get one of the few rooms at Gremium.

Hotel Spirit (☎ 00421-2-54 77 75 61; www.hotelspirit .sk; Vanéurova 1; s/d 990/1430Sk) Handy to the train station, this highly appealing avant-garde hotel is all angles and colour. Rooms are rather spartan though.

> ## Transport
> **Distance from Vienna** 65km
> **Direction** East
> **Boat** For information on boats to Bratislava, see p199.
> **Bus** Seven to 10 buses a day (1½ hours) connect Bratislava to Sudtirolerplatz in Vienna. Bratislava's main bus station is about 1km east of the town centre.
> **Car** Head east on the A4 from Vienna till the Fischamend junction, where you continue on Bundesbahn 9, which passes through Petronell and Hainburg and eventually ends at the Slovakia border, just south of Bratislava.
> **Train** Seven trains daily (1¼ hours) make the trip between Vienna Südbahnhof and Bratislava's main train station, which is 1.3km north of the old town.

BADEN

On the eastern edge of the Wienerwald, the spa town of Baden (full name Baden bei Wien) has a long history. The Romans liked visiting its medicinal springs. Beethoven heard about its healing properties and came here hoping to find a cure for his deafness. The town flourished in the early 19th century after being adopted by the Habsburgs as their favourite summer retreat.

Baden exudes health and 19th-century affluence (despite the slight whiff of sulphur from the thermal springs), an impression endorsed by the many Biedermeier-style houses. The town's reputation as a health spa rests on its 14 **hot springs**, which are enriched with sulphur, chlorine and sulphates. There are various indoor and outdoor pool complexes for medicinal or frivolous purposes. Predominantly in the latter category is the large **Thermalstrandbad**; the tourist office has a list of all health spas in town. The town attracts plenty of promenading Viennese on the weekends; all and sundry make for the **Kurpark**, a magnificent setting for a stroll. Rows of white benches are positioned under manicured trees in front of the bandstand, and elaborate flowerbeds complement monuments to famous artists (Mozart, Beethoven, Strauss, Grillparzer etc).

The **Rollett Museum** is the best museum in town. It covers aspects of the town's history, but the most unusual exhibit is the collection of skulls, busts and death masks amassed by the

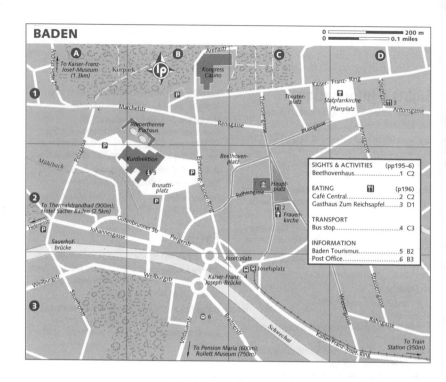

SIGHTS & ACTIVITIES   (pp195–6)
Beethovenhaus.....................1 C2

EATING   (p196)
Café Central..........................2 C2
Gasthaus Zum Reichsapfel........3 D1

TRANSPORT
Bus stop.................................4 C3

INFORMATION
Baden Tourismus......................5 B2
Post Office..............................6 B3

founder of phrenology, Josef Gall (1752–1828). The **Kaiser-Franz-Josef-Museum**, north of the town's centre, displays local folklore, while **Beethoven's former house** has Beethovenesque exhibits.

Sights & Information

Baden Tourismus (☎ 02252-226 00-600; www.baden
.at; Brusattiplatz 3; ☻ 9am-6pm Mon-Sat, 10am-1pm
Sun May-Sep, 9am-5pm Mon-Fri Oct-Apr) Has listings and
prices for thermal baths.

Beethovenhaus (Rathausgasse 10; adult/child €2.50/1;
☻ 4-6pm Tue-Fri, 9-11am & 4-6pm Sat & Sun)

Kaiser-Franz-Josef-Museum (☎ 02252-411 00; Hoch-
strasse 51; adult/child €2.50/1; ☻ 2-6pm Tue-Sun Apr-Oct)

Rollett Museum (☎ 02252-482 55; Weikersdorfer Platz
1; adult/child €2.50/1; ☻ 3-6pm Wed-Mon)

Thermalstrandbad (☎ 02252-486 70; www.baden-bei
-wien.at; Helenstrasse 19; pool entry adult/child €5.60/2)

Eating

Café Central (☎ 02252-48 454; Hauptplatz 19; coffee
€2.40-3; ☻ 7am-9pm Tue-Sat, 8am-9pm Sun) A '60s-
style café that's a bit on the dark side but full of character.

Gasthaus Zum Reichsapfel (Spiegelgasse 2; mains €6-11;
☻ 5-11.30pm Mon, Wed & Fri, 11am-2pm & 5-11pm Sat
& Sun) Rustic restaurant featuring plenty of local wine and
daily specials.

Transport

Distance from Vienna 30km
Direction South
Bus There's an hourly bus between the Vienna
Staatsoper and the centre of town (40 minutes).
Car Take the A2 south to the Baden exit, from where
Bundesbahn 210 runs 3.5km west to the town.
Train Regional and S-Bahn trains run to and from
Baden up to four times an hour from Südbahnhof
(20 to 30 minutes). The 'Lokalbahn' tram from
Karlsplatz does the same job, but takes longer (one
hour, every 15 minutes).

Sleeping

Hotel Sacher Baden (☎ 02252-484 00-0; www.sacher
-baden.at; Helenstrasse 55; s/d from €74/106) Four-star
hotel, associated with the Sacher in Vienna.

Pension Maria (☎ 02252-430 33; Elisabethstrasse 11;
s/d €38.50/60; ℗) Pleasant *Pension* with a swimming
pool and off-street parking.

Transport	198
Air	198
Bicycle	198
Boat	199
Bus	199
Car & Motorcycle	199
Public Transport	200
Taxi	202
Train	202
Travel Agents	202

Practicalities	202
Accommodation	202
Business	202
Children	203
Climate	204
Courses	204
Customs	204
Disabled Travellers	204
Discount Cards	204
Electricity	205
Embassies	205
Emergencies	205
Gay & Lesbian Travellers	205
Holidays	206
Internet Access	206
Maps	206
Medical Services	206
Metric System	207
Money	207
Newspapers & Magazines	207
Post	208
Radio	208
Safety	208
Telephone	208
Television	209
Time	209
Tipping	209
Toilets	209
Tourist Information	209
Visas	210
Women Travellers	210
Work	210

Directory

Directory

TRANSPORT
AIR

Flughafen Wien Schwechat, Vienna's international airport, is served by over 80 airlines and receives flights from as far away as Auckland, and as close as Linz. **Austrian Airlines** (☎ 05 17 89; www.aua.com) is the national carrier.

Bratislava's MR Štefánika Airport, in Slovakia, is only 60km east of Vienna, and close enough to make it an alternative to Schwechat.

Airlines

Air Berlin (☎ 0810-1025 73 800; www.airberlin.com)

Air France (Map pp240-3; ☎ 502 22-240; www.airfrance .com; 01, Kärntner Strasse 49)

Alitalia (Map pp240-3; ☎ 505 17 07; www.alitalia.com; 01, Kärntner Ring 2)

Austrian Airlines (Map pp240-3; ☎ 05 17 89; www.aua .com; 01, Kärntner Strasse 11)

British Airways (Map pp240-3; ☎ 7956 7567; www .britishairways.com; 01, Kärntner Ring 10)

Delta Air Lines (Map pp240-3; ☎ 7956 7023; www.delta .com; 02, Gredlerstrasse 3)

German Wings (☎ 01 5029 100 70; www.germanwings .com)

KLM (☎ 0900-359 556; www.klm.com)

Lauda Air (Map pp240-3; ☎ 05 17 89; www.laudaair .com; 01, Kärntner Strasse 11)

Lufthansa (Map pp246-7; ☎ 0810-1025 80 80; www .lufthansa.com; 06, Mariahilfer Strasse 123)

Sky Europe (☎ 998 555 55; www.skyeurope.com)

Swiss (Map pp240-3; ☎ 0810-810 840; www.swiss.com; 01, Marc Aurel Strasse 4)

For a complete listing, look under *Fluggesellschaften* (airlines) in the *Gelbe Seiten* (Yellow Pages) section of the Wien telephone book.

Airports

Schwechat airport (flight inquiries ☎ 7007 22233; www.viennaairport.com) lies 20km southwest of the city centre. Facilities include a handful of restaurants and bars, banks and ATMs, money-exchange counters, a supermarket, a post office, car rental agencies and a 24-hour left-luggage counter. Getting to/from the airport is possible using the following transport options:

Bus Link (☎ 05 17 17; www.oebb.at; one-way/return €5.80/10.90, children under six free, children 6-15 €2.90/5.40; from Westbahnhof ☯ 5.30am-11pm, from Wien-Mitte ☯ 4.30am-12.30am, every 20-30 min) The Westbahnhof service calls in at Wien Südbahnhof station, the Wien-Mitte service is direct.

C&K Airport Service (☎ 444 44; one-way €22) C&K car service is a better and cheaper option than a taxi as its rates are fixed. On arrival at the airport, head to its stand to the left of the exit hall; when leaving Vienna, call ahead to make a reservation.

City Airport Train (☎ 252 50; www.cityairporttrain .com, German only; return adult/child up to 15 €15/free; ☯ 5.37am-11.07pm, every 30 min) Departs from Wien-Mitte; luggage check-in facilities and boarding card issuing service.

Schnellbahn 7 (☎ 05 17 17; www.oebb.at; one-way €3, €1.50 with city transport passes; ☯ 4.35am-9.39pm Mon-Sat, every 30 min) Cheapest way to get to the airport; departs from Wien Nord and passes through Wien-Mitte.

Only 60km from Vienna, **MR Štefánika airport** (☎ 0421 2 4857 3353; www.airportbratislava .sk), serving Bratislava, is a viable option for travellers. Buses run between Štefánika and Schwechat seven times daily; a return fare costs €14.30. Sky Europe, Slovakia's premiere no-frills airline, connects Bratislava with a bunch of European capitals on a daily basis.

BICYCLE
Hire

Vienna is simply made for cycling. Over 700km of cycle tracks criss-cross the city, which means you're often more concerned about running into pedestrians than being run over by cars and buses. Note that many one-way streets do not apply to cyclists; these are indicated by a bicycle sign with the word *ausgen* alongside it. Popular cycling areas include the 7km path around the Ringstrasse, the Donauinsel (Danube Island), the Prater and along the Danube Canal (Donaukanal). See the Walking & Cycling Tours chapter (p105) for two cycle tour suggestions. If you're planning to do a lot of cycling pick up a copy of Argus' comprehensive *Stadtplan Wien für RadfahrerInnen*, which maps out cycle paths in Vienna. Hire bikes from any of the following:

Pedal Power (Map pp244–5; ☎ 729 72 34; www.pedal power.at; 02, Ausstellungsstrasse 3; 1-hr/½-/full-day rental €5/17/27; ☒ 8am-7pm Apr-Oct) Pedal Power also offers tours of the city; see p52 for more information. Child seats and helmets are €4 extra a piece.

Radverleih Floridsdorfer Brücke (Map pp238–9; ☎ 278 86 98; 21, Donauinsel Parkplatz; 3-gear bicycles/mountain bikes per hour €3.50/6; ☒ 9.30am-sunset Mon-Fri, 9am-sunset Sat & Sun Mar-Oct) Handy for the Donauinsel and Alte Donau (Old Danube), Floridsdorfer Brücke also has tandem bikes, BMX, beach cruisers and scooters for hire.

Vienna City Bike (☎ 0810-50 05 00; www.citybikewien .at, German only; bicycles €2 per hour) The City of Vienna's new initiative to provide the public with bikes, Vienna City Bike consists of bike racks in and around the Innere Stadt and Ringstrasse lined with bicycles to rent. You need a credit card or a bank card from an Austrian bank to rent the bikes; just swipe your card in the machine provided and away you ride. Don't lose the bike though – €600 will be deducted from your card.

Bicycles on Public Transport

Bicycles can be carried on carriages marked with a bike symbol on the S-Bahn and U-Bahn from 9am to 3pm and after 6.30pm Monday to Friday, after 9am Saturday and all day Sunday for half the adult fare. It's not possible to take bikes on trams and buses.

BOAT

The Danube (Donau) is a traffic-free access route for arrivals and departures from Vienna. Eastern Europe is the main destination; hydrofoil sailings to Bratislava take 1½ hours (one way/return €22/33.50; ☒ 9am Wed-Sun Apr & Sep-Oct, 9.30am Wed-Sun May, 9.30am daily Jun-Aug) while Budapest takes 5½ hours (one way/return €75/99; ☒ 9am daily Apr & Sep-Oct, 8am May-Jul, 8am & 1pm Aug). Bookings can be made through **DDSG Blue Danube** (Map pp240–3; ☎ 588 80; www.ddsg-blue-danube .at; 01, Friedrichstrasse 7; ☒ 9am-6pm Mon-Fri); ships dock at 02, Handelskai 265 (U1 Vorgartenstrasse).

Since the early 1990s the Danube has been connected to the Rhine by the River Main tributary and the Main-Danube canal in southern Germany. The MS *River Queen* does 13-day cruises along this route, from Amsterdam to Vienna, between May and September.

It departs monthly in each direction. In Britain, bookings can be made through **Noble Caledonia** (☎ 020-7752 0000); it also makes bookings for the MS *Amadeus*, which takes seven days to get from Passau to Budapest. In the USA, you can book through **Uniworld** (☎ 1-800-360 9550; www.cruiseuniworld.com).

For boat trips through the picturesque Wachau region northwest of Vienna see the Excursions chapter (p183).

BUS

Vienna has no central bus station; your arrival destination will depend on which company you're travelling with.

Eurolines (Map pp248–9; ☎ 798 29 00; www .eurolines.at; 03, Erdbergstrasse 202; ☒ 6.30am-8.30pm Mon-Fri, 6.30-11am & 4.30-8.30pm Sat & Sun) handles the bulk of Vienna's international bus connections and covers a plethora of destinations between England and Turkey. Its bus terminal is at Südbahnhof, on Arsenalstrasse (Map pp248–9). Check the website for your local Eurolines office, and prices to Vienna.

Austrobus has buses to Prague, leaving from 01, Rathausplatz 5 (one-way/return €20/34; ☒ 7am Mon-Sat, 2pm Sun); the journey takes six hours. Buy tickets directly from the driver, or in advance from **Columbus Reisen** (☎ 534 11-123; 01, Dr Karl Lueger Ring 8; ☒ 9am-5pm Mon-Fri, 9am-noon Sat).

Post buses (☎ 711 01; www.postbus.at, German only; information line ☒ 7am-8pm) are Austria's regional buses and basically go everywhere regional trains don't.

CAR & MOTORCYCLE
Driving

You're better off using the excellent public transport system than driving in Vienna. The city administrators have a penchant for one-way streets, the Viennese are particularly impatient drivers and parking is difficult and/or expensive in the centre. Most Viennese completely avoid driving in the Innere Stadt because of its notorious one-way system.

If you do plan to drive in the city, take special care of the trams: they always have priority and no matter how much you might swear at them, they're never going to deviate from their tracks just to suit you. Vehicles must wait behind trams when they stop to pick up or set down passengers. Like the rest of continental Europe, Viennese drive on the right.

Always carry proof of ownership of a private vehicle and your driver's licence. EU licences are accepted in Austria while all other nationalities require a German translation or an International Driving Permit (IDP). Third-party insurance is a minimum requirement in Europe: you'll need proof of this in the form of a Green Card.

The blood-alcohol limit in Austria is 0.05%. Speed limits are 50km/h in built-up areas, 100km/h on country roads (Bundesbahn) and 130km/h on motorways (Autobahn). On some country roads speed is restricted to 70km/h. Crash helmets are compulsory on motorcycles and children under the age of 14 and/or shorter than 1.5m must have a special seat or restraint.

A motorway tax (Vignitte) is imposed on all Autobahn; 10 day/two month/year passes cost €7.60/21.80/72.60.

Hire

For the lowest rates, organise car rental before departure. Holiday Autos (www.holidayautos .com) has low rates and offices or representatives in over 20 countries.

All the multinational rental companies are present in Austria. You should be able to make advance reservations online, or arrange something after arriving in Austria at the following:

Avis (Map pp240-3; ☎ 700 73 27 00; www.avis.at; 01, Opernring 3-5; ⌚ 7am-6pm Mon-Fri, 8am-2pm Sat, 8am-1pm Sun)

Denzeldrive (Map pp246-7; ☎ 897 55 28; www.denzel drive.at; 15, Europlatz (Westbahnhof); ⌚ 8am-8pm Mon-Fri, 8am-2pm Sat)

Europcar (Map pp240-3; ☎ 714 67 17; www.europcar.at; 01, Schubertring 9; ⌚ 7.30am-6pm Mon-Fri, 8am-1pm Sat, 8am-noon Sun)

Hertz (Map pp240-3; ☎ 512 86 77; www.hertz.at; 01, Kärntner Ring 17; ⌚ 7.30am-6pm Mon-Fri, 9am-3pm Sat & Sun)

Denzeldrive, Europcar and Hertz have desks at the airport. Rates start at around €60 per day but decrease for longer rentals. Check extra charges before signing an agreement; CDW is an additional charge starting at around €22 per day, theft protection another €7 to €8 per day and drivers under the age of 25 are often required to pay an additional €4 to €5 per day.

The minimum age for renting is 19 for small cars and 25 for prestige models and a valid licence of at least a year is required. If you plan to drive across the border, especially into Eastern Europe, let the rental company know beforehand and double-check any add-on fees.

Parking

Districts 1–9 and 20 are pay and display short-stay parking zones (Kurzparkzone) where a parking voucher (Parkschein) is required. These come in 30/60/90 minute lots (€0.40/0.80/1.20) and can be purchased from most Tabakladen (tobacconist shops), banks, train stations and Wiener Linien ticket offices. A free 10-minute voucher is also available. To validate a voucher, just cross out the appropriate time, date and year and leave it on your dashboard. The parking restrictions are in force from 9am to 7pm Monday to Friday (maximum 1½ hours parking) in the Innere Stadt and from 9am to 8pm Monday to Friday (maximum two hours) in other districts.

Kurzparkzone are found in all of Vienna's districts, but generally only on main thoroughfares. Look for blue signs circled in red with a single diagonal line. Disobeying the parking rules will incur an instant fine – ranging from €20 to €170 – and possibly a tow-away.

The MuseumsQuartier, Südbahnhof and Westbahnhof all sport private parking garages, along with the Ringstrasse; expect to pay anything between €1 and €3.50 per hour.

Automobile Associations

Two automobile associations serve Austria. Both provide free 24-hour breakdown service to members and have reciprocal agreements with motoring clubs in other countries; check with your local club before leaving. If you're not entitled to free assistance, you'll incur a fee for call-outs which varies depending on the time of day. The two associations are:

ARBÖ (Map pp246-7; 24-hr emergency assistance ☎ 123, office ☎ 891 21-0; www.arboe.at; 15, Mariahilfer Strasse 180; ⌚ 8am-6pm Mon-Fri, 9am-noon Sat)

ÖAMTC (Map pp240-3; 24-hour emergency assistance ☎ 120, office ☎ 711 99-0; www.oeamtc.at; 01, Schubertring 1-3; ⌚ 9am-6pm Mon-Fri, 9am-noon Sat)

PUBLIC TRANSPORT

Vienna has a comprehensive and unified public transport network that is one of the most efficient in Europe. Flat-fare tickets are valid for trains, trams, buses, the underground (U-Bahn) and the S-Bahn regional trains. Services are frequent, and you rarely have to wait more than five or 10 minutes. Public transport kicks off around 5am or 6am. Buses and trams finish between 11pm and midnight (except for night buses), and S-Bahn and U-Bahn services between 12.30am and 1am.

Transport maps are posted in all U-Bahn stations and at many bus and tram stops. Free maps and information pamphlets are available from **Wiener Linien** (☎ 790 91 05; www .wienerlinien.at; information line ☻ 6am-10pm Mon-Fri, 8.30am-4.30pm Sat & Sun), located in 25 U-Bahn stations. The Karlsplatz, Stephansplatz and Westbahnhof information offices are open 6.30am to 6.30pm Monday to Friday and 8.30am to 4pm Saturday and Sunday. Those at Floridsdorf, Spittelau, Praterstern, Philadelphiabrücke, Landstrasse and Volkstheater are closed on weekends.

Tickets & Passes

Tickets and passes can be purchased at U-Bahn stations – from automatic machines (with English instructions and change) and occasionally staffed ticket offices – and in *Tabakladen*. Once bought, tickets need to be validated before starting your journey (except for weekly and monthly tickets); look for small blue boxes at the entrance to U-Bahn stations and on buses and trams. Just pop the end of the ticket in the slot and wait for the 'ding'. It's an honour system and ticket inspection is infrequent, but if you're caught without a ticket you'll be fined €62, no exceptions.

Tickets and passes are as follows:

Single Ticket *(Fahrschein)* – €1.50; good for one journey, with line changes; costs €2 if purchased on trams and buses (correct change required)

Vienna Shopping Card *(Wiener Einkaufskarte)* – €4; for use between 8am and 8pm Monday to Saturday; only good for one day after validation

24-Hour Ticket *(24 Stunden Wien-Karte)* – €5; 24 hours unlimited travel from time of validation

Strip Ticket *(Streifenkarte)* – €6; four single tickets on one strip

72-Hour Ticket *(72 Stunden Wien-Karte)* – €12; 72 hours unlimited travel from time of validation

Weekly Ticket *(Wochenkarte)* – €12.50; valid Monday through Sunday only

The Vienna Card *(Die Wien-Karte)* – €16.90; 72 hours of unlimited travel from time of validation plus discounts at selected museums, attractions, cafés and shops; comes with information brochure. Only available from hotels and ticket offices.

Eight-day Ticket *(8-Tage-Karte)* – €24; valid for eight days, but not necessarily eight consecutive days; punch the card as and when you need it

Monthly Ticket *(Monatskarte)* – €45; valid from the 1st of the month to the last day of the month

Children aged six to 15 travel for half-price, or for free on Sunday, public holidays and during Vienna school holidays (photo ID necessary); younger children always travel free. Senior citizens (women over 60, men over 65) can buy a €2 ticket that is valid for two trips; inquire at transport information offices.

Buses

Buses go everywhere, including inside the Ring (unlike trams), and either have three digits or a number followed by an 'A' or 'B'. Very logically, buses connecting with a tram service often have the same number, eg, bus 38A connects with tram 38, bus 72A with tram 72.

Night Buses

Once trams, buses and the U-Bahn shut up shop for the night, Vienna's comprehensive 'Nightline' service takes over. Twenty one routes cover much of the city, and run from 12.30am to 5am on the half hour. Schwedenplatz, Schottentor and the Oper are starting points for many services; look for buses and bus stops marked with an 'N'. All tickets are valid for Nightline services.

S-Bahn

S-Bahn trains, designated by a number preceded by an 'S', operate from train stations, and are mainly used as a service to the suburbs or satellite towns. If you're travelling outside of Vienna, and outside of the ticket zone, you'll probably have to purchase an extension; check on maps posted in train stations.

Trams

There's something romantic and just plain good about travelling by tram, even though they're slower than the U-Bahn. Vienna's tram network is extensive; it's the perfect way to view the city on the cheap. Trams 1 and 2, which circle the Innere Stadt in opposite directions, are particularly popular with tourists as they provide a glimpse of the Ringstrasse's rich architecture. Trams are either numbered or lettered (eg 1, 44, J, D) and cover the city centre and some suburbs.

U-Bahn

The U-Bahn is a quick and efficient way to get around the city, albeit mostly underground and therefore lacking in visual stimulus. There are five lines, U1 to U6 (there is no U5). Plans are afoot to extend the U2 line across to Praterstern and beyond over the next few years. Platforms have timetable information and signs showing the different exits and nearby facilities. The whole U-Bahn system is a no-smoking zone.

TAXI

Taxis are reliable and relatively cheap by Western European standards. City journeys are metered; flag fall costs €2.50 from 6am to 11pm Monday to Saturday and €2.60 any other time, plus a small per km fee. A small tip is expected; add on about 10% to the fare. Taxis are easily found at train stations and taxi stands all over the city, or just flag them down in the street. To order one call ☎ 31 300, ☎ 60 160, ☎ 40 100 or ☎ 81 400. Don't count on taxis taking credit cards.

TRAIN

Like much of Europe, Austria's train network is a dense web reaching the country's far-flung corners. The system is fast, efficient, frequent and well used. **ÖBB** (24hr information ☎ 05 17 17; www.oebb.at) is the main operator, and has information offices all of Vienna's main train stations. Tickets can be purchased at ticket offices or on the train, but the latter will normally cost a little extra. Reservations incur a fee of €3, and are recommended for travel on weekends.

Vienna is served by a number of train stations, but has three main ones: Westbahnhof, Südbahnhof and Franz-Josef-Bahnhof. The big three all have left-luggage lockers (24 hours; €2 to €3.50), ATMs, currency-exchange counters, post offices and plenty of places to grab a snack. They usually close their doors from around 1am to 4am.

Westbahnhof (Map pp246–7; information office ☺ 7.30am-8.40pm Mon-Sat, 8am-8.40pm Sun) services trains to Western and northern Europe and western Austria and is connected to Vienna's public transport system by U-Bahn and tram. **Südbahnhof** (Map pp248–9; information office ☺ 6.30am-9.20pm) services trains to Italy, the Czech Republic, Slovakia, Hungary and Poland and has tram and bus stops. **Franz-Josefs-Bahnhof** (Map pp244–5; information office ☺ 6.40am-7.10pm) handles regional and local trains, including trains to Tulln, Krems and the Wachau region.

Smaller stations include **Wien Mitte** (Map pp240–3), **Wien Nord** (Map pp244–5) and **Meidling** (Map pp246–7). All have U-Bahn stops and the former two have connections to the airport.

TRAVEL AGENTS

Die Restplatzbörse (Map pp240-3; ☎ 580 850; www.restplatzboerse.at, German only; 01, Opernring 3-5; ☺ 9am-7pm Mon-Fri, 9am-noon Sat) This agent specialises in bargain flights and has 10 outlets across Vienna, including one at the airport.

Österreichisches Verkehrsbüro (Map pp240-3; ☎ 588 00; www.verkehrsbuero.at, German only; 04, Friedrichstrasse 7; ☺ 9am-5pm Mon-Fri) This major national agency organises everything under the sun.

STA Travel (Map pp240-3; ☎ 401 48; www.statravel.at, German only; 09, Garnisongasse 7; ☺ 9am-5.30pm Mon-Fri) STA has discounted flights for students. The staff members are helpful, friendly and speak English. There are five branches in the city.

PRACTICALITIES

ACCOMMODATION

Accommodation alternatives in the Sleeping chapter (p171) are separated into district groupings, and then listed in alphabetical order. Mid-range and top-end options are grouped together, followed by 'Cheap Sleeps' (anything under €70 for a double room). The average price for a double room in the Innere Stadt is around €130, but there are cheaper rooms in the surrounding districts. Peak season is June to September, Christmas and Easter; outside these times expect prices to drop and deals to become readily available. Prices quoted in the Sleeping chapter are summer rates.

BUSINESS

Vienna is Austria's business hub, and a traditional stepping stone between Eastern and Western Europe, even though its importance has dwindled since the fall of the Berlin Wall. It's also a major conference location, something Vienna's promotional machine pushes; the city's conference capabilities are seen as one of its five USPs (Unique Selling Points). For more information on conferences and conventions, contact the Vienna Convention Bureau (☎ 211 14-500; www.vienna.convention.at), which is part of the Vienna Tourist Board.

Starting a business can be a bit of a headache though, as there are a lot of bureaucratic hoops to leap through. The Austrian Business Agency's website www.aba.gv.at/en/pages is a good introduction point, as it has business contact listings and general information. The booklet *Business Contacts Austria* is a handy publication, with comprehensive business listings, as is the book *International Organizations in Vienna*, produced by the city authority. Helpful organisations in Vienna include:

American Reference Center (Map pp244-5; ☎ 313 39-0; 08, Schmidgasse 14; 🕙 9am-noon & 1-5pm Mon-Fri) This reference centre is linked to the US embassy, and has many publications in English about or from the USA. It's a resource for people undertaking research and not for the general public; appointments are necessary.

British Trade Council (Map pp240-3; ☎ 533 15 94; 01, Laurenzerberg 2; 🕙 by appointment)

US Chamber of Commerce (Map pp244-5; ☎ 319 57 51; 09, Porzellangasse 35; 🕙 9am-noon Mon-Fri)

Hours

Offices and government departments generally open from 8am to 3.30pm, 4pm or 5pm Monday to Friday. There are no real restrictions on shop opening hours but most open between 9am and 6pm Monday to Friday and until 5pm Saturday. Some have extended hours on Thursday or Friday until around 7.30pm.

Banking hours are from 8am or 9am to 3pm Monday to Friday, with extended hours until 5.30pm on Thursday. Many smaller branches close from 12.30pm to 1.30pm for lunch. Post offices open for business from 8am to noon and 2pm to 6pm Monday to Friday; some also open Saturday from 8am to noon. The main post office (Map pp240–3; 01, Fleischmarkt 19) is open 24 hours, and branches at Westbahnhof, Südbahnhof and Franz-Josefs-Bahnhof have extend hours.

Restaurants serve lunch between 11am and 3pm and dinner from 6pm to midnight and often close in between. Cafés tend to stay open the whole day; for more information see the Eating chapter (p115). Pubs and bars close anywhere between midnight and 4am throughout the week.

Centres

Much of Vienna's business is centred in and around the Innere Stadt. Vienna International Center (UNO City) in the 22nd district is where international organisations are based, including the UN (the third-most important base after New York and Geneva) and the International Atomic Energy Agency. Business Park Wien Süd is the biggest business park in Austria and is just beyond the city precincts, near Shopping City Süd. Facilities include offices as well as production, manufacturing and storage buildings.

CHILDREN

It was once said the Viennese love dogs more than they love children, and while this is true for some of the populace, attitudes, especially from the establishment, have changed in recent years. Vienna's museums, attractions and theatres are cottoning on to the idea that kids need entertaining, and that their parents are willing to fork out cash for such entertainment. The city now boasts two museums aimed directly at kids – Zoom (p82) and the Schönbrunn Kindermuseum (p102) – and many theatres and attractions, such as the Kunsthistorisches Museum and the Albertina, have children's programs over the summer months.

Fun for the little 'uns is not only restricted to indoors. The Prater, with its wide open playing fields, playgrounds and funfair, is ideal for children. Lainzer Tiergarten and the Donauinsel are just two more examples where kids can let loose and run off all their energy. Swimming pools are dotted across the length and breadth of the city and offer free access to children under 15 over the summer school holidays.

The city's facilities are also improving. The new trams are easily accessible with buggies or prams (the older ones, however, are a nightmare), as are U-Bahns and buses. Children aged six to 15 travel for half-price, or for free on Sunday, public holidays and during Vienna school holidays; younger children always travel free. Children's menus are popping up at restaurants more frequently and often children under 12 can stay in their parents' hotel room free of charge. Breast-feeding in public is a common sight and nappy changing ruffles no feathers.

Scan through the Districts (p47) and Entertainment chapters (p137) for museum activities, parks and swimming baths suitable for children and see the boxed text 'Top Five for Children' (p48) for best the city has to offer. A number of brochures on family activities are available from the children and teenager information offices listed under Tourist Information (p209) at the end of this chapter.

Pick up a copy of Lonely Planet's *Travel with Children* by Cathy Lanigan for helpful travelling tips.

Baby-sitting

The best idea is to check with the hotel you're staying at; the staff may be able to arrange a baby-sitter for you.

CLIMATE

Austria falls within the central European climatic zone, though the eastern part of the country (where Vienna is situated) has a Continental Pannonian climate, characterised by a mean temperature in July of above 19°C and annual rainfall usually under 800mm.

The differences in temperature between day and night and summer and winter are greater than in the west of the country. July and August can be very hot, and a hotel with air-conditioning would be an asset at this time. Winter is surprisingly cold, especially in January, and you would need to bring plenty of warm clothing. Damp maritime winds sometimes sweep in from the west, and the *Föhn*, a warm wind from the south, is not an uncommon occurrence throughout the entire year. Average rainfall is 710mm per year, with most falling between May and August.

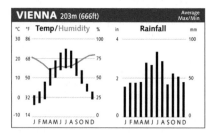

COURSES

Many places offer German courses, and they can usually offer the option of accommodation for the duration. Two of the better-known course providers are:

Berlitz (Map pp240-3; ☎ 512 82 86; www.berlitz.at, German only; 01, Graben 13; ☼ 8am-8pm Mon-Fri) Berlitz offers private, intensive and evening courses and has four offices in Vienna.

Inlingua Sprachschule (Map pp240-3; ☎ 512 22 25; www.inlingua.at; 01, Neuer Markt 1; ☼ 9am-6pm Mon-Fri) Courses at Inlingua run for a minimum of two weeks, and can either be taken during the day or at night. Classes are limited to eight students, and individual tuition is also available.

Check the *Gelbe Seiten* (Yellow Pages) under *Sprachschulen* (language schools) for more listings.

CUSTOMS

Theoretically there is no restriction on how much you can bring into Austria from other

EU states. However, to ensure these goods remain for personal use, guideline limits are 800 cigarettes, 200 cigars, 1kg tobacco, 10L of spirits, 90L of wine, 110L of beer and 20L of other alcoholic beverages. The same quantity can be taken out of Austria, as long as you are travelling to another EU country.

For duty-free purchases made outside the EU, you may bring 200 cigarettes or 50 cigars or 250g tobacco, plus 2L of wine and 1L of spirits into Austria. Items such as weapons, drugs (both legal and illegal), meat, certain plant material, and animal products are subject to stricter customs control.

DISABLED TRAVELLERS

Vienna is fairly well geared for disabled *(Behinderte)* travellers, but not exceptional. Ramps are common but by no means ubiquitous; most U-Bahn stations have wheelchair lifts but trams and buses don't (though buses can lower themselves for easier access and the newer trams have doors at ground level); and many, but once again not all, traffic lights 'bleep' to indicate when pedestrians can safely cross the road.

The tourist office can give advice and information. Its detailed booklet *Vienna for Visitors with Disabilities,* in German or English, provides information on hotels and restaurants with disabled access, plus addresses of hospitals, medical equipment shops, parking places, toilets and much more. Send an email (info@wien.info) for more details.

Organisations

Bizeps (Map pp246-7; ☎ 523 89 21; www.bizeps.at; 07, Kaiserstrasse 55/3/4a; ☼ appointments only 10am-4pm Mon-Fri) A centre providing support and self-help for people with disabilities.

Faktor i (Map pp246-7; ☎ 274 92 74; www.faktori.wuk .at; 05, Rechte Wienzeile 31; ☼ 1-5pm Mon & Tue, 9am-7pm Thu, information line ☼ 9am-5pm Mon & Tue, 9am-1pm Wed, 9am-7pm Thu) Faktor i is aimed at offering information to young people with handicaps.

DISCOUNT CARDS

The Vienna Card (*Die Wien-Karte*; €16.90) allows three days unlimited travel on the public transport system and a bunch of discounts at selected museums, cafés, *Heurigen* (wine taverns), restaurants, shops and guided tours. The discount usually amounts to 5% to 10% off the normal price or a free gift. It can be purchased at Tourist Info Vienna (see Tourist

Information p209), many hotels and at Wiener
Linien ticket offices.

ELECTRICITY
The current used is 220V. Sockets are the round
two-pin type, which are standard throughout
most of Continental Europe. North American
110V appliances will need a transformer if they
don't have built-in voltage adjustment.

EMBASSIES
The Austrian Foreign Ministry website (www
.bmaa.gv.at) has a complete list of embassies
and consulates.

Australia (Map pp240-3; ☎ 506 74-0; www.australian
-embassy.at; 04, Mattiellistrasse 2)

Canada (Map pp240-3; ☎ 531 38-3000; www.kanada.at;
01, Laurenzerberg 2)

Czech Republic (Map pp246-7; ☎ 894 321 25; www.mzv
.cz/vienna; 14, Penzingerstrasse 11-13)

France (Map pp240-3; ☎ 502 75 200 12; www.consul
france-vienne.org; 01, Wipplingerstrasse 24-26)

Hungary (Map pp240-3; ☎ 537 80-300; kom@huembvie
.at; 01, Bankgasse 4-6)

Italy (Map pp248-9; ☎ 713 56 71; www.ambitalia
vienna.org; 03, Ungargasse 43)

New Zealand (Map pp238-9; ☎ 318 85 08; www.nz
embassy.com; 23, Karl-Tornay-Gasse 34) Honorary
consulate only

Slovakia (Map pp238-9; ☎ 318 90 55; 19, Armbruster-
gasse 24)

Slovenia (Map pp240-3; ☎ 585 22 40; 01, Nibelungen-
gasse 13)

Switzerland (Map pp248-9; ☎ 795 05-0; www.eda
.admin.ch/wien; 03, Prinz-Eugen-Strasse 7)

UK (Map pp248-9; ☎ 716 13-0; www.britishembassy.at;
03, Jauresgasse 12)

USA (Map pp240-3; ☎ 319 39; www.usembassy.at;
4th fl, Hotel Marriott, 01, Gartenbaupromenade 2-4)

EMERGENCIES
In case of emergency, dial the following:

Ambulance *(Rettung)* ☎ 144

Doctor *(Ärzte-Notdienst)* ☎ 141

Fire *(Feuerwehr)* ☎ 122

Helpline (in English) ☎ 713 33 74; ☼ 9.30am-1pm &
6.30-10pm Mon-Fri, 6.30-10pm Sat

Police *(Polizei)* ☎ 133

Women's Emergency Line *(Frauennotruf)* ☎ 71 719

GAY & LESBIAN TRAVELLERS
Vienna is reasonably tolerant towards gays and
lesbians, more so than the rest of Austria, and
gay bashing is virtually unknown here (unlike
in ostensibly more gay-tolerant cities like Amsterdam or Berlin). The situation is improving
all the time; recently, the restricting federal stat-
ute 209, which set the consenting age for sex
between men at 18 (it is 14 for heterosexuals)
was repealed. There is no set age of consent for
lesbian sex, apparently because the legislators
decided there was no discernible difference between mutual washing of bodily parts and intimate sexual contact. While lesbians welcome
the lack of legislation, they see this as a typical
(male) denial of female sexuality.

Information on the gay and lesbian scene
(Schwullesbische Szene) is quite comprehensive.
The Vienna Tourist Board produces the handy
Queer Guide, a booklet listing gay bars, restaurants, hotels and festivals, and the *Vienna Gay
Guide*, a city map with gay locations marked
on it. Both are freely available at the Tourist
Info Wien office (p210), the organisations listed
below and at many gay and lesbian *Lokale* (bars).
Xtra and *Night Life* (www.nightlifeonline.at), two
free monthly publications, are additional sup-
plements and are packed with news, views and
listings, but they're only in German. Online, the
websites www.gayboy.at, www.rainbow.or.at
and www.gayguide.at are helpful.

Events to look out for on the gay and lesbian calendar include the Regenbogen Parade
(Rainbow Parade), the Life Ball, Wien ist Andersrum and Identities (Vienna's Queer Film
Festival). See the City Life chapter (p7) for more
details. Bars, venues and clubs in the *Schwullesbische Szene* are listed throughout the Entertainment chapter (p137).

Organisations
Homosexuelle Initiative Wien (HOSI; Map pp244-5;
☎ 216 66 04; www.hosiwien.at, German only; 02, Novara-
gasse 40; ☼ 5-10pm Tue-Thu, telephone counselling 6-8pm
Tues, 7-9pm Wed & Thu) HOSI is a politically minded gay
and lesbian centre with regular events.

Rosa Lila Villa (Map pp246-7; www.villa.at; 06, Linke
Wienzeile 102) Probably the best organisation in Vienna
for information, the Rosa Lila Villa has telephone counselling, a small library with books in English, and advice and
information on what's on offer in the city. The **lesbian
centre** (☎ 586 81 50; lesbenberatung@villa.at; ☼ 5-8pm
Mon-Fri) is on the ground floor, and the **gay men's centre**
(☎ 585 43 43; schwulenberatung@villa.at; ☼ 5-8pm
Mon-Thu) is on the 1st floor.

HOLIDAYS

Basically everything shuts down on public holidays. The only establishments open are bars, cafés and restaurants and even some of these refuse to open their doors. Museums like to confuse things – some stay closed while others are free. The big school break is July and August. This is a time when most families go on holiday so you'll find the city is a little quieter and some businesses, restaurants and entertainment venues are closed. See the City Life chapter (p7) for details on festivals and events.

Public holiday are:

New Year's Day *(Neujahr)* 1 January

Epiphany *(Heilige Drei Könige)* 6 January

Easter Monday *(Ostermontag)*

Labour Day *(Tag der Arbeit)* 1 May

Ascension Day *(Christi Himmelfahrt)* 6th Thursday after Easter

Whit Monday *(Pfingstmontag)* 6th Monday after Easter

Corpus Christi *(Fronleichnam)* 2nd Thursday after Pentecost

Assumption *(Maria Himmelfahrt)* 15 August

National Day *(Nationalfeiertag)* 26 October

All Saints' Day *(Allerheiligen)* 1 November

Immaculate Conception *(Mariä Empfängnis)* 8 December

Christmas Day *(Christfest)* 25 December

St Stephen's Day *(Stephanitag)* 26 December

INTERNET ACCESS

All top hotels have plugs for connecting your laptop to the Internet, but as yet it's not possible to organise an ISP in Austria for a short period (minimum contracts run for 12 months) so you'll have to arrange one from home. AOL's access number in Vienna is ☎ 585 84 83, Compuserve's is ☎ 899 330 and Eunet's is ☎ 0049-180 570 40 70.

Vienna has dozens of places offering public access to online services. Free access is available at Amadeus branches (p167), Café Florianihof (p130), Flex (p147) and rhiz (p143; free after 9pm), but there aren't many terminals. Bücherei Wien (p95) also has free Internet access; just turn up with your passport and log on.

If you're not prepared to wait, try any of the following reliable and relatively cheap Internet cafés:

BigNet (Map pp240-3; ☎ 205 06 21; 06, Mariahilfer Strasse 27; ☺ 8am-2am) BigNet has branches at Kärntner Strasse 61 and Hoher Markt 8 in the Innere Stadt; both are slightly more expensive and keep shorter hours than Mariahilfer Strasse.

G-Zone (Map pp240-3; ☎ 407 81 66; 01, Universitäts-strasse 11; ☺ 10am-11pm Mon-Fri, 2-11pm Sat & Sun)

Speednet Café (Map pp246-7; ☎ 892 56 66; 15, Europlatz, Westbahnhof; ☺ 7am-midnight Mon-Sat, from 8am Sun) You'll find Speednet Café lurking at the back of Westbahnhof beside the post office and another in the Innere Stadt at Morzinplatz 4.

Internet access normally costs anything between €4 and €6 for an hour's connection.

MAPS

For most purposes, the free map of Vienna provided by the tourist office will be sufficient. It shows bus, tram and U-Bahn routes, has a separate U-Bahn plan, and lists major city-wide sights. It also has a blow-up of the Innere Stadt. For a street index, you'll need to buy a map. Freytag & Berndt's 1:25,000 fold-out map, available at most book stores, is very comprehensive, but its Buchplan Wien (scale 1:20,000) is the Rolls Royce of city maps and is used by locals.

MEDICAL SERVICES

EU and EEA (European Economic Area) nationals receive free emergency medical treatment, although payment may have to be made for medication, private consultations and non-urgent treatment. Inquire before leaving home about the documentation required. British citizens normally need to show an E111 form (available from post offices) or a European Health Insurance Card (which will replace the E111 form by the end of 2005) to take advantage of reciprocal health agreements in Europe, so it's worth getting one if you're travelling through the Continent. However, in Austria you only need to show a British passport, though if you're staying a long time in Vienna it would facilitate matters if you get a certificate from the health insurance office, the **Gebietskrankenkasse** (Map pp238–9; ☎ 601 22-0; www.gkkwien.at, German only; 10, Wienerbergstrasse 15-19; ☺ 8am-2pm Mon-Thu, 8am-1pm Fri). This office can also tell you the countries that have reciprocal agreements with Austria (the USA, Canada, Australia and New Zealand don't).

Nothing, however, beats having full health insurance.

Emergency Rooms

The following hospitals *(Krankenhäuser)* have emergency rooms open 24 hours a day, seven days a week:

Allgemeines Krankenhaus (Map pp244-5; ☎ 404 00; 09, Währinger Gürtel 18-20)

Hanusch-Krankenhaus (Map pp246-7; ☎ 910 21-0; 14, Heinrich Collin Strasse 30)

Lorenz Böhler Unfallkrankenhaus (Map pp244-5; ☎ 331 10; 20, Donaueschingenstrasse 13)

Unfallkrankenhaus Meidling (Map pp238-9; ☎ 601 50-0; 12, Kundratstrasse 37)

If you require a dentist (Zahnarzt) after hours, call ☎ 512 20 78 (in German only); likewise if you need a pharmacy (Apotheke), dial ☎ 1550 (German only).

METRIC SYSTEM

The metric system is used. Like other Continental Europeans, Austrians indicate decimals with commas and thousands with points. You will sometimes see meat and cheese priced per dag, which is an abbreviation referring to 10g (to ask for this quantity say 'deca').

MONEY

Like other members of the European Monetary Union (EMU), Austria's currency is the euro, which is divided into 100 cents. There are coins for one, two, five, 10, 20 and 50 cents, and €1 and €2. Notes come in denominations of €5, €10, €20, €50, €100, €200 and €500.

See the Quick Reference (inside front cover) for exchange rates at the time of going to press. For the latest rates, check out www.oanda.com.

ATMs

Almost all central banks have ATMs (Bankomats), which accept credit, debit and Eurocheque cards. In outerlying districts they aren't as common but they're still numerous; Bankomats can also be found in the main train stations and at the airport. Just look for a green and blue horizontally striped neon sign which indicates a bank is equipped with a Bankomat.

Check with your home bank before travelling to see how much the charge is for using a Bankomat in Vienna; normally there's no commission to pay at the Austrian end.

Changing Money

Banks are the best places to exchange cash, but it pays to shop around as exchange rates and commission charges can vary a little between them. Normally there is a minimum commission charge of €2–3.50 so try to exchange your money in large amounts to save on multiple charges.

There are plenty of exchange offices in the Innere Stadt, particularly around Stephansplatz and on Kärntner Strasse. Westbahnhof also has one (🕒 7am-10pm), as does Südbahnhof (🕒 6.30am-10pm). Commission charges are around the same as banks, but quite often their exchange rates are uncompetitive.

American Express (Map pp240-3; ☎ 515 40; 01, Kärntner Strasse 21-23; 🕒 9am-5pm Mon-Thu, 9am-4pm Fri) exchanges cash as well as travellers cheques (AmEx travellers cheques for free, cheques of other institutions incur a small charge). It also has a travel section and financial services, and will hold mail (not parcels) free of charge for up to one month for customers who have American Express cards.

Credit Cards

Visa, EuroCard and MasterCard are accepted a little more widely than American Express and Diners Club, although a surprising number of shops and restaurants refuse to accept any credit cards at all. Plush shops and restaurants will usually accept cards, though, and the same applies for hotels. Train tickets can be bought by credit card in main stations.

To report lost or stolen credit cards, call the following:

American Express ☎ 0800 900 940

Diners Club ☎ 501 35 14

MasterCard ☎ 717 01 4500

Visa ☎ 711 11 770

NEWSPAPERS & MAGAZINES

English-language newspapers are widely available in Vienna, usually late in the afternoon of the day they're published. The first to hit the stands are the Financial Times and the International Herald Tribune. USA Today, Time, Newsweek, the Economist and most British newspapers are also easy to find. You'll find most titles sold at newsstands and pavement sellers, particularly around the main train stations and at U-Bahn stations on the Ringstrasse. Vienna's only home-grown paper in English was Austria Today (www.austriatoday.at), but now it's only available online.

Of the several German-language daily newspapers available, the magazine-size Neue Kronen Zeitung has the largest circulation by a long shot despite its sensationalist slant and lack of hard news. Serious papers include *Der Standard* and *Die Presse*; the former usually takes a stance on the left-hand side of the fence, the latter on the right. For entertainment listings and on-the-button political and social commentary, the winner hands down is Vienna's own *Der Falter*. This weekly publication comes out on Wednesday and is only in German, but the listings are quite easy to decipher. *City* is a cheaper, slimmed-down *Falter*, with none of the politics and less listings coverage. *Augustin*, Vienna's version of the *Big Issue*, is partially produced and sold by the homeless who receive a portion of the sales.

Austrian newspapers are often dispensed from bags attached to pavement posts, and rely on the honesty of readers to pay for the copies they take.

POST

Austria's postal service is reliable and easy to use. Post offices are commonplace, as are bright yellow postboxes. Stamps can also be bought at *Tabakladen* (tobacconists). Sending letters (up to 20g) within Austria or Europe costs €0.55 and worldwide €1.25. The normal weight limit for letter post (*Briefsendung*) is 2kg; anything over this limit will be sent as a package (from €3.70 within Austria, from €11.75 anywhere else). Up to 20kg can be sent via surface mail (*Erdwegpakete*).

Poste restante is *Postlagernde Briefe* in German; address letters *Postlagernde Sendungen* rather than post restante. Mail can be sent care of any post office and is held for a month; a passport must be shown on collection.

Franz-Josefs-Bahnhof Post Office (Map pp244-5; 09, Althanstrasse 10; ☉ 6am-10pm)

Main Post Office (Map pp240-3; ☎ 515 09-0; www.post .at; 01, Fleischmarkt 19; ☉ 24 hr)

Südbahnhof Post Office (Map pp248-9; 10, Wiedner Gürtel 1b; ☉ 7am-10pm)

Westbahnhof Post Office (Map pp246-7; 15, Europlatz; ☉ 6am-11pm)

RADIO

State-run stations include Ö1 (87.8 and 92 FM), which provides a diet of highbrow music, literature and science, and Ö3 (99.9 FM), a commercial outfit with pop music. Radio Wien (89.9 and 95.3 FM) is another state-run station, as is FM4 (103.8 FM). FM4 is the pick of the crop for alternative music and topical current

affairs; it broadcasts in English from 1am to 2pm and has news on the hour in English from 6am to 7pm.

SAFETY

Vienna is one of the safest cities in the world. At night it's not uncommon to see women walking home alone or elderly people walking dogs or using public transport. Tourists normally only experience petty crime, such as pickpocketing or the very rare money scam.

There are, however, a few places to avoid, especially at night. Karlsplatz station is a well-known spot for drugs and drug addicts, as is the Prater and Praterstern, and Mexikoplatz is supposedly a black-market centre. Südtirolerplatz and the S-Bahn and tram stations along Margareten- and Wieder Gürtel can be quite unnerving after dark.

TELEPHONE

Telekom Austria (☎ 0800-100 100; www.tele kom.at) is Austria's main telecommunications provider and maintains a plethora of public telephones throughout Vienna. These take either coins or phonecards and a minimum of €0.20 is required to make a local call. Every post office has a phone booth where both international and national calls can be made; rates are cheaper from 6pm to 8am Monday to Friday, and on weekends. Another option is call centres, which have recently been introduced into the telecommunications arena. They're generally found in the outlying districts and offer very competitive phone-call rates.

Austria's country code is ☎ 0043, Vienna's is ☎ 01. Free phone numbers start with ☎ 0800 or ☎ 0810, while numbers starting with ☎ 0900 are pay-per-minute. When calling from overseas drop the zero in the Vienna code; ie the number for Vienna's main tourist office is ☎ 0043 1 211 14-555. When calling a Vienna number from within Vienna, the Vienna code is not required; however, when calling Vienna from elsewhere in Austria (or from a mobile) the code needs to be used. National directory assistance is available on ☎ 11 88 77 and international on ☎ 0900 11 88 77.

To reverse the charges (ie call collect), you have to call a freephone number to place the call. Some of the numbers are listed below (ask directory assistance for others):

Australia ☎ 0800-200 202

Canada ☎ 0800-200 224

Ireland ☎ 0800-200 213

New Zealand ☎ 0800-200 222
South Africa ☎ 0800-200 230
UK ☎ 0800-200 209
USA (AT&T) ☎ 0800-200 288
USA (MCI) ☎ 0800-200 235
USA (Sprint) ☎ 0800-200 236

Mobile Phones

Austria's network works on GSM 1800, and is compatible with GSM 900 phones (*Handy* in German), but generally not with systems from the USA or Japan. *Handy* numbers start with 0699, 0676, 0664 and 0650. The major *Handy* networks – One, A-1 and T-Mobile – sell SIM cards with €10 worth of calls for €39. Telering, a smaller operator, has SIM cards for €30 with €30 worth of calls. Refill cards can be purchased from supermarkets and Trafik (tobacconist shops) for €20 or €40. Before buying an Austrian SIM card confirm that your phone is unlocked; check with your home network before leaving.

Rent mobile phones at **Tel-Rent** (☎ 700 733 340), located in the arrivals hall at Schwechat. Rental for a day/week, including phone and SIM card, costs €18/90. Additional weeks cost €54 and delivery or pick-up within Vienna is available for €26.

Phonecards

There's a wide range of local and international phonecards. You can save money and avoid messing around with change by buying a phonecard *(Telefon-Wertkarte)*; they come in various denominations, some of which give you extra calls for your money.

TELEVISION

Austria's state-run channels, ÖRF1 and ÖRF2, are never going to win any international broadcasting awards. ÖRF1 has sitcoms (both American and European), plenty of sport, dubbed movies (including *Colombo* almost every Sunday night) and a mixture of game, cooking and dating shows. ÖRF2 is more cultured, and regularly features documentaries, black-and-white Austrian movies, talk shows, operas, and unwatchable Alpine folk-music shows.

Many homes (and hotels) have satellite or cable and can pick up a whole host of TV channels from Germany and elsewhere, plus MTV, Eurosport, CNN, NBC and ATV, Austria's first domestic cable/satellite station.

TIME

Austrian time is on Central European time, one hour ahead of GMT/UTC. If it's noon in Vienna it is 6am in New York and Toronto, 3am in San Francisco, 9pm in Sydney and 11pm in Auckland. Clocks go forward one hour on the last Saturday night in March and back again on the last Saturday night in October.

Note that in German *halb* is used to indicate the half-hour before the hour, hence *halb acht* (half eight) means 7.30, not 8.30.

TIPPING

Tipping is part of everyday life in Vienna; tips are generally expected at restaurants, bars and cafés, and in taxis. It's customary to add a 10% tip, or round up the bill, while taxi drivers will expect around 10% extra. Tips are handed over at the time of payment: add the bill and tip together and pass it over in one lump sum. It doesn't hurt to tip workers, hairdressers, hotel porters, cloakroom attendants, cleaning staff and tour guides a euro or two. See the Eating chapter (p115) for tipping etiquette at restaurants.

TOILETS

Around 330 public toilets are scattered throughout Vienna, of which over 90 are wheelchair accessible. If they're attended, a small fee is required to use them, normally around €0.50. The toilet block on Graben, designed by Adolf Loos, is an Art-Nouveau masterpiece and worth visiting even if you don't have to go. The City Hall information centre (see below) produces a handy *Toiletten-Stadtführer* city map with toilets marked on it. Remember, *Damen* is for women and *Herren* is for men.

TOURIST INFORMATION

Airport Information Office (🕓 8.30am-9pm) This office is located in the arrivals hall.

City Hall (Map pp240-3; ☎ 525 50; www.wien.gv.at; 01, Rathaus; 🕓 8am-6pm Mon-Fri) The City Hall provides information on social, cultural and practical matters, and is geared as much to residents as to tourists. There's an info-screen with useful information.

Jugendinfo (Map pp240-3; ☎ 1799; www.jugendin fowien.at, German only; 01, Babenbergerstrasse 1; 🕓 noon-7pm Mon-Sat) Jugendinfo is tailored to those aged between 14 and 26, and has tickets for a variety of events at reduced rates for this age group. Staff can tell you about events around town, and places where you can log onto the Internet.

Niederösterreich Werbung (Map pp240-3; ☎ 536 100; www.niederoesterreich.at; 01, Fischhof 3/3; ☯ 8.30am-5pm Mon-Thu, until 4pm Fri) For information on Niederösterreich (Lower Austria), the province surrounding Vienna, this information office should be your first port of call.

Südbahnhof Information Office (Map pp248-9; ☯ 6.30am-midnight)

Westbahnhof Information Office (Map pp246-7; ☯ 7am-10pm)

Tourist Info Wien (Map pp240-3; ☎ 211 14-555; www .wien.info; 01, Albertinaplatz; ☯ 9am-7pm) This is Vienna's main tourist office, with a ticket agency, hotel booking service, free maps, and every brochure under the sun.

WienXtra-Kinderinfo (Map pp240-3; ☎ 4000 84 400; www.kinderinfowien.at, German only; 07, Museumsplatz 1; ☯ 2-7pm Tue-Thu, 10am-5pm Fri & Sat) Marketed firstly at children (check out the knee-high display cases), *then* their parents, this child-friendly tourist office has loads of information on kids activities and a small indoor playground.

VISAS

Visas for stays of up to three months are not required for citizens of the EU, the EEA (European Economic Area), much of Eastern Europe, Israel, USA, Canada, the majority of Central and South American nations, Japan, Korea, Malaysia, Singapore, Australia or New Zealand. All other nationalities require a visa; the Ministry of Foreign Affairs website, www .bmaa.gv.at, has a list of Austrian embassies where you can apply.

If you wish to stay longer you should simply leave the country and re-enter. EU nationals can stay indefinitely, but are required by law to register with the local magistrate's office *(Magistra- tisches Bezirksamt)* if the stay exceeds 60 days.

Austria is part of the Schengen Agreement which includes all EU states (minus Britain and Ireland) and Switzerland. In practical terms this means a visa issued by one Schengen country is good for all the other member countries and a passport is not required to move from one to the other. How this will apply to the 2004 EU member states remains to be seen; check with the local Austrian embassy for more details.

WOMEN TRAVELLERS

Overall, Vienna is a very safe city and women travellers should experience no special problems. Attacks and verbal harassment are less common than in many countries. However, normal caution should be exercised in unfamiliar situations.

The **Frauen Büro** (Map pp240–3; ☎ 4000 83 515; 08, Landesgerichtsstrasse; ☯ 8am-4pm Mon-Fri) has loads of pamphlets and brochures (mostly in German) on women's issues and can help with many problems you may have. A 24-hour hotline for women is listed under Emergencies in this chapter (p205).

WORK

EU nationals can work in Austria without a work permit or residency permit, though as intending residents they need to register with the police.

Non-EU nationals need both a work permit and a residency permit, and will find it pretty hard to get either. Inquire (in German) about job possibilities via local Labour Offices; look under *Arbeitsmarktservice* in the White Pages for the closest office. The work permit needs to be applied for by your employer in Austria. Applications for residency permits must be applied for via the Austrian embassy in your home country.

Teaching is a favourite of ex-pats; look under *Sprachschulen* (language schools in the *Gelbe Seiten* (Yellow Pages) for a list of schools. Outside that profession, you'll struggle to find employment if you don't speak German. Websites listing jobs include:

www.oeh.jobfinder.at Directed towards professionals; in German only.

www.studentenjob.com Specialises in student jobs; in German only.

www.jobpilot.at Comprehensive site with loads of professional jobs; in German only.

www.ams.or.at/sfa/index.htm Another site aimed at professionals, and only in German.

Social 212
Meeting People 212
Going Out 212

Practical 212
Numbers & Amounts 212
Days 213
Banking 213
Post 213
Phones & Mobiles 213
Internet 213
Transport 213

Food 214

Emergencies 214

Health 214
Symptoms 214

Glossary 214

Language

Language

It's true – anyone can speak another language. Don't worry if you haven't studied languages before or that you studied a language at school for years and can't remember any of it. It doesn't even matter if you failed English grammar. After all, that's never affected your ability to speak English! And this is the key to picking up a language in another country. You just need to start speaking.

Learn a few key phrases before you go. Write them on pieces of paper and stick them on the fridge, by the bed or even on the computer – anywhere that you'll see them often.

You'll find that locals appreciate travellers trying their language, no matter how muddled you may think you sound. So don't just stand there, say something! If you want to learn more German than we've included here, pick up a copy of Lonely Planet's user-friendly *German Phrasebook*.

SOCIAL
Meeting People

Hello.
Guten Tag.
Goodbye.
Auf Wiedersehen.
Please.
Bitte.
Thank you (very much).
Danke (schön).
Yes/No.
Ja/Nein.
Do you speak English?
Sprechen Sie Englisch?
Do you understand (me)?
Verstehen Sie (mich)?
Yes, I understand (you).
Ja, ich verstehe (Sie).
No, I don't understand (you).
Nein, ich verstehe (Sie) nicht.

Could you please ...?
Könnten Sie ...?
  repeat that
  das bitte wiederholen
  speak more slowly
  bitte langsamer sprechen
  write it down
  das bitte aufschreiben

Going Out

What's on ...?
Was ist ... los?
  locally
  hier
  this weekend
  dieses Wochenende

today
heute
tonight
heute Abend

Where are the ...?
Wo sind die ...?
  clubs
  Klubs
  gay venues
  Schwulen- und Lesbenkneipen
  restaurants
  Restaurants
  pubs
  Kneipen

Is there a local entertainment guide?
Gibt es einen Veranstaltungskalender?

PRACTICAL
Numbers & Amounts

1	eins
2	zwei
3	drei
4	vier
5	fünf
6	sechs
7	sieben
8	acht
9	neun
10	zehn
11	elf
12	zwölf
13	dreizehn
14	vierzehn
15	fünfzehn

16	sechzehn
17	siebzehn
18	achtzehn
19	neunzehn
20	zwanzig
21	einundzwanzig
22	zweiundzwanzig
30	dreizig
40	vierzig
50	fünfzig
60	sechzig
70	siebzig
80	achtzig
90	neunzig
100	hundert
1000	tausend

Days

Monday	Montag
Tuesday	Dienstag
Wednesday	Mittwoch
Thursday	Donnerstag
Friday	Freitag
Saturday	Samstag
Sunday	Sonntag

Banking

I'd like to ...
Ich möchte ...
   cash a cheque
   einen Scheck einlösen
   change money
   Geld umtauschen
   change some travellers cheques
   Reiseschecks einlösen

Where's the nearest ...?
Wo ist der/die nächste ...? m/f
   automatic teller machine
   Geldautomat
   foreign exchange office
   Geldwechselstube

Post

I want to send a ...
Ich möchte ... senden.

fax	ein Fax
parcel	ein Paket
postcard	eine Postkarte

I want to buy a/an...
Ich möchte ... kaufen.

aerogram	ein Aerogramm
envelope	einen Umschlag
stamp	eine Briefmarke

Phones & Mobiles

I want to make a ...
Ich möchte ...
   call (to Singapore)
   (nach Singapur) telefonieren
   reverse-charge/collect call (to Singapore)
   ein R-Gespräch (nach Singapur) führen

I want to buy a phonecard.
Ich möchte eine Telefonkarte kaufen.

Where can I find a/an ...?
Wo kann ich ... kaufen?
I'd like a/an ...
Ich hätte gern ...
   adaptor plug
   einen Adapter für die steckdose
   charger for my phone
   ein Ladegerät für mein Handy
   mobile/cell phone for hire
   ein Miethandy
   prepaid mobile/cell phone
   ein Handy mit Prepaidkarte
   SIM card for your network
   eine SIM-Karte für Ihr Netz

Internet

Where's the local Internet café?
Wo ist hier ein Internet-Café?

I'd like to ...
Ich möchte ...
   check my email
   meine E-Mails checken
   get Internet access
   Internetzugang haben

Transport

What time does the ... leave?
Wann fährt ... ab?

boat	das Boot
bus	der Bus
train	der Zug

What time does the plane leave?
Wann fliegt das Flugzeug ab?

What time's the ... bus?
Wann fährt der ... Bus?

first	erste
last	letzte
next	nächste

Where's the nearest metro station?
Wo ist der nächste U-Bahnhof?

Are you free? (taxi)
Sind Sie frei?
Please put the meter on.
Schalten Sie bitte den Taxameter ein.
How much is it to ...?
Was kostet es bis ...?
Please take me to (this address).
Bitte bringen Sie mich zu (dieser Adresse).

FOOD

breakfast	Frühstück
lunch	Mittagessen
dinner	Abendessen
snack	Snack
eat	essen
drink	trinken

Can you recommend a ...?
Können Sie ... empfehlen?

bar/pub	eine Kneipe
café	ein Café
coffee bar	eine Espressobar
restaurant	ein Restaurant
local speciality	eine örtliche Spezialität

What's that called?
Wie heisst das?
Is service included in the bill?
Ist die Bedienung inbegriffen?

For more detailed information on food and dining out, see the Eating chapter, p107.

EMERGENCIES

It's an emergency!
Es ist ein Notfall!
Call the police!
Rufen Sie die Polizei!
Call a doctor/an ambulance!
Rufen Sie einen Artzt/Krankenwagen!
Could you please help me/us?
Könnten Sie mir/uns bitte helfen?
Where's the police station?
Wo ist das Polizeirevier?

HEALTH

Where's the nearest ...?
Wo ist der/die/das nächste ...?

(night) chemist	(Nacht) Apotheke
dentist	Zahnarzt
doctor	Arzt
hospital	Krankenhaus

I need a doctor (who speaks English).
Ich brauche einen Arzt (der Englisch spricht).

Symptoms

I have (a) ...
Ich habe ...

diarrhoea	Durchfall
fever	Fieber
headache	Kopfschmerzen
pain	Schmerzen

Glossary

Abfahrt – departure (trains)
Achterl – 125mL glass of wine
Ankunft – arrival (trains)
Altwaren – second-hand goods
ANTO – Austrian National Tourist Office
Apotheke, Apotheken (pl) – pharmacy
Ausgang – exit
Autobahn – motorway

Bahnhof – train station
Bankomat – ATM
Bauernhof – farmhouse
Bauernmarkt, Bauernmärkte (pl) – farmers market
Besetzt – occupied, full (ie no vacancy)
Bezirk, Bezirke (pl) – (town or city) district
Beisl, Beisln (pl) – Viennese term for beer house
Biedermeier period – 19th-century art movement in Germany and Austria; applies particularly to a decorative style of furniture from this period
Briefsendung – letter; item sent by letter post
Börse – stock exchange

Briefmarken – stamps
Bundesbahn – country roads
Bundesland, Bundesländer (pl) – federal province (government)
Bundesrat – Federal Council (government upper house)
Christkindlmarkt, Christkindlmärkte (pl) – Christmas market

Dag – abbreviation for 10g
Denkmal – memorial
Dirndl – traditional Austrian folk skirt

EEA – European Economic Area, comprising European Union states plus Iceland, Liechtenstein and Norway
Einbahnstrasse – one-way street
Eingang, Eintritt – entry
EU – European Union

Fahrplan – timetable
Fahrrad – bicycle
Feiertag – public holiday
Fiaker – horse and carriage
Flakturm, Flaktürme (pl) – flak tower

Language

Flohmarkt – flea market
Flugpost – air mail
Föhn – hot, dry wind that sweeps down from the mountains, mainly in early spring and autumn
FPÖ – Freedom Party (political party)
Freikörperkultur – free body culture

Gästehaus – guesthouse, perhaps with a restaurant
Gasthaus, Gasthäuser – inn or restaurant, without accommodation
Gasthof – inn or restaurant, usually with accommodation
Gelbe Seiten – Yellow Pages
Glühwein – mulled wine
Graben – ditch
Gulasch – goulash

Haltstelle – bus or tram stop
Hauptbahnhof – main train station
Hauptpost – main post office
Herren – men
Heuriger, Heurigen (pl) – wine tavern

Jugendherberge – youth hostel
Jugendstil – Art Nouveau

Kaffeehaus, Kaffeehäuser (pl) – coffee house
Kellner/Kellnerin – waiter/waitress
Kino – cinema
Konsulat – consulate
Krankenhaus, Krankenhäuser (pl) – hospital
Krügerl – 500mL glass of beer
Kurzparkzone – short-term parking zone

Landeshauptmann – head of Austrian federal province
Landesmuseum – provincial museum
Lederhosen – three-quarter-length leather trousers
LIF – Liberal Forum (political party)
Lokal, Lokale (pl) – bar or pub
Luxuszimmer – luxury rooms

Magistratisches Bezirksamt – magistrate's office
Maut – toll (or indicating a toll booth); also Viennese dialect for a tip (gratuity)
Mehrwertsteuer (MWST) – value-added tax
Melange – Viennese version of cappuccino
Mensa, Mensen (pl) – university cafeteria
Menü – meal of the day. The menu (ie food list) is called Speisekarte
Münze – coins

Nationalrat – National Council (government lower house)

ÖAMTC – national motoring organisation
ÖAV – Austrian Alpine Club
ÖBB – Austrian federal railway
ÖVP – Austrian People's Party (political party)

Parkschein – parking voucher
Pension, Pensionen (pl) – B&B guesthouse
Pfarrkirche – parish church
Polizei – police
Postamt – post office

Postlagernde Briefe – poste restante
Prolos – Viennese word for working class

Radverleih – bicycle rental
Rathaus – town hall
Red Vienna – describes the period of socialist reforms instigated by the city government from 1919 to 1934
Ruhetag – 'rest day', on which a restaurant is closed

Saal, Säle (pl) – hall or large room
Sacher Torte – rich chocolate cake with layers of apricot jam
Sammlung – collection
Säule – column, pillar
Schiff – ship
Schloss – palace or stately home
Schrammelmusik – popular Viennese music for violins, guitar and accordion
Schwullesbische Szene – gay and lesbian scene
Secession – early 20th-century movement in Vienna seeking to establish a more functional style in architecture; led by Otto Wagner (1841–1918)
Selbstbedienung (SB) – self-service (restaurants, laundries etc)
SPÖ – Social Democrats (political party)
Stadtmuseum – city museum
Stallburg – stables
Stammlocal – regular watering hole
Studentenheime – student residences
Szene – scene (ie where the action is)

Tabak – tobacconist
Tagesteller/Tagesmenü – the set meal or menu of the day in a restaurant
Telefon-Wertkarte – phonecard
Tierpark/Tiergarten – animal park/zoo
Tor – gate
Tracht – traditional Austrian costume

Urlaub – holiday
U-Bahn – underground rail network (metro)

Viertel – 250mL glass (drinks); also a geographical district
Vignitte – motorway tax
Vürstelstand – like a Würstelstand (sausage stand) but for vegetarians

Wanderung – hiking
Wien – Vienna
Wiener Schmäh – the dark, self-deprecating Viennese sense of humour
Wiener Werkstätte – workshop established in 1903 by Secession artists
Wäscherei – laundry
Würstelstand – sausage stand

Zahnarzt, Zahnärte (pl) – dentist
Zimmer frei/Privat Zimmer – private rooms (accommodation)
Zeitung – newspaper

La·guage

Behind the Scenes

THE LONELY PLANET STORY

The story begins with a classic travel adventure: Tony and Maureen Wheeler's 1972 journey across Europe and Asia to Australia. There was no useful information about the overland trail then, so Tony and Maureen published the first Lonely Planet guidebook to meet a growing need.

From a kitchen table, Lonely Planet has grown to become the largest independent travel publisher in the world, with offices in Melbourne (Australia), Oakland (USA), London (UK) and Paris (France).

Today Lonely Planet guidebooks cover the globe. There is an ever-growing list of books and information in a variety of media. Some things haven't changed. The main aim is still to make it possible for adventurous travellers to get out there – to explore and better understand the world.

At Lonely Planet we believe travellers can make a positive contribution to the countries they visit – if they respect their host communities and spend their money wisely.

THIS BOOK

This 4th edition of *Vienna* was researched and written by Neal Bedford with assistance from Jane Rawson, who wrote the Arts and Architecture chapters. Mark Honan wrote the first two editions of this book; Neal Bedford coauthored with Mark for the 3rd edition. This guide was commissioned in Lonely Planet's London office and produced in Melbourne. The project team included:

Commissioning Editor Judith Bamber
Coordinating Editor Tegan Murray
Coordinating Cartographer Valentina Kremenchutskaya
Coordinating Layout Designer Indra Kilfoyle
Assisting Editors & Proofreaders Dan Caleo, Katie Evans, Cathryn Game & Martine Lleonart
Cover Designer Gerilyn Attebery
Series Designer Nic Lehman
Series Design Concept Nic Lehman & Andrew Weatherill
Managing Cartographers Mark Griffiths & Adrian Persoglia
Mapping Development Paul Piaia
Project Manager Charles Rawlings-Way
Language Editor Quentin Frayne
Regional Publishing Manager Amanda Canning
Series Publishing Manager Grabrielle Green

Thanks to Bruce Evans, Adriana Mammarella and Kate McDonald

Cover photographs Detail of the Fernwärme incinerator façade, Diana Mayfield/Lonely Planet Images (top); concert players dressed in Mozart costume, Sylvain Grandadam/Getty Stone Image Library (bottom); Roman inspired sculptures, Schloss Schönbrunn, Jon Davison/Lonely Planet Images (back)

Internal photographs by Richard Nebesky/Lonely Planet Images except for the following:
p74 (#1, 2, 3); p180 Mark Honan/Lonelyplanet Images; p74 (#4), p121 Dianna Mayfield/Lonelyplanet Images; All images are the copyright of the photographers unless otherwise indicated. Many of the images in this guide are available for licensing from Lonely Planet Images: www .lonelyplanetimages.com.

ACKNOWLEDGMENTS

Many thanks to the following for the use of their content:
Wiener Linien GmbH & Co KG for use of their Vienna U-Bahn & S-Bahn map

THANKS
NEAL BEDFORD

If I thanked all the people I've met on my Vienna travels, who've shared a beer, a thought and a recommendation with me, I'd take up a couple of pages. So I will limit this to those who directly helped with this book, and if I've left someone out I sincerely apologise, but my thanks go out to you all the same.

SEND US YOUR FEEDBACK

We love to hear from travellers – your comments keep us on our toes and help make our books better. Our well-travelled team reads every word on what you loved or loathed about this book. Although we cannot reply individually to postal submissions, we always guarantee that your feedback goes straight to the appropriate authors, in time for the next edition. Each person who sends us information is thanked in the next edition – and the most useful submissions are rewarded with a free book.

To send us your updates – and find out about LP events, newsletters and travel news – visit our award-winning website: www.lonelyplanet.com.

Note: We may edit, reproduce and incorporate your comments in Lonely Planet products such as guidebooks, websites and digital products, so let us know if you don't want your comments reproduced or your name acknowledged. For a copy of our privacy policy visit www.lonelyplanet.com/privacy.

First and foremost for putting up with my inane and unending questions, my undying debt goes out to Tiffany, Zsuzsa, Tom P and Tina. For allowing me to pick their brains – even though on holiday and not at all interested in thinking about home – 'ta' to Tom, Astrid, Marion and Vincent. To all those who joined me exploring this wonderful city and let me steal all their best ideas – thanks to Alice and the gang at Schleifmühlgasse, Hexi, Karin and Helmut, Mark, Martin and Anna, Peter, Sladjan, Vivi and Flo. A special thanks to Brian for entertaining me on the streets of Vienna with his wit and wisdom, and to Leo (and Brian once again) for his superb cycling skills.

This job could not have been completed without the help of the Vienna tourist office, all the knowledgeable museum staff across the city and the patient and friendly Statistik Austria staff. Last, but by no means least, a big, warm and wonderful thanks to the Kuzaras, my second family, Mum, for her unwavering support, and Dad, for his spelling brain and superb word choice.

JANE RAWSON
There is always room in my house and a beer in the fridge for Neal Bedford and Mark Elliott, all-round upstanding human beings and Vienna's finest expatriates.

OUR READERS

Many thanks to the travellers who used the last edition and wrote to us with helpful hints, useful advice and interesting anecdotes. Your names follow:

Heather Caldwell, Colin Chang, Helen Chipchase, Cehn Shing Chow, L Peter Deutsch, Tara Emery, Kristien Evans, Ronalie Green, Jarrod Hepburn, Janick Julienne Paul Levatino, Lianne Lim, Eddi Madgin, Darryl Munro, Piergiorgio Pescali, Shaun Phelan, Eva Claire Synkowski, Jason Tan, A Tomash, Niko Viramo, Viktor Weisshäupl, Dewi Williams

Notes

Notes

Notes

Notes

Notes

Notes

Notes

Notes

Notes

Index

See also separate indexes for Eating (p235), Shopping (p235) and Sleeping (p236).

A

accommodation 171-82, 202, *see also* Sleeping index 236
Actionism 26
air travel 198
airline offices 198
airports 198
Akademie der bildenden Künste 75-6, 108
Albertina 58
Albertinaplatz 55, 108
Alsergrund 95-7
Alte Donau 87, 113
Am Hof 63
ambulance services 205
amusement parks
 Böhmische Prater 98
 Wurstelprater 48, 85, 110
Ankeruhr 63-4
architecture 31-6
 baroque 32
 Jugendstil 34
 medieval 32
 modern 35-6
 neoclassical 32
 rococo 32
 Secession 34-5
Architekturzentrum Wien 80
Archiv des Österreichischen Widerstands 64
art galleries
 Akademie der bildenden Künste 75-6, 108
 Albertina 58
 Architekturzentrum Wien 80
 Bawag Foundation 55-6
 Generali Foundation 93
 KunstForum 61-2
 Kunsthalle 80
 Kunsthalle Project Space 93-4
 KunstHausWien 90, 111
 MUMOK 81, 108

000 map pages
000 photographs

Österreichische Galerie 91
Sammlung Essl 104, **25**
Art Nouveau, *see* Jugendstil
arts 21-30
Atelier Augarten/Gustinus Ambrosi-Museum 84, 110
Athena Fountain 75
ATMs 207
Augarten 84
Augustinerkirche 58-9

B

Babenbergs 40
baby-sitting 203
Baden 196
bars 139-44
bathrooms 209
Bawag Foundation 55-6
beer houses, *see* Beisln
Beethoven, Ludwig van 23
 Eroica Haus 103-4
 Pasqualati Haus 63, 108
Beisln 14
Bergkirche 192
Bestattungsmuseum 92
bicycle travel, *see* cycling
Blut, Eva 15
boat travel 199
 boating 156
 tours 51
Böhmische Hofkanzlei 64
Böhmische Prater 98
books
 history 38
 Top Ten 27
Brahms, Johannes 23
Bratislava 194-5, 194
Bratislava Castle 194
Bruckner, Anton 23
Brunnenmarkt 166
Brus, Gunter 26
Bücherei Wien 95
Bundeskanzleramt 61
Burggarten 76, 108
Burgkapelle 59
Burgtheater 108, 152
bus travel 199, 201
 tours 50
business hours 203

C

cakes, *see* Sacher Torte
car travel 199-200
 automobile associations 200
 parking 200
 rental 200
 road rules 199
castles & palaces
 Bratislava Castle 194
 Equitable Palais 107
 Hofburg 58-61, 107, **62**
 Palais Ferstal 63
 Palais Harrach 63
 Palais Kinsky 63
 Palais Schwarzenberg 83, **178**
 Primatial Palace 194
 Schloss Belvedere 91-2
 Schloss Esterházy 192
 Schloss Schönbrunn 101, **101**
cathedrals, *see* churches & cathedrals
Catholicism 12
cemeteries 99
 Hietzinger Friedhof 99
 Namenlosen Friedhof 98-9
 St Marxer Friedhof 90
 Zentralfriedhof 99
children
 activities for 48
 travel with 203
Chorherrenstift 188
Christkindlmärkte (Christmas markets) 11, 169
churches & cathedrals
 Augustinerkirche 58-9
 Bergkirche 192
 Burgkapelle 59
 Chorherrenstift 188
 Dominikanerkirche, Innere Stadt 54
 Dominikanerkirche, Krems 189
 Fischerkirche 191
 Franziskanerkirche 55
 Greek Orthodox Church 55
 Karlskirche 93, **33**, **93**

Katholische Kirche 191
Kirche Am Hof 63
Kirche Am Steinhof 103, **36**
Kirche zur Heiligsten Dreifaltigkeit 104
Michaelerkirche 62, 107
Minoritenkirche 62-3
Peterskirche 57, 107
Pfarrkirche St Veit 189
Piaristenkirche, Josefstadt 95
Piaristenkirche, Krems 189
Ruprechtskirche 65
Schottenkirche 63
Serviten Kirche 97
Stephansdom 6, 53-4, 107, **40**
St Martin Cathedral 194
Votivkirche 66, 108
cinema 28-30, 153-5
 Top Ten 29
Cistercian Abbey 193
City Hall, *see* Rathaus
classical music 149-52
climate 204
climbing 156
clothing 163
clubs 146-7
coffee 118
coffee houses, *see* Kaffeehäuser
composers 23
costs 6, 17-18
courses 204
credit cards 207
culture 11-17
customs 11
customs regulations 204
cycling 156, 198-9
 tour 112-14

D

dance 152-3
Danube Canal 18, 83
Danube Island, *see* Donauinsel
disabled travellers 204
Döbling 103-4
dogs 13

Dom- & Diözesanmuseum 53
Dominikanerkirche, Innere Stadt 54
Dominikanerkirche, Krems 189
Donauinsel 18, 48, 87, 113, **9**
Donauinselfest 9
Donaustadt 87-8
Donauturm 87-8, 113
Dürnstein 188

E
economy 17-18
Eisenstadt 191-3, 192
electricity 205
Elisabeth (Empress) 59-60
embassies 205
emergencies 205
emergency rooms 206-7
environmental issues 18-20
Equitable Palais 107
Ernst Fuchs Privat Museum 103
Eroica Haus 103-4
Esperanto Museum 60
Eugene, Prince 92
exchange rates, *see inside front cover*

F
Fasching 9
fascism 45
fashion 15, *see also* Shopping index 235
Favoriten 98
Fernwärme 95, 112, **19**
ferris wheel, *see* Riesenrad
festivals
    Christkindlmärkte 11
    Donauinselfest 9
    Fasching 9
    Frühlingsfestival 9
    ImPulsTanz 10
    International Haydn Festival 192
    Jazz Fest 10
    KlangBogen Festival 10
    Lange Nacht der Museen 11
    Langer Nacht der Musik 10
    Life Ball 10
    Musikfilm Festival 10
    Opernball 9
    Opern Festspiele 191
    OsterKlang Festival 9
    Queer Identities 10
    Regenbogen Parade 10
    Seefestspiele 191
    Silvester 11
    Soho in Ottakring 10
    Viennale Film Festival 11
    Volkstimmefest 10
    Wien ist Andersrum 10
    Wien Modern Festival 11
    Wiener Festwochen 10
Feuerwehr Centrale 63
Fiaker 51
Figaro Haus 54
film, *see* cinema
fire services 205
Fischerkirche 191
Flaktürme (flak towers) 84, 110, 111
Fleischmarkt 55
Flohmarkt 166, **49**
Floridsdorf 87
food 13-15, 115-36, *see also* Eating index 235
    booking 117
    business hours 117
    costs 117
    customs 118
    self-catering 117
    tipping 117
    university cafeterias 123
football 155
former civic armoury 63
Franziskanerkirche 55
Franz Josef statue 76
Franz Josef I 43, 99
Freud, Sigmund 12
    Sigmund Freud Museum 97
Freyung 166
Frühlingsfestival 9
Fuchs, Ernst 103

G
gardens, *see* parks & gardens
Gasometer 98
gay travellers 141, 205
Generali Foundation 93
geography 18-19
German 17
Globenmuseum 59

Gluck, Christoph Willibald von 23
golf 156
government 18
Graben 56, 107, **56**
Greek Orthodox Church 55
gyms 156

H
Habsburgs 41
Handke, Peter 28
Haneke, Michael 29
Haus der Musik 48, 55
Haus des Meeres 94
Haydn, Josef 23, 94, 192
Haydn-Museum, Eisendstadt 192
Haydn Museum, Mariahilf 94
Heeresgeschichtliches Museum 89-90
Heiligenkreuz 193
Hermesvilla 99-100
Heurigen (wine taverns) 14, 86, 97, 144-6
Hietzing 99-100
Hietzinger Friedhof 99
hiking 156
Historisches Museum der Stadt Wien 93, 111
history 37-46
    Babenbergs 40
    baroque 41
    books 38
    Counter-Reformation 41
    early years 39
    fascism 45
    Habsburgs 41
    Jews 44
    post-WWII 45
    Red Vienna 43
    reform 42
    Republic 44
    Turks 42
Hitler, Adolf 45, 76
    apartment 76
Hochstrahlbrunnen 82
Hofburg 58-61, 107, **62**
Hofmobiliendepot 95
Hofpavillon Hietzing 100
holidays 12, 206
Hollein, Hans 36
holocaust 64
Holocaust-Denkmal (memorial) 64, **45**
horse & carriage rides, *see* Fiaker

horse racing 155
hospitals 206-7
hostels 172
hot springs 195
hotels 172
Hundertwasser, Friedensreich 36, 90
    Fernwärme 95, 112
    Hundertwasser Haus 111
    KunstHausWien 111
Hundertwasser Haus 90, 111

I
ice skating 156-7
ImPulsTanz 10
in-line skating 157
Innere Stadt 52-65
    accommodation 173-6
    food 119-23
    shopping 161-6
International Haydn Festival 192
Internet access 206
itineraries 48-50

J
Jazz Fest 10
Jelinek, Elfriede 28
Jews 44
Johann Strauss Residence 84
Josefstadt 95
Joseph II 42
Josephinum 95
Jubiläumswarte 103
Judenplatz 64, **45**
Jüdisches Museum 56
Jugendstil 25-6, 34
Justizpalast 75

K
Kaffeehauser 14
Kahlenberg 104
Kaiserappartements 59
Kaisergruft 56, 107
Kalke Village 90
Karikaturmuseum 189
Karl-Marx-Hof 104
Karlskirche 93, **33**, **93**
Karlsplatz 108, 111
    tours 108
Karmelitermarkt 109, 166
Kärntner Strasse 57, 106, **138**
    tours 106-8
Katholische Kirche 191

Kirche Am Hof 63
Kirche Am Steinhof 103, **36**
Kirche zur Heiligsten
    Dreifaltigkeit 104
KlangBogen Festival 10
Klimt, Gustav 26, 91
Klosterneuburg 104
Kloster Und 189
Kohlmarkt 57, 107
Kokoschka, Oskar 24
Krems 189-90, 189
Kriegsministerium 82
Kuenringerburg 188
KunstForum 61-2
Kunsthalle 80
Kunsthalle Café **142**
Kunsthalle Project Space
    93-4
KunstHausWien 90, 111
Kunsthistorisches Museum
    6, 77-9, 108, **78**
Kurpark 195

L
Lainzer Tiergarten 100
Landstrasse 89-91
Lang, Helmut 15
Lange Nacht der Museen 11
Langer Nacht der Musik 10
language 17, 211-15
Leopoldstadt 109
    tour 109
Leopold Museum 80-1,
    108, **81**
lesbian travellers 141, 205
library, see Bücherei Wien
Liechtenstein Museum
    96
Liesing 104
Life Ball 10
Lipizzaner Museum 59
literature 27-8,
    see also books
live music 147-9
Loos, Adolf 35
    Loos Haus 62, 107
    public toilets 56

M
magazines 207-8
Mahler, Gustav 23
Majolikahaus 94
maps 206
Maria Theresia 42
Mariahilf 94
Mariahilfer Strasse **160**
Mariensäule 63

Marionettentheater 152
markets
    Brunnenmarkt 166
    Christkindlmärkte
        (Christmas markets)
        11, 169
    Flohmarkt 166, **49**
    Freyung 166
    Karmelitermarkt 109,
        166
    Naschmarkt 6, 108,
        166, **49**
Marx, Karl 104
Mayerling 193
medical services 206
Melk 186
metric conversions,
    see inside front cover
Michaelerkirche 62, 107
Michaelerplatz 62, **39**, **62**
Minoritenkirche 62-3
mobile phones 209
money 204-5, 207, see
    also inside front cover
Mörbisch 191
motorcycle travel 199-200
movies, see cinema
Mozart, Wolfgang Amadeus
    23
    Figaro Haus 54
    statue 76
MUMOK 81, 108
Museum für angewandte
    Kunst 82, 110
Museum für Völkerkunde 59
Museum für Volkskunde 95
Museum Judenplatz 64
museums
    Atelier Augarten/
        Gustinus Ambrosi-
        Museum 84, 110
    Bestattungsmuseum 92
    Dom- & Diözesanmu-
        seum 53
    Ernst Fuchs Privat
        Museum 103
    Esperanto Museum 60
    Globenmuseum 59
    Haus der Musik 48, 55
    Haydn-Museum,
        Eisenstadt 192
    Haydn Museum,
        Mariahilf 94
    Heeresgeschichtliches
        Museum 89-90
    Historisches Museum
        der Stadt Wien
        93, 111

Josephinum 95
Jüdisches Museum 56
Karikaturmuseum 189
Kunsthistorisches
    Museum 6, 77-9,
    108, **78**
Leopold Museum 80-1,
    108, **81**
Liechtenstein Museum
    96
Lipizzaner Museum 59
MUMOK 81, 108
Municipal Museums
    94
Museum für ange-
    wandte Kunst 82,
    110
Museum für
    Völkerkunde 59
Museum für Volkskunde
    95
Museum Judenplatz 64
Mythos Sisi 59-60
Naturhistorisches
    Museum 76, 108
Neidhart-Fresken 64-5
Neue Burg Museums 60
Pathologisch-
    anatomische Bun-
    desmuseum 96
Pratermuseum 85
Puppen & Spielzeug
    Museum 65
Rollett Museum 195
Schönbrunn Kindermu-
    seum 48, 102
Schubert Commemora-
    tive Rooms 94
Sigmund Freud Museum
    97
Slovak National
    Museum 194
Strassenbahn Museum
    90-1
Technisches Museum
    103
Theatermuseum 57
Uhren Museum 65
Wachau Museum 188
Wiener Kriminal-
    museum 86, 109
Zoom 48, 82
MuseumsQuartier 6, 79-80,
    108
music 22-4
Musikfilm Festival 10
Mythos Sisi 59-60

N
Namenlosen Friedhof 98-9
Naschmarkt 6, 108, 166, **49**
Nationalbibliothek 60
NationalPark Donau-
    Auen 87
Naturhistorisches Museum
    76, 108
Nazis 45
Neidhart-Fresken 64-5
Neubau 95
Neue Burg Museums
    Ephesus Museum 60
    Hofjagd und Rüstkam-
        mer 60
    Sammlung Alter
        Musikinstrumente
        60
Neue Kronen Zeitung 16
Neue Wilde 25
Neusiedl am See 190
Neusiedler See 190-3
New Year's Eve,
    see Silvester
newspapers 16, 207-8
nightclubs 146-7

O
Odeon 109
open-air cinema 154
opera 149-52
    bookings 139
Opern Festspiele 191
Opernball 9
OsterKlang Festival 9
Österreichische Galerie
    91
Ottakring 103

P
palaces, see castles &
    palaces
Palais Ferstal 63
Palais Harrach 63
Palais Kinsky 63
Palais Schwarzenberg
    83, **178**
Palmenhaus 102, 108
parks & gardens
    Augarten 84
    Belvedere gardens 91
    Burggarten 76, 108
    Kurpark 195
    Liechtenstein Museum
        gardens 96
    NationalPark Donau-
        Auen 87
    Prater 85, 110, 114, **85**

parks & gardens continued
Schlosspark 192
Schönbrunn gardens 102
Stadtpark 83, 110, 111
Volksgarten 75
Parlament 75, 108
Pasqualati Haus 63, 108
Pathologisch-anatomische Bundesmuseum 96
Pensionen 172
Penzing 103
Peterskirche 57, 107
Petržalka 194
pets 13
Pfarrkirche St Veit 189
phonecards 209
Piaristenkirche, Josefstadt 95
Piaristenkirche, Krems 189
pickpocketing 208
Planetarium 84-5
planning 204-5
Podersdorf 190
police services 205
politics 8, 18, 38
population 6, 11
postal services 208
Postsparkasse 82, 110
Prater 85, 110, 114, **85**
Pratermuseum 85
Primatial Palace 194
psychoanalysis 12
pubs 139-44
Puppen & Spielzeug Museum 65

Q
Queer Identities 10

R
radio 16, 208
Rainer, Arnulf 24
Rathaus 75, 108
recycling 19
Red Vienna 43
Regenbogen Parade 10
religion 12
Riesenrad 85, 110, **85**
Ringstrasse 32-3, 65-83
accommodation 176-7
food 123-5
road rules 199
Rollerblading, see in-line skating

000 map pages
000 photographs

Rollett Museum 195
Roman ruins 65, 107, **39**
Rudolf, Archduke 193
Ruprechtskirche 65
Russen Heldendenkmal 82
Rust 191

S
S-Bahn 201
Sacher Torte 13, **14**
safety 12
St Martin Cathedral 194
St Marxer Friedhof 90
Sammlung Essl 104, **25**
sausage stands 14, **9**
Schatzkammer 60-1
Schiele, Egon 24, 91-2
Schlegel, Eva 24
Schloss Belvedere 91-2
gardens 91
Oberes Belvedere 91-2, 111
Orangery 92
Unteres Belvedere 92, 111
Schloss Esterházy 192
Schloss Schönbrunn 101, **101**
Schlosspark 192
Schmetterlinghaus 61
Schnitzel, see Wiener Schnitzel
Schönbrunn 6, 100-3
Kindermuseum 48, 102
Palmenhaus 102
Schloss Schönbrunn 101, **101**
Schönbrunn gardens 102
Tiergarten 102-3
Wagenburg 102
Wüstenhaus 102
Schottenkirche 63
Schottentor 108
tour 108
Schubert, Franz 23, 94, 97
Schubert Commemorative Rooms 94
Schubert Geburthaus 97
Schwarzenberg, Karl von statue 82
Schwarzenbergplatz 82-3, 111
Schwedenplatz 112
Schweizertor 108
Secession 26, 34-5, 76-7, 108

Second Vienna School of Music 23
Seefestspiele 191
Seegrotte Hinterbrühl 193
Serviten Kirche 97
shopping, see also Shopping index 235
bargaining 161
business hours 161
markets 166
taxes & costs 161
Sigmund Freud Museum 97
Silvester 11
Simmering 98-9
skiing 157
Slovak National Museum 194
Snow Globes 168
Soho in Ottakring 10
Spanische Hofreitschule 61
Spanish Riding School 61
Spittelau incinerator, see Fernwärme
Spitz 188
sporting events
Vienna Marathon 10
sports 16
Staatsoper 106, 151, **151**
Stadtbahn Pavillons 94, 111, **110**
Stadtpark 83, 110, 111
tour 110
Stadttempel 65
Stephansdom 6, 53-4, 107, **40**
Stephansplatz 53-4
Stift Klosterneuburg 104
Strassenbahn Museum 90-1
Strauss the Elder, Johann 23
Strauss the Younger, Johann 23
Denkmal (statue) 83, **22**
residence 84
student residences 172
swimming 157-8

T
Tanzquartier Wien 152
taxis 202
Technisches Museum 103
telephone services 208-9
Temple of Theseus 75
Theater an der Wien 151
Theatermuseum 57
theatre 22-4, 152-3
bookings 139

Thermalstrandbad 195
Third Man, The 28
tour 51
time 6, 209
tipping 117, 209
toilets 209
tourist information 209-10
tours 50-2, 105-114
boat 51
bus 50
cycling 112-14
Karlsplatz to Schottentor 108
Kärntner Strasse Loop 106-8, 107
Leopoldstadt 109-10, 109
Schwedenplatz cycling roundtrip 112-14
Stadtpark to Karlsplatz 110
tram 51
walking 51, 106-11
train travel 201, 202
travel agents 202
Treasury of Slovakia 194
TV 16, 28-30, 209

U
U-Bahn 201
Uhren Museum 65
UN 88, 113
Universität Wien 75
UNO City 88, 113, **87**
Urania cinema 110, 114, **113**

V
Viennale Film Festival 11
Vienna Boys' Choir 59, 150
Vienna Marathon 10
Vienna Workshop, see Wiener Werkstätte
visas 210
visual arts 24-6
Volksgarten 75
Volksoper 151-2
Volksprater, see Wursteprater
Volksstimmefest 10
Votivkirche 66, 108

W
Wachau Museum 188
Wagenburg 102
Wagner, Otto 35
Hofpavillon Hietzing 100
Majolikahaus 94

Postsparkasse 82, 110
Stadtbahn Pavillons 94, 111, **110**
walking tours 51
Weingut der Stadt Krems 189
Weissenkirchen 188
Wieden 92-4
Wien ist Andersrum 10
Wien Modern Festival 11
Wienerwald 18, 193-4
Wiener Festwochen 10
Wiener Kriminalmuseum 86, 109
Wiener Porzellanmanufaktur 109
Wiener Porzellanmanufaktur Augarten 86
Wiener Schnitzel 116, **116**
Wiener Werkstätte 26
Willendorf 188
Wine 186
wine taverns, *see* Heurigen
women travellers 210
work 210
Wurstelprater 48, 85
Würstelstand (sausage stand) 14, **9**
Wüstenhaus 102

Z
Zentralfriedhof 99
Zoom 48, 82
zoos
    Lainzer Tiergarten 100
    Schönbrunn Tiergarten 102

EATING
Aida 107, 119, **106**
Amacord 128
Amerlingbeisl 132
Aromat 132-3, **133**
Atelier Augarten 110, 125
Bagel Station 133
Bayou 125
Beim Czaak 119
Bodega Marqués 122
Breakfast Club 134
Café Bräunerhof 120
Café Central 121, **121**
Café der Provinz 130
Café Dommayer 135
Café Drechsler 133
Café Engländer 119
Café Florianihof 130
Café Gloriette 135
Café Griensteidl 107, 121-2

Café Hawelka 120
Café Hummel 130-1
Café Landtmann 124
Café Prückel 125
Café Rüdigerhof 133
Café Sacher 108, 120-1, **14**
Café Schwarzenberg 125
Café Sperl 129
Café Tirolerhof 121
Canetti 129
Centimetre II 133
Chang 133
Chrinor 129-30
Coffeeshop Company 119-20
Contor 126
Demel 107, 121
Die Grossmutter Kocht 133-4
Diglas 120
Do-An 134
DO & CO 119
Drei Husaren 120
É Tricaffé 122
East to West 122
Eat It 124
EN 122
Etap 135
Expedit 120
Figlmüller 120
Fromme Helene 131
Gasthaus Wickerl 131
Gaumenspiel 130
Gelateria Hoher Markt 122
Gesundes 126
Govinda 134
Griechenbeisl 120
Haas & Haas 119
Halle 124
Happy Buddha 135
Immervoll 120
Indian Pavillon 127
Kantine 125
Katholisches Studenthaus Mensa 123
Kent 135-6
Kiang im Achten 131
Kim Kocht 131
Konoba 131
Korso 121
Kramer & Gutierrez 128
La Gondola 134
La Pasteria 132
Livingstone 122
Lusthaus 114, 126
MAK Café 125
Maschu Maschu 122-3

Meinl am Graben 121
Motto 128
Mr Lee 127-8
Music Academy Mensa 123
Naschmarkt Deli 128
Nudel & Strudel 123
ON 131
Palais Schwarzenberg 127
Pan e Wien 127
Pars 131
Piccini Piccolo Gourmet 129
Plutzer Bräu 130
Podium 130
Quell 136
Ra'an 132
Ra'mien 129
Rosenberger Markt Restaurant 123
Ruben's Brasserie 132
S-Bar 132
Saigon 129
Salettl 135
Samrat 131
Schilling 130
Schloss Concordia 135
Schöne Perle 109, 126
Schweizerhaus 126
Side Step 131
Soupkultur 123
Steirereck 127
Stomach 132
Strandgasthaus Birner 113, 126
St Josef 130
Summer Stage 112, 132
Tancredi 128
Tichy 134
Toko Ri 128
Trzesniewski 123
Ubl 128
Una 124, **124**
Universität Mensa 123
Vegi Rant 132
Vestibül 124
Vinissimo 129
Wegenstein 134
Wild 110, 127
World Restaurant 136
Wrenkh 122
Würstelstand am Hoher Markt 123
X-Celsior Caffé-Bar 125
Yoga 129
Yohm 121
Zu den 3 Buchteln 128
Zu den Zwei Liesln 134
Zum Alten Fassl 128-9

Zum Inder 126
Zum Schwarzen Kameel 122
Zur Alten Kaisermühle 126-7

SHOPPING
Aida 161
Altmann & Kühne 162
Amadeus 168
Art Deco 161
Babettes 167
Black Market 165
Bobby's Food Store 167
Boutique Charme 162
Braun & Co 162
British Bookshop 161
Café Sacher 162
Das Möbel 169
Demel 162
Dominici 162
Dorotheum 162
Douglas 163
Es Brennt 165
Eva Blut 169
Feiner Naturkostladen 165
Freytag & Berndt 163
Generalli Center 168
Gerngoss 169
Gesundes 167
Glasfabrik 163
Helmut Lang 163
Humanic 163
J & L Lobmeyr 163
Kaufhaus Schiepek 165
Kräuterdrogerie 170
La Pasteria 170
Loden-Plankl 165
Lollipop 169
Lomoshop 167
Lucky Star Organix 165
Lugner City 170
M. Frey Wille 167
Manner Fabriksverkauf 170
Meinl am Graben 164, **164**
Mörtz 168
Niedermeyer 164
Orator 169
Österreichische Werkstätten 164
Pachisi 167
Palmers 164
Piccini Piccolo Gourmet 168
Pischinger Fabriksverkauf 170
Polyklamott 168
Prada 162
Rave Up 168

Ringstrassen Galerien 167
Shakespeare & Co 165
Shipping 165
Shu! 168
Song 166
Staud 170
Steffl 164
Substance 169
Swarovski 164
Szaal 170
Teuchtler 170
Unger und Klein 166
Virgin Megastore 168
Wein & Co 166
Wiener Porzellanmanufaktur Augarten 167
WOKA 162
Wolford 165
Xocolat 165

SLEEPING
Academia 180
Accordia 177
Albatros 179
Alla Lenz 179
Altwienerhof 181

Appartement Pension Riemergasse 173
Attaché 178
Auer 180
Avis 180
Celtes 182
Das Triest 178
Das Tyrol 178
Do Step Inn 182
Favorita 181
Fünfhaus 182
Grand Hotel 176
Hotel-Pension Continental 179
Hotel-Pension Suzanne 174
Hotel Adlon 177
Hotel Am Schottenfeld 179
Hotel Am Schubertring 176
Hotel Am Stephansplatz 173
Hotel Amadeus 175
Hotel Ambassador 174
Hotel Arkadenhof 180
Hotel Atlanta 180
Hotel Austria 173
Hotel Boltzmann 180

Hotel Donauwalzer 181
Hotel Fürstenhof 180
Hotel Imperial 176
Hotel Im Palais Schwarzenberg 178
Hotel Kaiserin Elisabeth 173
Hotel Kärntnerhof 173
Hotel Marriott 177
Hotel Orient 175
Hotel Post 175
Hotel Sacher 174, 175
Hotel Viktoria 181
Hotel Wandl 174
InterContinental 177
Jugendgästhaus Wien-Brigittenau 177
Jugendherberge Myrthengasse 180
Kolping Wien-Zentral 180
König von Hungarn 174
K & K Maria Theresia 179
Laudon Court 179
Le Meridien 176
Mercure Wien Zentrum 175
Parkhotel Schönbrunn 181
Pension Am Operneck 174

Pension Atrium 179
Pension Carantania 179
Pension Falstaff 180
Pension Hargita 181
Pension Kraml 178
Pension Nossek 175
Pension Pertschy 175
Pension Wild 181
Quisisana 179
Radisson Sas Palais Hotel 177
Rathauspark 176
Schlossherberge am Wilhelminenberg 182
Schlosshotel Römischer Kaiser 174
Schweizer Pension 176
Singerstrasse apartments 174
Sophienalpe 182
Starlight 175
Theater-Hotel 179
Thüringer Hof 182
Westend City Hostel 181
Wombat's 182
Zur Wiener Staatsoper 174

Index

000 map pages
000 photographs

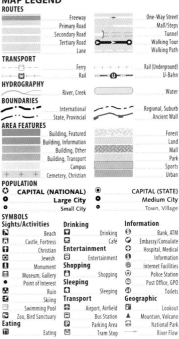

MAP LEGEND

ROUTES
- Freeway
- Primary Road
- Secondary Road
- Tertiary Road
- Lane
- One-Way Street
- Mall/Steps
- Tunnel
- Walking Tour
- Walking Path

TRANSPORT
- Ferry
- Rail
- Rail (Underground)
- U-Bahn

HYDROGRAPHY
- River, Creek
- Water

BOUNDARIES
- International
- State, Provincial
- Regional, Suburb
- Ancient Wall

AREA FEATURES
- Building, Featured
- Building, Information
- Building, Other
- Building, Transport
- Campus
- Cemetery, Christian
- Forest
- Land
- Mall
- Park
- Sports
- Urban

POPULATION
- ✪ **CAPITAL (NATIONAL)**
- ● **Large City**
- ○ Small City
- ◉ CAPITAL (STATE)
- ● Medium City
- ○ Town, Village

SYMBOLS

Sights/Activities
- Beach
- Castle, Fortress
- Christian
- Jewish
- Monument
- Museum, Gallery
- Point of Interest
- Ruin
- Skiing
- Swimming Pool
- Zoo, Bird Sanctuary

Eating
- Eating

Drinking
- Drinking
- Café

Entertainment
- Entertainment

Shopping
- Shopping

Sleeping
- Sleeping

Transport
- Airport, Airfield
- Bus Station
- Parking Area
- Tram Stop

Information
- Bank, ATM
- Embassy/Consulate
- Hospital, Medical
- Information
- Internet Facilities
- Police Station
- Post Office, GPO
- Toilets

Geographic
- Lookout
- Mountain, Volcano
- National Park
- River Flow

Map Section

Greater Vienna	238
Central Vienna	240
Northeast Vienna	244
Southwest Vienna	246
Southeast Vienna	248
Vienna Transit Map	250

GREATER VIENNA

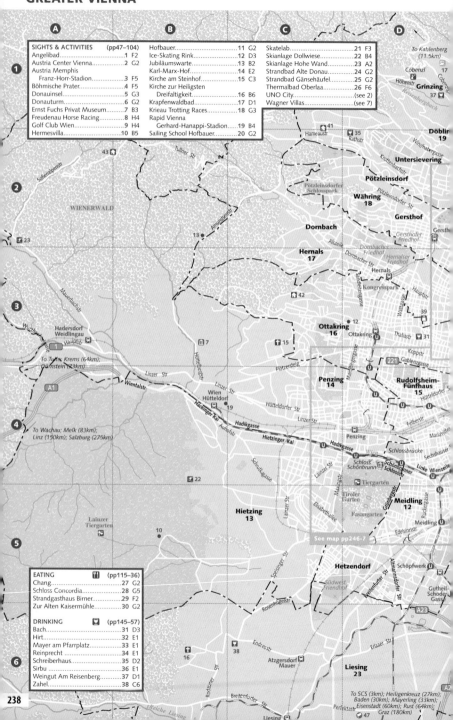

SIGHTS & ACTIVITIES (pp47–104)
Angelibad.....................................1 F2
Austria Center Vienna.................2 G2
Austria Memphis
  Franz-Horr-Stadion..................3 F5
Böhmische Prater.......................4 F5
Donauinsel.................................5 G3
Donauturm.................................6 G2
Ernst Fuchs Privat Museum.........7 B3
Freudenau Horse Racing.............8 H4
Golf Club Wien...........................9 H4
Hermesvilla...............................10 B5
Hofbauer...................................11 G2
Ice-Skating Rink........................12 D3
Jubiläumswarte..........................13 B2
Karl-Marx-Hof............................14 E2
Kirche am Steinhof.....................15 C3
Kirche zur Heiligsten
  Dreifaltigkeit...........................16 B6
Krapfenwaldbad.........................17 D1
Krieau Trotting Races.................18 G3
Rapid Vienna
  Gerhard-Hanappi-Stadion.....19 B4
Sailing School Hofbauer............20 G2
Skatelab...................................21 F3
Skianlage Dollwiese..................22 B4
Skianlage Hohe Wand..............23 A2
Strandbad Alte Donau..............24 G2
Strandbad Gänsehäufel.............25 G2
Thermalbad Oberlaa..................26 F6
UNO City...............................(see 2)
Wagner Villas.........................(see 7)

EATING (pp115–36)
Chang.......................................27 G2
Schloss Concordia......................28 G5
Strandgasthaus Birner................29 F2
Zur Alten Kaisermühle................30 G2

DRINKING (pp145–57)
Bach..31 D3
Hirt..32 E1
Mayer am Pfarrplatz..................33 E1
Reinprecht 34 E1
Schreiberhaus...........................35 D2
Sirbu..36 E1
Weingut Am Reisenberg.............37 D1
Zahel.......................................38 C6

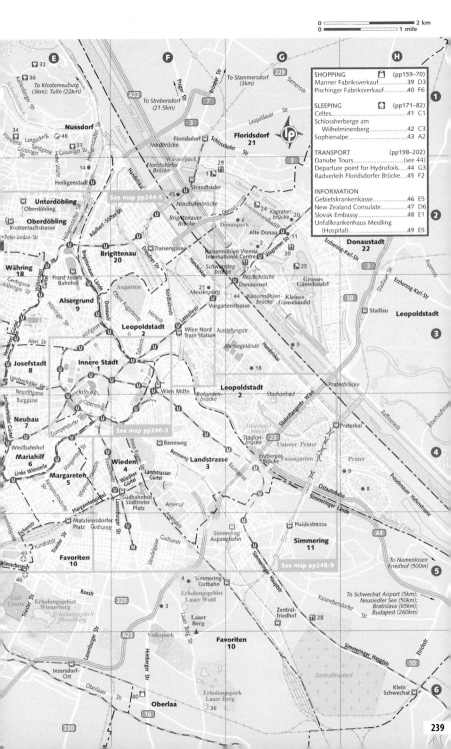

CENTRAL VIENNA

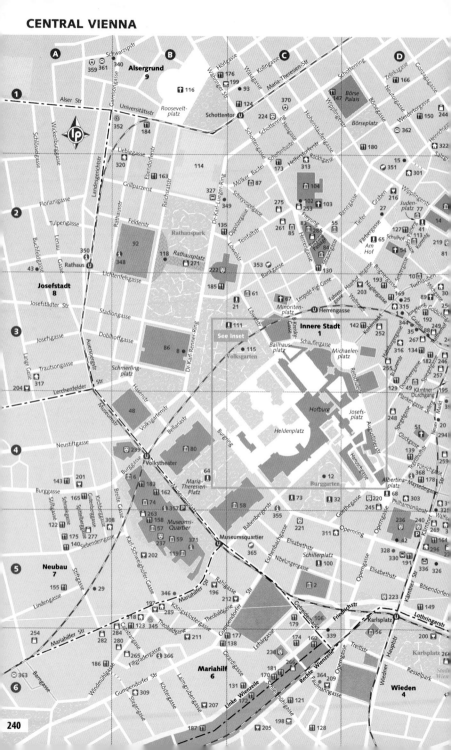

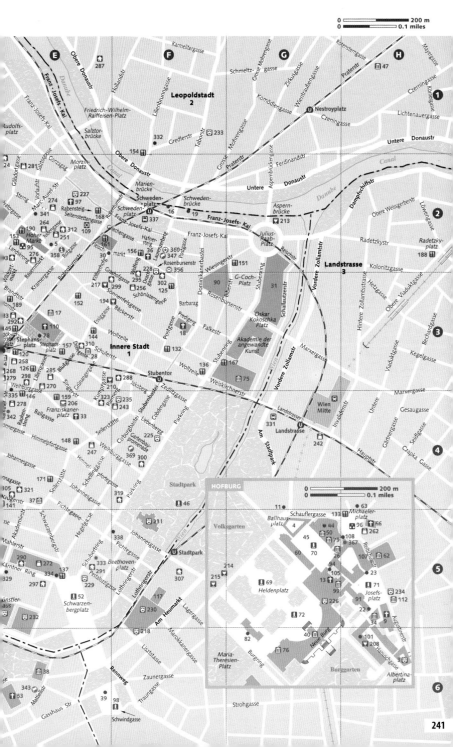

SIGHTS & ACTIVITIES (pp52–83)
Adolf Loos' Public Toilets.................1 D3
Akademie der bildenden Künste 2 C5
Albertina.......................................3 H6
Amalia Wing..................................4 G5
Ankeruhr.......................................5 E2
Architekturzentrum Wien.................6 B4
Archiv des Österreichischen
  Widerstands...............................7 D2
Athena Fountain............................8 B3
Augustinerkirche............................9 H5
Bawag Foundation........................10 G4
Bundeskanzleramt........................11 G4
Burggarten..................................12 C4
Burgkapelle.................................13 G5
Böhmische Hofkanzlei...................14 D2
Cityrama.....................................15 D2
DDSG Blue Danube Canal Tour
  Departures................................16 F2
DDSG Blue Danube Office.........(see 339)
Dom- & Diözesanmuseum.............17 E3
Dominikanerkirche........................18 F3
Donau Schiffahrt Pyringer-Zopper....19 F2
Donnerbrunnen............................20 D4
Empress Elisabeth Monument.........21 C3
Entrance to Prunksaal....................22 H5
Entrance to Spanish Riding School
  (Training Session Viewing)............23 H5
Ephesus Museum....................(see 40)
Equitable Palais............................24 E3
Erste Österreichisches Sparkasse......25 D3
Esperanto Museum.......................26 G5
Feuerwehr Centrale.......................27 D2
Figaro Haus..................................28 E3
Flakturm......................................29 A5
Fleischmarkt................................30 E2
Former Civic Armoury...............(see 27)
Former Kriegsministerium..............31 G3
Franz Josef Statue.........................32 C4
Franziskanerkirche........................33 E4
Globenmuseum............................34 H5
Grabenhof...................................35 D3
Greek Orthodox Church.................36 F2
Harry Lime's Apartment...........(see 234)
Haus der Musik.............................37 E4
Historisches Museum der Stadt Wien.38 E6
Hochstrahlbrunnen........................39 E6
Hofjagd und Rüstkammer
  Collection.................................40 G6
Hoftafel- und Tafelkammer........(see 50)
Holocaust-Denkmal.......................41 D2
Hop On Hop Off Vienna Line..........42 D5
Ice-Skating Rink............................43 A2
Imperial Chancery Wing.................44 G5
In der Burg Courtyard....................45 H5
Johann Strauss Denkmal.................46 F4
Johann Strauss Residence...............47 H1
Justizpalast..................................48 B4
Jüdisches Museum........................49 D3
Kaiserappartements......................50 G5
Kaisergruft.............................(see 51)
Kapuzinerkirche...........................51 D4
Karl von Schwarzenberg Statue......52 E5
Karlskirche..................................53 E6
Kirche Am Hof.............................54 D2
KunstForum.................................55 C2
Kunsthalle Project Space................56 D6
Kunsthalle...................................57 B5
Kunsthistorisches Museum.............58 C4
Leopold Museum..........................59 B5
Leopold Wing..............................60 G5

Liechtenstein Town Palace..............61 C3
Lipizzaner Museum........................62 H5
Loos Haus...................................63 H4
Maria Theresia Statue....................64 B4
Mariensäule.................................65 D2
Michaelerkirche............................66 H5
Minoritenkirche............................67 C3
Monument against War and
  Fascism....................................68 D4
Monument to Archduke Karl...........69 G5
Monument to Emperor Franz..........70 G5
Monument to Emperor Josef II........71 H5
Monument to Prince Eugene of
  Savoy......................................72 G5
Mozart Statue..............................73 C4
MUMOK......................................74 B4
Museum für angewandte Kunst......75 G3
Museum für Völkerkunde..........(see 24)
Museum Judenplatz......................77 D2
Musikmeile Wien Servicestelle........78 E3
Mythos Sisi..................................79 G5
Nail Studded Stump................(see 24)
Nationalbibliothek...................(see 40)
Naturhistorisches Museum.............80 B4
Neidhart-Fresken..........................81 D2
Palace Gates................................82 G6
Palais Ferstal................................83 C2
Palais Harrach..............................84 C2
Palais Kinsky...............................85 C2
Parlament...................................86 B3
Pasqualati Haus............................87 C2
Pestsäule.....................................88 D3
Peterskirche.................................89 D3
Postsparkasse...............................90 F3
Prunksaal....................................91 H5
Puppen & Spielzeug Museum....(see 113)
Rathaus (City Hall).......................92 B2
Reisebuchladen............................93 C1
Renaissance Swiss Gate.................94 G5
Roman Ruins...............................95 H5
Roman Ruins...............................96 E2
Ruprechtskirche............................97 E2
Russen Heldendenkmal.................98 F6
Sammlung Alter
  Musikinstrumente..................(see 40)
Schatzkammer.............................99 H5
Schiller Statue............................100 C5
Schmetterlinghaus.......................101 H6
Schottenkirche
  Museum Entrance.....................102 C2
Schottenkirche............................103 C2
Schottenstift...............................104 C2
Schweizerhof..............................105 G5
Secession Building........................106 C5
Spanish Riding School...................107 H5
St Michael's Gate.........................108 H5
Stadtbahn Pavillons................(see 200)
Stadttempel................................109 E2
Stephansdom..............................110 E3
Temple of Theseus.......................111 C3
Theatermuseum...........................112 H5
Theatershop..........................(see 238)
Uhren Museum............................113 D2
Universität Wien..........................114 B2
Vienna Sightseeing Tours.........(see 42)
Volksgarten................................115 C3
Votivkirche.................................116 B1
Wiener Eislaufverein.....................117 F5
Wiener Eismarkt...........................118 B2
Wiener Prozellanmanufaktur.....(see 24)
Zoom...119 B5

EATING 🍴 (pp119–25)
Aida...120 E3
Amacord....................................121 C6
Amerlingbeisl..............................122 A5
Bagel Station..............................123 C1
Bagel Station..............................124 B5
Beim Czaak.................................125 F3
Billa Supermarket........................126 B5
Bodega Marqués..........................127 D2
Breakfast Club.............................128 C6
Café Bräunerhof..........................129 D3
Café Central................................130 C2
Café Drechsler.............................131 C6
Café Engländer............................132 F3
Café Griensteidl...........................133 H5
Café Hawelka..............................134 D3
Café Landtmann..........................135 B2
Café Prückel................................136 F3
Café Sacher...........................(see 303)
Café Schwarzenberg.....................137 E5
Café Sperl...................................138 C6
Café Tirolerhof............................139 D4
Centimetre II...............................140 A5
Coffeeshop Company...................141 E4
Demel..142 D3
Die Grossmutter Kocht.................143 A4
Diglas..144 E3
DO & CO...................................145 E3
DO & CO...............................(see 3)
Do-An..................................(see 172)
Drei Husaren...............................146 E4
É Tricaffé....................................147 C1
East to West...............................148 E4
Eat It...149 D5
EN...150 D1
Expedit.......................................151 G2
Figlmüller....................................152 E3
Gelateria Hoher Markt.................153 E2
Gesundes...................................154 F1
Govinda.....................................155 A5
Griechenbeisl..............................156 F2
Haas & Haas...............................157 E3
Haas Haus............................(see 145)
Halle..158 B5
Immervoll...................................159 E4
Indian Pavillon............................160 C6
Interspar Supermarket..................161 E2
Kantine......................................162 B4
Katholisches Studenthaus
  Mensa.....................................163 B2
Korso...164 D5
La Gondola.................................165 A4
Livingstone.................................166 E5
MAK Café...................................167 F3
Maschu Maschu..........................168 E2
Meinl am Graben.........................169 D3
Mr Lee.......................................170 C6
Music Academy Mensa.................171 E4
Naschmarkt Deli..........................172 C6
Nudel & Strudel..........................173 C2
Piccini Piccolo Gourmet................174 C6
Plutzer Bräu................................175 A5
Ra'an..176 B1
Ra'mien......................................177 C6
Rosenberger Markt Restaurant.......178 D4
Saigon.......................................179 C5
Soupkultur..................................180 D1
Toko Ri......................................181 C6
Trzesniewski...............................182 D3
Una...183 B4
Universität Mensa........................184 B1

Wild..188 H2
Wrenkh..189 E3
Würstelstand am Hoher Markt......190 E2
X-Celsior Caffé-Bar......................191 D5
Yohm...192 D3
Zum Schwarzen Kameel...............193 D3

DRINKING 🍷🍷 (pp147–55)
Alt Wien..194 F3
American Bar..................................195 D3
Aux Gazelles..................................196 B5
Bar Italia Lounge..........................197 B5
Café Anzengruber..........................198 C6
Café Stein......................................199 B1
Club U...200 D6
Das Möbel......................................201 A4
Donau..202 B5
Esterházykeller.............................203 D3
First Floor.............................(see 109)
Frauencafé.....................................204 A3
Goodmann......................................205 C6
Kleines Café...................................206 E4
Kunsthalle Café......................(see 56)
Mango Bar......................................207 B6
Onyx Bar................................(see 145)
Palmenhaus....................................208 H6
Roxy..209 C6
Santo Spirito.................................210 E3
Titanic..211 B6
Top Kino Bar..................................212 C5
Urania...213 G2
Volksgarten Pavillon.....................214 F5
Volksgarten....................................215 F5
Why Not?.......................................216 D2
Zwölf Apostelkeller......................217 E3

ENTERTAINMENT 🎭 (pp155–66)
Akademietheater............................218 F6
Artis International..........................219 E3
Bundestheaterkassen....................220 D4
Burg Kino......................................221 C5
Burgtheater...................................222 B2
Cinemagic......................................223 D5
De France.......................................224 C1
Gartenbaukino...............................225 F4
Hofburg concert halls....................226 G5
Jazzland..227 E2
Kammeroper...................................228 F2
Kasino am Schwarzenbergplatz......229 E5
Konzerthaus...................................230 F5
Kursalon.......................................231 F5
Musikverein...................................232 E5
Österreichische
   Filmmuseum.......................(see 3)
Odeon..233 F1
Palais Pálffy...................................234 H5
Porgy & Bess.................................235 F4
Staatsoper....................................236 D5
Tanzquartier Wien.........................237 B5
Theater an der Wien......................238 C6
Top Kino..............................(see 212)
Volkstheater..................................239 B4
Wien-Ticket Pavillon.....................240 D5

SHOPPING 🛍 (pp161–7)
Altmann & Kühne..........................241 D3
Amadeus..242 G4
Art Deco..243 F4
Black Market..................................244 D1
Boutique Charme...........................245 D4
Braun & Co....................................246 D3

British Bookshop............................247 E4
Dominici...............................(see 258)
Dorotheum....................................248 D4
Douglas...249 D3
Es Brennt.......................................250 D3
Feiner Naturkostladen...................251 E2
Freytag & Berndt...........................252 D3
Freyungmarkt.................................253 C2
Gerngross.....................................254 A6
Glasfabrik......................................255 D3
Heiligenkreuzerhof
   Christmas Market.....................256 F3
Helmut Lang..................................257 D3
Humanic...258 E3
J&L Lobmeyr..................................259 D4
Karlsplatz Christmas Market.........260 D6
Kaufhaus Schiepek.........................261 C2
Loden-Plankl..................................262 H5
Lomoshop.......................................263 B5
Lucky Star Organix........................264 C6
Mörtz...265 B6
Naschmarkt....................................266 C6
Niedermeyer..................................267 D3
Österreichische Werkstätten.........268 E3
Pachisi..................................(see 273)
Palmers..269 D5
Prada..270 E3
Rathausplatz Christmas Market.....271 B2
Ringstrassen Galerien...................272 E5
Ringstrassen Galerien...................273 D5
Shakespeare & Co..........................274 E2
Shipping...275 C2
Song...276 E2
Spittalberg Christmas Market.......277 A5
Steffl...278 E4
Swarovski......................................279 E3
Teuchtler.......................................280 B6
Unger und Klein.............................281 E2
Virgin Megastore...........................282 A6
Wien & Co......................................283 E3
Wiener Prozelanmanufaktur...........284 B5
Woka.....................................(see 278)
Wolford..285 E3
Xocolat..286 C2

SLEEPING 🏠 (pp173–7)
Accordia..287 E1
Appartement Pension
   Riemergasse..............................288 F3
Das Tyrol.......................................289 B5
Grand Hotel...................................290 E5
Hotel am Schubertring..................291 E5
Hotel am Stephansplatz.................292 E3
Hotel Amadeus..............................293 E2
Hotel Ambassador.........................294 D4
Hotel Austria.................................295 F3
Hotel Bristol..................................296 D5
Hotel Imperial...............................297 E5
Hotel Kaiserin Elisabeth................298 E3
Hotel Kärntnerhof.........................299 E3
Hotel Marriott...............................300 F4
Hotel Orient..................................301 D2
Hotel Post.....................................302 F3
Hotel Sacher..................................303 D4
Hotel Wandl..................................304 D3
Hotel zur Wiener Staatsoper.........305 E4
Hotel-Pension Suzanne..................306 D5
InterContinental............................307 F5
K+K Maria Theresia........................308 A5
Kolping Wien-Zentral....................309 B6
König von Hungarn.........................310 E3

Le Meridien...................................311 C5
Mercure Wien Zentrum.................312 E2
Österreichischer
   Judendherbergswerk..................313 C2
Pension am Operneck....................314 D4
Pension Nossek.............................315 D3
Pension Pertschy...........................316 D3
Pension Wild..................................317 A3
Quisisana......................................318 B5
Radisson SAS Palais Hotel.............319 F4
Rathauspark...................................320 B2
Schlosshotel Römischer Kaiser......321 E4
Schweizer Pension..........................322 D1
Singerstrasse Apartments.............323 E4
Starlight..324 E2

TRANSPORT (pp198–202)
Air France......................................325 D4
Alitalia...326 D5
Austrian Airlines.....................(see 335)
Austrobus......................................327 B2
Avis...328 D5
British Airways..............................329 E5
Bus to Baden.................................330 D3
City Air Terminal............................331 G4
Delta Air Lines..............................332 F1
Die Restplatzbörse..................(see 328)
Europcar..333 E5
Hertz...334 E5
Lauda Air.......................................335 E3
Lokalbahn Tram to Baden..............336 D5
Night Bus Departures....................337 F2
ÖAMTC..338 F5
Österreichisches Verkehrsbüro......339 C6
STA Travel.....................................340 B1
Swiss Air.......................................341 E2

INFORMATION
American Express...........................342 E4
Australian Embassy........................343 E6
Berlitz...344 D3
BigNet...345 B5
British Bookshop....................(see 247)
British Trade Council...............(see 347)
Canadian Embassy.........................347 F2
City Hall Information Centre..........348 B2
Columbus Reisen...........................349 B2
Frauen Büro...................................350 A2
French Embassy..............................351 D2
G-Zone..352 B1
Hungarian Embassy.......................353 C2
Inlingua Sprachschule...................354 D4
Jugendinfo....................................355 C4
Main Post Office............................356 F2
MuseumsQuartier
   Information Centre.....................357 B4
Niederösterreich Werbung............358 E2
Police..359 A1
Police..360 F2
Post Office......................................361 A1
Post Office.....................................362 D1
Post Office.....................................363 A6
Reisebüro Mondial.........................364 C6
Slovenian Embassy.........................365 C5
Slowakische Zentrale
   für Tourismus............................366 B6
Spanish Riding School Office.........367 H5
Tourist Info Wien...........................368 D4
US Consulate..................................369 F4
Vienna Police Headquarters..........370 C1
WienXtra-Kinderinfo......................371 B5

NORTHEAST VIENNA

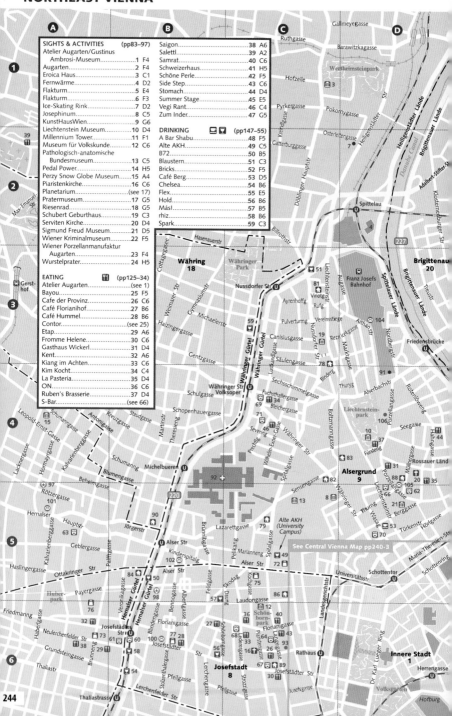

SIGHTS & ACTIVITIES	(pp83–97)
Atelier Augarten/Gustinus	
Ambrosi-Museum...................1	F4
Augarten...................2	F4
Eroica Haus...................3	C1
Fernwärme...................4	D2
Flakturm...................5	E4
Flakturm...................6	F3
Ice-Skating Rink...................7	D2
Josephinum...................8	C5
KunstHausWien...................9	G6
Liechtenstein Museum...................10	D4
Millennium Tower...................11	F1
Museum für Volkskunde...................12	C6
Pathologisch-anatomisch	
Bundesmuseum...................13	C6
Pedal Power...................14	H5
Perzy Snow Globe Museum...................15	A4
Piaristenkirche...................16	C6
Planetarium...................(see 17)	
Pratermuseum...................17	G5
Riesenrad...................18	G5
Schubert Geburthaus...................19	C3
Serviten Kirche...................20	D4
Sigmund Freud Museum...................21	D5
Wiener Kriminalmuseum...................22	F5
Wiener Porzellanmanufaktur	
Augarten...................23	F4
Wurstelprater...................24	H5

EATING	(pp125–34)
Atelier Augarten...................(see 1)	
Bayou...................25	F5
Cafe der Provinz...................26	C6
Café Florianihof...................27	B6
Café Hummel...................28	B6
Contor...................(see 25)	
Etap...................29	A6
Fromme Helene...................30	C6
Gasthaus Wickerl...................31	D4
Kent...................32	A6
Kiang im Achten...................33	C6
Kim Kocht...................34	C4
La Pasteria...................35	C6
ON...................36	C6
Ruben's Brasserie...................37	D4
S-Bar...................(see 66)	

Saigon...................38	A6
Salettl...................39	A2
Samrat...................40	C6
Schweizerhaus...................41	H5
Schöne Perle...................42	F5
Side Step...................43	C6
Stomach...................44	D4
Summer Stage...................45	E5
Vegi Rant...................46	C4
Zum Inder...................47	G5

DRINKING	(pp147–55)
A Bar Shabu...................48	F5
Alte AKH...................49	C5
B72...................50	B5
Blaustern...................51	C3
Bricks...................52	F5
Café Berg...................53	D5
Chelsea...................54	B6
Flex...................55	E5
Hold...................56	B6
Mäsl...................57	B6
rhiz...................58	B6
Spark...................59	C3

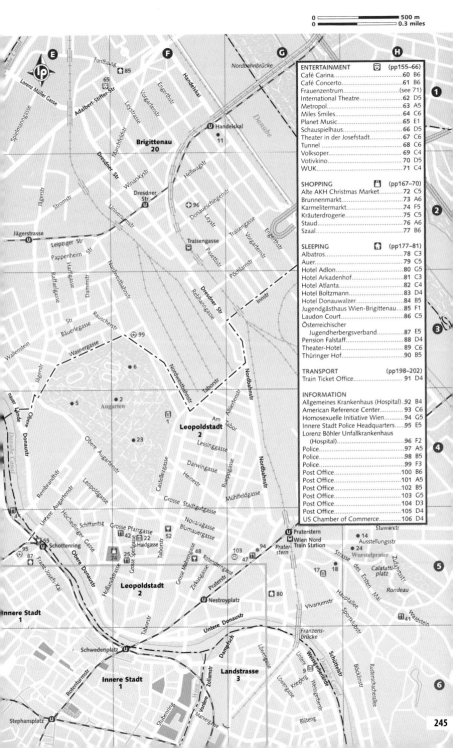

ENTERTAINMENT 😊	(pp155–66)
Café Carina	60 B6
Café Concerto	61 B6
Frauenzentrum	(see 71)
International Theatre	62 D5
Metropol	63 A5
Miles Smiles	64 C6
Planet Music	65 E1
Schauspielhaus	66 D5
Theater in der Josefstadt	67 C6
Tunnel	68 C6
Volksoper	69 C4
Votivkino	70 C4
WUK	71 C4

SHOPPING 🛍	(pp167–70)
Alte AKH Christmas Market	72 C5
Brunnenmarkt	73 A6
Karmelitermarkt	74 F5
Kräuterdrogerie	75 C5
Staud	76 A6
Szaal	77 B6

SLEEPING 🛏	(pp177–81)
Albatros	78 C3
Auer	79 G5
Hotel Adlon	80 D5
Hotel Arkadenhof	81 C3
Hotel Atlanta	82 C4
Hotel Boltzmann	83 D4
Hotel Donauwalzer	84 B5
Jugendgästhaus Wien-Brigittenau	85 F1
Laudon Court	86 C5
Österreichischer Jugendherbergsverband	87 E5
Pension Falstaff	88 C6
Theater-Hotel	89 C6
Thüringer Hof	90 B5

TRANSPORT	(pp198–202)
Train Ticket Office	91 D4

INFORMATION	
Allgemeines Krankenhaus (Hospital)	92 B4
American Reference Center	93 C6
Homosexuelle Initiative Wien	94 G5
Innere Stadt Police Headquarters	95 E5
Lorenz Böhler Unfallkrankenhaus (Hospital)	96 F2
Police	97 A5
Police	98 B5
Police	99 F3
Post Office	100 B6
Post Office	101 A5
Post Office	102 B5
Post Office	103 G5
Post Office	104 D3
Post Office	105 D4
US Chamber of Commerce	106 D4

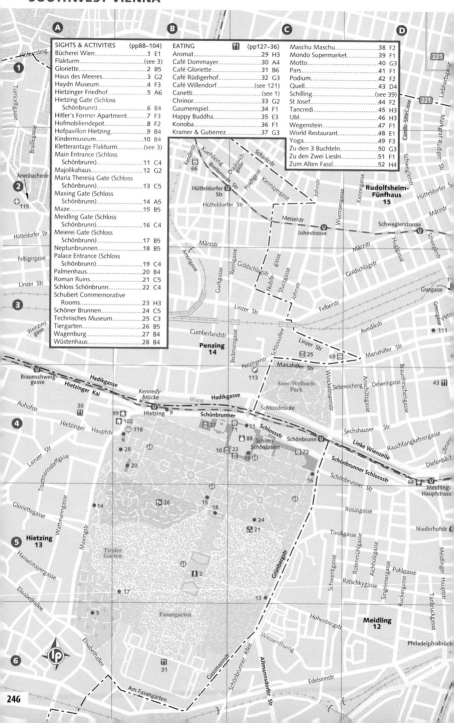

SIGHTS & ACTIVITIES (pp88–104)

Bücherei Wien.....1 E1
Flakturm.....(see 3)
Gloriette.....2 B5
Haus des Meeres.....3 G2
Haydn Museum.....4 F3
Hietzinger Friedhof.....5 A6
Hietzing Gate (Schloss Schönbrunn).....6 B4
Hitler's Former Apartment.....7 F3
Hofmobiliendepot.....8 F2
Hofpavillon Hietzing.....9 B4
Kindermuseum.....10 B4
Kletterantage Flakturm.....(see 3)
Main Entrance (Schloss Schönbrunn).....11 C4
Majolikahaus.....12 G2
Maria Theresia Gate (Schloss Schönbrunn).....13 C5
Maxing Gate (Schloss Schönbrunn).....14 A5
Maze.....15 B5
Meidling Gate (Schloss Schönbrunn).....16 C4
Meierei Gate (Schloss Schönbrunn).....17 B5
Neptunbrunnen.....18 B5
Palace Entrance (Schloss Schönbrunn).....19 C4
Palmenhaus.....20 B4
Roman Ruins.....21 C5
Schloss Schönbrunn.....22 C4
Schubert Commemorative Rooms.....23 H3
Schöner Brunnen.....24 C5
Technisches Museum.....25 C3
Tiergarten.....26 B5
Wagenburg.....27 B4
Wüstenhaus.....28 B4

EATING (pp127–36)

Aromat.....29 H3
Café Dommayer.....30 A4
Café Gloriette.....31 B6
Café Rüdigerhof.....32 G3
Café Willendorf.....(see 121)
Canetti.....(see 1)
Chrinor.....33 G2
Gaumenspiel.....34 F1
Happy Buddha.....35 E3
Konoba.....36 F1
Kramer & Gutierrez.....37 G3

Maschu Maschu.....38 F2
Mondo Supermarket.....39 F1
Motto.....40 G3
Pars.....41 F1
Podium.....42 F2
Quell.....43 D4
Schilling.....(see 39)
St Josef.....44 F2
Tancredi.....45 H3
Ubl.....46 H3
Wegenstein.....47 E1
World Restaurant.....48 E1
Yoga.....49 F3
Zu den 3 Buchteln.....50 G3
Zu den Zwei Liesln.....51 F1
Zum Alten Fassl.....52 H4

See NorthEast Vienna Map pp244-5

See Central Vienna Map pp240-3

SHOPPING	(pp167–70)
Amadeus	76 F2
Babettes	77 H2
Eva Blut	78 F2
Flohmarkt	79 G3
Generalli Center	80 F2
Lollipop	81 F1
Lugner City	82 E1
M.frey Wille	83 F3
Naschmarkt	84 H2
Orator	85 F2
Polyklamott	86 G3
Rave Up	87 G3
Schonbrunn Christmas Market	88 C4
Shul	89 F1
Substance	90 F2

SLEEPING	(pp177–82)
Academia	91 F1
Alla Lenz	92 F1
Altwienerhof	93 F1
Avis	94 F1
Do Step Inn	95 E2
Fünfhaus	96 E3
Hotel am Schottenfeld	97 F1
Hotel Fürstenhof	98 E3
Hotel Viktoria	99 B4
Hotel-Pension Continental	100 G2
Jugendherberge Myrthengasse	101 F1

DRINKING	(pp147–55)
Blue Box	53 F2
Café Savoy	54 G2
Europa	55 G2
Futuregarden Bar & Art Club	56 G2
Lo:sch	57 E4
Orlando	58 G3
Schikaneder	59 H2
Shebeen	60 F1
Shultz	61 G2
Subzero	62 G2
Tanzcafé Jenseits	63 G2
U4	64 D4
Wirr	65 F1

ENTERTAINMENT	(pp155–66)
Breitenseer Lichtspiele	66 B2
English Cinema Haydn	67 G2
Filmcasino	68 G3
IMAX Wien	69 C3
Jirsa Theater Karten Büro	70 G1
Marionettentheater	71 C4
Orangery	72 C4
Raimund Theater	73 E3
Stadthalle	74 E2
Vienna's English Theatre	75 G1

Parkhotel Schönbrunn	102 B4
Pension Atrium	103 E1
Pension Carantania	104 E2
Pension Hargita	105 F2
Pension Kraml	106 F3
Westend City Hostel	107 F3
Wombal's	108 D3

TRANSPORT	(pp198–202)
Denzeldrive	109 E2
Lufthansa	110 F3
Ärbo	111 D3

INFORMATION	
Bizeps	112 E2
Czech Republic Embassy	113 C4
Faktor i	114 H2
Hanusch-Krankenhaus (Hospital)	115 A2
Police	116 G3
Police	117 F3
Post Office (Schloss Schönbrunn)	118 B4
Post Office	119 G3
Post Office	120 F2
Rosa Lila Villa	121 G3
Speednet Cafe	(see 123)
Westbahnhof Information Centre	122 E2
Westbahnhof Post Office	123 E3

See pp244-

A B C D

Stephansplatz

Hofburg

Hetzgasse

36

Blüteng 13

Weissgerberlände

Schüttelstr

Böcklinstr

Stubentor

Vordere Zollamtstr

Markergasse

Kegelgasse

Löwengasse

12

22

Innere Stadt
1

Wien Mitte

Landstrasse

Marxergasse

Rotunden-
brücke

Burggarten

Parking

Stadtpark

Landstrasse
3

Rasumofskyg

Kundmanng

Geusaugasse

Erdberger
Lände

Böcki

Openring

Kärntner Ring

Schubertring

Lothringerst

Stadtpark

Am Heumarkt

Rechte Bahngasse

Linke Bahngasse

Reisnerstr

Salesianergasse

Rochusgasse

Ungargasse

Hainburger-

Wasser-

Erdbergstr

Hagenmüllen

Collnerg

Hagenmüllen

Friedrichstr

Karlsplatz

Karlsplatz

Neulinggasse

Neulinggasse

Arenbergpark

34

Landstr

Apostelgasse

Hörnesgasse

Baumgasse

Kardinal-
Nagl-Platz

Rechte Wienzeile

Margaretenstr

See Central Vienna Map pp240-3

Wiedner Haupt

Kühbuch

21

39

Jauresgasse

Barichgasse

Barmherzengasse

27 29 10

Schleifmühlgasse

Gusshausstr

Schwindg

Wohlleben

Palais
Schwarzenberg

31

15

18

Juchgasse

Petrusg

Kardinal-
Nagl-Platz

Paulanergasse

Frankenberggasse

38

Rennweg

Boerhaavegasse

Esslarngasse

Waag
gasse

Floragasse

Taubstummeng

Argentinierstr

Rennweg

Schützen-

gasse

Strohgasse

Oberzellergasse

19

Wieden

Taubstummengasse

Schloss
Belvedere

Obere Bahngasse

Rennweg

Steingasse

Wieden
4

Theresianumgasse

Belvederegasse

Botanic
Gardens

4

Gerlgasse

Keilg

Hegergasse

Aspangstr

Wiedner Hauptstr

Mayerhofgasse

Favoritenstr

Jacquingasse

Fasangasse

Kölblgasse

Landstrasse
3

Mommsengasse

14

Johann-Strauss-Gasse

Goldeggasse

Weyringergasse

1
Alpine
Garden

Holflweggasse

Mohsgasse

Kärchergasse

A.-Blamau Gasse

Rennweg

Landstrasser

28

Rainergasse

Kolschitzkygasse

Landstrasser Gürtel

Wiedner Gürtel

32

37

Schweitzer
Garten

Kelsenstr

Lebend

Schönburgstr

Südtiroler
Platz

Südtiroler
Platz

Südbahnhof

Chegastr

11

Wiedner Gürtel

Schelleingasse

Blechturmgasse

Laxenburger Str

Sonnwendgasse

Favoritenstr

Humboldtgasse

Arsenal

Lilienthalgasse

Franz-Grill-Str

Landgutgasse

30

16

Dampfgasse

Hasengasse

Sützenbruggasse

Klagbaumg

Kepler gasse

Keplerplatz

Favoriten
10

5

Gudrunstr

Erlachgasse

Pernerstorfergasse

Columbusgasse

Favoritenstr

Wielandgasse

Herndlgasse

Gudrunstr

Arsenalstr

Gänsbachergasse

Brehm

Neilreichgasse

Herzgasse

Quellenstrasse

Buchengasse

Reumannplatz

2

Gellertgasse

Erlachgasse

Quellenstr

Abegggasse

Geiselberg-Str

Rotenhofgasse

Davidhofgasse

Leebgasse

Rotenhofgasse

23

Reumann-
platz

Buchengasse

Steudelgasse

Puchsbaumgasse

Schrötterschgasse

Davidhofgasse

Ettenreichgasse

Lader-Berg-Str

Inzersdorfer Str

Augelgasse

Antons-
platz

Favoritenstr

Kudlichgasse